Hope you enjoy
the book!

#137

The Perfect Life

AN AUTOBIOGRAPHY

By Monte J Perepelkin

The Perfect Life

Monte Perepelkin

This book is for anyone who has faced adversity, self-doubt, or hopelessness, or felt disadvantaged at some point during their life.

In order to successfully navigate through life as a quadriplegic, the value in having and maintaining reliable caregivers is extremely important. Therefore, I want to dedicate this book to the many nurses and caregivers who have worked with me throughout this long journey, especially one in particular who has had my back without fail for the past fourteen years, John Szabo. My life would never have been possible without people like you. Thank you!

I would also like to thank Alberta Health Services for providing me with the financial support to live on my own through the self-managed care program.

To my mom, Betty: I am thankful for your honest effort in raising me the best you could despite the adversities we faced. The experiences we have shared together throughout our lives has brought us closer and shaped me to become the man I am today. For that, I am eternally grateful and would not trade it for anything. Love you, Mom!

My one regret is that I cannot hand my stepdad, Bill, a copy of this book. Since he played a large role in influencing pretty much every good thing that ever became of me, it would have been a pleasure to hear him say, "I told you so." It seems, in more ways than one, he knew how this story was going to end before I did.

Very special thanks to my daughters, Danielle and Haylee, for their support and encouragement throughout this process. They have always stood by me, even in my darkest hours. Without them, I am not sure that I would be here today. Love you both very dearly.

Thank you to Laurie Ann Ross for painting the beautiful sunset for the cover of this book.

Most of all, I am thankful to our Creator, Jehovah, for giving me the strength, ability, and determination to endure this life and write this autobiography. (Psalm 83:18)

TABLE OF CONTENTS

AUTHOR'S NOTE

Music is a universal language that can provide the soundtrack to our lives. Songs often define moments in time for us, and memories of those moments can be instantly triggered by those songs as we age. Even people with dementia are not immune to this phenomenon. You hear an old tune that was playing in the background on your first date, for example, and BOOM...a treasured moment in time lights up for you. Or you hear a song on the radio that serendipitously accompanies the emotion you are currently experiencing, and suddenly you find yourself relating to the lyrics.

For this reason, I list the name and artist of certain songs at the end of select chapters throughout my autobiography. Because this music adds another dimension to the story, I invite you to listen to the music after reading each chapter that has such a list. Doing so may intensify your perception of the moods and emotions I was truly feeling, further enhancing your reading experience. In our digital age of the internet, we can access this music in a matter of seconds. Simply scan the QR code with your smart phone, and the song should immediately begin to play. You can download the QR code reader app for free on any smartphone. If you are reading this in ebook format, simply click or tap on the link above the QR code. Or you can look up the song on YouTube. Throughout my autobiography, you will also find the occasional QR code after certain paragraphs. Scanning the code with your smartphone will take you to a photo or video that pertains to the story. To make the most of your reading experience, I encourage you to take advantage of this technology.

INTRODUCTION

As a person who has always been fascinated with looking back on life and trying to figure out why I did or did not do something, and why certain things happened or did not happen, writing my autobiography has been an educational, therapeutic, and enlightening process. While it taught me much about myself personally, it also enabled me to make sense of certain things and connect the dots—so to speak—by helping me recognize some of the reoccurring pitfalls I have found myself in. Second-guessing ourselves and trying to make sense of certain things, especially if they don't seem to make sense, is human nature. However, just as memory serves to remind us that touching something hot will burn our hand, the experiences we have encountered during times past can be of significant value in learning a great deal about ourselves, especially when we take the time to analyze each notable occurrence with a degree of humility—conceding that not every decision we made was justifiable or even correct. That's when many occurrences that didn't seem fair or make any sense start to make perfect sense. One thing I've learned while digging through my memory banks is that for the majority of life's situations, it's our choice as to which fork in the road we travel down, but every once in a while, the road chooses us. How we walk that road is up to us.

In hindsight, my decision to race dirt bikes may not have been the best choice, but then again, hindsight is twenty-twenty. At the time, taking up cross-country racing, which would lead to motocross and arenacross, seemed like the thing to do. Although I entered the sport relatively late in life—compared to most who take up off-road motorcycle racing—I considered myself a decent rider. And after learning the ropes of handling a dirt bike while riding the trails of my adoptive province, Alberta, racing was an inevitable choice for a competitive-by-nature guy like me to make. Pushing myself to be the best I can be has always been in my blood; therefore, sanctioned racing filled that need perfectly. You're up against dozens of other riders who think they're good enough to make a statement on a motorcycle. Even if the best you can do is to finish a cross-country or motocross race, you've made a statement. That, in itself, says something about your character and ability to ride a dirt bike. Of course, for most of those who enter racing, it's about finishing on the podium and winning championships. That's when you're making a big statement!

As anyone with experience will attest, dirt bike racing is not for the faint of heart. It's a sport that takes no prisoners, especially motocross and its offshoots: supercross and arenacross. Motocross is the original "extreme sport" and one of the most physically demanding endeavors on the planet. Like any motorized sport, it is dangerous. That is part of the attraction for those who choose to pursue it. Fortunately, fatalities and spinal cord injuries are relatively few and far between when taking into account the tens of thousands of people who race dirt bikes worldwide. Injuries, however, are common to all three of the sport's major disciplines. The more years a rider is active—except in rare instances—the more injuries he will accumulate. For many, the accumulation of injuries will see them enter into forced retirement from the sport. Injuries in motocross, supercross, and arenacross are so prevalent that anyone who races accepts the fact that an injury is inevitable at some stage in their career. If they don't, they are seriously deluding themselves. It's not a matter of "if" but "when" an injury will happen.

Knee injuries are some of the most common in motocross, supercross, and arenacross—injuries to the anterior cruciate ligament (ACL) being at the top of those that affect ligaments. A broken collarbone, acromioclavicular (AC) joint sprain, broken wrist, broken or sprained ankle, broken arm, and broken leg belong in the "most likely to occur" injuries category. Any one of these will see most riders return to the sport after recovery. In Canada, only a handful of dirt bike racers have been killed or suffered a spinal cord injury.

Life-altering injuries have claimed both amateurs and professionals in Canada, as they have in every country that includes dirt bike racing in their sports catalog. Whether you're a middle-of-the-pack amateur or an elite pro champion, one mistake—big or small—can dramatically change your life forever. The best known Canadian dirt bike paraplegic is Blair Morgan, a rider who not only made a huge statement in motocross and arenacross, but in snowcross as well. Morgan was a superstar by any definition of the word: a multi-time Canadian National Motocross champion as well as a multi-time World Snowcross champion and five-time Winter X-Games gold medalist. Morgan was a fan-favorite in the sport for his sheer speed and determination, and after his many come-from-behind victories. On September 21, 2008, he broke his spine while practicing at the Montreal Supercross and was paralyzed from the middle of his back down. When I heard the news of his crash and injury, my heart went out to him. I could definitely relate.

Racing dirt bikes, however, makes up just seven of the forty-seven years I have been alive. While paralysis encompasses seventeen of those years. In this autobiography, I give you an in-depth account of my life as a quadriplegic, woven into a narrative that dates back to when I was two years old—when I miraculously escaped becoming paralyzed. From that frightful moment when I was a toddler until I crashed in an arenacross twenty-eight years later, it seems I was walking on borrowed time.

My autobiography also delves into my experience with being introduced to the Jehovah's Witness faith by my parents at a young age, which I abandoned after leaving home only to find myself on a lifelong search for the true meaning of God—a search that culminates after losing my father, grandmother, and a close friend.

In order to commit my autobiography to paper, I poked away over four million keystrokes—one key at a time—with a mouth-stick between my teeth. I mention this not to dramatize my efforts, but to underscore the resilience of the human spirit to triumph over adversity. During the course of writing this book, as difficult and uncomfortable as it was in some instances—not that I'm claiming to have confessed all my sins; that would take a series of books—I made a genuine effort at providing an authentic and forthright account of my life. In doing so, I have laid bare a journey that has taken me from childhood to convicted criminal, and then to maturing into adulthood and enjoying a brief encounter with what I believed was the perfect life. I had it all: a beautiful and dedicated wife, two wonderful children, a thriving carpentry business, a dream home on seven acres of land with a panoramic view of the Alberta Rockies, and a dirt bike racing career that brought me fulfilment. Then my seemingly perfect life evaporated within the blink of an eye, only to be rediscovered once I came to terms with my injury. This process led me, after clawing through a dark forest of loss and adversity, further than I ever imagined in understanding why we are here—that there is indeed a time for every purpose. In the process of revealing my story, I relate the many lessons this life has taught me. I hope you will enjoy taking this journey with me.

CHAPTER

1

Déjà Vu

On February 12, 1999, thirty-four days after my thirtieth birthday, I was in Lethbridge, Alberta, at the Canada Games Sportsplex— later renamed the Enmax Centre Arena. The arena is home to the Lethbridge Hurricanes WHL hockey team and further serves as a multi-purpose venue, hosting pretty much anything, from world class concerts to national curling championships, international basketball games, skating events, banquets, and even three-ring circuses. On that particular night, the Canada Games Sportsplex was ground zero for rounds three and four of the Alberta Arenacross Championship. That was my reason for being there, not as a spectator, but to compete in the 125cc Pro class. Because the event was part of the provincial title hunt, the Lethbridge Arenacross, as it was referred to, was for all intents and purposes a big event, and it catered to a fairly decent-sized crowd. With a seating capacity of 5,479 at the time, the Canada Games Sportsplex provided the perfect stage for Western Canada's best arenacross racers to duke it out.

It was shortly before 7:00 p.m. I had just returned to the arena from one of the town's Italian restaurants with my wife Nicole and some friends. We had enjoyed a nice, relaxing dinner. The calm before the storm. Now it was time for me to get focused, time to slip into racing mode. Although I was already familiar with the race track—I had set up my pit area and participated in scheduled practice earlier in the day—I decided to walk the course one last time before the event began. I headed out to the arena floor, where the hockey rink and playing surface markings had been replaced by between 100 and 150 truckloads of dirt carefully sculpted into an arenacross track. My pulse, still beating normally, was ready to ratchet up a few notches. I loved the intensity of racing a dirt bike. I liked flying through the air on a two-hundred-pound (90.7 kg) machine. Poetry in motion, some call it. I felt the adrenaline slowly beginning to course through my veins. My anticipation of getting the racing underway was electric. While I was walking the track, I could see people settling into their seats, getting ready for the action to begin.

The track was prepped beautifully, with perfectly formed corners and every jump symmetrically placed as if it were sculpted from clay with God's own hands. While walking the course, I made mental notes, choosing my lines—lines I believed would give me an edge over the competition. Although I had already done exactly that in the afternoon, re-familiarizing myself one last time wouldn't hurt. I was there to win, and I left nothing to chance.

With consistent, tacky soil, the course looked sublime. The fresh, moist soil emitted an all-too-familiar odor, creating a somewhat nostalgic atmosphere. Upon walking around to the final section, I noticed the maintenance crew had made a significant change to the small triple-jump. To my amazement, the take-off was somewhat steeper and definitively more difficult...even dangerous! But it was just one more challenge to deal with. I didn't dwell on the change. During practice—earlier in the afternoon—I would rail around the corner, grab third gear, and sail over the triple with ease. I was feeling awesome and excited to be taking part in this arenacross, my third of the season. The week before, I had raced in Saskatoon, Saskatchewan—a town close to my heart—where I had recorded fifth and third-place finishes respectively. And the week before Saskatoon, I was in Red Deer, Alberta, for rounds one and two of the Alberta Arenacross Championship, where I ended up watching from the stands because of a broken clutch.

http://montejperepelkin.com/photos-1

After exiting the track, I walked over to my pit area. I didn't have to worry about checking my bike again, as prepping and maintenance were being looked after by my very good friend Chris Bonneau. Chris had agreed to be my pit mechanic for the series. I knew I was in good hands. All that was left for me to do was get ready to race. Every veteran dirt bike racer has a certain checklist they go through as they prepare for battle. For me, it was all about the goggles, making sure they were super clean, with two fresh tear-off lenses loaded onto them. As any racer knows, clear vision is an essential piece to the winning formula. And when it's cold outside—like it is in Alberta during the month of February, even inside the arena—fogged lenses can be an issue, especially when you're breathing heavy. However, I had learned a little trick…fabric softener! Rub a small amount into the goggle lens with a soft cloth, and problem solved. I slipped into my brand-new racing gear, generously provided by my apparel sponsor, AXO: jersey, pants, chest protector, gloves, and helmet. Dressed to the nines and feeling like a rock star…I was ready to race! There's something extraordinarily special about wearing brand-new gear. It somehow gives you the impression that you're a little bit faster the first time you wear it.

It was time to head out to the starting line, where Chris had my bike warmed up. As I walked over to the starting area, I could see that my gate pick wasn't too great—fourth from the far outside. That's what a seventh gate pick—pulled from a hat containing numbered slips of paper—will get you. But that was OK. I liked a challenge. Throwing a leg over my two-stroke Yamaha YZ125, I got comfortable and took the bike over from Chris. With a few seconds to spare, I looked up and around at the crowd in the arena: people were sitting in their seats, some glancing at their programs; others had their eyes directed on the starting gate. This was it—show time! The announcer began introducing each rider over the PA system. When my name came up, I nodded and put my hand up for a quick wave, surprised the man behind the microphone had actually pronounced my last name correctly. Then, as per tradition, the national anthem was played, and everyone stood to pledge their allegiance. Not particularly fond of the opening ceremonies, I was glad when they were over. I just wanted to race.

Even though this first race of the evening was just a qualifier, it was still very important. With only two spots advancing from this heat race, it meant I needed to finish top two or else ride the semi-qualifier. Failing in the semi—God forbid—I would have to face one final attempt in the form of the last chance qualifier, or LCQ as it is known in racing jargon. In other words, if I didn't nail a berth for the main in the first qualifier, it entailed a lot of extra racing. This was something I, not to mention my rivals, desperately wanted to avoid.

In order to conserve energy for the main event, you needed to qualify first time out. Failing to qualify at all meant watching from the seats with the fans, or heading back to the hotel to watch a movie.

Feeling a slap on the back of my helmet from Chris let me know the thirty-second board was up. It was time to get serious. Beginning my pre-start ritual, I checked, at least a couple of times, to make sure the fuel valve was turned on—didn't want to be running out of gas during the race. Next, I clapped my hands together briskly till it hurt, to feel the blood flow through my fingers. Then I did a few neck and torso stretches, with a final vigorous headshake to clear away any unwanted outside interference, thus bringing all my senses into pinpoint crystalline focus.

While sitting on the line, waiting for the thirty-second board to go sideways, a familiar odor permeated my senses. It was the aroma of racing fuel after it's been burnt, lingering among the exhaust fumes. It's a sweet, pleasant odor. Almost perfume-like. A motocrosser's cologne, if I may call it that. The thirty-second board went sideways, and that meant the gate would drop within five seconds. Because these indoor races have short start straights, that first jump out of the gate was paramount. And being that I'm five foot ten inches, 165 pounds—while some of these kids next to me were barely 120 pounds soaking wet—I desperately needed that advantageous burst off the line. The first corner, being a left turn, meant I needed a half bike length lead or so in order to squeeze off the riders lined up on the left of me while I drifted into their line down the start straight towards the first turn in pursuit of that elusive holeshot. Every rider wanted it; only one would get it. Being at the front of the pack, going into turn one, doesn't guarantee you will win the race, but it certainly gives you an edge. And you're definitely not going to get stuck in the first turn if there's a pileup.

My right hand had the throttle gripped tightly, holding it about halfway open. The motor was screaming at the top of its RPMs as my left hand's middle finger engaged the clutch, just enough to load up the rear suspension. Meanwhile, my right hand's middle finger held in the front brake. Feeling as if I was seated upon a rabid beast that was chained to a wall, with its prey just inches out of reach, my reflexes were on full alert and razor sharp. I was ready to attack! With intense, pinpoint concentration, my eyes were fixated on the little metal tab on the ground in front of me, which held the start gate up. Once that moved, it was go time!

After watching the amateur races earlier that day, I knew the gate would drop right after my three count: *Thousand one, thousand two, thousand three.* Then the tab would move and the gate would shake slightly. That was my cue. While releasing the clutch, with tactile precision—like I had practiced a thousand times—I turned the throttle hard, wide open, right to the stop, as if trying to break the cable. At that moment, I felt my front tire rub, just slightly, against the gate as it fell to the ground in front of me. Precisely what I was hoping for. Every racer just knows when they've nailed the perfect start before they're even ten feet out of the gate. It's one of the most sublime feelings you get from racing a dirt bike, whether it's arenacross, supercross, or motocross. With a slight tactile feathering of the clutch, I grabbed second gear right away, continually holding the throttle firmly wide open as I shifted my weight to the center of the bike. My feet were planted firmly on the pegs as I squeezed the motorcycle tightly between my legs. Nearing the end of the start straight, with the aid of my peripheral vision, I could discern that I was clear of everyone on either side. Perfect! This allowed me to drift to the inside and get hard on the brakes to take the nearest rut, and then I was tight around the start corner and in first place. What a sensation that was! It almost felt as if I had already won. No matter what happened next, at least I'd gotten the holeshot. That was an accomplishment in its own right, especially at this level of racing. With my Yamaha performing perfectly, the feeling was nothing short of amazing. It was almost euphoric, like there was nothing that could possibly go wrong.

For most of the local competitors, this arenacross was only their first or second time they had raced since last fall, when the outdoor motocross season came to an end. This gap in racing causes most riders to tense up, which results in arm-pump. Arm-pump is a common phenomenon in racing arenacross. It happens when you grip the handlebars tightly for an extended period of time without ever relaxing, inducing your forearms to tighten so much you can barely hang on. It happens more commonly if you haven't been on a motorcycle for a while or you're not relaxed enough. Having just returned from Southern California—where I'd been practicing and testing for two weeks just before the arenacross series began—I had a considerable amount of seat time on my bike. This allowed me to feel relaxed and confident on the track—I knew I was capable of winning this heat. Nevertheless, while overeagerly attempting to maintain the lead, I made the smallest mistake exiting the first turn on lap two and got passed by a fellow competitor. I was ticked off big time! Not that he passed me, but that I had made a minuscule error, like some rookie. Which I wasn't. It's amazing how close in proximity two riders can be to each other in a racing situation; all it takes is a split-second mistake, and he is by you just like that. Second place, however, still qualified me for the main, and after sensing that I was starting to gap the rider behind me, I decided not to pursue the new leader. Instead, I focused on riding smoothly. My objective at this point was simple: ride my lines, rail the corners, and hit all my marks to set up a comfortable distance between myself and third place. My number one concern was getting to the main event. If I maintained second place, then I was golden.

By the end of lap three, my experience as a racer told me I had enough distance between myself and third; I didn't need to protect the inside line anymore. This allowed me to ride wider in the corners and carry more speed. This translated into a quicker lap time. After jumping the big crowd-pleasing step-up, I came around to the corner before the small, altered triple. Thus far into the heat, I hadn't attempted to jump it yet; like the rest of my competitors, I'd chosen to double in and single out instead. Knowing that jumping the triple was determinately faster in terms of lap times made it a critical obstacle to dial in before the main event. Having successfully jumped it a number of times earlier in the day, I had no reservations to go for it now that I had some breathing room between myself and the rider behind me. Because the track crew had changed the trajectory of this triple, I fastidiously rounded the corner nice and wide to carry a little extra speed. On my approach to the triple, with the throttle held wide open to the stop, I feathered the clutch slightly to grab third gear and went for it. As my front wheel hit the face of the jump, I gripped the bike tightly between my legs and launched up and forward. Upon nearing the apex of my trajectory, however, I felt the back end of my bike still rising, pushing the front end downward, as if I was about to go over the bars. Then that "uh-oh" moment hit me. I was becoming a passenger, and my options to regain control of the bike were slim. I knew I was in trouble. Suddenly everything went silent. The sands of time began to float instead of fall. It was as if reality was moving in slow motion. In an attempt to correct in mid-air, I hit the throttle and leaned back, hoping the centrifugal force of my rear wheel would lift the front end. But the maneuver had little effect. Gravity took over from there. I was definitely a passenger now. My heart was in my throat. Suddenly the front wheel of my bike planted itself into the face of the landing. The momentum carried me over the bars head first into the ground, where the chin guard of my helmet dug into the moist, hard-packed soil. My head stopped instantly and abruptly while my neck absorbed the energy created by the weight and velocity of my body. Rolling onto the ground in ragdoll fashion, I lay motionless while the bike bounced over me and fell on its side. I was aware I'd just gone down hard... Just how hard would soon become apparent. For some reason, I wasn't rendered unconscious by the crash. At that very moment, a warm, pleasant wave transferred through my entire body, as if a powerful drug had just been injected into all my veins at once. That's when the realization hit me: *I'm paralyzed!* Then the strangest thing happened. I experienced what amounted to the strongest déjà-vu-like phenomenon I had ever felt in my entire life. But it wasn't quite the same as the more common déjà vu moment, the intuition that an experience has occurred before. This was different. This was the recollection of a memory that I had long forgotten but suddenly remembered. The memory of *knowing* this was going to happen to me. That's when a momentary sense of panic set in, and I silently began to reject the revelation: *No way! It can't be! This can't be real!*

Lying there on the track, unable to move, an unexpected feeling of what I can only describe as bliss suddenly came over me. There was literally no pain at all. In essence, I felt nothing, not even the slightest sensation. It was as if I was alive inside a body that wasn't connected to my brain. In the thirty seconds or whatever it took before someone came over to check on me, I was surprised by how much data could pass through my mind. I reflected on how perfect the last twenty-four hours had been. I remembered coming home from work just yesterday thinking I had the perfect life, and how Nicole and I were excited about this weekend in Lethbridge—her mother was babysitting our two kids so we could have Valentine's Day weekend alone. And just last night, how we'd gone for a nice romantic dinner together and then headed back to our hotel, where we relaxed in the establishment's hot tub before returning to our room for the evening and making love before falling asleep. As I stared helplessly through my goggles at the dirt around me while lying motionless on the track, I realized that the intimate contact I'd once known as an able-bodied man with Nicole had just come to an end. While reflecting on how that part of my life would never be the same again—that nothing would ever be the same again—a momentary sadness enveloped me. I was paralyzed. The entire experience felt incredibly surreal, as if it were all a dream. A bad dream. I was experiencing every dirt bike racer's worst nightmare. I wanted to wake up. But I was awake.

For some reason, I recalled the last song we'd heard on the radio during the drive back from dinner less than an hour ago, "What It's Like" by Everlast, and the formidable irony it portrayed. I thought about my little girls and how this would affect their lives. How just a couple of days ago, I'd come home from work and chased my eighteen-month-old around the house, caught and tickled her as she giggled. How I'd gone skating later that evening with my five-year-old in our backyard on a skating rink that I had built—I'd skated around the rink while she'd sat up on my shoulders and yelled, "Go faster, Dad!" Then I thought about work and how it was strange that all my current jobs had been completely finished just prior to this race—and how that was so very much out of the ordinary in itself. I couldn't ever remember a time in my career as a contractor when that had ever happened. There was always something on the go. It was as if something had been preparing me for this moment, and somewhere in all of that I found a certain peace. Over the course of those thirty seconds or so, I somehow came to terms with the fact that my entire life was about to change. Dramatically! Even though I knew exactly what had just happened, that this was permanent, the small amount of anxiety and fear I was experiencing began to dissipate.

At this point, the race must have been red-flagged and all motors shut off—there was a deafening silence. No more roar of the bikes. I did hear voices. Mumbled voices. Probably spectators engaged in subdued conversation while looking down on the rider who'd just crashed. A rider who wasn't moving... Me.

While lying on the track for what felt like an eternity, finally, someone approached and asked me if I was all right. Completely cognizant, in a clear, calm voice, I replied that I couldn't move anything. He made some motion that I surmised was to summon help. Next, the EMS crew came onto the scene of my crash. The crowd, nearly silent now, knew that whatever had happened to me was serious. One of the EMS people began to ask me a series of questions. What's my name? Do I know where I am? After answering correctly, the paramedic asked if I was able to wiggle my fingers? My answer: "No. I can't move anything." As the expression of controlled panic illuminated her face, the female paramedic hesitantly reassured me that everything would be fine. But I knew different. Life as I had known it was over. A new journey awaited me. As the next few grains of sand floated through the hourglass, I twisted my eyes upward, past the immediate foreground of my line of vision, and looked at the ceiling of the arena—at least I could do that—and unceremoniously accepted this new adventure.

Finally, after what seemed like another eternity, now with a neck brace in place and my helmet removed, I was very delicately placed on a stretcher—as if I were made of glass—and carried off the track. That was when the crowd began clapping and cheering loudly—a customary gesture when an injured rider appears to be okay and is cleared to safety. I know they were all hoping the best for me. And it was best, under the circumstances, that they didn't know I was paralyzed. It was time for the other guys to resume racing. The show had to go on. Besides, apart from being paralyzed, I was feeling no pain whatsoever. I was alive, conscious, stable, and breathing…so I was okay. I could have been dead. People have died racing dirt bikes. I was a bit confused, though, about what had just happened and wished I could turn back the clock. But life doesn't work that way. The best way I can describe how I felt at this point is that there was a reassuring silence inside my head indicating that I would come out the other side of all this.

Once I had been carried off the track, I was placed in an ambulance that was waiting in the wings for the ride to the hospital. It was time for me to leave the building. Nicole, my dear, loving wife, had joined my side. The look on her face was controlled, but I could tell she was freaking out inside. I knew my wife, and I could tell she was horrified! I forced a weak smile, but it probably wasn't very convincing. It was probably pathetic. I knew she wanted to comfort and reassure me, but she was too distraught to even go through the motions. I wanted to comfort and reassure her that I would be fine, but words didn't materialize from either one of us. Perhaps this wasn't the time for words. They would come later.

As I lay completely immobilized in the ambulance, the young female paramedic recommended in a shaky nervous tone that giving me a powerful sedative to put me out might be my best option right now. Considering there wasn't any pain to feel, I wondered if perhaps remaining conscious might be useful. However, after a quick examination of the situation, sleeping like a baby in the company of dreams wasn't such a bad idea either, and I decided that postponing this nightmare until I awoke in the morning, or whenever, suited me just fine. The final image my eyes took custody of before nodding off was the terrified expression on the paramedic's face as she attempted to reassure me, once again, that everything was going to be okay. I wanted to believe her, but the terror-stricken expression on her face painted a much different scenario than the one she was trying to sell. With that, she injected me with a syringe full of mercy, sending me off to dreamland. Before drifting off, I had just enough time to register one final thought: *Maybe I should say a prayer.*

Cue music: "Sleep Like a Baby Tonight" by U2

https://www.youtube.com/watch?v=9llw-hfafdw

CHAPTER

2

Encumbrance

While driving past a beautifully manicured golf course on a warm day in early autumn, I happened to peer over and notice three perfectly formed moguls of grass surrounding the sand trap on the eighth hole. *Hmmm, bet I could triple jump that on my motocross bike*, I thought to myself. Unable to resist the temptation, I pulled over to the side of the road, unloaded my bike, got suited up in riding gear, and within minutes, there I was, blitzing across the fairway on my Yamaha YZ250. Quite frankly, the impeccably landscaped paradise of greenery was begging to be violated by the crispy brand new tires on my motorcycle. If I hadn't known better, I'd have sworn I'd just died and gone to heaven!

Upon riding slowly over the three mounds, to assess the situation first, a couple of golfers across the fairway were pointing at me. Therefore, in courteous fashion, I gave them a friendly wave, but they didn't look too happy. Then, for some strange reason, an annoying beeping sound began to fill the air—as if a garbage truck was backing up. Nevertheless, on a mission, I blocked the irritating noise from my mind and shredded around the eighth green in perfect motocross form, dumping the clutch and grabbing a handful of throttle while looking back to watch the roost pour from my rear tire as it tore through the flawlessly manicured putting green like a chainsaw through butter. Deciding it was probably time to jump the symmetrically perfect triple and hightail it out of there, I rounded my way across the fairway, grabbed another gear, and set course to fulfill every motocrosser's dream. Suddenly, that irritating beeping sound grew even louder.

Becoming annoyed, I silently ranted, *Would someone please turn that off already!* But then, after closing my eyes for a moment, I realized the beeping was coming from inside my head. That was when this brief escape from reality began to fade off into oblivion and the perpetual uninterrupted tone of my heart beating on a monitor, beep-beep-beep-beep, became genuinely real. After awakening, I found myself lying in a hospital bed, unable to move a single muscle. Tubes were protruding from my nose. Meanwhile, the rhythmic sound of a ventilator inhaling and exhaling oxygen into my lungs filled the room. Saddened by the fact that the fantasy of shredding across the terrain of an impeccably groomed golf course on a motocross bike was nothing more than a dream, my mind quickly synchronized with reality, and I recalled the events that had led to this disconcerting situation. I mouthed the words, "No way!" followed by softly whispering to God: *This is going to be my new life? I don't know that I have the strength for this.* Sensing my condition was permanent, I further pleaded, *Please, God! Help me get through this.*

Noticing I was awake, a strange woman in a sparkling white uniform—obviously stationed in my room—quickly approached and filled in a few details. *Must be a nurse*, I thought. Feeling groggy and zombie-like, I watched her lips move and learned it was Monday, February 15th, 1999, around 9:00 AM. I was in the ICU ward of the Foothills Hospital in Calgary, Alberta. And due to a series of surgeries, I had been unconscious for three days. Fleeting thoughts rushed through my mind. I tried to focus on the nurse as she kept speaking. Not knowing when I would exactly wake up, the doctors had sent my family and friends home to get some sleep. Those were the next words to cascade from her lips. Nicole was staying with our friends Chris and Anne Bonneau, who conveniently lived just five minutes away from the hospital. Believe it or not, this was good news, as it provided a few much-needed moments to gather and collect my thoughts before getting bombarded with visitors—moments I spent contemplating the inescapably eerie feeling of somehow knowing this was going to happen. But I didn't have any answers. That mystery wouldn't be solved until later in life.

When a doctor finally came around to inform me of everything that had happened over the past three days, my first question was, "When can I go home?" He just peered at me with this puzzled expression on his face and replied, "Let's not worry about that quite yet." After revealing that my chances of recovery were slim to none—I was going to be a quadriplegic the rest of my life—the impassive doctor boldly stated that regaining the ability to breathe on my own at this point would be nothing short of a small miracle. Nevertheless, ignoring even my own intuition that this was permanent, I refused to accept this reality without a fight. And with my invincible, cocky attitude, I replied, "I'm going to walk out of here, you know." Shaking his head in disbelief, the frustrated doc left the room.

A few minutes later, I could overhear him talking in the hall amongst a group of physicians, saying, "This guy actually thinks he's going to walk out of here." They all laughed. The joke was on me. Upon overhearing their taking pleasure in my reasoning—as delusional as it might have been—as if it were the punchline to a great joke at a comedy club, I became angry. I vowed to myself that the first thing I was going to do after my recovery was punch that doctor square in the face. Thereafter, for the next hour, I vigorously kept trying to move my arms and legs—to the point that beads of sweat were pouring from my forehead. Determined never to give up, I decided right there and then… Paralysis was not going to break me!

Sometime later, a neurosurgeon met with me to explain in great detail exactly what had happened. As a result of the motorcycle accident, my fourth vertebra was completely crushed, leaving the spinal cord in that area badly bruised. During surgery, he had cleaned out the bone fragments and built a new vertebra with bone from my left hip. Then he'd reinforced the area with a stainless-steel plate spanning from my third to fifth vertebrae. Once the doctor finished explaining the nitty gritty of everything, he pulled out an MRI scan of my lower back and pointed to a previous injury. Concluding that it seemed to have happened quite some time ago, he directed my attention to an area where the spinal cord was narrowed from having been pinched by the vertebrae. An injury—in his opinion—that appeared to have been a mere millimeter from paralyzing me. After mentioning the events of being run over by a car at two years old, the neurosurgeon glanced at me with his eyebrows raised and said, "Seems as if you were walking on borrowed time."

One of the most difficult moments during those first few days of consciousness was when Nicole brought our daughters in to visit me. Because of all the medical paraphernalia attached to my body, Haylee, barely eighteen months old, was terrified of me. That broke my heart more than anything. Danielle, five at the time, just sat on my bed and asked when she and I could go to another movie together. The sadness of that possibility never happening was overwhelmingly emotional. To think I might never hold my daughters in my arms again was something I wasn't ready to accept. While fighting back the tears, I shifted my focus toward believing in the only option that seemed acceptable: a full recovery!

* * *

After a two-week stay in ICU, I was moved up to the rehabilitation unit. For those two weeks, my days consisted of staring at the ceiling and being turned on my side three times per day for twenty minutes while they pounded on my back to loosen up the phlegm in my chest. After this procedure, the nurse would suction them clean with a tube. Although I couldn't feel a thing, this was NOT fun! The highlight of my two-week stay in ICU was when Chris smuggled me in some screamin'-hot chicken wings. Believing I would have problems swallowing, the hospital kept feeding me gross pudding-type foods. I was constantly hungry. I figured if I died eating a chicken wing, then so be it. Those may have been the best wings I ever tasted. There was one thing that smug doctor WAS wrong about. Because of being on a ventilator, he guaranteed me that I would get pneumonia. But I never did.

Immediately after my neck brace came off, I began physical therapy. Chris and Anne, who visited nearly every day, taped a picture to the wall in my room of a pelican with a frog in his mouth. The frog, with his head partway down the bird's throat, had his hands wrapped tightly around the pelican's neck. The caption appropriately read... "Never Give Up!"

http://montejperepelkin.com/photos-2

During the course of the next four months, I would recover the ability to breathe on my own, nearly full use of my neck, and the capacity to shrug my shoulders. Interestingly, I never even realized how or when that transition took place. With the neck brace on, I was unable to notice. All I know is that while lying on the track—right after my crash—the only thing I could move was my eyeballs. Unfortunately, the most important recovery I was hoping for didn't happen. No matter how desperately I tried, there was no motor recovery below my shoulders, no arm function whatsoever. One thing I never did get used to was a nurse coming around every few hours to shove a tube in my penis to drain my bladder. Especially when the nurse was male. Even though I had no sensation in that area, the idea of it all felt as if I was somehow being violated. The procedure gave me the heebie-jeebies every single time. All I can say is thank God I couldn't feel it.

My stepdad, Bill, having suffered a stroke two years prior, was on disability leave. To help out, he chose to stay with Nicole and the kids at our acreage home outside of Calgary. Meanwhile, Mom had to continue running her reflexology business during the week in Wetaskiwin, Alberta. She'd drive to Calgary on weekends. Convinced he would get me walking again, Dad would come to the hospital every single day and perform reflexology treatments on my feet. If there were ever any doubts in my mind that Bill didn't love his stepson, they were completely erased after witnessing firsthand the dedication he displayed throughout this difficult time. The two of us certainly shared more than a few teary conversations together, one of which involved the events surrounding the aftermath of his stroke. Deeply moved by my reaction at the time to drop everything and drive straight to Wetaskiwin to be by his side in the hospital, Dad, although emotional while relating the experience, also seemed surprised. I responded, equally choked up, "What did you expect? You're my Dad! After all the time we spent together while I was a kid, of course I care about and love you." In the wake of contemplating his heartfelt display that afternoon, I learned that Bill had been just as unsure about me as I'd been about him. Perhaps it's normal to question the devotion of a step-family member. After all, I wasn't his biological son, and he wasn't my biological father.

One surprising visit I encountered during my hospital stay was from a member of a competing motocross sanctioning body, which also hosted off-road events—there were three different racing organizations operating in Alberta. Not writing this book in the interest of purposely exposing anyone, I'll keep this individual's identity to myself. During his brief visit, it was clear he was nudging me to sue the sanctioning body that had hosted the event I was injured in. Apparently, after learning the details of how and on which obstacle I'd broke my neck, he was adamant I had an undisputable lawsuit to file. But I already knew that, and I'd decided not to sue anybody. The track crew, other than maintenance, aren't allowed to make changes to the racecourse after practice. Therefore, by drastically changing the trajectory of the triple jump, the race crew violated that rule. And to further add to the legitimacy of the situation, in the very next pro qualifying race—just minutes after breaking my neck—another pro rider crashed in a similar manner that I had on the exact same obstacle. Instead of breaking his neck, though, he got lucky and broke his collar bone. Then, after finally realizing the jump wasn't safe, the track crew brought out a Bobcat and quickly adjusted the obstacle to a safer trajectory.

As for my decision not to sue the sanctioning body, that was something I only needed about two seconds to think about. I had walked the track prior to the race and even ridden two laps before attempting the jump. Therefore, to sue under those circumstances, in my opinion, wouldn't have been in good conscience. After all, it's not like I'd come around the first lap, attempted the jump, and been fully surprised by the change. Personally, I believe that people these days, instead of taking responsibility for their decisions, are all too willing to sacrifice their integrity for a quick payday. I'd known the risks, and the decision to attempt the obstacle had been of my own accord. To draw any other conclusion would've been dishonest. Considerably persistent, however, before my visitor left, he placed a business card from an attorney on the table next to my bed—in case I changed my mind. Apparently, this lawyer was quite eager to speak with me. Anxious to get rid of the card, however—before anyone saw it and started asking questions—when the next nurse came around to stick a catheter up my penis and relieve my bladder, I instructed her to throw it in the trash. I'm sure my visitor felt compassion for me and sincerely believed I was entitled to be compensated for the life-altering injuries I'd incurred. But his agenda seemed to be transparently self-serving. If my accident had occurred under the auspices of his sanctioning body, would he have come around and encouraged me to sue him?

* * *

After learning about the long-term seriousness of my injury, the off-road racing community was very supportive. On a daily basis, I received cards and letters expressing gratitude and appreciation for my contribution to off-road racing in Canada. The Lethbridge club even held an auction that raised nearly $20,000 for my family. This was a heartwarming gesture at a time when we seriously needed the money. And Pete Issler—whom I'd had a falling-out with in 1996—managed to put our differences aside and fill in temporarily with one builder I had a contract with until they could find another finishing carpenter to replace me. However, other than family of course, the bulk of my appreciation has to be directed towards Chris and Anne Bonneau for their undying devotion. Coming to visit regularly and catering to my every need, they seriously went above and beyond the definition of any friendship I have ever experienced.

Over the course of my 134-day stay in the hospital, I had several visits from friends, family, racing colleagues, work associates, and even a few fans. One of these stood out considerably. Chris, being my liaison to the outside world, informed me that one particular guy—an amateur racer in his early twenties—kept asking if it was alright to visit me. After giving Chris the okay, sure enough, the young fellow came with his girlfriend the very next day. I'll back up a few months to fill in the details of how this young amateur racer became acquainted with me. Every year, the Wild Rose Motocross Association would host their annual Turkey Scramble race at Blackfoot Motocross Park in Calgary. The event was always held on the Sunday afternoon of Canadian Thanksgiving weekend in October. Basically, the racecourse consisted of a twenty-minute lap around the park, with a mixture of motocross/hare scramble terrain. And other than the overall winner getting his name engraved on the club trophy—sort of like the Stanley Cup—the race never meant anything. There wasn't any money or points involved. It was just for fun. Nonetheless, this event stood out as one of my favorite races of the year. And for some silly reason, just once, I really wanted to win the overall. My two previous attempts had resulted in second-place finishes. Well, as circumstance would have it, in 1998—four months before succumbing to paralysis—I finally achieved my goal and won the race.

During the course of this endeavor, however, I apparently lapped this same young man who had visited me in the hospital. In doing so, I'd impressed upon him a familiar awe that I'd once felt. After listening to his star-struck recollection of my passing him on the course that day, I couldn't help relating it to similar sentiments of my own, when a pack of pros had passed me at a cross-country race less than seven years prior, while I was an up-and-coming amateur. Hearing the desire and enthusiasm in this young man's voice to one day become a pro racer was like looking at myself seven years before in the mirror. And for the first time since my injury, I had a moment of clarity. I silently reasoned, *If only I'd had the chance to give my twenty-three-year-old self some advice, I might not be in this hospital bed.*

Understandably, considering the severity of my injury, a common question many people often asked was "Do you regret becoming a motocross racer?" And as if scripted from a novel where the main character continually fails to ever admit he made a mistake, my reply was always the same, "No way!" After which, the person who'd asked me the question would smile back and say, "That's good." I would falsely reason that becoming paralyzed could have happened while driving to work or walking my dog for that matter. A car could have veered off out of nowhere, hit me, and left me paralyzed. Therefore, at least it happened while doing something I enjoyed. In reality, however, that was a load of crap! The truth is I put myself at risk every time I raced on the edge of that proverbial razor blade. Therein lies the issue with a majority of professional sports: Athletes get so used to living that close to the threshold of catastrophe that it becomes second nature. That is, until they miscalculate and fall off the edge of the razor blade. Even still, because we can't turn back the clock and undo what's been done, our egos convince us that it was worth it. Except, that's a lie; it's not worth it. If given the chance to go back in time and walk away from racing, I would do it in a heartbeat! Dismissing the opportunity to hold my kids and raise them as an able-bodied father, to deny them and myself of that, would be an unforgivable crime against the essence of life itself. Unfortunately, there are no do-overs in this life.

Admittedly, the type of injury that I sustained does happen to people as a result of any number of common occurrences each and every day. It doesn't have to be complicated or dramatic. A simple fall from a stepladder can do the trick. But it happened to me because of unnecessary risks I willingly imposed on myself, thus revealing the provocative lesson of my painfully obvious erroneous lifestyle. Plain and simple, by racing motorcycles, I exposed myself and the well-being of my family to unnecessary risk—I put my personal pursuits ahead of theirs. Does that mean I sit around holding on to regret and hating life? Absolutely not! Doing the best I can with what I have while learning from past mistakes is what gives me contentment, that and knowing even the worst situations can often have a silver lining. I just needed to find out what that silver lining was.

One of the most difficult transitions of paralysis involved accepting the fact that the remainder of my life would be spent in a wheelchair. Still wanting to believe a full recovery was just over the horizon, when the guy came around to size me up and fit me with a power wheelchair, I was hesitant and even declined at first. Bob was the fellow's name. I can still recall Bob distinctly warning me—because the process of getting a power chair doesn't happen overnight—I might regret not having that independence once released from the hospital. Of course, he was right! Fortunately, I didn't prolong the process more than a few weeks before coming to my senses. My first time sitting in that chair was an experience in itself. It felt as if I were getting a new body part. Over time, that's exactly what it became…an extension of me. If I wasn't in bed, I was always in that chair; it literally became a part of me. If it broke down, I was stranded. Fortunately, having raced motorcycles, adapting to driving the chair with my chin was a breeze. Soon I was zooming around like the mischievous rabbit who made fun of the cautious tortoise. I guess some things never change.

Shortly before my release from the hospital, I encountered a situation that gave me a much-needed dose of reality. Still looking toward and hoping for a full recovery, this little event finally set me straight. While the nurse was putting my socks on one morning, I would have sworn I could feel her touching my leg. Accordingly, I began to get excited. After all, that's what I had been hoping for all along: first, sensation, and then motor function would return. Later that same morning, when the spinal cord specialist popped in to see me, I voiced my enthusiasm in believing my legs were beginning to regain sensation. To which he answered, "Well, let's see," and he proceeded to roll up my pant leg and begin tapping his pen against my lower leg. Immediately, I piped up and said, "Yeah! I can feel that!" Except, from my vantage point, I couldn't actually see his pen making contact with my leg. All I saw was his arm making the motion. That was when I realized he was tricking me, and I recanted. "You're not actually tapping my leg, are you?" I asked him. The considerate doctor simply shook his head, verifying that he wasn't. He explained how the act of watching something touch you can often facilitate the false perception of sensation. Then he offered me this advice: "Focus on what you have today and don't worry about tomorrow. Whatever recovery may happen in the future, you can deal with then. But for now, this is your life. The sooner you accept this reality, the sooner you can begin living again."

The doctor's counsel was something I desperately needed to hear. From that day forward, instead of waiting for a miracle that I knew wasn't going to happen, I started focusing on making the best of my new life. Instead of dreading to wake up in the morning, I would welcome first light and embrace each new day with anticipation of whatever it had in store for me, great or small. First thing I did was head down to the hospital restaurant with Dad and have a grilled cheese sandwich with a side of fries and gravy—my favorite as a kid. That moment marked my first real step towards recovery.

As for the young amateur racer who came to see me that day, he and his girlfriend became regular visitors. She, being a hairdresser, even cut my hair during one visit. You could say we became friends. Then, all of a sudden, they stopped visiting. I found this rather odd, but I had enough other visitors and things to think about, I didn't dwell on it. I soon enough learned that he had committed suicide. Needless to say, I was utterly in disbelief. This was a good-looking kid with a beautiful girlfriend and a great job. All I could think was *What problems could he possibly have that were worse than mine?* After all, I was the one lying in a hospital bed, paralyzed from the neck down.

Nevertheless, even after four and a half months in the hospital, I was never able to shake the eerie sensation of waking in the morning, feeling as if I was in a hotel room, wondering how I'd gotten there. Following a session of deep contemplation about trying to understand why I had ended up a quadriplegic and why a kid with seemingly everything going for him would resort to such drastic measures as suicide, surprisingly, I found some much needed strength and determination. As much as my situation seemed impossible to bear at times, never once was I even close to my breaking point. Somewhere in all that, while lying in a hospital bed paralyzed, I considered myself fortunate. I decided it was time to stop looking for answers and start living my life.

When the time finally arrived to return home, it felt as if I were being released from prison. Saying goodbye to hospital food, a cramped room, and constant interruptions all night when I was trying to sleep in exchange for being with my children in my own house was definitely a welcome milestone. That first drive up the long driveway towards our house was an extremely emotional experience. Though it had been less than five months since the accident, it felt as if I hadn't been home in years! Thankfully, Frank and Tony—owners of one home builder I had a contract with—were kind enough to build me a wheelchair ramp so that I could get into my house. Going through the front door in my powerchair for the very first time and recognizing the familiar aroma of our newly built house—sort of like that new car smell—intensified my emotions to the point where my eyes welled up with joy. Finally, no more hospital smell!

Being at home with my wife and children felt like finding the first two pieces of a jigsaw puzzle that fit together. For the first time in nearly five months, something in my life felt normal. That was when the sand in the hour glass of my life finally began to fall at the natural rate of gravity. Time stopped crawling. My kids, as young as they were, were probably more excited than I was. Eager to show me the rabbits they'd found in the old barn on our property and kept in a big cage as pets, their enthusiasm at finally having their dad home was unmistakably noticeable. Surprisingly, my daughters had no reservations whatsoever about me being paralyzed. In fact, it seemed they enjoyed helping me when I needed it. Asking for help, however, was not something I was very good at. Rather than ask for simple assistance, I'd often suffer for hours with my arm or leg in an awkward position.

http://montejperepelkin.com/photos-3

A short while after being released, I returned to the hospital for a follow-up session of physical therapy. I was supposed to keep up regular weekly visits, but I never did. Not particularly fond of ever having to spend any amount of time in the hospital ever again, I canceled my remaining appointments. Other than the annual check-ups with my appointed spinal cord doctor, I was on my own. Upon returning from that final visit to the hospital—Chris and Anne took me in their truck—something rather pathetic, yet amusing, still sticks out in my mind. While sitting in the front seat next to Chris, I felt the sudden urge to spit. After asking Chris to hit the button and roll down my window for a second, I attempted to spit outside. However, because of my severely reduced lung power, it ended up trickling down my chin. Anne burst out laughing and wiped my face with a Kleenex. As if it wasn't already bad enough that I couldn't move, I couldn't even spit. Talk about losing everything!

One thing I now had plenty of was time to reflect on my life. Not in a nostalgic sort of way—I was too young for that—but just taking stock of where I'd been in order to figure out where to go from the point at which I had so suddenly and unexpectedly found myself. Having always been a planner, not having any foresight or prospects with regards to my future was somewhat disconcerting. As an able-bodied man, I had accomplished quite a bit in my thirty years of life. There was a lot to consider, some of it painful, some of it bittersweet, some of it joyful, and some of it inspiring. Because of being raised by my wonderful mom, Betty, and stepdad, Bill, I'd acquired a strong work ethic and entrepreneurial spirit from them. Just when I thought I'd had it all figured out and my life was pointing in the right direction, my world had been flipped upside down. Unsure as to what my next move might be, one thing I did know…I needed a plan. And taking a trip down memory lane was a good place to start.

Cue music: "My Silver Lining" by First Aid Kit

https://www.youtube.com/watch?v=DKL4X0PZz7M

CHAPTER

3

Twenty-Eight Years Earlier

Unlike most people, I am blessed—or cursed, depending on how you want to look at—with distinct memories that stretch back to almost the very beginning. I don't quite remember being in my mother's womb, as some people claim to, but I do remember being a toddler. Though many memories are hazy, like looking through a foggy windowpane, some remain quite vivid. By the time I reached primary school age, my recollections of that time become clearer. My teen years and beyond reach a point of crystal clearness. Okay, here we go. This is my journey from the beginning. It began on a Thursday in 1969, January 9th to be precise, in Tisdale, Saskatchewan. Nearby Hudson Bay, Saskatchewan, where my parents lived, wasn't equipped to deliver babies. Hudson Bay, a typical small town in the east-central area of the province, was a place where nothing much ever happened and everybody knew pretty well everybody else. The town's population of roughly 1,500 at that time mostly relied on the lumber industry for its livelihood.

I was born on the cusp of a new era. A flamboyant Pierre Trudeau was well into his first year of being Canada's prime minister. There were lots of societal changes going on, the most powerful youth culture in the history of the planet was growing up, the economy was booming, and pop culture was thriving. Perhaps the most monumental of all human achievements took place in 1969, when, in July, Apollo 11 astronauts Neil Armstrong and Edwin Aldrin Jr. took mankind's first walk on the moon. And to keep up with our kind's penchant for war and large-scale slaughter, the Vietnam War was raging. It would continue to escalate well into the early 1970s, when I first started to become cognizant of my sentience. Needless to say, I have no memories of those historic events, but I do have some recollections of the more dramatic personal incidents that would severely affect my life.

The year was 1971; I was two years old, lying in my bed, unable to sleep. I felt like I was tied into a knot. Aware that it was somewhat late, my disquieting posture was generated from the sound of my parents fighting in the next room. Distinct shouting, emanating from both of them like a cat and dog going at it, echoed through the darkness. Feeling moderately concerned, but not afraid, I heard my mom shout, "I'm not coming back!" The slamming of a door startled me into an upright position. Having discerned her upset demeanor through my open bedroom door, I said as she walked down the hallway, "It's okay, Mom. You can sleep with me. My bed is warmer anyway." Upon hearing my voice, she entered my room and crawled next to me in bed. She gently caressed the side of my face, and I instantly felt a sense of solace. I fell asleep very soon after.

That, in a nutshell, was the end of my parents' marriage and what sparked an instantaneous deviation from what was my then current course in life. The sequence of events that unfolded after that—at a rapid pace—would have a subsequent impact on my life forever. Had my parents stayed together, who knows what direction I would have taken. One can only speculate. "What ifs" can grow to be troublesome companions that butt into our lives like unwanted company as we age, especially during moments of doubt and when reflecting on the past. Is cause and effect the result of making decisions, a matter of rolling the dice, or fate? I have my own opinions on that, but I'd rather just tell my story and let the chips fall where they may.

Waking up the following morning after my parents' altercation, the first feeling I remember experiencing was that now I was in charge; it was up to me to look after Mom. Surprisingly, even at that young age, I understood exactly what had transpired. Yet there was no feeling of trepidation at all. According to Mom, my dad, whose name was Roy, never really took any interest in me. Therefore, he never spent any quality time with me. Perhaps this explains why I have virtually no memories of my biological father from childhood. My memories of him date back to later in my life. As a toddler, to me, Roy was just a guy who had lived with my mom—I never thought of him as my dad. Accordingly, throughout my entire life, I've always lived under the preeminent shadow of feeling born without a father. I say that not in the spirit of pity or regret—it simply is what it is. It's important to mention that I mean no disrespect to Roy. I feel no resentment towards him. We all make choices in life based on our resolve and the knowledge we possess at the time. It's not my place to judge him. Many years later, Roy remarried and had four beautiful children, whom I'm sure he is a wonderful father to. Perhaps he just wasn't ready to be a dad when I came into his young life. I did, however, spend a considerable amount of time with my mom. Because of her marriage breakup, we became a closer team than I'm sure we would have if there had been no divorce. Perhaps overcompensating for her leaving my father, while I was growing up, Mom would allow me to get away with more than she should have.

* * *

A few months before Roy and Betty's argument that fateful evening, an unforgettable event would take place that contributed to the demise of my parents' marriage. As it turns out, it's also my very first memory. I was playing on the driveway at my babysitter's place roughly six feet behind a parked vehicle. Roy, who was a truck driver, wasn't around a whole lot. Mom, twenty-five years old at the time, was employed as a bookkeeper during the day at a local nightclub. I was a quiet, well-behaved kid who could play contently on his own for long periods of time. Sitting cross-legged, with my back more or less centered to the rear bumper of the vehicle, I was playing with my toy truck. It was a warm day, with the sun shining brightly. I didn't have a care in the world and was amusing myself with my toy truck. I can still remember exactly what I was wearing: a yellow shirt and red corduroy pants. Red was and still is my favorite color. Upon hearing the front door of the house open and close, I looked over to see who it was. From my vantage point, I could only see the person's head. It was the lady visiting my babysitter. I turned my focus back to making *vroom-vroom* sounds and continued playing with my truck. I did not realize, however, that it was the visitor's car I was sitting behind. Next, I heard the thump of the car door slamming, followed by the engine starting. Although fairly certain she'd seen me, my immediate inclination was to get out of there. Before I even had a chance to react, however, the car unhesitatingly began to back up. Now in panic mode, I scrambled to move out of the way, but it was too late. The bumper smacked me square in the back of the head, and under the car I went. Having heard or felt the thump of my head making contact with her rear bumper, the driver stopped the automobile and stepped out. Meanwhile, there I was, ear mashed into the concrete and with my legs folded over and behind me—basically rolled in to a ball. I remember the situation being somewhat uncomfortable. Even a flexible gymnast would have had a hard time getting into that position. I was beneath the center of the vehicle, tangled up in such a way that my line of sight was conveniently facing the driver's side. When the woman stepped out of the automobile, I could clearly see her legs and feet. That was my only view. In an effort to peer under the car and inspect underneath, she proceeded to bend down on one knee. That was when our eyes locked. Not uttering a sound—I wasn't crying and never even made a peep—we stared at each other for what seemed like an eternity. My only thoughts were: *That's right, you just backed over me. Thanks for ruining my entire day, lady! Now, how about getting me out from under here?*

After continuing to stare bewilderingly into my eyes, the reality of the moment and what she had done must have finally sunk in. In an instant, her face changed from absolute confusion to full-blown hysteria. A loud shriek emanated from deep down in her throat, followed by the words "OH MY GOD!" Her scream, more terrifying than anything else, had me wondering if perhaps this predicament was worse than I thought. The way I was pinned underneath the car made it impossible to move my head and ascertain the situation for myself. Other than the fact that it was extremely uncomfortable, I don't remember feeling any obvious pain. And throughout the entire ordeal, never once did I cry or murmur a single complaint. This was probably more disconcerting to the woman than the fact that she had run over me. It's important to note that the wheels of her vehicle hadn't run over me at all. Fortunately! Or I might not have been around to write this book.

I don't recall much of what happened after that. An ambulance was summoned to free me from beneath the car and rush me to the Hudson Bay hospital. The attending physician, expecting Mom to be a total basket case after hearing that her son had just been run over by a car, decided he'd better go to her place of employment and deliver the news in person. Clearly, this doctor didn't know my mother. When he walked into Mom's office, she looked up, took one glance at him, and, before he was able to utter a single word, instantly knew the reason for his presence. As circumstance would have it, three days earlier, she'd had a vivid dream of this exact situation, right down to the distinct detail of the doctor visiting her at work to inform her of what had happened to me. Because she already knew the outcome, she wasn't alarmed at all. I didn't find out about Mom's dream until much later in life and, honestly, never really thought much of it.

According to the paramedics who were on the scene at the babysitter's driveway, I remained in good spirits throughout the entire ordeal. And after they finally got me out from underneath the car, unaware of the seriousness of my injury, at one point, I even stood up in protest, trying to convince everyone I was just fine. I can't say who deserves the credit for the attitude I displayed that day. I was simply a two-year-old child reacting on instinct when I attempted to get up to prove I could handle the situation on my own. Of course, I was far from able to handle it on my own—I had a severely broken pelvis. When all was said and done, just as Mom's dream had reassured her, I ended up being just fine. Ironically, roughly twenty-eight years later, I would be paralyzed in a racing accident. Considering that I could very easily have been paralyzed from being run over by my babysitter's visitor, some would say it was my fate, destiny, or whatever you want to call it to end up like this. From that point of view, it seems I was living on borrowed time. Were there lessons to be learned? Lessons I needed to learn? I don't know the answers to those questions, but I can tell you this unequivocally: A life-altering injury such as paralysis will test you beyond your limits. And IF it doesn't break you, it will teach you more about life and yourself than you ever believed possible.

* * *

I've often wondered how my memory is able to reconstruct with vivid detail these occurrences from such an early age. Perhaps something that dramatic is more apt to stand out. It was fairly significant, after all. Nevertheless, I've come to realize that events such as this, when they happen early in life, determine our resolve in terms of how we handle future obstacles and hardships that face us later on. We will either embrace a difficult situation and conquer it or succumb to it and allow the situation to break us. We can choose to be either an egg or a rock. Personally, I prefer letting the situation break itself against me. Well, except for that one time, but I'll get to that later. Unfortunately for Roy, he was home on a day off work when I was run over in the babysitter's driveway. As I could have been home with him, or should have been by Mom's account, she was furious with him. In his defense, however, it was the early 1970s—a time when dads just weren't into the parenting role like they are today. Besides, this wasn't the first time, or the last, that a child was at the babysitter's place while a parent had the day off work. It's easy to have twenty-twenty hindsight. From my mother's point of view, however, this accident was the proverbial "straw that broke the camel's back" in their marriage. After four years of marriage, Roy and Betty went their separate ways and later divorced.

Mom and I were on our own, and I recall moving around a lot after leaving Hudson Bay. Interestingly, because we didn't own a car and money was in short supply, hitchhiking became a regular mode of transportation for us. I recollect one instance in particular—I don't remember where we were going, but it was dark outside—when a semi truck stopped to pick us up. We climbed into the big cab, and I crawled into the sleeper area. I had a painful toothache that affected my entire mouth. For some reason, Mom thought chewing gum would help. It didn't! That was the first time I ever remember crying, and not because of the scary truck driver. He was really nice, actually. The pain in my mouth was unbearable, and it's probably a big part of why I still dislike going to the dentist even today.

I suppose one could conclude that hitchhiking with a toddler wasn't the smartest thing to do. But hey, who's judging. It was the seventies. We were poor and pretty much homeless for a while. In retrospect, we could have sued the lady or her insurance company for backing over me. However, other than spending an extended stay in the hospital, I was fine. Even though she desperately needed money, Mom considered it wouldn't have been in good conscience to take such action. Fortunately, Saskatchewan healthcare covered the expenses of the doctors and my hospital stay. After their marriage tanked, my father never contributed financially to Mom's and my well-being. Because Mom and I didn't have it easy by any means, Roy's actions, or lack thereof, taught me a valuable lesson that left a significant impression on me. Growing up without a father for the first five years of my life affected me psychologically in many ways, including the hardship of living hand to mouth. The lessons learned from this experience instilled within me a strong conscience when it came to financial responsibilities. Later in life, I would learn firsthand what the collateral damage can be when you divorce while raising a child or children.

It wasn't until well into my late teens that I found out Roy had reneged on his financial contributions to raise an estranged son—never mind paying alimony to his ex-wife. I definitely lost a little respect for him upon learning those details; in the process, I gained more for my mom. Betty never tried turning me against my father, which so often is the case when marriages run afoul and there are children caught in the middle. Mom could have easily justified such an injustice as grist for the mill. However, I'm sure it didn't help that she was a very prideful person and therefore never asked Roy for help. But in my opinion, a mother shouldn't need to ask for financial support, as it really comes down to honor, responsibility, integrity, and dignity.

I'm aware that my narrative paints a rather ugly portrait of my biological father, but that's not my intention; it's simply a component of this story that is impossible to omit. Besides, as you will soon discover, I'll be using the same brush of impartiality to paint my own portrait throughout this book. I don't hold a grudge or resent Roy at all. In fact, there are several qualities about him—some of which I'll get to later—that I admire. Besides, I'm quite certain Roy would have preferred to do things differently with regards to his ex-wife and son. Only he knows the reasons why he didn't, and I never asked him. After getting remarried, he had four more kids and raised them to adulthood, of which he did, for all intents and purposes, a fine job. I believe he had learned his lessons and did his best not to repeat the same mistakes. I know there are things that I've done or didn't do with my children that I would like to do over and correct. God knows I've certainly made an overabundance of errors throughout my life. I'm quite certain most of us—if we're honest—have a few regrets here and there when it comes to our past. Nobody's perfect, and we all make mistakes. However, there's a difference between living with regret and recognizing the missteps in one's life.

As an adult, I read a profoundly informative book by Henry Cloud entitled *Integrity*. In the book, Cloud defines what he believes is the hallmark of true character, stating that when a person possesses such a quality, they have the ability to see oneself clearly and accurately while maintaining the desire and strength to self-correct—when needed. I would add that in order to view ourselves honestly and be able to make those necessary adjustments that Cloud describes, we must first ignore our precious little egos and cultivate a spirit of humility. Further testing of our character is when someone else makes negative comments about us. Let's face it, to resist the natural inclination to defend oneself can be difficult. To counteract that knee-jerk reaction—of taking offence or retaliating—with sincere self-examination to see if there's any truth to it, that's the backbone of humility. Speaking personally, I certainly haven't mastered it. But I keep trying. Unfortunately, pride is that which blinds us from humility.

CHAPTER

4

The Art of Shoplifting

After moving around different parts of western Canada, living like gypsies, Mom and I finally settled in Vancouver, British Columbia. I was around three years old, and we would live in this vibrant city for approximately the next two years. Times were tough, and money was tight, causing Mom to transition from one job to the next in an effort to find the right one that could afford us a modestly comfortable living. Desiring the privacy of a single dwelling as opposed to an apartment building, Mom found a decent rental unit. The house was comfortable and affordable. It came with a developed basement, which could be sublet to help pay the bills. Betty did manage to scrape enough money together to finally purchase a vehicle. One of the things we enjoyed was going to the airport to watch the jet airplanes land and take off. As it was free entertainment, we did that quite regularly. I still enjoy plane watching to this day. There's a certain magnificence in how something that large can leave the ground and fly so gracefully.

As time went on, Mom kept working mostly in bartending and waitressing positions. I imagine that was about the best she could get with a ninth-grade education. Nevertheless, I have a lot of admiration for her. She was surviving in an industry that couldn't have been easy for a young single mother in the 1970s. From the pictures I've seen of her, I don't hesitate to say that Betty was an attractive woman. I'm sure that played in her favor while working as a bartender or waitress, both at getting the jobs and carrying them out. It's human nature to gravitate towards beauty. Considering how independent and prideful Mom was, taking the easy road and opting for welfare was inconceivable to her.

Not long after moving into our house, Mom became very sick and had to be hospitalized, with no one to look after me and no financial assistance from anyone. Her sister, Corrine, who also lived in Vancouver, kept me overnight but worked full time during the days. Therefore, all she could do—before heading to work each morning—was drive me to the hospital, where I would stay with Mom all day in her room. But that didn't jive for very long. The nursing staff quickly saw what was going on, and soon social services got involved, placing me in a temporary foster home until my mother returned to health. Terrified of what might happen to me while in foster care, this was precisely what Mom was trying to avoid. However, the social worker handling the case was quite understanding of our situation. She reassured us that I would be cared for very well and placed with a qualified family who had a long-standing, spotless reputation. The social worker was right. They were awesome, and generous too. My temporary parents bought me an entire wardrobe of brand-new clothes, along with some new toys, something I did not have plenty of. Their kindness was a great distraction from what was nothing short of a scary situation. At this juncture in our lives, Mom and I really only had each other; therefore, I did miss her terribly.

To complicate things, the doctors couldn't figure out why my mother was sick. Apparently, one of her legs had become swollen, and they didn't know why. She had been shot in the foot at a young age by her brother while he'd been cleaning his gun. Unbelievable, yes!

How does something like that even happen? I've never been given a satisfactory explanation. Her doctor believed that may have had something to do with her leg problem. Assuming it was some sort of infection, the doctor administered a full spectrum of antibiotics through IV, which seemed to clear up whatever it was. I was only in foster care for about two weeks before I returned home with Mom, who was back to full health. Soon after being discharged from the hospital, she landed decent full-time employment with Johann Strauss—a classy hotel—working in the lounge as a waitress. Finally, our lives began to resemble some sort of normalcy—not that I knew the difference between what was or wasn't normal. But I could tell Mom was happier. She even found a young woman to rent the basement from us. Her name was Louise. Immediately taking a liking to me, Louise and I got along really well.

* * *

Our lives settled into a routine, and I felt a certain stability in it— at least, as stable as it can get for a single mom raising a young kid. One day, my mother, who was a rather sociable person, met a woman named Mary. This kind woman was willing to look after me during the days while Mom was at work. On the surface of things, the chance meeting of Betty and Mary seemed like a heaven-orchestrated occasion. But for me, there proved to be a life-influencing element attached to the deal. At least, one could come to that conclusion in retrospect. Then again, if Mary hadn't come into our orbit to unwittingly provide the spark to ignite a character trait that may have already been within me, it may well have occurred in some other fashion.

Mary had a daughter, Kelly, who was two years older than I. Kelly and I became very close friends. Mary seemed to be a decent mother, and Betty trusted that I was in good hands. What she didn't know, however, was that Mary was somewhat naïve in her ways. Mary was quite a bit older than my mom and also a single mother, raising Kelly on social assistance. Her other children were older, living on their own. I don't recall seeing Kelly's dad at any time. I don't know if she actually ever saw much of him herself.

One afternoon, I accompanied Kelly to the store in order to buy a carton of cigarettes. Because Mary wasn't a smoker, it may have been my mom—a smoker—who sent us while we were visiting. It seemed like nearly every adult smoked back then, and I had a severe aversion to it. The odor of cigarette smoke was simply detestable to me and still is. The store was just down the street; therefore, it wasn't unusual for Kelly and myself to be sent out on our own, even though we were nearly in the downtown core of Vancouver. These days—because we were only four and six years old—that would be considered grounds for child endangerment. But in the seventies, it was normal for little kids to roam the streets. Well, at least, it was normal for us.

On the way to the store, Kelly held my hand, kind of like a big sister looking after her little brother. Instead of going to the corner store where we were supposed to go, however, we went a block farther to the supermarket. I didn't care. What did it matter to me? But there was a reason Kelly headed to the supermarket. Little did I know that this would be my first lesson in shoplifting. It was quite simple really. The cartons of cigarettes at the corner store were behind the counter, making them impossible to steal. But during the 1970s, it still wasn't uncommon for grocery stores to keep cartons of cigarettes on open shelves along with everything else, usually in the coffee aisle. Maybe it was because both contained ingredients that were habit forming or it was somebody's idea of a joke. At the time, however, there wasn't much public awareness of the addictiveness of nicotine and caffeine.

Not long into the 1980s, however, cigarettes were relocated from store shelves to behind the counter, in most cases under lock and key.

Needless to say, the plan was to steal the carton of cigarettes and keep the money to buy candy, pop, and potato chips. Kelly had it all figured out. Not your typical six-year-old, Kelly was pretty crafty to think of that, but I'm skeptical that she came up with that concept on her own. I'm quite confident she picked that little stunt up from someone else—perhaps her older siblings. The deed was easy for us to accomplish. After all, who would suspect a couple of kids as young as we were of coming into a store to steal something, especially cigarettes. We just walked out the front door, carrying them in plain sight. Immediately after getting outside the store, we ran for a little bit—not that we were being chased—but the adrenaline rush just inclined us to. I'd never done anything like that before. Quite honestly, the whole experience was exhilarating and kind of fun too.

Soon after the cigarette-stealing caper, Kelly and I were swiping candy and trinkets every day from every little retail outlet in the neighborhood. We'd walk in with a dime, buy a little bag of one-cent candies, and leave with pockets full of miscellaneous treats. My only thought was: *Why didn't I think of this?* Occasionally, Mary would ask how we acquired the goods, for which Kelly always had a clever answer. She was a quick thinker. Surprisingly, Mary never suspected a thing. Shoplifting had become a part of my everyday life. Not long after, I witnessed Kelly taking money from her mom's purse, something I would eventually do to my mom. Learning these devious skills from Kelly was another one of those life-altering moments that would inevitably lead to unpleasant consequences down the road. For clarification, in no way am I painting Kelly with the brushstrokes of a scapegoat. I may have only been four years old, but I knew what we were doing was wrong. However, the fact that it was wrong got lost within the inertia of excitement we experienced. I can't speak for Kelly, but the reward from stealing simply outweighed and, over time, desensitized any sense of right and wrong I might have had in that regard, as whatever guilt associated to the acts were buried under a cloud of minimization. To me, it wasn't a big deal. I mean, there were so many cartons of cigarettes, so much candy, etc. Who was going to miss the few items we purloined? All that needed to be done was to restock the shelves. Looking back at these instances—perhaps because of the unsheltered life we were exposed to at the time—it's quite evident that Kelly and I knew more about the adult world than our childlike minds should have been capable of knowing.

* * *

Mom would meet my future stepdad, Bill Perepelkin, shortly after I turned five. According to Mom, Bill showed sincere fatherly compassion towards me and immediately began treating me as if I were his own son. That's what drew Betty to Bill, and they soon developed a romantic relationship. I can honestly say that not once do I remember Roy, my biological father, ever coming to see me. It was almost as if he never existed. From an optimistic point of view, it could be considered a blessing that I never formed a relationship with him. That way, I had nothing to miss. However, speaking as a parent, it would kill me if my kids never missed me. Not long into Mom and Bill's relationship, the three of us would move to Manitoba. Our destination was the province's capital city, Winnipeg, where my soon-to-be stepdad was offered a job with Transair airline. Knowing I enjoyed watching the planes land and take off, one day after work, Bill brought home a miniature-scale airplane of a Boeing 747—the coolest toy I had ever seen. Not surprisingly, it wasn't long before Bill and I became close. I instantly took a liking to him. He was a good man, and I believe kids pick up on that before adults can.

Mom and Bill bought a double-wide mobile home in Lockport, a small unincorporated community some twenty-eight kilometers outside of Winnipeg. Lockport, located near the Red River, was a nice place, actually…for a trailer park! Our lot backed onto Gunns Creek, with lots of trees on the other side of the creek. It wasn't your typical trailer-park-type setting. After living in a big city, it was kind of pleasant finding myself in something that approximated a rural paradise. Mary and Kelly would follow us from Vancouver, but they chose to live in Winnipeg—about twenty-five minutes from Lockport. Mom and Bill remained close friends with Mary while we lived in Lockport. On occasion, Kelly and I would continue to see each other on weekends, but not nearly as often. With all the kids living in that little trailer park, it didn't take me long to make friends in Lockport. Bill even bought me a new bicycle that year. It was purple, with a big banana seat that had colorful flowers printed all over it. I thought it was pretty cool. Bill taught me how to ride the bike in front of our new home. That day is still quite vivid and a great memory. Clearly, my mom's life, and my life, had definitely been improved by the presence of Bill. Mom was happy, and so was I. In no time, I began calling Bill Perepelkin "Dad."

Kindergarten was the next adventure in my journey through this life. Unfortunately, I soon discovered that school was quite boring. The best part was taking a bus to school every day. I felt so grown up. A particular memory that's alive and well involves a set of circumstances that occurred after arriving home from school one afternoon. It was one of those beautiful prairie autumn days. The sky was blue, and the sun bright. Big, crunchy leaves covered the landscape. There were loads of mature trees throughout the trailer court, adding to the allure of living there. A corner store was located only a few blocks from where we lived, and I desperately wanted to ride my bike there. With no money, however, and in an effort to find some spare change, I went into my parents' bedroom and started going through some of their drawers. I don't know where Mom was at the time, but she was around, probably somewhere outside. Finally, I came across a bunch of coins in a jewelry box on their dresser. I'd hit the jackpot. They weren't like normal coins, though, or at least not like any I had seen before. Taking a couple of the bigger ones, off to the store I went. Upon arriving at the corner store—knowing they weren't regular coins—I asked the lady behind the counter if she would accept them, and if so, how much were they worth. From my recollection, she was somewhat advanced in age. However, when you're five, everyone seems old. She looked at the coins for a few seconds and then went to talk with someone else about them. That was when my active imagination kicked in, wondering if perhaps this lady knew my mom and was planning to call her. Knowing full well Mom would tan my butt if she knew what I was up to, I figured my goose could very well be cooked. My heart began to race. This was, after all, my first solo malfeasance. Just before making a break for it and getting my juvenile little butt out of there, the lady returned to inform me how much the coins were worth. Surprisingly, it was a lot more than I was expecting. After purchasing a pop, a bag of chips, and stuffing my pockets with a bunch of bubblegum packages, each one containing a lick-on tattoo, I went outside to enjoy the spoils.

Upon arriving back at home—now with tattoos plastered up and down both my arms—Mom enquired as to where the tattoos had come from. Unfortunately, I hadn't thought that part through. Consequently, this led to my first experience in getting busted. Apparently, I wasn't the quick thinker my partner in crime Kelly was. I just fessed up to the entire operation. Mom was furious. Considering my thieving career had spanned nearly two years already, I'd had a fairly good run. But sooner or later, everyone eventually gets caught. The smell of those tattoos on my arm is still quite vivid; it was sweet with a sort of baseball card bubblegum odor. I thought they were pretty darn cool. Mom, however, did not. She rubbed my skin raw with soap and water until they finally came off.

When Bill came home from work, in an effort to retrieve the coins, he took me back to the store. Turned out they were vintage and exceedingly more valuable than what the store owner had given me. Bill explained the situation to the store clerk—that I wasn't supposed to take the coins—but it was to no avail. The owner told a tale of how they'd already been taken to the bank and deposited. This made Mom even more furious, and I received my very first spanking from Bill. His prescribed method of punishment was roughly five lashes with his belt on my butt. Surprisingly, it didn't really hurt all that bad. Consequently, that form of discipline didn't suffice as a deterrent to stealing. Mistakenly, instead of punishment for doing something wrong, I viewed the strap as punishment for getting caught. Therefore, being the resourceful and fearless child I was, I simply stepped up and became craftier at evading getting caught. And stealing from my parents would become a pattern.

One day after school, during my walk home from the designated school bus drop-off point—two blocks our home—another enticing opportunity came along. Upon passing by our neighbor's yard, I noticed this really cool airplane just sitting there on the corner of their lawn about three feet away from the sidewalk. It was one of those miniature gas-powered airplanes that had a real motor and propeller. Considering my fascination with aircraft, I just had to have it! After a brief look around to see if anyone was watching, I grabbed it and ran home to hide it under our deck. Unbeknownst to me, however, one of the residents inside the trailer had seen me take the plane and phoned my mom moments later. I would have preferred she just come out to scold me and take the plane back.

Mom soon came outside, acting like everything was kosher, and started asking me about my day. Having no clue that she already knew, I was a pretty cool cucumber at this juncture. Then she informed me that the neighbor had called to ask if we might have seen anyone take an expensive toy from their yard. Still maintaining my cool, I replied, "What kind of toy was it? Maybe I can help her look for it." Then, all of a sudden, Mom got dead serious. By this point, it would be safe to assume she was getting fed up with my shenanigans, and she further explained how imperative it was that I return the airplane immediately along with an apology for taking it. I sheepishly complied. Later, Mom sat me down and proceeded to tell me that a lady was coming over from social services in about an hour to take me away to live in a foster home where bad kids go when they keep doing bad things and don't listen to their parents. Too smart for my own good, however, I knew all along that she was just trying to scare me or perhaps teach me a lesson. She even went so far as to take me for a walk to the store and buy me a kind of going-away pop while telling me that she would miss me, really trying to pour it on. But I still wasn't buying it. Somehow I knew she was bluffing, and so I just played along.

Little did I know, however, there actually was someone coming over who would, in fact, try to reason with me in an attempt to explain that what I'd done wasn't acceptable. But I didn't take the situation seriously at all. Later in life, I was made aware that the lady who came to give me a dressing down really was a social worker. But she wasn't there to take me away. Just as I suspected, she was attempting to scare me straight. I commend my parents' effort at trying something different, but the fact that I knew it was an empty threat negated its effect completely. The only emotion I remember feeling from that incident was amusement. Unfortunately, by this juncture, my conscience was practically numb to the fact that stealing was wrong. After learning to enjoy the art with Kelly, it seemed that no form of punishment was effective at extinguishing the pleasure I got from acquiring desired items. With the self-adopted philosophy that it was only considered wrong if you got caught, stealing became a welcomed challenge—second nature to me.

Shortly after their failed attempt at scaring me straight, Mom and Dad must have thought perhaps God might have a chance at restoring the conscience of their misguided son, and they enrolled me in Sunday school. That was when I learned the story of Noah's Ark and the concept of God, a concept that I found both fascinating and confusing, sparking a flurry of questions for my poor Sunday school teacher. These included: How did Noah get all those animals in the ark? How did he know to build the ark? What if he didn't finish on time? Who is God? What does he look like? Where does he live? I was extremely intrigued. But the teacher gave me little-kid answers that didn't make a whole lot of sense or answer my questions to the degree that I was capable of understanding.

I attended Sunday school a few more times, but the teacher would only allow me to ask one question per session. Besides, her kindergarten-type answers just created more questions than they answered anyway. I couldn't help but think what a big waste of time this whole going-to-school-on-Sunday thing was. However, we did get a free candy bar at the conclusion of each lesson. We were only supposed to take one treat. Of course, I always palmed an extra one. My dear, loving parents were doing their best to correct my waywardness, but I'm not sure there was anything they could do. After spanking the living daylights out of me—more than once—they tried to scare me by threatening to send me away. I was a tough nut to crack. Nevertheless, as much as my strong will proved to be a detriment in certain areas of my life, it would prove to be immensely helpful when focused in the proper direction.

* * *

That same year, I really wanted a pet; a dog, in particular, might be more accurate. After searching the newspaper, we found a little female Terrier Toy Poodle mix for $25.00. I emptied my piggy bank, which Mom kept hidden, and began counting my money. Short about ten bucks, Mom and Dad were kind enough to make up the difference, and off we went to pick up my new canine. She was just a pup, maybe six weeks old at most. Mom often read nursery rhymes to me when I was younger, and "Georgie Porgie" was always my favorite, so accordingly, I named my female dog George. Due to her ornery nature, the name suited her to a T. I don't know if Dad was as keen on having a dog as Mom and I were. He'd get quite perturbed whenever she would do her "business" on the floor. I'd swear George would poop on the floor just to get Bill riled up. It was quite funny, actually—Mom laughing at Dad, who would curse under his breath. I don't believe he ever really liked George.

The next adventure—or change in the status quo—that arrived in my life would be a baby sister. The day she came home with Mom from the hospital, I'd never seen Bill so excited. According to Mom, I had always wanted a baby sister with blond hair and blue eyes. Well, that's exactly what I got. They named her Monique, but we always called her Nikki. I couldn't help but feel a little bit left out at the time, though, as all the attention was now focused on her. However, Bill was good at keeping the attention he gave to his biological daughter and stepson as balanced as possible…eventually.

Sometime around the birth of my sister, my parents began studying the Bible with Jehovah's Witnesses. At the time, it seemed of no consequence, but I would later learn otherwise. Not long after, Betty and Bill got married. It was a small ceremony in someone's house. Afterward, they went to Las Vegas for their honeymoon. While they were holidaying in the Entertainment Capital of the World, Nikki and I stayed with Mary and Kelly in Winnipeg. One particular event remains clear in my mind from that period of time: Kelly, my mentor for better or worse, took me to a movie theater to see an actual motion picture. I thought it was the greatest thing in the world. The movie we saw was something about rockets, and I believe—if memory serves me—we even saw it twice, back to back. That's how awesome I thought it was.

http://montejperepelkin.com/photos-4

After my parents returned from their honeymoon, I finished kindergarten and was now ready to move up in the world as a first-grader. I hoped grade one, and being a year older, might add some new excitement to my life. I literally could not wait to turn seven.

CHAPTER

5

Tadmore

Summer of 1975 would prove to be a life-altering time for the Perepelkin family. So far, Mom and I had lived in three western Canadian provinces: Saskatchewan, British Columbia, and Manitoba. Now we were back in the province where we'd started, in a small hamlet in Saskatchewan called Tadmore. This is where I would spend the rest of my childhood as well as most of my teenage years. Along with my maternal grandparents, four of my mother's brothers lived there, too. Mom's family made up a third of the town. Mary and Kelly wouldn't follow us this time. They moved back to Vancouver, and that would be the last I would see of them—except for a couple of visits during family vacation years later.

Upon reflection of Kelly and my experiences with her, it is hard to imagine how young we actually were and the shenanigans we so adroitly pulled off. Looking back now at my own kids, when they were four and six years old, it's difficult to fathom what I was like. From the things I was doing and the knowledge I had at such a young age, I think it's safe to say I had street smarts when most kids of my age were lucky to have backyard smarts. Strangely, I never at any time felt like the little kids Kelly and I were. Somehow it seemed that we were able to see the world through adult eyes. The two of us had a similar way of thinking in that we never saw obstacles—only solutions. And being that we were both extremely resourceful, that mindset served us well in our endeavors. Understanding consequences, however, that's where we came up short. I've often wondered—from time to time—how Kelly might be doing, because we did have some interesting memories together and shared a unique connection. I do remember missing her a great deal after moving to Tadmore.

A genuine prairie farming community, Tadmore is not unlike the fictional town Dog River, which was home to the popular Canadian sitcom *Corner Gas*. The series ran from 2004 to 2009. Fortunately, I had already encountered the opportunity to acclimatize to a small community after we had moved from Vancouver, B.C., to Lockport, Manitoba. Tadmore—about the same size as Lockport—is located in the middle-eastern section of Saskatchewan. It's only forty-five minutes driving distance from Manitoba, about four hours north of the U.S. border states of Montana and North Dakota. Most people, when they think of Saskatchewan, picture flat, boring prairies, where you can watch your dog run away for two days. True, parts of the province are very much like that, but not where we were. In our area, it was quite beautiful, with lots of trees, bushes, and plenty of elevation changes—a very scenic place to grow up.

There was a main street in Tadmore, four side streets, and one back street that ran parallel with the main. Between the main and back street sat three average-sized blocks that made up the town. This tiny hamlet even had a general store that sold basic everyday groceries, with a spectacular selection of candy, pop, and potato chips. The odor that would captivate one's senses when you walked in still lingers in my memory. It was sweet, as if the feeling of jubilation fused itself to the smell of bubblegum, thus instilling an instant sense of small-town euphoria. Every time I entered that little store, a simple state of happiness would always come over me, like the kid in the proverbial candy store, if you will.

In 1975, Tadmore had a whopping population of about sixty, sixteen of whom were part of my mom's family. Mom had nine siblings: five brothers and four sisters. Four of her brothers lived in Tadmore. At that time, two of them were married with children. This meant I had seven cousins living in close proximity. Uncle Ernie, Mom's oldest brother, had three kids: a boy one year older than I named Randy; Barbara, who was two years younger; and finally Ricky, who was just a baby. Then there was Larry. He had four kids: a boy and three girls. The eldest, Kim, was a year older than I, with the rest all two years apart starting with Kelly (not to be confused with my partner in crime), who was a year younger than I. Next were Candice and Kerri. Uncle Jim, the fourth-youngest brother to my mom, was living with his girlfriend in a little house roughly a block from us. Uncle Tim was the youngest of all. He still lived at home with my grandparents. Tim was only ten years older than I and still going to high school. All of my mom's older brothers worked for the Canadian National Railway. Mom's parents, whose names were Ada and William, were simply Grandma and Grandpa to me. Last but not least, there was my mom's Aunt Mabel, who lived by herself. She was quite up in age and kept to herself. The rest of Mom's siblings lived elsewhere. To avoid a bombardment of characters, I will only mention them when relevant.

One cool aspect of where we now lived was the aurora borealis or northern lights. On a clear summer night, the phosphorescent display would radiate over the backdrop of a dark sky in spectacular fashion. I have fond memories of standing out in the middle of a field with my cousins, the northern lights directly above us—which we took in with youthful amazement—as we shouted boisterously. The sound waves of our shouting seemed to cause the luminescent colors to dance across the canvas of the universe. After witnessing something so fascinating, it seems rather unorthodox not to believe in a Creator.

Before moving to Tadmore, my parents had purchased a quaint little bungalow for $2,000. Oh, how times have changed; a typical bathroom renovation costs more than that these days. The bungalow was 1,000 square feet in size and needed a little work, although I wouldn't quite call it a fixer-upper. The property it sat on was enormous, with a spacious garden in the backyard. My new home was on the middle block of town. Railway tracks ran in front of us. The regular sounds of a train going by, at all hours of the day and night, soon became commonplace. Two huge grain elevators were operating there at the time—also a noisy affair, especially during the harvesting season. But these were sounds of the prairies; wheat and railways opened up the prairie provinces. Saskatchewan became known as the Breadbasket of Canada because of it.

We moved during the summer shortly after I finished kindergarten in Lockport. Mom, Dad, and some friends of theirs loaded up our belongings into a big rental truck, and off we went, headed for the land of living skies. Dad drove the truck; I rode shotgun. I thought it was pretty neat he could handle such a big vehicle. Mom and my little sister—who'd just had her first birthday—followed in our car. Once we arrived, our first stop was Grandma and Grandpa's house, which was right in town. They had two milking cows and a barn full of chickens in their backyard, indicative of the farming community this really was. They didn't even have a bathroom in their house. There was an outhouse in the backyard where you did your business—a first for me!

* * *

Our trip west from Manitoba to Saskatchewan went smoothly. Shortly after we arrived at Grandma and Grandpa's house, however, I experienced my first encounter with material loss. It was a rather big letdown. For my dad, my loss proved to be disappointment, anger, and frustration. Dad had parked the big truck in my grandparents' long gravel driveway. As it was a beautiful sunny day, mid-afternoon in July, scorching hot, the first thing I wanted to do was ride my purple bicycle. Lucky for me, it was the last thing loaded. Dad, however, was dead set against letting me loose to roam the streets of Tadmore. But I hounded and hounded him until he finally gave in and begrudgingly unloaded the bike for me to ride. I got on that big, flowery banana seat, and I was gone. Freedom at last! The independence that bicycle afforded me was coolness in itself. After a few minutes, I returned to Grandma and Grandpa's. Just then, one of my cousins came outside. His name was Kelvin. He was visiting with his parents. They lived in British Columbia. Kelvin was three years older than I, so he would have been nine. First thing I did was show him my new bike, and he asked to take it for a spin. I was a bit hesitant about giving into his request at first, but I thought, *What the heck, he's my cousin*, and I wanted to become buddies with him.

Off Kelvin went while I sat on the wooden steps waiting. As it was scorching hot outside, I went into the house to cool off and get a glass of water. With an old, bent-out-of-shape metal ladle, Grandma poured me a fresh glass of crystal clear water from a metal bucket on the porch. They had to pump their water from a well, and somehow that made it taste extra special—ice cold too. When Kelvin finally came back, he leaned my bike up against the back of the big moving truck and came into the house. Shortly after that, my dad went outside to drive the truck over to our new home. The game plan was that I'd follow Dad over to the house on my bike. Because I had no idea Kelvin had put my bike where he did, I stood there on the wooden steps with Grandma as I watched him back out of the driveway right over my bike, mashing it into the ground into a purple scrap-metal pancake. Watching this precarious situation unfold before my eyes, my heart sank to the ground as a lump formed in the back of my throat. Unable to utter a single syllable, I stood in disbelief, mortified! The truck was so big and powerful that Dad couldn't tell he'd run over anything until he saw the wreckage appear in front of him. When he jumped out of the truck, having mentioned several times that he didn't want me riding my bike unsupervised, wow, was he ever angry.

Kelvin's dad came outside to see what all the commotion was about. When confronted, Kelvin denied any responsibility. So much for becoming buddies. I wanted to wring his neck. My uncle offered to buy me a new bike, basically underscoring the fact that I was telling the truth. Dad, however, refused to accept it. That was his way of teaching me the importance of looking after and taking responsibility for my bike—not to mention the fact that I should have listened to him when he'd said "no" in the first place. At the time, however, I thought the entire incident was so unfair. My bike was gone, and I never enjoyed a decent one again until I was fifteen. It was a yellow BMX bike and a real racing model. Unfortunately, it was stolen two weeks after I got it. Again, I had not heeded Dad's warning to lock up the bike, and I had to shoulder the blame for it being swiped. Indicative of my stubborn nature, however, and as painful a lesson as these were, they would still prove to be ineffective in teaching me anything about obeying my parents or that I should consider the consequences of my follies. Instead, I just kept paying the price over and over, ignoring the obvious conclusion that if we look closely enough and are honest with ourselves, nearly everything that happens to us—good or bad—is a direct result of a decision or choice we made. There are very few exceptions to this fundamental principle. The reason many of us fail to recognize this fundamental principle is that we lack accountability. Quite simply, blaming someone else for our unfortunate circumstance is more comfortable to our ego. For me, I alternatively saw the situation as entirely Kelvin's fault and therefore learned absolutely nothing from my loss. Throughout this eventful life, I've come to learn a valuable truth: From every loss we incur, there is a lesson to be gained. However, in order to benefit from that lesson, a person must first possess humility.

* * *

We began settling into our new home, new life, and the change of scenery that came with it. But without a bike, I had to walk everywhere. Dad, considering himself somewhat of a handyman, began changing things here and there around our new home. He fixed up the kitchen, replaced a couple of windows, and I helped him build a shed and shingle its roof. My new stepdad clearly had some basic carpentry skills. I believe Mom was kind of a dreamer in some ways, though, with grand visions of a little castle for us to live in. She had poor Dad building this huge fence all around the house. The idea of a six-foot fence around our dainty shack just didn't seem right in that little town. Nevertheless, Dad, always willing to please his wife, got right to it and started installing thick fence posts. However, Bill had one particularly annoying disposition. As hard as he worked, he rarely ever completely finished a project, a habit that drove my mother nuts. Therefore, all that remained of our castle walls was a line of huge fence posts surrounding our property. Ironically, Dad leaving projects half-completed around the house had the reverse effect on me. When I start a project, I'm determined to finish it.

Perhaps the best thing about Tadmore was Crystal Lake, a lake resort only two miles away. It was a place I would frequent regularly once I got older. My friends and I would go swimming regularly during the hot prairie months. The lake itself is three-quarters of a mile long and one-half mile at its widest point. This small but beautiful body of water is spring fed with crystal clear ice-cold water; hence its name, Crystal Lake. The resort, surrounded by plenty of cabins, had a healthy mix of both spruce and poplar trees encompassing the areas around it. Although it was a small lake, it had two beach areas, one on each side, with a small store at each. Crystal Lake even had a nine-hole golf course and a drive-in movie theater. That very summer, I would see my first movie there with a couple of my uncles. We watched *Night of the Living Dead*. Six years old at the time, I remember being terrified beyond words while wondering if there were such a thing as zombies as we drove home that evening. I don't think I slept a wink that night.

Our first summer in Tadmore went by fast, and I soon started grade one in Canora, located at the junction of Highways No.5 and No.9. Canora was only a twenty-minute drive from where we lived, but it was an hour-long ride every day, each way, on the school bus. Being that we were at the end of our bus route meant getting up much earlier than I would have liked and then getting home late too. That first year wasn't so bad—except for my crabby teacher. She was a mean, bitter woman. One of the kids in our class would often uncontrollably pee herself in class. Our callous grade one teacher would become angry and call her a "stupid kid." It was an awful display by someone who should have been setting an example. I felt so sorry for the poor girl once that I scolded the teacher by saying, "Why do you have to be so mean?" Needless to say, I was not her favorite student after that.

Mom was home every day when I'd return home from school during grade one. However, grade two was a different story. Dad took on a new job for Dowie's Stationary in Yorkton as a traveling salesman of office equipment, and Mom accepted a position at the Holiday Inn—also in Yorkton. Therefore, to avoid the forty-five-minute commute each way, Mom and my sister stayed in Yorkton with a relative during the week while Dad traveled all over southern Saskatchewan selling office equipment. As for me, I stayed with Grandma and Grandpa while attending grade two. I only saw my parents on weekends. I think they were financially strapped at the time, although we didn't really lack anything, and I didn't feel like we were poor. Staying with my grandparents was extremely boring. Therefore, while the weather was nice, I spent the majority of my time outside. Being a self-reliant little dude, upon returning from school, I'd check in with Grandma and then go outside to play by myself in the ditch across from the cemetery. In an effort to capture gophers, I'd build little homemade traps. The cemetery, however, always gave me the creeps, especially after watching *Night of the Living Dead*. You can be sure that anytime I was in the vicinity of that churchyard, I kept a constant lookout for zombies—in case they decided to dig themselves out from their graves. I took that matter seriously!

This was an extremely lonely period in my life, and I often cried myself to sleep at night. Being all alone at my Grandma and Grandpa's, I longed for the companionship of my little girlfriend, Kelly, wishing that she would have moved to Tadmore with us. The only thing I remember looking forward to was watching *The Six Million Dollar Man*, which was my favorite television show. Lee Majors played the lead role of Colonel Steve Austin, an astronaut who suffered severe injuries when he crashed an experimental aircraft. He was then "rebuilt" in an operation that cost six million dollars. His right arm, both legs, and left eye were replaced with "bionic" implants that enhanced his strength, speed, and vision far above human norms: He could run at speeds of sixty mph (97 km/h), his eye had a twenty to one zoom lens with infrared capabilities, and his bionic limbs all had the equivalent power of a terminator cyborg. Austin then used his enhanced abilities to work for the OSI (Office of Scientific Intelligence) as a secret agent, where he would solve crimes involving national security. The drama aired on the ABC network as a regular series for five seasons from 1974 to 1978. Fascinated by the entire concept of being bionic, I loved watching *The Six Million Dollar Man* and never missed an episode!

Once the notorious prairie winter arrived, my mood and loneliness got even worse. After coming home from school and checking in as usual with Grandma—now that it was too cold to play outside for any length of time—I'd break into my parents' house just to be at home, my own home. I'd stay there and watch cartoons, and then I'd return to Grandma's house for the night. I think being at home, even if it was just for an hour, gave me a sense of comfort. Looking back now, I'm surprised Grandma never wondered where I was. As for Grandpa, he just sat on a chair next to the kitchen, smoking cigarettes all day. Can't say that I ever remember him moving from that spot. Under his chair was a large metal tray filled with cigarette butts. I never really got to know my grandfather or connect with him. He always seemed grumpy and unapproachable. He died a year later from emphysema. Go figure!

On a blustery day, early in 1976, I got off the school bus, headed to my grandmother's, said hello, and then followed my usual routine of going home for an hour. This time, however, upon leaving to head back to my grandma's, I failed to close the front door all the way. As a result, while I was at school, my parents came home early the next day, a Friday, and found the front door wide open with a big snowdrift literally in the middle of our living room. When I heard Mom and Dad talking about it with Grandma, they concluded that someone must have broken in, and they were about to call the police. That was when

I came forward and confessed to what I had been doing every day after school. Surprisingly, my parents weren't angry at all. In fact, I think they felt guilty. Mom quit her job shortly afterward and once again became a stay-at-home housewife. Having been somewhat of a free spirit and accustomed to working outside the home, I don't know if she was particularly fond of living the domesticated lifestyle. Being at home full time while raising two children was probably never her natural inclination in life, but she never complained, and she was the best mother she could be.

* * *

Other than the usual trials and tribulations of a little kid's life—with sneaking off from Grandma's house to my own, unattended home, and the snow drift incident being the basic highlights—1976 proved to be a rather uneventful year for me. As the year was winding down into its final hours, my parents, along with a couple of my aunts and uncles, were out celebrating New Year's Eve. I was babysitting a few of my younger cousins at home. It was just ten days before my eighth birthday, but obviously, Mom and Dad believed I could be entrusted with the care of four kids, which included my sister Nikki. They were all asleep, though, so it wasn't a big deal. I did check on everyone periodically before eventually falling asleep on the couch myself. Quite often, I was enlisted with responsibilities that at times, probably exceeded the abilities of most kids my age. Luckily for my parents, there were no dire consequences. I remember sitting on the sofa in our living room that evening listening to Johnny Cash on our 8-track stereo. Mom first introduced me to music at three years of age, buying me hit singles records known as 45s. I'd listen to the vinyl records on a little blue record player that she bought me for my fourth birthday. The three favorites I recall playing all the time were: "Eve of

Destruction" by Barry McGuire, "Wild Thing" by The Troggs, and "Do It Again" by Steely Dan. And there was my all-time favorite song, "Mah-Na Mah-Na," by Mahna Mahna and the Snowths. That crazy tune always cracked me up. Though I was never inclined to play an instrument, listening to music would forever become an integral part of my life.

At one point during this time period, early spring 1977, our family took a trip back to Manitoba, and Grandma came with us to help with my sister. My parents hadn't been able to sell the mobile home that was back in Lockport, so we went there to set up movers so that they could transport the trailer to Tadmore. Having more or less forgotten about the trailer, I returned home from school one day to find the monstrous contrivance parked next to our house. This thing was huge and took up a big portion of our yard. Even though the double-wide trailer was considerably nicer than the place we were now living in, my parents decided to sell it. Problem was, no one wanted to buy it, and by the time summer came around, that trailer would still be parked next to our house. Mom and Dad were beginning to lose hope that anyone was ever going to buy it. Since they didn't exactly want to give it away, dear old Dad came up with the craziest plan I'd ever heard. I was only eight years old, and his wacky idea even had me scratching my head. The harebrained scheme he devised was to buy the property behind us from his sister and move the existing dilapidated old house that she lived in off the property. The plan was to pour a big slab of concrete—for a foundation—and build walls to create a bottom story for this huge double-wide trailer to sit on top. Unbelievably, he wanted to jack this trailer eight feet off the ground, thus creating a massive 2,700-square-foot two-story home. Everyone in town was telling poor Dad he was crazy, further stating that the first big wind would blow the entire structure right over. And I didn't exactly doubt them either.

For a man who, I'll be honest with you, didn't have a lot of ambition when it came to finishing projects around the house, this was a huge undertaking. Remember those fence posts he put in? Well, they were still there, but no fence. However, this time, Dad seemed exceptionally motivated. I think all the naysayers just lit a fire under his butt, because he did it. He actually pulled it off, and our house became the talk of the town. Several times, I would see a car drive really slowly as it passed by to check out the "wonder" of Tadmore. As in "I wonder how they got that trailer up there." Some people would even stop and point. It was kind of funny.

After we moved into our newly renovated house, I found it somewhat unusual having the main living area upstairs, but nevertheless, it was pretty clever. That's not to say I wasn't freaking out when the first Saskatchewan windstorm hit us later that year. You could literally hear the wind blowing across and crinkling the tin roof all night long. I don't know that I slept a wink that night. However—though I didn't realize it at the time—the best part of this house was that my bedroom was downstairs and at the opposite end of my parents' sleeping quarters. It was perfect once I got older for sneaking out at night. Looking at that house today, you would never suspect it was ever a trailer.

* * *

Grade two was finally done, and we had the summer of '77 to look forward to. I figured out by then that I really didn't like school. I found it totally boring and remember thinking many times while sitting in class, *Okay, I get it already. Do we really need to go over this a million times?* The *Dick and Jane* stories were pathetically mind-numbing. These books were meant to entertain little kids while teaching them to read. Being from a different era, they seemed extremely old-fashioned to me. For the uninitiated, Dick and Jane were a little boy and girl, and their stories revolved around their family and pets. Maybe there was a deeper agenda there in teaching us about family values and all that stuff, but they stirred about as much interest in me as watching paint dry—which, by the way, pretty much sums up the majority of my scholastic experience. Towards the end of grade two, however, I had begun developing friendships at school. Because I was a fairly social child—never intimidated or insecure, with other boys anyway—making friends came easily. Be that as it may, having a ton of friends was never my style.

Saskatchewan summers were the best. The weather was really hot, with very little rain, and when it did rain, it was hard and fast. This meant we kids could spend the majority of our time outdoors. Being the imaginative adventurer that I was, you'd almost never find me in the house. I did finally get a new bike that summer, except it wasn't exactly new—it was used and basically a piece of junk. But it had two wheels, and I could ride it, which translated into mobility and freedom. I rode my bike everywhere, usually accompanied by one of my cousins. That summer, I really got to know our little town. As my sister Nikki was getting older—she'd have been about three now—I began taking more of an interest in her. With my yellow wagon, I'd often pull her around everywhere I went. It was kind of cute. Being the big brother, I was very protective of my sister—not even allowing my parents to discipline her. Unfortunately, my innocent gestures certainly didn't do her any favors later in life.

http://montejperepelkin.com/photos-5

Mom would plant a huge garden that year and every year afterwards. Even though I was only eight years old, she delegated a fair bit of responsibility, having me do the weeding and watering. I was even cutting the lawn with a push mower by now. Aside from doing my expected chores every day, Mom, being a business-minded person, had assigned a small monetary reward for certain odd jobs that I'd do for her around the house and in the garden. Never afraid of hard work, I welcomed earning a little spending money and enthusiastically took on anything she threw at me. The little grocery store in Tadmore let me establish a tab with them, and that made me feel really grown up. Having credit gave me a sense of maturity, so you can bet I took that responsibility very seriously. It never amounted to more than a couple dollars, and I always made sure to pay my bill whenever I had money. I would often take Nikki to the store in my wagon and buy her a popsicle. Now that Mom was home full time life was pretty good. Tadmore was beginning to feel like home.

Mom, having the entrepreneurial spirit in her, was regularly involved in some sort of small business venture. Oddly enough, one of her entrepreneurial escapades involved me. With the aforementioned plan of sending me from door to door in every little town within driving distance of Tadmore, Mom bought a bunch of Lord's Prayer plaques one day from a wholesale catalog for two dollars each. Her intent was that I'd sell them for six dollars apiece and we'd split the profit right down the middle. I thought it was a dumb idea at first and really wasn't into it at all. After making a couple of sales, however, my attitude changed completely. The plaques had a gold frame with black velvet inside, where the entire Lord's Prayer was imprinted in gold lettering. They were quite nice, and who could resist buying the Lord's Prayer from a little kid? Mom even started recruiting some of my cousins to come with us, but I didn't like that too much. I wanted all the sales to myself. Yet having some company did make the sales outings more enjoyable.

Looking back, I can see that even by this early age, I was already quite the little entrepreneur myself. I quickly ascertained the plaques could just as easily sell for eight dollars—without Mom knowing, of course—and double my profits. Greedy? Not by my way of thinking. Mom set her price and got her price. Now that I was making four bucks on every plaque I sold, I really started raking in the dough. I sold a ton of those godly treasures of spiritual goodness in every little town within a few hours' drive from where we lived, earning myself some serious spending money in the process. I was motivated! In retrospect, however—because these plaques featured the Lord's Prayer—I realize now that wasn't such a good idea. At the time, however, to me, they were just some gold plaques that people could hang on their wall, a product to be sold like anything else. I wasn't cognizant of them being from the Bible…where it says, "You received free, give free." So, I'm sorry, dear God! Selling those plaques did keep me busy and out of trouble, though. More importantly, the experience gave me ambition like I'd never felt before. The more I sold, the more money I made. My reward was based on performance, and that suited me perfectly. I hadn't realized it at the time, but it was clear that I, like my mother, had the entrepreneurial bug in me. My life might have been much easier if I'd figured that out right then and there.

Being on the road, selling office equipment for Dowie's Stationary out of Yorkton, Bill wasn't home during the week. He did considerably well at that profession, and it wasn't long before he became their top salesman. Sales suited Dad to a T—clearly his forte. Everyone just loved him. With a gift for the gab, that man could have sold snowmobiles in the dessert—if he'd wanted to. He would always be home on weekends, though. That was when he'd take us swimming or to a movie in the evening. We were always doing something fun. To make it even more enjoyable, we'd often invite one of my cousins to come along. Bill was a fun dad. Strangely, Betty never came with us. It was almost always Dad, my sister, and me. Maybe Mom felt deserving of a break from us and treasured some downtime for herself. Bill was very generous too—often times a little too generous. I could tell even at only eight years old that Mom "wore the pants," so to speak, when it came to finances, which, in retrospect, was probably a good thing. Bill was kind of like a big kid when it came to money—probably why I liked him so much.

Tadmore was buzzing with excitement, and times were great economically for Saskatchewan during this era. Dad even found a better job selling Ford vehicles at Formo Motors in Preeceville. As Preeceville wasn't that far from Tadmore, it allowed him to be home every night. It wasn't long before he excelled at selling cars. Always maintaining a servile attitude towards people, Bill had the perfect demeanor for a career in sales. I believe the personality he possessed really helped him ascend in that occupation. By his second year with Formo Motors, Dad was already winning awards for being one of the top salesmen in all of Canada. Since we lived in optimum farming country, every farmer from miles around would come to buy a truck from Dad. He practically became a legend in the sales industry—the *go-to* guy!

CHAPTER

6

Enter Jehovah's Witnesses

After a long, hot summer, which always seemed to end too quickly considering my dislike of school, I entered grade three. Looking back at 1977, I'd have to say it was a peculiar year indeed. Shortly after moving into our lofty and unique two-story abode, Betty and Bill decided to become foster parents—a noble deed I didn't really understand at the time. We soon had a fifteen-year-old girl named Ramona living with us. It seemed a little weird at first, but she was really nice to me and pretty cute too. I had a little crush on her. Not expecting me to be up that late, I got to see my very first pair of boobs one night when she came out of the shower. I wasn't spying on her. I just needed to pee. Although I never had any issues or confrontations with Ramona, I do know that she was a troubled teen at the time. On one occasion, she got busted for stealing my parents' car while we were attending Sunday service. Other than making sure it didn't happen again, Mom and Dad never did anything about it. After all, what could they do? It wasn't like they could spank her. Ramona wouldn't stay with us for very long, though. Shortly after turning sixteen, she moved back home. Her stay with us must have been a positive experience for Ramona, because she always kept in touch after moving out. She and Mom later became close friends.

Another prominent occurrence that happened in 1977 would have a significant impact on my immediate and distant future. Although my parents had begun to study the Bible with Jehovah's Witnesses back in Lockport, after relocating to Tadmore, they never continued with it, and they never made any real significant changes in their lives, at least none that I noticed. Well, those persistent JWs must have come knocking again, because we started attending the Kingdom Hall—the place of worship used by Jehovah's Witnesses—on Sundays again. In contrast to most Christian churches, Kingdom Halls are characteristically modest, functional structures with pragmatism front and center and devoid of religious iconography. Before Betty became a Jehovah's Witness—other than being baptized at birth as a Catholic—I was not subjected to any religious denomination and attended no churches. It was only later that I noticed how understated Kingdom Halls were compared to conventional religious buildings. As I had nothing to compare the Jehovah's Witness religion to, I had no problems with it per se. As far as I was concerned it was just another Christian faith.

For the very first time in my life, however, we didn't celebrate Christmas when it came around that year. I was not impressed! To a kid, Christmas Day is one of the best and most anticipated days of the year. After all, it involves the receiving of gifts. Dad sat me down one day to explain how there was no such thing as Santa Claus, and that it was actually he who ate the cookies and drank the milk, not Santa. Well, I already knew that. I wasn't some naïve child who believed a man in a red suit flew around on a sleigh propelled by flying reindeer, delivering presents to every house on the planet in one night. After Dad finished clarifying the obvious truth about Santa Claus, I looked at him with a furrowed brow and said, "Really, Dad? I figured that out at four years old." All he said was, "Oh, well, okay then." To which I replied, "Okay what? That doesn't mean you have to stop buying me presents." To this, he responded, "We don't need a special day in order to buy you something. We can do that any day." Under my breath, in a slow, condescending tone, I retorted, "Is that right? Well, we'll see about that." Needless to say, that was the end of Christmas as I knew it, at least for the immediate future.

Adding insult to injury, when my birthday came, we didn't celebrate that either. Mom and Dad revealed the details as to why we weren't going to be celebrating these events and holidays any longer. In all honesty, their explanation did make sense to me…if I believed in God, that is. Because it is a well-known fact that Jesus wasn't actually born on December 25th, one of Dad's theories about Christmas was that the holiday was probably fabricated by none other than the devil himself, Satan, further pointing out that if you take the "n" in the name "Santa" and move it to the end, it spells "Satan." Although I did find that little tidbit of information interesting, if not a stretch of the imagination, my reply to him centered around the fact that if I didn't believe in God, then what did it matter? Since there was obviously no such thing as Santa Claus or the Easter Bunny, I concluded that God probably didn't exist either. By deduction, if there is no God, then there is no such thing as Satan. After my explanation, Dad looked at me and said, "How can you not believe in God?" I'll go out on a limb and say that the debate I had with my stepdad that day was seemingly deep for a nine-year-old boy, but I didn't think like your average child. In the end, I wished that I'd just kept my mouth shut, because, the next thing I knew—in an effort to convince and teach me that there is a God—my stepdad and I were having a weekly hour-long Bible study together. That was in addition to the three meetings a week we were already attending at the Kingdom Hall in Sturgis. Considering all the changes that were going on in my life, it felt like too much too soon. It seemed like this whole JW belief system was about cheapening out. No presents? What kind of deal was that? For the uninitiated, Jehovah's Witnesses don't celebrate Christmas, Easter, Valentine's Day, Halloween, Thanksgiving, birthdays, etc. In accordance with Bible standards, however, they do celebrate weddings, anniversaries, and the commemoration of Jesus's death, albeit not in the context of Easter.

Dad was certainly making an earnest commitment to this JW way of life. Quite frankly, it was a little much for my liking. Going to the meetings three times a week wasn't so bad; it was the going from door to door every Saturday morning to preach the "good news" that had me worried. What if I went to a house where someone from school knew me? That would've been excruciatingly embarrassing. I can remember saying a silent prayer as we'd walk up to each house, asking God, *Please don't let it be anyone I know from school.* Perhaps my prayers were answered, because I don't know that it ever happened. And surprisingly, as long as I didn't know them, I wasn't afraid talking to people, and some even accepted magazines from me. Interestingly, if you believe in the Bible, the necessity for all Christians to preach about God's Kingdom is recorded in many of the gospels, one example of which is Mathew 24:14.

* * *

The winter of 1977–78 dragged on, and I was happy when spring finally arrived. One day towards the end of grade three, I convinced Mom to write me a note allowing me to leave the school premises at lunchtime. Kids who took a bus to school weren't allowed to leave the schoolyard. Although this rule was for our own safety, to me, it was like being kept a prisoner. We had to eat our food in the lunchroom over the noon hour. Being that I was exceptionally responsible and fairly street smart for my age, Mom had no qualms writing the requested note. In fact, she seemed excited about the idea. And since I was still selling the Lord's Prayer plaques, making my own money, she didn't have to fork out any money for my lunch at a restaurant. Upon handing my teacher the note, which she accepted without question, I scurried off to have lunch at one of the local restaurants in downtown Canora. It took only a few minutes to get there on foot. Walking downtown by myself, I must say, was a pretty cool feeling, and it had an empowering effect on me. Up to this point, since moving to Tadmore, I had been a good little camper and managed not to get into any serious trouble—at least nothing that required a spanking. Well, that was about to change. What I did next REALLY got my adrenaline pumping!

After finishing my gravy-covered fries at the restaurant, I walked over to the local hardware store, which was called McLeod's. I headed straight for the sports equipment. My plan was to steal a soccer ball. The strategy was to inconspicuously move the item close to the front door without anyone noticing. Then, to convince the clerk I was just browsing, I would walk around the store with nothing in my hands. Next, I'd wait until there were no customers—that was when the cashier headed to the back of the store. At that point, I'd make a calculated bee-line for the door and grab the ball on my way out. My plan worked perfectly. Although I had become proficient at shoplifting small items, I'd never done anything on this scale before. This was "big time" for me. While it was exhilarating, at the same time, it was scary as hell, leaving me to feel a little lightheaded and slightly nauseous from the ordeal. The rush and gratification I felt from getting away with the misdeed, however, was all too familiar. Getting caught at that moment might have been the best thing for me, but I totally got away with it. For that reason, a new feeling would emerge: confidence! If that wasn't bad enough, I went back to school and became the hero of recess. This was another factor that did me no favors: infamy for my actions. It was a recipe for disaster.

Summer of 1978 arrived, and it was a memorable one at that. I was getting older, and with that came more freedom. As my baby sister got older, however, I began to notice some distinct favoritism from my father. He would let her get away with murder in comparison to how he treated me. Okay, she was his blood; I wasn't. And girls tend to get away with more because they are the apple of Dad's eye. Boys can count on Mom to be a little more forgiving when it comes to reprimanding. Today, I understand all that. As a nine-year-old, it was treachery and betrayal of the highest order, and I soon realized that my standing in the way of their disciplining Nikki hadn't been such a good idea after all. Mom definitely noticed the favoritism and even voiced her opinion to Dad on more than one occasion. However, overhearing my mother criticizing her husband's favoritism toward his biological daughter was something I didn't need to hear. It made me even more upset and further validated my feelings.

* * *

Considering that I had no reservations about breaking the rules, the years leading up to and including 1978 were a culmination of events that would inevitably contribute to the perfect recipe for the makings of a rebel. Looking back, I can see how a simple string of events would drastically mold my future. It wasn't all doom and gloom, though. Growing up in a small town would provide a compendium of memorable adventures that shaped my life in a positive way. Actually, the summer of 1978 was one of my favorites as a child. My sister Nikki—now four years of age—and I could interact at a much higher level for the first time. Nikki and I became even closer as brother and sister, especially since I pretty much looked after her a majority of the time. Our mother, with her entrepreneurial spirit and all, didn't like to stay still for too long. I think if you were to have asked her at a young age what she wanted to be when she grew up, a housewife would have been last on her list. I didn't mind, though, Mom would often pay me to look after Nikki. Being a little entrepreneur myself, I welcomed every opportunity. That summer, Dad offered me $20 to cut and rake the grass on the vacant lot next to us. I know that seems like a lot—and a "twenty" went a long way back then—but it wasn't when taking into consideration the land was roughly half an acre in size. With a motorized lawnmower, it would have been one thing, but I had to cut the grass with a push mower, not to mention the fact that the grass was eight inches tall. I may have been a lot of things, but lazy was never one of them. I enjoyed working hard. While working in the hot, blazing Saskatchewan sun—listening to "Da Do Ron-Ron" by Shaun Cassidy time and time again on my little blue record player—I raked that entire lot all by myself. Admittedly, I loved that silly song. I was unaware at the time that the tune was a cover of The Crystals' smash hit of 1963, produced by the notorious Phil Spector. It was a huge hit for Cassidy as well, basically launching his career in the late seventies as a teen heartthrob.

Shortly after collecting my hard-earned twenty bucks, I decided it was time to clean out and reorganize the garage. The task took me all day to complete, but I must say it was pristine once I was finally done. When Dad returned from work that day, instead of giving me an "attaboy" all he said was "It's about time." Bill had some great qualities as a father, but handing out compliments was never one of them. One thing about my stepdad, however, he was very generous when it came to helping others. Shingling roofs, pouring concrete, and building stairs were just a few of the jobs I remember doing with him for people in our Kingdom Hall congregation—all for free, no less. In fact, to anyone who needed a hand with something, everyone in our congregation was very helpful and giving of their time. Money was never even discussed. Too bad more people aren't like that.

While cleaning out the garage, I noticed Dad had accumulated quite a collection of tools and leftover material from when he'd built our house. This sparked an idea inside me. My one-year older cousin Kim and I were always talking about building a fort together. I called her up, mentioned the tools and building materials I'd found in the garage, and suggested it was time to build our fort. Off we went, searching for the perfect location. With plenty of wooded area in and around Tadmore to choose from, after some extensive searching, we finally decided on a location near my grandma's house. Although this particular spot wasn't exactly convenient for hauling material, it had the perfect formation of trees to build a treehouse. It was almost as if someone had planted those trees just for us. After taking measurements, we'd go back to my place, make the cuts with Dad's power saw, and haul the boards back to the site to begin construction. It took a couple of days, but when we finally finished construction, it was awesome! And very secluded too. Our little fort even had two stories, carpeted floors, and a window to look out of. Looking back, for a couple of nine and ten-year-old kids, I'd say we outdid ourselves. Little did I know that someday I would make my living in the building trade, working as a finishing carpenter.

That summer of 1978 would be the first time I met Bill's parents, known to me as my new grandma and grandpa. They lived in Langley, British Columbia, a municipality in the Greater Vancouver Regional District. I traveled there on a Greyhound bus with one of Dad's sisters, Aunt Marna—who lived near Tadmore—and her daughter Tracey, who was my sister's age. Meanwhile, my parents drove down in the family car. My new grandma and grandpa seemed nice and were very accommodating. I even had my own private room to sleep in until my parents arrived a few days later. While staying in that room, I noticed some empty pop bottles by the bed. I knew I could fetch twenty cents each for them back home at our little store. Being the little hooligan I was, I put two of them in my suitcase. Well, a couple of days later, Grandma, while helping me find a shirt, started digging around in my suitcase. And of course, she discovered the empty pop bottles. I didn't think it was that big of a deal, but to my new grandma, it sure was. She even called me a little thief! Can you imagine…? Yours truly a little thief? Not wanting to ruin the holiday atmosphere we were all enjoying, however, Grandma waited until the very last day of our vacation before informing my parents of the misdeed. As punishment, Dad gave me one of the hardest spankings of my life that day… right on the bare bum, a first for me. Mom, on the other hand, was not impressed. Scolding Bill right in front of me, she stated how the situation would have been handled much differently if any of the kids from his side of the family had taken a couple of measly pop bottles. After all, it wasn't like I was stealing the family silverware.

According to Bill, however, no matter how insignificant the amount or what it was, stealing is stealing. Can't say I disagree with him. Again, Mom's view on the matter—even if she was right about the argument of favoritism—didn't do me any favors, considering my perspective on the issue of right and wrong. I bring this incident up for another reason: Like I mentioned, it was one of the hardest spankings of my life. It hurt like hell! Normally—after a spanking like the one I had received—most kids would think twice before pulling another five-finger discount, but not this little criminal. It didn't even faze me. Instead, I was extremely upset with myself for getting caught in the first place. My primary grievance was situated around how stupid it was of me to put the empty pop bottles in my suitcase that early. I should have waited until the last day, when we were packing up to head home. Then I would have been scot-free.

For a kid who had a great deal of compassion toward others, who was clearly a hard and determined little worker, and who had such a positive attitude towards life, it seems almost inconceivable that someone of that mindset could have had such a distorted view of right and wrong. Considering how we are all an apprentice to life's lessons, each with our own personal albatross standing between us and advancement, personal experiences will continue to be our most effective teacher. Yet many of us instinctively deceive ourselves by stubbornly refusing to surrender to the most essential lessons necessary in championing our becoming a better human being. Conquer that, and you've conquered your biggest obstacle.

* * *

While visiting with Grandma and Grandpa during family vacation that particular year, I noticed something that made a significant impact on me in a positive way. It had to do with how Bill's father—my new grandpa—treated his wife. I've often heard of how we will either follow in the footsteps of our parents or do the complete opposite. Well, Grandpa, in my opinion, really didn't treat Grandma very nicely, verbally that is. He often yelled at her with a demeaning tone and belittled the poor woman quite regularly. It's not that I'm saying he was a terrible person by any means. I just thought he could have been more considerate towards Grandma's feelings. By contrast, however, Bill conducted himself very respectfully around my mother. Never once can I remember him saying a single demeaning word towards her. Dad would do just about anything to make Mom happy. He definitely loved her and always tried to make her feel beautiful. His sterling example certainly set the tone for me once I got older. And for that reason, I have always tried to cultivate an attitude of respect towards women. Admittedly, there were times when that was easier said than done. Unfortunately, overwrought emotions can lead us to do or say things we later regret. And like the arrow released from a bow, you can't take it back. Even though Dad made mistakes, just as I admittedly have with my own children, I always respected him and recognized how he was often a great role model for me. My overall positive attitude towards women is a direct reflection of how my father, Bill, treated my mother. For that, I am thankful.

CHAPTER

7

Vindicated

Summer of '78 came to an end with grade four kicking off the new school year. For some reason, near the onset of summer, Mom came up with the wild idea for us to raise a bunch of chickens—to save money. What she really meant was *Monte would raise the chickens*. Like all chickens after they hatch, they started out as adorable little chicks endowed with soft yellow fur. Real cute and cuddly. There had to be at least twenty of them. On the other hand, once they were fully grown, they weren't so cute anymore. And quite stupid! Hard to believe they taste so good. I raised them on the property next door to us in the old house my father's sister used to live in. Because I was home all day, looking after the chickens during summer holidays wasn't a big deal. Once school began, though, that meant getting up extra early to feed and water them every morning. That wasn't cool.

After about a month into grade four, upon feeding them in the morning, I began discovering a dead chicken every once in a while. It was soon determined that a weasel was getting into the chicken coop at night and selecting a midnight snack for himself every now and then. One day, around mid-October, while I was at school, Grandma came over and butchered all our chickens for us. I was happy about that. When I arrived home from school, there was blood and feathers everywhere, not to mention the awful odor radiating throughout and around our house—it was disturbingly unpleasant.

As soon I walked in the door, Mom immediately started lecturing me. Then Grandma started in on me as well, accusing me of not feeding the chickens properly. Apparently, Grandma could tell they were malnourished and their stomachs were empty. Bewildered at what to say, knowing I'd fed those stupid chickens every single day, I stood there, speechless, wondering what else could I have done. Considerably upset—to say the least—I remember leaving the house in tears, which soon turned to anger. Walking aimlessly, I headed for the railway tracks and decided to run away from home, resolving in my heart never to return.

After strolling along the tracks for what felt like roughly an hour, I forgot about what had happened and why I was even running away in the first place. My little journey now became an adventure. It's amazing the things you can find wandering around where people haven't been for years: skeletons of dead animals, clothing, old bottles, and wrecked cars parked off in the bushes. In one junked vehicle, I looked in the glove box and found an unopened condom. Not quite sure of its intended purpose yet, I knew one thing for certain: It wasn't bubblegum! I'd learned that little tidbit of information a year earlier while using a public restroom that had a dispenser on the wall where someone had written; *DO NOT BUY THIS BUBBLEGUM.* Of course, knowing me, I had to know why. That's when I discovered it wasn't bubblegum. So this time, I simply put the unopened square package in my back pocket, with the intention of exploring its usage someday, and continued walking along the railway tracks. The tranquility of the stillness and silence that existed away from the business of life out in the middle of nowhere that evening was satisfyingly calming. I genuinely enjoyed the serenity that materialized as a consequence of the peaceful inactivity surrounding me—nature's organic relaxation therapy.

I continued along on my journey, and though I was the only person around, that didn't mean I was alone. There were plenty of animals coming and going. Rabbits have always been my favorite, and I certainly saw my share of them on this day. Then a skunk came across my path. Knowing they will spray you with that awful stench of theirs, I knew to stay away from him. A fox even graced my presence for a moment, but it ran away when I tried to move toward him. There were deer, mice, gophers, and even a stray cat to keep me company. As a result of having a highly acute sense of smell, I took notice of the various odors one encounters out in the country, most of which are quite pleasant. For instance, the aroma of a freshly cultivated field—you can smell the rich nutrients emanating from the moist soil. In the case of it being harvest season, the fragrance of a fresh-cut swath sends forth a remarkably crisp clean scent. Encountering these natural conditions within nature had my mind completely distracted from why I was out there in the first place. In the process of maturing with age, when it comes to triggering memories, I've come to realize how powerful a person's sense of smell can be. Often times, when I'm out in the country, certain odors will trigger vivid memories of my childhood—details that were thought to be long forgotten.

Considering that it was beginning to turn dusk and the temperature was noticeably cooler, I was beginning to realize that my radical plan didn't involve any real forward thinking. For instance; where was I going to sleep? Since cozying up in the ditch for the night wasn't all that appealing, suddenly I wasn't as furious with everyone as I'd once been. With daylight fading fast, I knew it would soon be dark. Coupled with all the crazy ghost stories floating around Tadmore, being out in the middle of nowhere in the darkness wasn't even moderately okay with me. Nearly every week, someone had a new tale to tell—not that I ever truly believed any of the stories, but some of them sure did get the little hairs on the back of my neck standing up. Cousin Kelly had told everyone he'd seen a werewolf standing by Grandma's woodpile and described it as having two hind legs like a horse, with hooves instead of feet. That made me think of a story Grandma had once revealed. She'd described hearing someone walk in during the middle of the night while she was in bed only to wake in the morning to find a single set of two-legged muddy hoof prints on the floor from the door to her wood stove. Sheesh! I was the biggest skeptic when it came to stuff like that, but being alone in the dark wasn't exactly what I had in mind when I'd run away. I needed to figure this out, and fast, before it actually got dark and those darn zombies came looking for me. Plus, I knew Mom would be worrying about me by now, and I didn't want that. The darker it became, the more my discontent with the chicken fiasco subsided—I was ready to go home.

Finally, I came upon a roadway where the train tracks intersected, and as circumstance would have it, just then, a vehicle was coming up the road. It was one of my uncles; he saw me and immediately stopped to offer a ride while asking what the hell I was doing way out here. I surmised that a search party was likely out looking for me by now—it was nearly dark. But since there were no such things as cell phones back then, and my uncle was driving home from work, I figured he likely didn't know anything about what was going on. Therefore, I simply told him that I was out for a nature hike along the tracks and had just lost track of time, after which I enthusiastically accepted a lift and climbed into the cab of his truck. He drove back into town and dropped me off in front of our house. Mom was sitting outside under the lights at our front door, and never in a million years would I have guessed what happened next. Instead of the heavy scolding I was bracing for, as I approached, she stood up and immediately began apologizing. I learned that after Dad had come home from work, he'd explained to her that I was, in fact, fulfilling my responsibilities by feeding the chickens every day, because he often checked on them before going to work. Dad would get up and leave for work after I left for school each morning. And he further said that the reason the chickens weren't getting their food was because of the family of weasels living under the old house in which the chickens were kept. The weasels were eating the food as well as killing the odd chicken now and then.

Then Dad pulled into the driveway—he had been out driving around, looking for me—and I could tell he was upset, though not in the usual get-out-the-belt kind of way—this was different. He walked up with his finger pointed right at me and said, "Don't you ever do that to us again! You had your mother and me worried sick over you!" Then, after affirming that he recognized how hard I was working around the house, Bill wrapped his big burly arms around me, gave me a huge hug, and told me that he loved me. After all that, Mom felt bad for blaming me and actually said she was sorry. I don't think there was ever a time— that I can remember—when one of my parents actually apologized to ME! Usually it was always the other way around. That was the first time Bill ever said he loved me, and because of the emotion he showed, I knew he meant it. Since he never handed out much in terms of verbal affirmation, I was inclined to believe that nothing I ever did was good enough. Like the time I cleaned and organized the garage on my own accord—it took me all day, yet his reply was something to the effect that it was about time. Granted, he said it in a joking way. However, a peer into the past, with greater understanding, reveals to me that he was—in all likeliness—feeling proud of me for taking the initiative. He just held back from expressing it. And after meeting Bill's dad, I doubt he got many compliments from his father either. Seems parents just weren't big on words of affirmation towards their children back in those days, which is too bad, really! A little recognition now and then can go a long way in contributing to the development and self-esteem of a child. In the aftermath of this situation, I did feel better, and Dad's reaction made this whole unpleasant incident worth it. Although it wasn't entirely unpleasant, my three-mile voyage along the train tracks was quite enjoyable. That is, until it had started getting dark.

* * *

Grade four would come and go with no birthday and Christmas celebrations again. I think, however, that Mom must have felt sorry for me that second Christmas without the exchanging of gifts, because I have distinct memories of her letting me go to my cousin Kelly's house on Christmas morning to watch him and the rest of their family open presents. I'm not sure how Mom thought that would help, but believe it or not, it actually did. I got to see firsthand as an observer how short-lived the joy of opening presents on Christmas Day truly was. I can distinctly recall one of my cousins, roughly an hour later, saying, "I'm bored." I also learned something about myself that day too. The whole time I was at cousin Kelly's, observing him and the rest of my cousins opening their presents, I can honestly say that at no time did I feel any jealousy or resentfulness because I didn't get any presents. I'm thankful to have been born the kind of person who is not of the jealous type. It's been my observation that jealousy, or envy, is a relative of hate and counterproductive to a happy, fulfilling life. Personally, I've witnessed it chew up too many people.

Nevertheless, outside of receiving no presents, I was starting to get used to the whole idea of not celebrating the holidays. After all, it really wasn't that big of a deal. Besides, every once in a while, Mom or Dad would buy Nikki or me a toy completely out of the blue—usually something we really wanted. This, in turn, taught me that receiving a gift when you're NOT expecting it is far more enjoyable then when you are. Therefore, I never did feel as if something was lacking from my life just because we didn't celebrate Christmas or any other holiday for that matter.

One memory that remains clear in my mind pertains to our Sunday morning routine before heading to the Kingdom Hall. Dad, Nikki, and I would wake up roughly thirty minutes before our 9:30 AM departure. Mom, on the other hand, would be up two hours ahead of time getting ready in her bathroom. My parents had their own private ensuite, and for the next two hours—every twenty to thirty minutes—Mom could be heard walking back and forth between the coffee pot in the kitchen and her beauty salon/makeup area in the washroom. This sequence of events eventually culminated in Dad, Nikki, and I waiting in the car as Mom continued putting on the last finishing touches to her wardrobe. Then, after two minutes or so, Bill would become impatient and begin honking the horn for her to hurry-up! Now frustrated, he'd look at me and say, "How can it take her so long to get ready?" To which I'd reply, "Dude, don't look at me. I have no idea." Finally, not pleased with her husband's honking and rushing, Mom would angrily enter the car and say, "You know I hate being rushed. Besides, we have plenty of time." After which, I'd yell from the back seat, "You look great, Mom," and she'd reply, "Thank you, Monte. At least someone notices." Dad, attempting to rectify the disgruntled mood, would quickly retort, "Oh, c'mon, you know I always think you're beautiful!" One thing I did like about going to the Kingdom Hall, after the services were over, the four of us would go out for our Sunday family dinner—usually an all-you-can-eat Chinese buffet. Bill loved Chinese food.

Although I was fascinated by the concept of the possibility of there being a God, I was very skeptical of it actually being reality. Believing in something I couldn't see, feel, or hear was a difficult proposition for me. For that reason, the probability of there being a God seemed like a stretch to me. Conversely, I soon learned that the more I participated with my dad in going to meetings and such, the more rewarded I was for it…by him. That simplified things, motivating me to take an avid interest in the Jehovah's Witness way of life—strictly for the rewards I received from Dad, of course. But over time, as unintentional as it was, I learned and retained a considerable amount of Bible knowledge, a lot of which made practical sense in terms of living the best life possible—not that I would benefit from that wisdom anytime soon. I had my own ideas. When I was ten years old, Dad rounded up a brown suit for me to wear to Sunday services. I reluctantly tried it on, not being much of a mister dress-up. Surprisingly, it didn't look half bad on me. In fact, I thought it looked pretty darn good—for a hand-me-down. After Mom sized me up, she said, "You'll make a fine young man someday." She snapped a photo of me, standing outside, on our way to the car as we prepared to leave for the Kingdom Hall. For some reason, I couldn't help but take her statement as an insult, and I wondered, *What about today? Aren't I a fine young man today?*

http://montejperepelkin.com/photos-6

As a result of attending Kingdom Hall meetings, we became friends with some other JWs and often participated in a multitude of good, wholesome family activities. There was no question that these were really salt-of-the-earth people, and I could definitely see a distinct difference in how they and their children acted compared to my non-JW friends. You never heard them swear, and the entertainment they subjected themselves to contained no violence or immorality. As I peer over my past, it's quite clear that some of those positive influences rubbed off on me and found their way into my adult life. I can honestly say, even to this day, my parents have never heard a curse word come from my lips. It's not that I never swore, just never, out of respect, around them. And as I got older, it was rare that I cursed at all. Violence was never of any interest to me either, and it has further become an aspect of life in this world that I truly despise. A few things, however, didn't stick, stealing being one, of course.

Summer of 1979 finally arrived. Dad and I would go by ourselves that year to Vancouver by train, where we would visit his folks and attend a four-day Jehovah's Witness convention. The convention was held at the big football stadium where the BC Lions played before BC Place was even built. As I have already mentioned, Bill's mother and father lived in Langley, and they lent us their old truck to drive to Vancouver and back, a roundtrip of about one hundred kilometers (sixty-two miles) or so. Dad would try and sell Grandma and Grandpa on coming with us for some spiritual nourishment, but they weren't having any part of it. The weather was extremely hot, and there was a massive number of people at the convention, but for a ten-year-old, attending a four-day JW preaching seminar was mighty boring. Dad, having sensed my discontent, rewarded my soldiering through the event by taking me to a movie. We saw *Moonraker*, a James Bond flick. That was the coolest movie I'd ever seen. I still remember the character they called "Jaws" in the movie; he could bite through a steel cable. Though I knew it had to be fake, the entire movie would fascinate me for quite some time. After all, James Bond is one cool cucumber.

I also noticed that 007 had a lot of sexy girlfriends. The best part of that Vancouver trip, though, was taking the train. I thoroughly enjoyed sitting in the glass dome car all day while taking in the breathtaking scenery as we played board games. Taking the train certainly is a peaceful and methodical way to travel. I can still remember the sound of the wheels going click-click, click-click at a constant and consistent rhythm as we slept. It was very hypnotic. Throughout my childhood and into adulthood, Dad and I would go on several trips together, just the two of us. Nikki would occasionally accompany us, but usually, it was just Dad and me. Bill was an awesome stepdad!

* * *

Ever since I can remember, Mom had struggled with her health. When I was in grade five, she got very sick and became partially paralyzed, spending a long time in the hospital. Both she and Bill were getting frustrated by now, as this had been a recurring theme going on for several years. After both of them adamantly insisted, their doctor finally referred Mom to a specialist, and his final diagnosis was that Mom had multiple sclerosis. Although I didn't have a clue what MS was at the time, this was devastating news for my parents, especially Mom. In a nutshell, MS is an inflammatory disease that damages the insulating cover of nerve cells in the brain and spinal cord. This damage disrupts the ability of parts of the nervous system to communicate, resulting in a wide range of physical and mental impairments, signs and symptoms that can make life hell for the afflicted. MS can take several forms, with new symptoms either occurring in isolated attacks or building up over time. Dad, who had been reading about reflexology, learned that it had favorable results in helping people with MS. Thereupon, he began taking a class to learn the skill. It wasn't long before Bill was giving her foot treatments in the hospital nearly every day. I would stay home and look after Nikki—sometimes even missing school to do so. I didn't mind that at all.

Mom soon came home from the hospital, but she wasn't her usual self for at least a couple of months. This left me to continue looking after things in her place while Dad was at work. I would cook dinners, clean the house, look after my sister, and make my own lunch for school. Feeling as if there was never any time for myself, I do remember being overwhelmed at times by the expectations placed on my young shoulders, and the food didn't taste as good either. At ten years old, needless to say, I wasn't a very good cook. Grandma would often bring food over to help out, which was a welcomed relief. Dad wouldn't arrive home from work until well after 6:00 PM, and I don't remember him ever cooking supper, except on Saturday nights, when he would make his famous chili while watching *Hockey Night in Canada*. The man certainly made a mean bowl of chili, a recipe I later acquired for myself. *Hockey Night in Canada* was a Saturday night ritual in our household. Without fail, Dad could be found perched on the sofa, watching the game and yelling at the TV while eating either a bowl of chili or a big bowl of popcorn. Good luck getting his attention during those three hours—never happened! The theme song of that iconic CBC hockey coverage is forever implanted in my memory. Too bad they replaced it. I miss the old song. Mom, on the other hand, couldn't be bothered with hockey, or any sports for that matter. Saturday was her night to let loose, when she was healthy. Once Mom returned to better health, things would eventually calm down and return to normal for me. If there was such a thing as normal. Both of my parents swear that it was the reflexology treatments that helped Mom recover from what the full blunt of living with MS usually does to a person and how debilitating it can be. She would struggle with the disorder periodically throughout her entire life, yet she would always bounce back and keep it from progressing. To this day, she is still walking around and a going concern, not staying still for any period of time. She never gives up. Mom is convinced reflexology has kept her going all these years, and I can't say that I disagree.

* * *

In the fall of 1979, I found myself in grade five. At that stage in your life, time seems to drag on and on, but in retrospect, it was flying by. I was already past the halfway mark of elementary school. Although I wasn't exactly what could be called an ideal and committed student, I did manage to get through every grade without ever having to repeat a year. Fortunately, I was blessed with a high enough IQ to absorb my lessons without having to work very hard at them. Doing homework wasn't ever part of my scholastic experience. Normally, upon arriving home from school, I was on my own. In fact, I had to look after my sister. But grade five was a bit of a game changer for me, at least as far as my disliking the academic world went. My teacher that year was Mr. Kozak. He turned out to be one of my favorites. Mr. Kozak, though strict, was a great teacher. His style of teaching resonated with me, and I actually enjoyed learning from him. School became slightly more interesting for me. Every year, during parent/teacher interviews, the teachers would all say the exact same thing, "Monte is very intelligent, but he doesn't apply himself." Mr. Kozak, on the other hand, was the first teacher to recognize that because I learned so quickly, I often became bored in class, thus causing my mind to wander. Out of all the teachers I had studied under, my marks were the best with Mr. Kozak. He had me excited about learning and enjoying school, which in itself lends credence to the difference an understanding teacher who goes the extra distance with his or her students can make.

Autumn and winter morphed into spring of 1980. This particular spring, however, reawakened my desire to take something that wasn't mine. This time, it was food. Basically, for lunch every day, I had a sandwich and an apple, which I made myself most mornings before heading out. B-o-r-i-n-g! As per custom, I would sit with all the other kids in the lunchroom and get to see what they brought to eat every day. To my disappointment, they always had really cool things like homemade cookies, cake, pastries, and Wagon Wheels. I mentioned something to Mom about it one evening, and her reply was that she'd see what she could do for me the next shopping trip. The following week, I noticed Mom had bought a box of Wagon Wheels and some Dad's Cookies. I thought, *Okay, not homemade, but I can live with that.* The next day at lunchtime, feeling somewhat excited about my dessert— after eating my sandwich—I went to bite into the Wagon Wheel, but it fell apart in my hand. It was hard as a rock. The cookies? Yeah, stale and old as the freakin' hills. I was not happy. Mom must have bought them from the bargain bin.

I decided it was time to take things into my own hands. Accordingly, at school the next day, my plan was to go through some of the other kids' lunches and swipe a cookie or maybe a Rice Krispies square. With gym class just before lunch break, I told the gym teacher I had to use the washroom. Instead, I snuck back into our homeroom and started going through lunches. Not being greedy, I just took two items: a big chocolate chip cookie, homemade of course, and a marshmallow square. Not wanting to leave them with no dessert at all, I took from two different lunches. And in the spirit of not being mean, I made sure to leave some sort of treat behind. So far, my plan was working perfectly. Lunchtime arrived, and for once, I had some awesome snacks—except the kid I'd taken the cookie from knew something was up and said to me, "I had a cookie like that in my lunch yesterday. Where did you get that?" Keeping my cool, I replied, "My mom made a bunch of these cookies last night. I guess she has the same recipe as your mom." This kid, though, wasn't buying my story. He went straight to Mr. Kozak, saying that I'd thieved his cookie. Consequently, the teacher pulled me aside, discreetly, to enquire. Of course, I denied the accusation. Nevertheless, Mr. Kozak wasn't fooled by my big puppy-dog-eyed denial. He called my mom, who came to the school that afternoon. Mr. Kozak, extremely considerate of the situation, kept the circumstances quiet from everyone else. When speaking with my mom—because of the compassion and understanding he displayed—I actually felt he was on my side. Mom, on the other hand, never spoke of the incident ever, nor did I receive any discipline for what I'd done. In fact, instead of the usual strap I was expecting that evening, Dad simply cautioned me not to ever eat other kids' lunches. "You don't know who made it or whether they washed their hands" was his only reprimand.

* * *

With summer of 1980 finally upon us and another school year behind me, I would actually go to visit my biological father Roy for the first time. Wow! The anticipation for this face-to-face get-together infused me with both an apprehensive and exciting feeling. After all, I was getting to an age where curiosity about my father was something that started occupying my mind. For me, it was about seeing what he was like and if I was at all similar to him. As Roy had never left that logging town, Mom and Ramona—our one-time foster care girl, now a family friend—would drive me to Hudson Bay, Saskatchewan. As it was a good two-hour drive from Tadmore to Hudson Bay, Ramona came along for the ride to keep Mom company. Upon arrival, we drove straight to Roy's apartment, parking in the building's lot, where we'd meet and greet. Mom and Ramona headed back to Tadmore right after that, choosing not to go up to the apartment. During the introduction process, we discovered that Roy had a girlfriend. She was in the parking lot with Roy and about twenty years his junior. At the age of eleven, I didn't even notice how much younger she was, but Mom sure did. I heard all about it once I returned home after the visit. And if I didn't know better, from the way she went on and on about how young she was, I'd say she was a little bit jealous. As far as I was concerned, if she was twenty years younger—way to go Roy!

During the visit, I could tell Roy was a methodical, laid-back kind of guy, never in a hurry. He was a good-looking man for sure, and I could see why my mother had married him. The one thing I really didn't like about him, though, was that he smoked…and heavily! He did, however, drive an extremely cool truck that any boy would appreciate back then. It was a "Big Green Machine" Chevy half-ton. And whenever we went anywhere, I always sat in the middle between Roy and his girlfriend. I'll never forget the time I changed the radio station and Roy said to me, "Don't touch that, Monte." I thought to myself, *Touchy about your radio, hey?* The way he talked was unique, very slow and disciplined, almost like he was singing—kind of a cross between John Wayne and Johnny Cash. I have a fairly vivid memory of everything we did that visit. After all, it was the first of only two notable visits I had with him. Before this, the only other time I remember seeing Roy was a couple of years before, when he'd popped in one afternoon while passing by Tadmore. Luckily, I'd been home, and that afternoon, we'd made a brief trip to Canora, where he'd purchased a toy fire truck for me. After that, he'd returned me home and continued on his journey.

There were three things most notable during that particular weeklong sleepover visit with Roy. The first highlight was the day I went to work with him. Being a logging town, Roy worked in the bush, loading logs onto big semi-trailer trucks. It was a cool experience to watch up close—from a safe distance, of course. He even let me ride in the cab with him for about an hour as he loaded one of the trucks. It was a rough and bumpy ride. He did that all day long, from early in the morning till quite late. As cool as it was to watch him load trucks, after a while, it became boring. Thereupon, I decided to go do some exploring in the forest. When lunchtime arrived, Roy took me for a walk in the bush while explaining how much he enjoyed the quiet peacefulness of the forest. That's when I discovered we had at least one thing in common. Because his job involved working in a noisy machinery-prolific environment, I understood where he was coming from. As we walked through the trees, I could tell he was looking for something, so I enquired what it was. Roy answered that he was looking for the perfect place to lie down and rest his head for a few minutes. Eventually finding a pristine location for both of us—a spot for him and a spot for me—he put his cap over his eyes and lay on the mossy ground. With my inquisitive mind, I kept talking, asking him questions and such. I didn't realize I was cramping his style and defeating the very purpose of why we were there. Becoming frustrated with my chattiness, he finally said, "You have to be quiet, Monte, and listen to the sounds in the forest. It's very peaceful." So I did. We lay there for about twenty minutes, absorbing the fresh intoxicating aroma of the forest. The odor of decomposing wood and leaves filled the air with a sweet perfume, and the unprocessed scent from all the pine trees was both stimulating and soothing to one's sinuses. Even though it was a hot day in mid-July, the oxygen was heavy and moist— nature's version of an air conditioner in the shade, with a heavy dose of tranquility to make it perfectly relaxing. It was truly an experience that could never be artificially replicated. Roy and I were certainly alike in loving the peace that nature has to offer. Another similar aspect of our personalities that I picked up on that day was working long hours while never complaining about his job. Roy certainly was a hard worker. It was evident that he enjoyed working, and evidently, I inherited the work gene from him—not that my mom was a slacker by any means.

The second thing that stood out to me during that visit happened on one of the days I stayed home with his girlfriend while Roy went to work. She took me shopping downtown to one of the local stores to buy me something to play with. She was very nice and catered to me constantly. When we arrived at the store, I decided a puzzle was a great way to keep myself occupied for the rest of the day. After scouring through the selection of puzzles they had on hand, I finally found one that I liked. It was a picture of a train going through the mountains, like the one my stepdad and I'd taken to Vancouver. However, it also just so happened to be the most expensive one they had.

Now, I was a smart kid. Knowing what things cost and how it all worked, I noticed things like price tags and had a good concept of money. Therefore, upon witnessing what happened next, I knew exactly what was going on. After all, I didn't just fall off the turnip truck. After peeling the price tag off the puzzle I chose, she replaced it with a price tag of lesser value. She tried to hide it from me, but I saw. She switched the price tags! A kindred spirit, perhaps? Laughing to myself, I recalled figuring out that little trick while out shopping myself one day. Conversely, it was funny to see someone else do it, especially an adult, no less. This was before computers and scanners, so it was easy to get away with then. She was pretty cool in my book, especially after seeing her switch the price tags.

Lastly, on the final day of my visit—Sunday afternoon, after attending Catholic Church service—Roy's girlfriend told me they were going to have a nap, and while handing me a pair of headphones to plug in to their 8-track stereo and listen to music, she asked me if I'd be okay for an hour on my own. Knowing that I loved music, she suggested listening to the new Rod Stewart album they'd just purchased…hint-hint. *Yeah, okay. I get it*, I thought to myself. Like I didn't know they were going to be playing checkers with each other. What is it with Sunday afternoons anyway? Mom and Bill always played checkers then too. In case you're wondering, "playing checkers" is an innocent metaphor for an adult activity. The Rod Stewart album, *Blonds Have More Fun*, coincidently had one of my favorite songs on it, "Do Ya Think I'm Sexy"—a big hit at the time. Ever since I'd seen Stewart perform the song live on TV at the Grammys a year earlier, it had been a favorite of mine.

All in all, the trip was great! And even somewhat enlightening, to spend time with my biological father. I don't know that we were similar in every way, but I could definitely see some characteristics in him that I related to. To look at us side by side, it was easy to tell I was my father's son. The next time I would see Roy wouldn't be for a couple of years—and then not again until my wedding day. Rarely ever phoning me, he obviously wasn't a telephone guy. On the other hand, Roy's mother, Irene, my grandma, kept in touch regularly, always sending me $50 for Christmas every year. Then, without fail, she'd call me on my birthday every year. Like Roy, I never saw much of Grandma Irene either, but every once in a while—when passing through—she'd pop in for a brief visit.

You might think that spending time with my biological father for the first time since I was two years old would have had a profound impact on me, or given me some kind of feeling of connection, but really, it didn't. I knew who he was, of course, and acknowledged it completely, but I never got emotional about the fact that he wasn't a part of my daily life. I saw it for what it was—nothing more, nothing less. Because he was never in my life, we never did bond as a father and son. While growing up, my stepdad, Bill, filled that void quite well. I never felt that I was missing anything. How do you miss something you never had? It's about acceptance and being happy with, and thankful for, what you do have. I've found plenty to be grateful for in the dad I had, in Bill—probably more so now than ever!

CHAPTER

8

Moving On

Sitting in my wheelchair back at my home outside of Calgary, reminiscing about my past in an effort to move on into my future and further come to terms with my new life, proved to be a cathartic experience. Never the type to vegetate mindlessly in front of the TV, I spent a lot of time thinking about how to discover my new self within my old self. Not the type of person to shrink away from any challenge, I believed that I could bounce back from anything. I was always a take-charge kind of guy, and this situation wasn't about to change that. I did, however, wonder how paralysis might affect my life expectancy. After a brief internet search on the subject, I soon learned that spinal cord injury did not substantially reduce life expectancy—unless you were on a ventilator. With current medications and trained caregivers, life expectancies for those with SCI is only slightly lower than the national average. Being past the one-year mark of my injury, I'd already beaten one statistic: surviving the first year. Mortality rates are significantly higher—mostly due to suicide and medical complications—during the first year after injury than during succeeding years, especially for those who suffered other severe injuries in addition to the SCI.

I knew that although I didn't have places to go and people to see, I did have things to do. And I was fortunate enough to have a few tools at my disposal to do that. If I was going to become paralyzed, I couldn't have picked a better time in history to do it. Thanks to the personal computer and one of its offspring, the internet—with its endless possibilities, like email and chatroom communication—and the word processor, I was not isolated from the great big world around me. And thankfully, while in the hospital, my recreational therapist had built a special mouth stick, which was molded to fit my teeth. This allowed me to operate a ball mouse and type on a computer keyboard by gripping the stick in my mouth. Following my release from the circumstantial confines of a hospital room, first thing on the agenda was to set up the computer in our den for me to use. My good friend, Chris Bonneau, built me a platform to raise and angle the keyboard to a specific location, and with a little practice, I quickly adapted to this new and somewhat unusual method of using a computer. Some days, I felt like a woodpecker poking away on my keyboard, but it worked pretty darn good, and that was all that mattered.

With the internet being the hot new craze in 1999, it opened up a whole new world to me, something that would prove to be both a blessing and a curse. On my journey through cyberspace, I stumbled upon a website called Spinewire. Spinewire, which later rebranded to CareCure, is a website dedicated to helping people with spinal cord injuries as well as keeping everyone up to date with the latest and greatest advancement in spinal cord injury research. Basically, it's an online community of people from around the globe who have some form of spinal injury. As well as news on research, CareCure offers medical advice from professional nurses, doctors, and researchers on every subject you can think of. From bowel programs, depression, to sex after injury, they cover everything. This website, being extremely educational and helpful, became a safe haven to anyone with a SCI (spinal cord injury)—especially for yours truly.

Interestingly, everyone on this particular message board—supposedly well-versed in spinal cord research—kept predicting that within five years, medical science should have a cure for anyone with a damaged spinal cord. That was seventeen years ago. As much as that was sweet music to my ears, I was somewhat skeptical. After educating myself in the complexities of the human spinal cord and central nervous system, a cure stemming from what primitive knowledge we had in the area of neural biology seemed highly unlikely, at least in my lifetime. Nevertheless, this website proved very beneficial and therapeutic by connecting me with others who were going through similar trials and tribulations while dealing with such a drastic life-altering change as paralysis. It's peculiar how reminiscing with others who were going through similar hardships made it somehow easier to bear. Perhaps knowing you're not the only one in the world dealing with the challenges of spinal cord injury washes away or at least dilutes the bitter attitude of "woe is me." I would discover that eighty percent of spinal cord injuries occurred among males; although statistics are prone to change over time. No doubt, with females being more active in almost as many diverse extreme sports as males these days, the chances of them becoming the victim of an SCI has risen. As the median age of the general public increases, the average age at injury increases over time also. When I had my accident, the average age was roughly thirty, exactly the age I was. Now it's up to around forty.

Another beneficial aspect of the internet in 1999 was listening to the live streaming audiocast of the AMA Supercross series on Saturday nights. Without fail, every Saturday evening—during race season—I could be found in my office listening to the live feed. The announcers did such an amazing job at relaying to listeners the live excitement that it felt as if you were right there in the middle of the action. If you couldn't be there, this was definitely the next best thing. Although it was true that I regretted pushing the limits of racing, I still loved it! Once racing gets in your blood, it becomes a part of you.

* * *

The spring of 2000—usually a time to get ready for the start of the upcoming motocross or cross-country racing season—brought along what would be one of the first rays of hope for me as far as doing something really worthwhile with my time. Surprisingly, it would keep me involved in the sport that had meant so much to me. The Canadian Motosport Racing Corporation (CMRC) asked if I'd be interested in writing a regular column for their organization's in-house magazine. CMRC, which had seen the light of day in Canada some nine years earlier as CMC (Continental Motosport Club), had practically reinvented the sport of motocross in Canada from grassroots up to pro, which, under CMA sanctioning, had seen a steady decline from the mid-1980s onward. By adding new tracks to the national championship lineup and attracting outside corporate sponsors like Snapple, Export A, Monster Energy Drink, Rockstar Energy Drink, the series was picked up and broadcast on network television, thus attracting all the top pros, who inevitably migrated away from a sinking CMA. CMRC had provided Canadian motocross with a new lease on life. Today it has expanded its reach worldwide—thanks to the internet—with live lap-scoring and live streaming audio/video of the Rockstar Energy Drink/CMRC Motocross Nationals. By 1999 CMRC had displaced the CMA as the sport's national sanctioning body and ushered motocross into a new "golden age." Therefore, being asked by CMRC's founder/president, Mark Stallybrass, to join his magazine's writing staff was definitely an honor. There was only one little problem, though. My first reaction, which I kept to myself, was: *Me writing…for a magazine? I don't even know how to write! I failed and never did complete grade ten English.* Nevertheless, in the spirit of trying anything once, I gave it a shot and wrote my very first article for the July 2000 issue of *CMRC Magazine.* The editor probably took one look at all my broken sentences and shook his head in disbelief. Given my no-holds barred, tell-it-like-it-is personality, Nicole came up with the perfect title for my column: "The Full Monte!"

The following year, Performance Publications Group in Toronto bought the magazine from CMRC—it came with the sanctioning body's 7,000+ membership mailing list. PPG's owners, Blake and Perry Breslin, were the publishers of, among others, a well-known and respected Canadian motorsport magazine called *Performance Racing News* (PRN). It covered everything from four-wheel racing to two-wheel racing, including everything from Formula 1 to NASCAR and motocross to road racing. Their new acquisition, however, would focus mainly on the burgeoning Canadian motocross scene, which now featured big hitters from the U.S., Europe, and Australia to give our homegrown boys a run for their money. The Breslin brothers also intended to take the magazine, which had initially been aimed at the CMRC's amateur and pro racing membership, to a nationally distributed publication aimed at motocross fans. To my astonishment, PPG asked me to join their team and keep writing. Rechristened *Motocross Performance and Off-Road Racing*—later shortened to *MXP* (*Motocross Performance*)—the magazine was officially launched in January 2002. Before long, I was covering events, interviewing racers, and writing a variety of different pieces for the publication, which slowly but surely was spreading across the country as the "voice of Canadian motocross." To my surprise, after working closely with their founding editor-in-chief, Wil De Clercq, my writing skills quickly sharpened. Although he made suggestions and sometimes requested specific writing assignments, I was given carte blanche. All I had to do was meet my deadlines. Never missing a single issue, I wrote for *MXP* until late 2007, when, after becoming somewhat disconnected from the racing scene, the decision to bow out gracefully and keep my opinions to myself felt like the right choice. *MXP*, meanwhile, has enjoyed a longevity that few if any rival publications have been able to uphold in Canada. Today, it ranks as the No.1 motocross magazine in the country, with a strong online presence.

http://montejperepelkin.com/photos-7

I fully enjoyed writing for *MXP*, and it came into my life at a time when I needed something…anything, to give me a new purpose now that I was no longer an able-bodied man and would no longer be practicing my occupation of finishing carpenter. In a way, it was ironic how the opportunity to start reinventing myself was provided by the very same sport that had so dramatically changed my life. In some ways, it was bittersweet to write about motocross. But hey, I knew the sport from an insider's perspective. I knew a lot of the riders and behind-the-scenes players personally. And I still felt passionate about the sport. In other ways, the experience helped build up my confidence again, the confidence I'd had in myself before my accident. If I put my mind to something, I could carry through and do pretty much anything. With *MXP* I had proven to myself that I actually could write more than just a grocery list. Not only that, my motocross journalism experience would eventually lead to writing this autobiography. While writing for *MXP*, however, and many years after, the thoughts of writing an autobiography were never of any interest to me. That would come later. I still had a lot of soul-searching to do, not to mention really get my life in order. There were some serious dramas and new challenges still waiting in the wings for me. But escaping into my past always seemed to bring solace in to my life.

* * *

Not long after returning home from the hospital, I acquired an old van that was adapted with a wheelchair lift. Though somewhat of a beater, it sufficed as transportation. Besides, for $1,500, beggars can't be choosers. At least, as long as I had a chauffeur, usually Nicole, I was able to get around. Needless to say, Nicole was stuck doing the majority of my care. Fact is, we didn't have a choice. Around the clock care would have cost a fortune. Besides, as intrusive as our lives had already become, we didn't exactly want a caregiver hanging around more than they needed to. As a result, finding someone to come in for a couple of hours at a time while living out on an acreage was a challenge, because of the distance. This led to the unfortunate consequence of my poor wife having far too much on her plate. Within four short months of returning home from the hospital, Nicole was nearing her breaking point. Adding insult to her already diminished mental capacity, every time someone would call or pop over, the attention was always directed at me. Very seldom did anyone bother to ask how she was faring. Obviously, I was the one suffering with the physical injury. The consequences, however, were felt just as much—if not more— by her as well. At one point, due to the loss of control, I remember Nicole sitting at the foot of our staircase screaming uncontrollably at the top of her lungs. Meanwhile, I sat helplessly and watched. There was nothing I could do. While part of me felt compassion, another part of me was angry that she couldn't cope with the situation. Truth is, neither of us were equipped with the mental skills to console each other. I was oblivious to what she needed, and likewise, Nicole was toward me.

Part of the solution was to sell our acreage and move to a smaller home in the city. Living in the acreage home certainly wasn't the ideal situation. Being a two-story, I wasn't able to get upstairs. We had purchased a queen-size bed, and our formal dining room became my bedroom. Meanwhile, Nicole slept upstairs with our daughters. But it just wasn't practical to remain where we were—for any number of reasons—and the time had come to face another reality of my confinement to a wheelchair: selling our home and moving back to the city. We had our property listed, but selling an acreage is much different than selling a home in the city. Because of their specific nature, it wasn't uncommon for an acreage to sit on the market for months or even years before finding a buyer. Unfortunately, our situation couldn't afford to wait that long. In addition to our already complicated state of affairs, since I was generally the one who initiated physical affection in our relationship, Nicole and I hadn't shown any genuine expressions of love toward each other for months. And because my body had changed so drastically, I wasn't exactly feeling all that secure about the idea of physical intimacy anyway. Seemingly, everything still worked—I could still get erections—but the whole concept just seemed foreign and unfamiliar, which equated to a very unhealthy scenario for even the strongest relationship. Unfortunately, there are no clear-cut answers on how a husband and wife are supposed to adapt to such a life-altering change. Adding fuel to a wildfire that was already threatening our marriage, I began looking for comfort online, and I soon found myself engaging in conversations with a girl from another country. At first, it started out innocent and harmless, as it usually does, but before long, the situation proved significantly otherwise. That was when I learned about the effects of emotional infidelity, the consequences of which are equally as serious as physical infidelity. When Nicole learned of my conversations, she was justifiably furious and heartbroken.

Both of us still wanting to work things out, we began weekly counseling sessions with a therapist. I immediately put a stop to the online conversations, and for about a month, it seemed there might be light at the end of the tunnel. However, that light proved to be nothing more than an illusion we created while looking forward to a future version of ourselves where I was once again able-bodied. Knowing how happy we were before the injury, the two of us couldn't seem to shake the hope of once again living that reality. It really was a sad situation, one that I'd often cry myself to sleep at night thinking about. Deep down, I knew this paralysis was permanent and no amount of mental therapy was going to change that. Besides, the counselor was able-bodied; what could she possibly know about our situation? Sadly, the writing was on the wall. Our marriage was doomed! All I could do was sit back and watch it disintegrate.

Not helping matters, Nicole's family offered very little assistance to our situation. While I was in the hospital and Nicole needed her parents to babysit our daughters for a couple of hours, her mother expected to get paid every time. Then, once it was evident that my injury was as life-altering as it was, the advice Nicole's parents offered her was to leave me while she was still young… She could easily find someone else and even have more kids. I went from being their favorite son-in-law to a piece of clothing you just throw away once it's outlived its usefulness. One of Nicole's own sisters once asked her, "How can you even lie next to that?" as if being paralyzed meant I was no longer a human being. Needless to say, those insensitive comments certainly took their toll on my self-worth as a man, but in the end, they were just words.

Nicole, not akin to the same mentality as her family, was appalled by their attitude. Yet there wasn't much she could do either; they were her only support anchor. Recognizing that we've all said things we later regretted, I chose not to take their thoughtless remarks personally. Besides, that would have done me more harm than them. They were just thinking of their daughter's well-being and future, a daughter who was now being pushed to the extremes of mental anguish because of an accident that had occurred in the pursuit of my own happiness. I couldn't really fault them for that, and I hold no animosity towards them for their insensitivity. We've all made mistakes and said stupid things throughout our lives. I know I certainly have, more times than I'd like to remember. In writing about these particulars, my only intention is to paint an accurate portrait of what my family went through and the odds we were up against. I'm sure that anybody who ends up paralyzed, regardless of what caused it, faces similar scenarios. It was part of our reality, and to give an accurate portrayal of our circumstances, I feel it is something that needs to be included in my narrative. There are no hidden agendas here. I harbor no resentment or ill will towards Nicole's family, or anyone, for that matter. Holding a grudge serves no benefit. In fact, it's a detriment to our own advancement in becoming a better human being. I'm reminded of a quote I once came across by actress Carrie Fisher, best known for her role as Princess Leia in the original *Star Wars* trilogy: "Resentment is like drinking poison and waiting for the other person to die."

One afternoon, during an argument Nicole and I were engaged in, we managed to actually laugh at ourselves in even the darkest of moments. Out of frustration, not expecting to hit her target, Nicole picked up a banana and hurled it across the room at me. Not being able to move out of the way, however, her aim proved far more accurate than she'd anticipated. The banana bulls-eyed me square in the head. If I remember correctly, I definitely deserved it. At times, I would forget that my predicament didn't just affect me; it affected Nicole as well, who meant everything to me. There was no question; we certainly loved each other. The multi-dimensional situation we were in was simply far too complicated for us to solve. A combination of the physical and psychological effects caused by such a life-altering injury, with two little girls who needed to be raised, an acreage to upkeep, bills to pay, and constantly dealing with caregivers, would have been challenging for any marriage. The circumstance we were facing could easily be compared to a Volkswagen Bug towing a 20-foot RV up a never-ending hill. Regardless of what you put in the gas tank, sooner or later, the engine is going to fail.

In spite of the disastrous storm clouds looming overhead, one afternoon, while interacting with my children, I'd managed to unceremoniously stumble upon that illustrious silver lining I kept looking for. Part of my daily routine included sitting on the couch while my daughters, Danielle and Haylee, gathered around, playing dolls, tea party, and everything else a young girl's imagination could think of. The big kid in me would have me playing along with them—usually trying to make them laugh. Funny faces and voice impressions from children's movies were a big part of my repertoire. On one particular afternoon, however, three-year-old Haylee, while sitting on the floor at my feet, looked up at me with those big blue eyes of hers and said, "Daddy, I'm glad you got in a wheelchair." And after enquiring why, she responded, "Because now you're home all the time to play with us." Danielle, overhearing her sister's comment, chimed in and agreed. The two of them, not oblivious to the emotion I was trying to conceal, came over and gave me a giant, much-needed hug. Only a child could produce tears of joy from saying such a thing. While contemplating my youngest daughter's heartfelt remark, I came to a valuable realization… She was right! That was when I began to recognize the burden that had been lifted from me: not having to worry about the next race or push myself to be more successful in business. I woke in the morning with a freed mind and spirit. Evidently, somewhere along the way, I'd crossed the line from having enough to sustain a happy life to having far more than we ever needed. I had completely lost sight of contentment and, more importantly, what truly mattered in life. Fortunately, thanks to this injury, my three-year-old daughter set me straight. My silver lining was an opportunity that few parents get these days: the ability to spend quality time with their children on a daily basis during their most precious and formidable years. Though a seemingly steep price to pay, I wouldn't trade it for anything.

Not long after becoming acquainted with my silver lining, however, we finally found a buyer for our acreage—except it was too little too late. Though still living together, Nicole and I had already decided to amicably part ways. Selling the acreage meant moving out on my own and living apart from my daughters. Not knowing what the future held, becoming paralyzed wasn't nearly as difficult to accept as the prospect of living separate from Danielle and Haylee. They had literally become my entire world. Thankfully, I was temporarily distracted with the desperation of finding a new place to call home. Not being confident that I would be able to live by myself meant living in some sort of assisted facility. Knowing full well that life in an old-age home would drive any thirty-one-year-old testosterone-filled man to the brink of suicide, I was somewhat concerned about my options. Fortunately, not unlike every other bleak situation throughout my life, before I even had a chance to worry, an opportunity conveniently presented itself. I acquired the phone number to a special facility called the 4th Dimension, which especially catered to victims of spinal cord injury. Because ten clients at time was all they could accommodate, however, I was warned of a possible long wait, as the list was lengthy, and that was if I met their criteria for getting accepted in the first place. Although forewarned not to get my hopes up, needless to say, hope was all I had.

After one phone call that entailed a brief explanation of my dire circumstances, to my amazement, they were willing to meet with me the very next day and assess whether or not I qualified. Then, after a brief interview with the lady who ran the place, Earla, I was informed of a room that would be soon available, and it was mine if I wanted it. There was only one hitch: the room wasn't available until two weeks after the new owners took possession of our acreage. Fortunately, and once again, my great friends Chris and Anne came to the rescue and generously allowed me to stay with them until then. As circumstances would have it, Chris's home was accessible and even had a wheelchair shower. Sadly, Chris had a brother who had also been in a wheelchair but who had passed away three years prior. I couldn't have asked for better accommodations. Meanwhile, my soon-to-be ex-wife and our daughters took temporary refuge with her parents.

I can distinctly recall. the day before moving out of the house I had designed and built, much of it with my own two hands, sitting on the sofa watching a movie with my girls. Haylee was under my left arm while Danielle was nestled under my right. But my mind wasn't focused on the movie. Instead, like a scratched vinyl record skipping and playing the same lyrics over and over, my mind kept spinning through a repetitive cycle of wondering how or when I would ever experience this level of closeness with my daughters in an assisted living facility. As a result, with each of their adorable little heads pressed tightly against my paralyzed torso, my eyes began to well up with tears. All I could do before embarking on this unknown journey was savor these remaining moments and hope and pray for the best.

Cue music: "Shape of Things to Come" by Audioslave

https://www.youtube.com/watch?v=TMdqDxpGo9g

CHAPTER

9

Thou Shalt Not Steal

In 1981, I was twelve years old and some seven months away from becoming a teenager. Like any kid, I couldn't wait to join that illustrious group. It was the last day of grade six, with summer holidays straight ahead in the proverbial headlights of life... *Woohoo*! My mom's fifth brother, Uncle Keith—third youngest of the boys—and his wife Beverly lived in Canora at the time. They had two children, both girls, Tracey and Terri. They later had a boy, Robbie. Tracey and Terri were closer to my sister Nikki's age. As per custom, to kick off the summer holiday, we only had a half-day of school. I had been told by Mom to go to my uncle and aunt's house in Canora after school instead of coming home on the bus. The plan was that Mom would pick me up from their place later in the day. Knowing that after checking in with my aunt, I would be heading downtown on my own, I was cool with Mom's arrangement.

Upon arriving at my uncle's house, I found the babysitter there, watching Tracey and Terri. My Aunt Bev wasn't home from work yet, and Uncle Keith was away all week. He worked for the CN Railway as a welder and wasn't normally home during the week. When I walked in the front door, my little cousins were happy to see me. The sitter was lying on the couch, engrossed in watching television. He was actually tuned into a soap opera, *Another World*. Considering he was male and in his early twenties, I thought that was rather strange. I thought of soaps as something mothers and grandmothers watched. I think my little cousins were bored. They definitely weren't into soaps at their age. With my mom being an aficionado of the show herself, I was familiar with some of the characters, including Rachel and Mack. This particular soap was very popular in its heyday among housewives and, apparently, this young babysitter. At his age, you wouldn't have caught me dead in front of a TV watching *Another World* or any other sappy soap opera.

Being that it was lunchtime, I asked Tracey and Terri if they were hungry. In unison, they said they were. I guess Mr. Babysitter was too busy to fix them lunch. After snooping through the kitchen cupboards, I found some Kraft Dinner and asked the girls if they wanted some. Again in unison, and very enthusiastically, they said they did. Aunt Bev came home from work a short time later, and feeling more comfortable now that auntie was there for my cousins, I wandered off downtown. It was about four blocks away. As usual, I had a plan—a devious one! I went in to the Rexall drugstore, purloined a ten-dollar ornament, and walked out the door. I made sure to be quick and get out of there before anyone noticed me. My plan was to return in about an hour and ask for a refund. I needed to kill some time, so I walked around town, checking out different stores. For a little town of roughly 1,700 inhabitants, there was a surprisingly large number of retail in Canora. When I figured enough time had elapsed since steeling the ornament, I returned to the Rexall store. I walked straight to the till and explained to the cashier that I'd bought the item for my mom but had changed my mind about it, and wanted to get her a scarf instead. It was something they didn't sell in the drugstore, so I didn't have to worry about being confronted with an exchange. Obviously, I didn't have a receipt. The cashier looked at me and must have thought I had an honest face, because she gave me a refund for the item—no questions asked. I thought to myself, *That worked out pretty well,* and headed to the arcade. Ten dollars in quarters went a long way back in those days. I played Pac-Man, Defender, Space Invaders, and some new games I hadn't tried before. I was a quick study of most things, but wasn't an ardent gamer. Therefore, the quarters ran out after a couple of hours, and my pockets were once again empty. Not quite ready to head back to my relatives' place just yet, the smart kid I thought I was decided to do something incredibly stupid. It worked the first time, so why not try it again, right?

Like most pharmacies, the floor at Rexall was raised behind the counter—at the back of the store—giving the pharmacist/owner a bird's eye view of customers coming and going. And since the store was quite small—three aisles front to back—it wasn't hard for him to keep an eye on everyone. Probably suspicious of me visiting the store for a third time in a few hours' time, he saw me attempt the same scam again. What's worse, Canora being a small town, everyone knew everyone else, including my uncle's family and my mom. And it just so happened that at the time I got busted, there were two boys in the store who knew me from school. It was shaping up to be a very unpleasant afternoon. After a brief interrogation—albeit a friendly one—the store owner called my mom. She was at my uncle's by this time. While we waited for her to arrive, the kind pharmacist took me to the back of his store and asked me questions about school and what I wanted to do over the holidays. I believe his intentions were to keep me calm. Having never been caught stealing in a situation such as this, I was in unfamiliar territory.

Once Mom arrived, the owner spoke with her just out of earshot of me. Not being able to hear anything they were saying, all I could do was sit and watch the expression on my mother's face. They chatted for what seemed like eternity. In reality, it might have been five minutes—time has a way of slowing down in situations like this. Every once in a while, Mom would turn to look at me—and not in a happy, fun way. No, the appearance of absolute disappointment was deeply engraved in her face. If looks could kill, by the time they finished talking, I'd have been reduced to a mere pile of smoldering ashes.

During the twenty-minute car ride home, which also seemed to take forever, Mom just stared straight ahead and never once looked at me. Every time I looked over towards her, the vein in her temple kept pulsating as if it might explode at any moment. Not a word was spoken between us, and I sure wasn't going to be the one to initiate a conversation. Once we arrived home, she sent me straight to my room, where I just waited, lying on the bed, wondering what was going to happen next. As is the case with the calm before a storm, I didn't have to wait long. Like a hurricane, Mom entered my room with her thick, two-inch-wide purple and black leather belt. That was when it really hit the fan. There was no bending me over her knee, no warning whatsoever; that purple belt just started flying. Let me tell you, she was angry! She kept swinging until she was finally out of breath. Fortunately for me, that didn't take long. Physically speaking, neither of my parents were in very good shape.

After the dust settled, surprisingly, there were no welts or marks on my body, but oh boy, that one had stung. I'd never seen my mom react like that. Ever! She'd actually lost it—her temper that is. Looking back, I understand why Mom was so upset. Up until this point, she'd more or less always stuck up for me. This time was different. I'd embarrassed her. This was a matter of pride. With the small-town drama and gossip that constantly circled around, her son being known as a "shoplifter" was a tough pill to swallow. Regretfully, not realizing it at the time, because of my actions, I'd completely disrespected her. And even though the punishment seemed harsh, it was well deserved. The problem, however, was that receiving the strap did not intimidate me. Otherwise, I would have thought twice before stealing. Unfortunately, getting the strap was beginning to feel like a rite of passage that went with growing up. It failed as a deterrent measure.

I've often pondered why Mom had a tendency to stick up for me or shift the blame on occasion even when it was clearly my fault. Understandably, that too was a matter of pride. Mom raised me on her own until I was five; therefore, she felt that my actions were a direct reflection of her parenting. Generally speaking, many parents are guilty of this mentality. They mistakenly see their child's misbehavior as a reflection of themselves. As a result, they fall prey to the knee-jerk reaction: *My child would never do that… Someone else MUST be to blame!* That's not to say that children don't or can't pick up bad habits from their parents, but in my case, that wasn't applicable. Mom and Dad are two of the most honest people I know—they wouldn't steal a nickel from anyone.

Three days after getting caught at the drugstore, retribution came calling—or so I thought. I was out riding my crappy secondhand bike down one of the streets in our little town. On this particular day, my chain kept falling off the front sprocket. It wasn't the first time, and when it happened, grease would get on my pant leg. This was irritating me. Being the type of kid who cared about what he wore, wrecking a pair of pants that I liked wasn't cool. After concluding that the rear wheel must have slid forward and loosened the chain, I went home to make the repair. It was an easy adjustment to make, and within two minutes, I was done. To make sure the chain wasn't going to fall off again, I climbed aboard my bike and pedaled hard for about a block. So far so good. Then, after slowing down but not stopping, I reached down with my right hand to check the tension of the chain to make sure it wasn't loose again. Bad idea. Just as I grabbed the chain between my right index finger and thumb, my finger got caught between the sprocket and chain, after which the most gut-wrenching sound of bone being crunched resonated through my entire body—similar to the crinkling of a plastic water bottle, except this was my index finger being squashed between the chain and sprocket. Immediately, the pain made its pulse-enhancing debut and rushed directly to my brain. The worst part was that I had to pedal a full revolution to get my finger out. What was left of it anyways.

Upon freeing my finger and making a quick inspection of the carnage, I wrapped my hand in the t-shirt I was wearing, dropped my bike, and ran home. With each beat of my heart, blood would squirt from my finger and send a wave of spine-piercing pain up my arm. I ran into the house and screamed, "I cut my finger off!" Luckily, Mom was home. Not even asking to see the damage—she could tell by all the blood that it was bad—we both ran to the car and drove off to Canora. I had never seen Betty drive that fast before. She had the car matted as fast as it would go; the speedometer needle was well past 100 mph. Because Dad was a top-selling car salesman at Formo's, he always got to choose a demo to drive, which was usually a brand new luxury car. That particular day, however, he had taken our other "beater car" in for some long-overdue repairs, leaving his new car for Mom to drive. Good thing he did. We arrived at the hospital in record time, dashed into emergency, and in a jiffy, the doctor sewed up my finger. It wasn't quite as bad as I'd thought; just the very tip was cut off. Basically, my fingerprint was gone.

After all the drama had subsided, I could tell Mom was a nervous wreck. Putting on my bravest front, I said, "Don't worry, Mom. It's just the tip of my finger. I'll be fine." She just shook her head and replied, "One of these days, you're going to give me a nervous breakdown." Once the theatrics of the afternoon had settled down, I was stretched out on my bed, ruminating on the day's misfortune. I couldn't help but wonder if the events that had transpired three days ago were connected with what had happened to my finger. Could it be? Was I indeed being punished? It sure felt like it.

Being immersed in the Jehovah's Witness way of life, I definitely had a good understanding of the Ten Commandments, and I knew full well that one of them was not to steal. But did that really mean it was wrong according to my own self-appointed moral standards? My principles, or lack thereof, had been established at four years of age, hanging out with Kelly. Since then, I believed that as long as no one was getting hurt, stealing was a victimless crime. And it's not like I was causing anyone to go without food or lose their business. Furthermore, at most, it was only a few dollars here and there.

* * *

Later that summer Bill and I would go on our first of many fishing trips to Flin Flon, which is located on the border of Manitoba and Saskatchewan. Because Flin Flon was situated around numerous large lakes, it was a desirable destination for many freshwater fishing enthusiasts. We went with a few of our JW friends, and some of them really knew their way around the region's lakes. They had all the hot fishing spots dialed in. What an incredible experience that was! The scenery was spectacular, and wow, did we catch a lot of fish. What could be better than sitting in a boat in the hot sun, drinking pop, and eating snacks all day while catching fish? Dad was in his glory. I was too. One afternoon, we went ashore to a small island on one of the big lakes, cleaned a few of the fish we'd just caught, and then cooked them fresh on an open fire. That was the best fish I'd ever tasted. After that initial trip, Dad and I were hooked. We went every summer after that. Dad even bought a nice boat the following year, the kind with an open bow—lots of seating and great for fishing. This watercraft came with a powerful seventy-horse Johnson motor; great for water skiing. Remember, we lived only two miles from Crystal Lake. There weren't many fish in that lake, but it was the perfect size for water skiing, an activity we'd eventually do quite often during the summer months.

Summer holidays were coming to an end, and school was starting again in September. That year, however, instead of Canora, my parents decided to send me to grade seven in Sturgis, another small east-central Saskatchewan town. We lived on the border between the two school districts, giving us the option to choose. Because Dad worked in Preeceville, Saskatchewan—which is on the same route to Sturgis—and we went to JW services in Sturgis, I believe their decision revolved around keeping a better eye on me. Nikki began grade one that year. She would join me at the elementary school in Sturgis.

On the first day of school, Nikki and I walked to the bus stop. Since changing schools is a pretty big deal when you're a kid, I was feeling somewhat apprehensive. From a social perspective, I was basically starting from scratch—not to mention once again being "the new kid." As it turned out, adding a small element of familiarity to my first day, our bus driver was someone we knew. It was Dan, a fellow JW and a jolly fellow. That was a welcome surprise. The school year usually kicked off on a Friday, which gave us the weekend to get our supplies. In the past, Mom would always give me money and send me off to buy everything on my own. This particular year, Nikki needed supplies as well. Therefore, while at Yorkton Mall, Mom gave me $60 and sent me off with my sister. Normally, I'd get $40 just for myself, and that was barely enough. I'm not sure how Mom thought $60 was going to stretch far enough for both of us. I don't think all our school supplies can be purchased from the bulk discount bin at K-Mart, Mom! She did cough up another twenty bucks eventually.

When it came to buying school clothes, however, Mom would often take us to the Sally Ann store, as she called it. That's slang for the Salvation Army thrift store. Sometimes you could find some cool garments there, but I was going into grade seven now and starting to appreciate the difference between quality stylish clothing and secondhand stuff! When I was younger, I could actually get excited about going through racks of used clothing, looking for that diamond in the rough. But now, not so much. Maybe I'm sounding like I was a whiny little kid, but all the other kids had designer jeans and Nike running shoes. Why couldn't I? My parents could have easily afforded it, as they were doing well financially by this time. Sometimes it felt like my parents were cheapskates.

Fact of the matter was, there was no way I was going to wear cheap dollar-bin running shoes with my Sally Anne clothes to school that year. I needed to come up with a solution. Still a bit shaken up from allowing myself to get busted at Rexall, I scrapped the option of stealing what I desired. That was when I came up with a brilliant plan and sat down with Mom at the K-Mart coffee shop to explain. My proposal began by telling her that I wanted to buy my own clothes from now on, and I suggested that perhaps she could give me the amount that was fair and reasonable to spend on my school clothes and allow me to purchase them on my own. Secondly, I reasoned, because she often wasn't at home after school, she would need some help with Nikki every day. Then I explained how I could make sure Nikki kept up with homework, make her something to eat, get her to clean her room, and make lunches for school. My fee for all this: $35 a week. I knew I'd be doing it anyway, so I thought, why not capitalize on the opportunity before I ended up doing it for nothing. It was a long shot, but to my surprise, Mom readily agreed and even laughed, saying it was pretty crafty of me to come up with this little proposal on my own. I believe she was proud of my industriousness. I had one condition, though: She had to pay me for a month in advance so that I could go buy some decent school clothes. With a big smirk on her face, she replied, "You conniving little bugger!"

Mom gave me $140 plus another $60 for what she thought was fair. Combined with a few dollars I'd saved from working for Frank, the cattle farmer who lived next to us—I'd often help feed his cattle—I was off shopping. After finding a few "back to school" deals, I was able to stretch that money and get everything I wanted. In the end, I bought a couple of shirts, jeans, and a nice pair of Nike running shoes. I was stylin'!

If I were to say that we unnecessarily lived an underprivileged life, Mom would argue that compared to the way she was raised, we lived a life of luxury. And she wasn't wrong. Did I ever not have shoes to wear? Did I ever not have clothes to wear? No! I always had more than enough clothing. Just not the brand-name items I would have liked. And I never went hungry. I merely didn't have the kind of desserts the other kids had. In comparison, I can recall Mom telling me about, when she was a young girl, going to school barefoot. Why? Because she REALLY didn't have any shoes to wear, never mind if they were Nikes. For her, back in those days, having a pair of shoes to wear was considered a luxury. Granted, we were no longer living "back in those days." But I can imagine, growing up the way Mom did, it wasn't easy to overcome such a heavily ingrained disposition.

Although I have often resorted to unscrupulous behavior in order to attain what some might consider justifiable wants, it was through no fault of my parents' conservative upbringing. There were other contributing factors that perpetuated those components of my life. Consequently, once I matured and finally grew a conscience in regard to stealing, Mom and Dad's method of old-school parenting—whether by design or not—taught me a valuable life lesson: *Nothing is free in this world. If you want something, then go out and earn it!* In comparison, I have witnessed my share of parents who buy their kids far in excess of what they actually need, thus spoiling them and contributing to an all-too-common attitude we see today: *The world owes me a living.*

* * *

Grade seven got into full swing, with Mom taking full advantage of our new arrangement, which was identical to the old arrangement except now I was getting paid. Being the go-getter she was, she ambitiously began selling the popular Avon cosmetics. Mom was really fired up about being an associate of Avon—one of the first direct-selling companies in North America. Eventually, she worked her way up to sales rep, with several girls working under her. Mom even won a trip to Hawaii the following year and had her picture taken with the actor Jim Nabors while there. Nabors was the star of a sitcom during the 1960s called *Gomer Pyle*. The sitcom was so popular the networks would play reruns of it well into the 1980s.

My daily routine of looking after Nikki was running smoothly. I think she listened to me better than she did Mom or Dad. Let me tell you, she was a stubborn child sometimes. I wonder who she ever inherited that from! Throughout my childhood, I was a tidy kid. Nikki, on the other hand, not so much. She would drive me bonkers sometimes. I even remember spanking her on the bum, just with my hand, though. Being a kid myself, I soon learned that bribing my sister was the most effective way to get her to follow instructions. Food and taking away her favorite toy was my best ammunition with Nikki. She loved her snack foods and dolls.

As is the case with all boys, grade seven was a changing point for me. Puberty and all that weird stuff got a hold of me. It just so happened that my locker was next to that of the cutest girl in our class. Her name was Rene. Wow, did I have a crush on her. Rene was blond, with long, curly hair and the cutest face. At that age, it's really just about the face. I didn't notice her body until much later. Rene really was a beauty. Shortly after my innocent infatuation with Rene began, I remember getting ready for school one morning and looking at myself in the mirror. My hair was all over the place, having just gotten out of bed. That was when I realized never once did I ever comb my disheveled locks before going to school. I couldn't help but wonder: *What was I thinking? Rene must think I live with a bunch of baboons or something.* From that day on, I washed my hair every single morning and styled it with a blow dryer. Soon, I learned that looking good takes a lot of work. I had to get up fifteen minutes earlier just to wash and style my hair. Sheesh! But nothing ever became of us, not even a single date, and it wasn't for lack of trying. I did come very close once in grade ten. She wanted to go, but her dad said no way! Considering my reputation by grade ten, I can't say that I blame him.

Being an athletically gifted kid, gym class would be my favorite part of the school day. Badminton became my favorite sport, next to volleyball and floor hockey. After learning the rules and strategies that went with the competitive side of badminton, I exceled quickly. By grade nine, I was the best our school had to offer. This provided me the opportunity to participate in tournaments at neighboring schools. In grade ten, I never lost a single game at any tournament and was the first student in our school to ever beat our gym teacher and badminton coach, Mr. Poppowich. He was good, really good! No one could even touch him at badminton—until I came along, that is. I never asked him, but I wonder if he was an ex-badminton pro from college or something. All the same, from the displeased look on his face, I don't think he felt too groovy about losing to me that day. You can be sure that I never let him forget about it either.

Due to the fact that I went to school in Sturgis, the same town as our Kingdom Hall meetings, grade seven presented a few changes to my lifestyle. With several kids in my school who were from JW families—two of whom were in my grade, I had to watch my Ps and Qs. Anything I did at school would get back to the elders in our congregation, not to mention dear old Dad. Therefore, I had to tread lightly. Every Wednesday at lunchtime, I had to attend a Bible study with Corey, one of the two boys in my grade who was a JW. Just as I suspected, my parents' decision to send me to school in Sturgis was definitely to keep a close eye on me. We studied with an older girl, Eunice, who attended grade twelve at our school. Corey and I would walk to her house during lunch break for a half-hour Bible study. I can't speak for Corey, but I dreaded Wednesdays. Quite frankly, this believing-in-God thing and the accompanying hoopla was really wearing me thin. Don't get me wrong; if I had believed at the time there was such an all-powerful, all-knowing being, then I would have been all in. For believers, studying the Bible was no doubt very nourishing spiritual wisdom. But quite frankly, as time went on, I simply couldn't come to terms with the possibility of it being true. Even though I might have periodically wondered if He were punishing me for my thieving ways, I had far too many reasons not to believe in God. I wondered, if God loves us so much, why would He allow an innocent baby to die of crib death? Or any number of atrocities that befall good-hearted innocent people? Especially when He supposedly has the power to prevent it. My reasoning behind such conviction lay within a very simple conclusion: If I were crossing the street and saw a little kid about to get hit by a car, and I was in a position to prevent it, I wouldn't hesitate for a second. So why doesn't God prevent innocent people from suffering? That and many other similar reasons made believing in God nearly impossible for me.

Towards the end of grade seven, while downtown at lunchtime, I witnessed something rather interesting. A kid one grade ahead of me got busted for stealing a package of twenty-five-cent jawbreakers. I even saw him put it in his pocket. Unfortunately, the store manager did also. This kid was clearly an amateur thief. And really, you're fourteen and stealing a twenty-five-cent package of jawbreakers? The interesting aspect of this was being on the witnessing end of things. With firsthand knowledge of what it felt like to get caught, I couldn't help but feel a little compassion for the poor kid, especially considering what his parents were likely going to do to him afterward. Coincidently, the next day at school, there was an announcement on the intercom instructing all students to stay clear of that particular store during the lunch hour on school days. In fear of getting robbed blind every day, the manager was likely getting annoyed with having to keep an eye on every kid who entered. The little rebel I was, of course, went to said store just to see if they'd kick me out. They didn't!

Eventually I found my groove, made new friends, and got comfortable with my new surroundings as grade seven came to its conclusion. But even though I had, to my own amazement, somehow managed to keep my nose clean—for an entire school year, no less— old habits do die hard, and a return to my former ways was just around the corner.

CHAPTER

10

Is There Really a God?

There are some perplexing details of my life in this chapter that even I haven't completely come to terms with. For that reason, I never revealed to anyone the specifics. At this point, though, they are quite pertinent to the overall story, and further, they led to my writing another book, one that deals with the matter of my finding an answer to the question posed in the title of this chapter.

On a Friday evening in mid-May, 1982, roughly six weeks before grade seven ended, I was at home watching *The Dukes of Hazard*—an American television series that aired on CBS for seven seasons starting in 1979. Being a fan of the program, especially Daisy Duke, I was sitting on our living room sofa, focused on the TV. After all, what red-blooded thirteen-year-old boy didn't have a crush on Daisy? I suppose that bright orange '69 Dodge Charger, dubbed the "General Lee," was pretty cool too.

While watching Bo and Luke, the show's two main protagonists, jump over a pond in their Charger, with Sheriff Rosco P. Coltrane always in hot pursuit, I heard Mom calling me. Luckily, a moment later, my show went to commercial break. Mom and I were home alone that evening. Dad was out of town delivering a vehicle, and Nikki was having a sleepover at one of our cousins. In answer to Mom's beckoning, I walked down the hall into my parents' bedroom—Mom was sitting on the bed going through mail. With a cold, sober expression on her face and concerned tone, she said to me, "Listen, do you hear that?" Pausing for a couple of seconds to be still, I could hear the distant sound of a baby crying, and it was coming from under my Mom and Dad's bedroom—our garage. Immediately, I headed downstairs to check it out. Upon entering the garage, I turned on the lights and walked around to inspect, but nothing out of sorts was to be seen or heard. After returning upstairs and explaining my discovery to Mom, or rather lack thereof, I advised her that it was probably her brother, Tim, playing a prank on us. "He's likely outside with a tape recording of a crying baby, laughing at us right now," I said.

Not accepting my explanation, Mom was adamant that was not the case. Supposedly, Tim was away for the weekend. By now, I could tell she was somewhat disturbed by the mysterious crying and seemed deeply concerned…scared even. Still, I concluded that if it wasn't Tim, then one of her other brothers was pranking us. Mom's family loved doing things like that. Whatever the case, the mysterious crying had ceased. In an attempt to comfort her, I said, "I'm sure there's a perfect explanation for whatever it was. There always is," and as a consolation, I told her, should the noise return, to summon me again.

Not more than a few minutes later, with a disconcerted semblance on her face, Mom came out from her room to tell me the crying had resumed and it was much louder this time. To indicate her anxiousness, Mom was biting her fingernails. She was definitely scared. Without hesitation, I followed her to the bedroom. The sound was unmistakably more distinct than the previous time. Clearly, the well-defined sound of a crying infant was coming from our garage. Listening for a few seconds, I could discern it had all the hallmarks of a baby who had just woken up from a nap and wanted its mommy. Although the situation itself was nothing short of hair-raising, the whimpering baby sound didn't instill a sense of fear, at least not to me. Be that as it may, all these interruptions during one of my favorite TV programs was beginning to irritate me. Again, I headed for the garage to check it out.

Mom followed me this time, but she refused to enter the garage. She just stood by the door, poking her head in. Sure, Mom, *send me in alone*! On our way to the garage, I grabbed my baseball bat. Just in case. I wasn't afraid at all, simply determined to get to the bottom of this, but a little protection seemed in order. Being just a single-car garage, with only a small table saw, deep freezer, a few yard tools hanging on the walls, and a couple of metal shelf units containing various items, there wasn't much room for anyone or anything to hide. Nonetheless, after thoroughly inspecting every little nook and cranny, the result was same as the first time...nothing! No noise, no baby. Zilch! Finally, I said loudly, "Whoever is here, I want you to leave. You're freaking my mom out, and I'm trying to watch television!" Mom laughed, but not exactly wholeheartedly.

In the spirit of ruling out all possibilities, I decided to have a look outside. Because it was dark out, I grabbed a flashlight and walked around the outside of our house. Again, just like in the garage, there was nothing out of the ordinary to see and not a sound to be heard. In fact, it seemed mysteriously extra quiet. Living out in the prairies, there are usually sounds of crickets or frogs filling the night air. Feeling nothing more than annoyed by this point, I went back upstairs. And since the crying had seemingly stopped, I told Mom—if it started again—to simply ignore it. I reassured her that it could be a sick cat or perhaps the wind—even though I was sure it wasn't either of those things. Quite frankly, at this point, I didn't know what to think. I just wanted to get back to Daisy. Returning to the living room, I finished watching what remained of the show and then went to bed. Because Mom was so freaked out, I decided to sleep upstairs in my sister's room, which was next to my parents' bedroom. Convinced it wasn't anything to worry about, I went right to sleep as if nothing happened. Upon waking up the next morning, I completely forgot about the entire incident.

Later that day—Saturday, about mid-afternoon—I was standing on the approach of our driveway with three of my cousins, Kimberly, Candace, and Kelly. It was a typical Saskatchewan spring afternoon, with nary a cloud in the sky. Grandma was in the house, visiting with Mom. For some odd reason, she'd chosen to park her car on the street and walk to our house. Normally, because of her bad knee, Grandma would park as close to her destination as possible—to avoid unnecessary walking. I had just finished washing Mom's car, and it was still parked on the lawn, leaving our driveway completely vacant. I just wrote off Grandma not parking in the driveway as one of those old folks' idiosyncrasies.

The three of us were standing at the entrance to our driveway, talking about taking a little trip on our bikes down to the creek to do some exploring. I was facing our house. while Kim, Candace, and Kelly were facing me—their backs to our house. While discussing the particulars of our little excursion, I happened to notice something unusual on our closed overhead garage door: a strange dark shadow. Normally, a shadow wouldn't grab my attention, but this one was moving. First thing I did was look around to see if it could be a reflection from something. There was nothing, however, to support that. And the sun was in the wrong position to even be a factor—the door was in the shade. With my mind now completely focused on this strange image, Kim noticed I was distracted from our conversation and asked what was up. Dumbfounded, I replied while pointing toward the garage door, "Do you guys see that?" They all turned around to look. The four of us just stood in silence for roughly five seconds with our eyes fixated on this peculiar image moving around on the garage door. Upon studying the obscure figure visually, I began to make out what it was: a dark shadow image of a man slowly twirling around, as if he'd been tied, standing, to a man-sized slowly spinning wheel. Curious, I began walking towards it. Upon advancing roughly ten steps—now twenty-five feet away—the figure suddenly detached from the garage door, swirled up into a ball, and shot off up into the sky. The four of us just stood in amazement as it quickly ascended vertically against the backdrop of the clear blue sky and faded out into a tiny black dot until it was gone.

The whole incident, from first seeing the unexplained phenomenon to it vanishing in the sky, probably lasted about twenty seconds. Curious if this thing had left anything behind, I bolted towards the house, but there wasn't a trace. Then, with a frenzy of excitement in our voices, all four of us ran into the house and explained to my mom and Grandma what we'd seen. Grandma and Mom turned to one another and began nodding knowingly. Grandma said, "It worked." Apparently, because of what had happened the previous evening—the crying baby incident—Grandma was there with Bible in hand to ask this spirit to leave. Well, IT WORKED all right, and the four of us witnessed IT leaving. But was it really some kind of spirit? I was already questioning God's existence, and the mysterious shadow on the garage door was just as difficult to wrap my mind around. My grandmother's role in all this—her belief that there was a disembodied spirit of some kind present in our house and that she'd banished it with her faith in God and the Bible—added a whole other layer to the mystery.

* * *

Roughly twenty-four hours earlier, Friday afternoon—more or less eight hours before Mom first heard the baby crying—I was engaged in some much-overdue spring cleaning chores around the house. I had the day off from school and was outside taking advantage of the warm weather. While working away, raking the leaves from under our Caragana shrubs, the entire time, my mind was vigorously preoccupied with the question of whether there really was a God. It was not exactly the kind of heady stuff most thirteen-year-olds would be thinking of, but the question weighed on me heavily. I was very much dedicated to trying to resolve the conundrum. Despite my age, I had always been somewhat of a deep thinker. In an attempt to understand how things worked, I'd often pursue answers to questions that were troublesome finding answers to. A perfect example of this would be when I was seven. For the simple reason of finding out how it worked, I removed the back cover from our alarm clock. It was one of those mechanical clocks that you had to wind by hand, with two little bells on top that rang when the alarm sounded. I just needed to know *what made it tick*. I was far too young to understand the mechanics of how it actually worked, but I saw the gears and moving parts that made it function. My curiosity was more about checking to see that it wasn't some magical force inside that couldn't be explained. In the end, my quest was satisfied. I wish everything in life was that simple to figure out. Throughout my childhood and even into early adulthood, I continued taking different devices apart for that very reason—to see how they worked. And with age, I got braver, sometimes dismantling machines that putting back together proved to be more than I bargained for, making otherwise working mechanisms no longer functional. At times, this drove my dear dad nuts. It may be said that sometimes I think too much—I've been told as much. Until my accident, however, the upside to constantly taking things apart rewarded me with being somewhat skilled at using my hands and good at fixing things when they were actually broken.

My parents' penchant for pushing me to attend JW meetings and constantly having to study the Bible, however, had me worried about wasting a considerable amount of time and energy on something that wasn't even real. My parents, and all like-minded folk who congregated at the Kingdom Hall, took that "belief in God" stuff very seriously, and they wanted their son to share their belief, for his own good, especially the directive from our Creator not to steal. Having acquired a certain degree of Bible knowledge by this time provided me with a basic understanding of the main characters, along with their roles and the stories surrounding them. All that did, however, was cause me to place the notion of God into the category of a fairy tale. But just in case there was a God, I did often pray. I knew that if I was ever convinced as to the nature of God, then I'd be one of His most faithful servants. I was desperate and willing to do just about anything to find the answer.

Frustrated with my prolonged inability to arrive at an answer, I stopped raking and began to plead with God for some sort of proof that the spiritual world did in fact exist. If these supposedly invisible spirit beings were indeed out there, I begged Him to show me—I just had to know for sure. Suddenly, I had the distinct sense that God WAS indeed listening. And from a series of thoughts, which without conscious provocation unexpectedly materialized in my mind, I was able to comprehend that my request would be answered—within the next twenty-four hours. Furthermore, in order that I'd know for certain that this was indeed God answering me, He revealed something about my distant future that only He could possibly know: At the age of thirty, I would become paralyzed in an accident and confined to a wheelchair. And during this accident, I would feel no pain whatsoever and not have a single scratch on my entire body. As is the case with anyone just into their teens, thirty seemed like a lifetime away. At this time, my parents were in their thirties, and they seemed old to me. Therefore, the thought of being in a wheelchair that far into the future never concerned me. Besides, if all of this was going to actually happen, then I'd know for sure there really was a God. That would make it all worthwhile. It was a huge price to pay for settling my doubts, sure, but if the Bible is correct, what we are experiencing here in this reality is not the real life anyway. Be that as it may, if I was going to be paralyzed, in jest, I respectfully requested living a good, healthy life before this tragedy occurred—the perfect life. And I even had some foresight in to what that perfect life might entail, after which, from what I understood, God had a request of His own—one that I promised I would do. The details of this request I will reveal later. In order to seal what I believed was a hypothetical covenant with God, being the imaginative thirteen-year-old boy that I was, I reached out my hand as if I were about to shake someone's hand and shook on it. No one was there, of course. It just seemed like something you do after a verbal agreement.

Finishing up with the yard work, I bagged up the leaves and went into the house to retrieve a cold glass of orange juice from the fridge. Mom, who was pouring herself a cup of coffee, enquired as to who I'd been talking with outside. Unbeknownst to me, she had been watching me through the window. I embarrassingly explained that it was nothing, that I was just playing around. Persistent, she insisted that it looked like I was definitely engaged in a conversation with someone. I kind of shrugged and said I was just talking to myself. Mom laughed and said something to the effect that I was a goofy kid. She didn't know the half of it. I don't doubt that if anyone would have overheard me talking out loud the way I did afternoon, they would have concluded

I was losing my marbles. I've often wondered that myself: *Am I crazy?* Wouldn't anyone who experienced what I had that day question his or her own sanity? It would be hard not to. After all, I didn't hear a voice, and there was no physical transaction. This experience consisted of nothing more than a series of distinct thoughts accompanied with a strong inclination that they were not my own. To be completely honest, this entire experience remains quite troublesome to me, which is why I'm hesitant to interpret any of it.

After hearing what my mom and I had heard and witnessing what my cousins and I had seen, most people would assume that I quickly became a firm believer in the Almighty. Strangely, my resolve as to whether or not God existed didn't change. At the time, I never really connected the dots between my appeals to God that afternoon and hearing the eerie sound of a baby crying or seeing the supernatural entity. More accurately, perhaps, I found it highly unlikely that this whole incident had any validity to it whatsoever and further concluded that this had to be a wildly amusing coincidence. Considering the fact that I was skeptical at best regarding the validity of God, I didn't take any of what occurred that afternoon seriously. And I can't state that I genuinely believed God was actually listening to me, let alone give any credence whatsoever to the fact that I would become paralyzed at the age of thirty. Following that prophetic day in 1982, never once did I remember or give any thought to becoming paralyzed. That didn't happen until the evening of February 12, 1999, when, just seconds after my life-altering injury, I felt something similar to déjà vu. It was at that moment that I suddenly had the strong inclination that I'd somehow known that I was going to spend the remainder of this life in a wheelchair. The finer details, though, wouldn't be completely revealed to me until an element of my agreement was fulfilled. I had some ways to go yet, some obstacles to clear out of the way and a few more crises to contend with.

When writing this experience out into words, I can understand how these events may seem a little far-fetched to some of you. Believe it or not, even though it happened to me, I have a hard time accepting that it was real myself. After all, I'm claiming to have had a conversation with God and even to have bargained with Him, a concept that seems rather silly when you think about it. I doubt God would ever bargain with anyone. I'm simply explaining what I felt at the time and how things transpired from my point of view. Though my recollection of that day is quite vivid to me today, my perspective of what happened— in terms of bargaining—may be distorted by what my thirteen-year-old self perceived it to be. Truth is, I don't know for certain what any of it meant, or if it means anything at all. But when I agree to do something, you can bet the farm that I'm going to do it.

* * *

Changing the subject to a lighter note, I would like to relate something humorous that happened later that year. One thing we never lacked in our family was a sense of humor—sometimes it could be deemed dark humor. This particular event, I like to call "The Big White Freezer Story." It concerns an old deep freezer that we kept in the very garage on which door the mysterious shadow appeared. It was a seriously old General Electric freezer, probably dating back to the late 1940s, and it weighed a ton. This thing should have been in a museum. As opposed to modern upright freezers, this one was flat, like a chest, with the door on the top that opened upward. To open the lid, though, you had to pull the big chrome latch on the front of it. The interesting aspect of this old freezer was that if you weren't wearing a good pair of rubber boots when grabbing the chrome latch, it would deliver a toe-curling jolt of electricity through your body. I suspect it wasn't grounded properly. I really disliked that appliance, and it seemed like I was always the poor schmuck getting sent to fetch food out of it for dinner. A pair of rubber boots solved the problem, but I got to bypassing that. After a few body-convulsing electrocutions, I became somewhat skillful at opening and closing the latch fast enough that I barely got much of a shock from it. When I returned to the kitchen, Dad would enquire, "Did it get you?" Then he'd laugh. Ha-ha…real funny Dad!

The events that occurred on this particular winter's day just might have been some well-deserved payback for the amusement Dad derived at my expense. In addition to tons of snow that winter, it was a cold one, with temperatures dipping down to -40° (C) at times. This, in effect, created a few plumbing issues in our home. Bill, being the jack of all trades, master of none that he was, had done all the plumbing himself when he'd renovated our house. Behind our big white freezer, there just so happened to be one section of four-inch plastic sewage pipe that would freeze every once in a while, usually when the temperature dipped down to aforementioned temperatures. This section of pipe also happened to be the main sewage line just before it went outside to our septic tank. Dad and I were in the garage one evening, trying to thaw this all-too-familiarly troublesome sewage pipe.

Our house, being an above ground two-story, didn't have a basement, and both bathrooms were upstairs. Good thing too! As we were on day two of these plumbing issues, everything was backed up, and by this time, both toilets were half full of poop and toilet paper—a disturbing scene that was accompanied by a fiercely repugnant odor. Nevertheless, after assisting Dad—while wearing the appropriate rubberized footwear—with pulling the electrocuting ice box away from the wall, there he was, behind the freezer, standing on a step ladder with a propane bottle torch, heating up the pipe. How can you heat up a plastic pipe with a torch and not melt it? Very carefully. Being that this wasn't his first rodeo, Bill was quite practiced at the endeavor. I was standing on the other side of the freezer, watching. Having done this before, we could always tell when the frozen blockage was freed by the sudden "swoosh" as the waste suddenly rushed through the pipe. However, that wasn't happening this time. Our usual method of thawing the pipe was proving to be unsuccessful. Dad decided to unscrew the clean-out cap located in the ceiling of our garage, just above where he was standing on the ladder. Come to think of it, unscrewing the clean-out cap may have been my idea. My reasoning was that perhaps the frozen section was further up the pipe and he was trying to thaw the wrong area. Dad, concluding that my idea had some validity, proceeded further up the ladder to unscrew the clean-out cover. I honestly had NO IDEA the series of events that would be set in motion by my innocent suggestion. It's pertinent to mention that Dad wasn't wearing rubber boots.

There he was, up on the ladder, jacket completely unzipped and with his shirt hiked up, exposing his rather large, bare belly. After loosening the clean-out, all of a sudden the cap—from intense pressure—went flying across the room, ricocheting off the wall and darn near hitting me in the head—good thing I ducked. Immediately after that, the accumulated waste from both bathtubs and toilets upstairs came gushing out, right on top of Dad's head. In an attempt to flee the waterfall of poop pouring out, he quickly jumped off the ladder. But he didn't account for the electrocuting freezer—now all wet—in his way. And while proceeding to shimmy his way to safety, he mistakenly placed both hands firmly on top of said freezer. That was when the situation turned momentarily strange. Dad suddenly stopped moving and stood motionless as waste continued pouring on top of him. *Why doesn't he move away?* I wondered. Instead, he just stood there with a peculiar look on his face and appeared to be vibrating. There was wet toilet paper stuck in his hair, and a piece was even dangling from his chin—it was vibrating too! I stood in bewilderment, trying to figure out what he was doing. Looking closer, I saw what appeared to be mud dripping down his face as his jowls quivered—it wasn't mud. That was when it hit me: *He's being electrocuted!* Instinctively, I ran over and quickly unplugged the freezer. Dad stepped back, looked me square in the eyes, and as if gasping for air after inhaling too much smoke—almost in a whispered voice—said while exuding a single puff of smoke from his mouth, "Whoa, that was rough."

After everything that transpired, I couldn't help myself and burst out laughing so hard there were tears running down my face. I couldn't wait to run upstairs and tell Mom. Dad hastily scolded me to stay with him and help get the mess cleaned up, further mumbling something about seeking revenge if I breathed a word. Of course, I didn't listen. This was far too entertaining not to share. Needless to say, Mom nearly peed herself laughing as I relayed the incident. This story—which became a family classic—always remained a bone of contention with poor Dad. Okay, this could have had a fatal outcome and would hardly have been humorous. But it turned out like some kind of Charlie Chaplin, Three Stooges, Laurel and Hardy, Abbott and Costello-type comedic episode, where all's well that ends well and you're rolling on the floor, hysterically laughing your socks off.

CHAPTER

11

You'll Break Your Damn Neck

Summer of 1982 was an eventful time for me, with several adventures that stand out considerably in my mind. One of these was our annual four-day JW convention in Saskatoon—the largest city in Saskatchewan. Saskatoon, being centrally located in the province, has served as the cultural and economic hub of the region for a long time, making it one of the more vibrant of prairie towns. It was near the middle of July, and our family was staying with my aunt and uncle and their three boys. Hanging out with my cousins was always a blast and it alleviated some of the boredom from listening to seminars all day long.

During this particular JW convention, I hung out mostly with Doug, who was three years older than I. In the evenings, I stayed with him in his room, sleeping on the floor in a sleeping bag. For some reason, I was more drawn towards Doug than the other two boys, probably because he was older. Later in life, I'd eventually become close friends to Doug's younger brother, Duane, who was one year my senior. For the duration of the four days, Doug kind of took me under his wing. During the daily sessions, to take a break every couple of hours, he and I would go for walks around the convention center. The two of us would engage in some fairly deep conversations. During one of these discussions, the subject of girlfriends came up. Doug was sixteen, but when it came to girls, he was not your typical guy. He had a soft, kind heart, and I could tell he respected women. While on one of these walks, we just happened to notice a couple of cute girls in front of us. It seemed they were doing the same thing we were—taking a break. I believe they noticed us as well and had purposely stopped walking so we would catch up to them. Doug and I stopped to say hi and asked their names. The girl I happened to like was named Deena. After chatting with the girls for a few minutes, we went on our way. While walking, I mentioned to Doug my interest in Deena, and he suggested asking for her phone number. However, I wasn't convinced there was enough courage in me to do THAT just yet. I decided to bide my time; as this was only the first of the four days, I felt I didn't need to rush into anything. The next day, we would meet up with the girls again, enabling me to learn a little more about Deena. Doug reassured me that he could tell she liked me as well and further encouraged me to ask for her number. Not only did she give me her digits, she wrote down her mailing address as well. Doug patted me on the back and said, "See how easy that was."

On the last evening of our stay in Saskatoon, Doug and I were hanging out in his room, listening to music. He introduced me to a British rock band, Rainbow, in particular, the album *Down to Earth*, released in 1979. *Down to Earth* was the fourth studio album by the band, whose full name had originally been Ritchie Blackmore's Rainbow. Blackmore was a founding member of the seminal British band Deep Purple. I've been a fan of Rainbow's *Down to Earth* album ever since, and I've found a few other tunes the band recorded to be enjoyable as well, further discovering over the years that music would often have a way of extracting a wide variety of emotions from me. One of the songs that caught my ear from the *Down to Earth* album was "Since

You've Been Gone," a lyrical satire about a guy who, because he loves her so much, really misses his girlfriend. As the tune played, I thought about the context of the song and what that kind of love might feel like. I even got a little teary. At the age of thirteen, I obviously had no concept of romantic love. How could I? My active imagination was simply fantasizing about what love might be like with Deena, or someone like her, which, in turn, persuaded some emotion out of me. That would be the first time a girl would have that effect on me. Doug noticed, but he was cool and didn't say anything.

When I returned to Tadmore after our trip to Saskatoon, the first thing on my agenda was drafting a letter to Deena. After writing a few different versions, I finally picked one. It wasn't too mushy or over the top. I mean, really, we'd just met. Deena wrote me back, and we talked on the phone a few times, but that was about all that ever materialized. Nevertheless, our brief interlude remains in my memory as a nice little romantic yet innocent experience that we both participated in, a pleasant memory that taught me something about myself: I had a sensitive side. Who knew?

* * *

That same summer, with a little tent trailer in tow, Dad and I drove out to his parents in British Columbia again. Bill had bought the little camping trailer a year earlier in an effort to cut the cost of paying for hotels. It was old and ratty, but I'd painted it ruby red, my favorite color. After that, the little trailer didn't look half bad. Opposed to the usual get-there-as-fast-as-we-can mentality, for this trip, Dad took the time to stop at various tourist attractions along the way. We spent our nightly downtime in various campgrounds along the way as we headed to the West Coast. One place in particular had a lake where tourists could rent two-person pedal boats. Before it got dark that evening,

Dad and I rented one of these boats and went for a tour of the lake. Once we were on the calm, clear waters of the lake, he wanted to fish, but our fishing rods were packed away in the car. That man loved fishing, no two ways about it. Nevertheless, as we were out pedaling around on the lake, Dad tactfully instigated a conversation with me about girls. He had a couple of beers in him by now and was feeling a little more relaxed than usual. He even let me have a beer—my very first! As the conversation progressed, he brought up the subject of sex. Awkward! Considering the fact that I was certainly feeling the effects of that beer, this was not a good time for me to be having a discussion about sex with my father. As I would later learn, I tend to be a little too honest when there's alcohol coursing through my veins. In turn, I said something to the effect that I probably knew more about sex than he did. Well, dear old Dad didn't take very kindly to that smart-alec remark. Smacking me across the head, he said, "Quit being a smart-ass, mister!" Bill always called me mister when he was angry with me—I got called that a lot! The gist of his advice that afternoon boiled down to the fact that I was far too young and shouldn't even be thinking about girls or sex yet. *Yeah, Dad. Tell that to my hormones*, I thought to myself. Not wanting to encourage our little "birds and the bees" conversation any further, however, I kept my mouth shut. After my innocent little escapade with Deena, I believe this was Dad's way of nipping that in the bud. He was right, though. I WAS far too young.

During our vacation, Grandpa took Dad and me up into the interior of British Columbia, where we fished for Rainbow Trout. After each of us caught our limit, we returned to my grandparents' place, where Grandpa smoked the fish in his homemade, redneck-style smokehouse. Let me tell you, those trout tasted amazing. It was like eating candy. Fishing with Grandpa was something we often did when Dad and I were on vacation in British Columbia. Some years later,

Bill's father would even take us salmon fishing on the Pacific Ocean. That was an awesome experience. One thing about Grandpa, he knew everything there was to know about where to fish, how to catch fish, how to clean fish, and how to cook fish. Okay, so that's four things— he knew a lot about fish. I, in turn, gained a considerable amount of knowledge about fishing while collecting some great memories in the process.

There is only one bad memory from that particular trip in 1982. Well, two if you count the smack on the head. But I deserved that. This unfortunate incident occurred one afternoon when I went swimming with one of Dad's sister's, Marna, and her daughter, Tracy. We went to a local pool somewhere near Grandma and Grandpa's. Dad was off buying Mom something from an aunt of his who owned a local clothing store in Langley. He wouldn't show it to me afterward. I deduced it must have been lingerie. Way to go, Dad! Meanwhile, at the pool, because Tracey was much younger than I, she and her mom hung out in the kiddie's area while I swam around in the main pool. At best, my swimming ability was mediocre. I certainly was no aquatic connoisseur. Nevertheless, after becoming bored with gracelessly splashing around, I decided to jump off the high dive board—something I'd never done before. The fearless little experimentalist in me proceeded to climb onto the diving board and bounce up as high as I possibly could. Then I plunged head first into the water. Piercing through the water, my hands touched the bottom of the pool, after which, to shoot myself toward the surface, I stood on the bottom and sprung my legs upward. Upon reaching the surface, however, it felt as if a vacuum or current was pulling my body downward. This prevented me from catching my breath and being able to swim. Floating back to the bottom, I again attempted to springboard myself back toward the surface. Still, a force kept sucking me back down. Frustrated, with every ounce of strength in me, I kicked and paddled, but to no avail. Not able to get any air, I thought for sure I was going to drown. Just when I was about to give up, someone finally jumped in, pulled me to safety, and saved my life. If I'd have gone under one more time, there's no doubt they would have been dragging my lifeless body out of the pool and giving me mouth to mouth.

After pulling me to safety, the guy asked if I was all right and suggested I keep to the shallow end. While lying by the edge of the pool, catching my breath, I looked across the pool and saw the lifeguard sitting on his high chair, reading a book. I was indignant and beyond belief that this person had totally neglected the duty he was entrusted with. After a brief gaze around the pool, I could tell that in addition to the so-called lifeguard, no one had even noticed me damn near drown. Thank God one person did. If not for him, my life could have been cut short right then and there. At the time, however, being embarrassed by the whole incident, I was glad no one noticed and kept that little perilous adventure to myself. Despite almost dying in a watery grave, I'd have to say this was my favorite trip out to the coast with Dad.

* * *

Summer of 1982 was coming to an end, with grade eight about to begin. And with it came an eye-opening experience—literally! Towards the end of grade seven, I began noticing something was not quite up to par with my eyesight. Sitting in the front row of class, I could barely read the notes written on the chalkboard. This was before whiteboards and the use of felt-tipped markers. Originally, the boards were black, later green, and teachers wrote notes on the boards with chalk. In frustration, I wondered, *How on earth can the kids sitting at the back read the blackboard if I'm having a hard time from the front?* I decided to ask one of the guys who sat at the back. He said reading the board was no problem. Okay, I had an eyesight problem.

After a visit to the optometrist, sure enough, I needed glasses. However, with the mindset that glasses were for nerds—something of which I could never be accused—I certainly wasn't happy about wearing spectacles. Nevertheless, after scouring through an assortment of frames, I picked out a pretty cool pair that looked more like sunglasses than they did eyeglasses. I'll never forget the day, about a week later, when I picked up my new frames from the optician's office in Canora and put them on for the first time. What an eye-opening experience that was. Walking around town, looking at everything with my glasses on, was nothing short of amazing. It was as if I was seeing for the very first time. I could see each individual leaf on trees instead of a green blur like before. I could read signs from a distance and see people's faces clearly from afar; the whole experience was quite exhilarating. It's interesting, really, without even noticing, how deteriorated something in our lives can become when it happens gradually, like my vision. I didn't realize how severely reduced my eyesight had become until I couldn't read anything that wasn't right in front of my face. Unless a person takes the time to evaluate themselves on a regular basis and has the willingness to make changes, life seems to get in the way and distract us from recognizing how bad a situation has become. And it's not until one's perception is fully restored that we realize how bad it really was.

As awesome as it was to see clearly, without a doubt, there was an adjustment period that I was never able to conquer, especially with my affinity toward sports. About a year later, I finally had enough of the eye glasses and switched to soft contact lenses. Wearing contacts was certainly more my style.

* * *

Later that fall, another unfortunate incident occurred that nearly put me six feet under. This happened while Dad and I were helping one of our congregation elders, Allen, on his farm with harvest. Finishing up for the day, we were out in the middle of his field, about to head back to the house for dinner. Dad was driving the combine. Allen hopped in his truck, and I climbed into the open-cab John Deere tractor. We headed for Allen's barn, which was about half a mile away, next to his house. Putting the old tractor into high gear, I cranked the hand throttle full on and began cruising along at a pretty good pace. Where the field ended, a relatively narrow trail turned toward Allen's yard and passed through roughly 200 feet of dense woodland. While cruising along, about to turn left on to this pathway, all of a sudden, the tractor veered off course, and I found myself bouncing two feet off the metal seat as the tractor carved a path through the densely populated bush. While hanging on for dear life, branches kept knocking me backward, making it impossible to reach the throttle or foot pedals. My main concern now was that I didn't fall off and run over myself. Just when I thought all hope was lost, Allen ran up out of nowhere, reached in, and somehow managed to turn the ignition switch off, successfully killing the engine. Once again, I was saved by the bell. I have no idea how he pulled off that maneuver—the rear wheels of the tractor were up to his shoulders—but I'm sure glad he did. Otherwise, I might have been a grease stain on the ground. Needless to say, Allen never trusted me to drive his John Deere again.

If that wasn't enough, once again, another hair-raising incident happened roughly three months after the tractor caper, when Dad decided to buy a snowmobile. He brought it home from work one day, totally out of the blue. And later that evening, he and I went for a spin. Dad was driving, and I was on the back. My cousin Kimberly happened to be walking past our house just as we were leaving, and she asked if she could hop on the back too. "Sure, why not," Dad replied. After climbing on the back with me, we headed out onto the field behind town. Being sandwiched between Kimberly and my dad, I couldn't see much of anything, but I could kind of tell where we were. I knew my way around the area probably better than anyone. Snow was falling quite heavily, and visibility was extremely poor, especially in the dark. And none of us were wearing goggles or even helmets for that matter. Not good!

Cruising along at about forty miles per hour, I began to get concerned. If my sense of direction was correct, we were approaching a section—square on—where the snow plow had created six-foot snowbanks on each side of the roadway. Unexpectedly, my "Spidey" senses began to tingle, and my mind was consumed with one thought: *Dad had better start slowing down. Otherwise, this may not end well for us.* Just as I was about to warn him, suddenly everything went still and quiet. And for the next few seconds, it was as if we were suspended motionless in space. It felt like something straight out of *The Twilight Zone.* Then, in what I perceived as slow motion, my body became extremely heavy from the impact of the snowmobile being pulled to the ground by gravity, and it knocked the wind out of both my cousin and me. After squirming around on the snow in an effort to regain the ability to breathe, we finally realized what had just happened. Dad had unknowingly hit the six-foot high ramp-like snowbank and jumped clear over the entire road. Including the giant snow bank on the other side as well. Roughly fifty feet! Good thing the snowmobile stayed level and we landed flat, or that could have been much worse, if not fatal. No one was hurt, thank God, but Dad's chest broke the handlebars completely off the snowmobile. The throttle and brake still worked, but with no way to steer the snowmobile—a mile from town in -25°C

155

weather—we were in a bit of a conundrum. Unfortunately, none of us were dressed for a long cold walk in the dark either.

Frustrated by the situation, I questioned Dad as to what he'd been thinking and why he hadn't slowed down. Surely, he'd known there was a road there. He commented that because of the snow falling, it had been hard to see. Biting my tongue, I so badly wanted to say, *If you can't see where you're going, then maybe you should slow down.* Getting home would be an interesting little adventure. For me, that is. We figured out that if I sat on the hood of the snowmobile and stretched my legs out towards the ski tips, I could steer the sled with my feet while Dad worked the throttle. At a snail's pace, the three of us made it all the way home without incident. We definitely lucked out that day and were fortunate to be in one piece, never mind alive. After our little near-death experience, Dad parked the snowmobile behind the house and never looked at it for the rest of the winter. He must have scared himself good! Every time Bill retold that story I always heard the words: *I saw my life flash before my eyes.* His comment, probably due more to the way he said it, made me chuckle every time.

* * *

One day, shortly after Christmas, during the holiday season break, I went outside in the morning to chop some wood for our furnace. I stepped out the door, and lo and behold, there was a brand-new Honda three-wheeler parked in our yard. We had gotten a huge dump of snow the night before; therefore, I could see fresh tracks from someone riding it earlier that morning. I couldn't wait to get on this thing, and I immediately phoned Dad at work to ask. Remarkably, I was free to go ahead and ride it, but was told to "take it easy"—those were his words. This was totally unlike Bill, causing me to wonder, *Okay, who is this man, and what has he done with my dad?* Apparently, Dad had bought this three-wheeler specifically for me, yet he'd never said a word about it. It was an outright surprise and completely out of character for him to do something like that. When it came to operating recreational vehicles, Dad was always very protective. For instance, the previous summer, he'd come into possession of a little dirt bike after making a side deal with a customer. Dad had sold a vehicle at work and had accepted an 80cc two-stroke motorcycle as a trade-in, which he planned to immediately sell and recoup his investment, something he did about six weeks later. I don't remember the make of motorcycle it was, but that dirt bike was the perfect size for me. Do you think he would ever let me ride it? Hardly! When I'd ask him, he would reply, "No, you'll break your damn neck!" Surely one can see the irony in that. Dad made it abundantly clear that his intention was never to buy the bike for me; he was trying to sell it as soon as possible. After constant begging and hounding, I was eventually allowed to ride it a few times, though. Strange thing about that: when I did get to ride it, there was no helmet or any protective gear whatsoever for me to wear. Same scenario with the three-wheeler. The entire time we owned that recreational vehicle, I never once wore a helmet—I didn't even own one. Evidently, Dad's regard for my personal safety was somewhat contradictory. Once I started riding and racing motorcycles, I wouldn't even consider going ten feet without a helmet on my head.

Nevertheless, that Honda three-wheeler was certainly a nice addition to the repertoire of activities I had to keep myself entertained while living in a small town. A multitude of fun times and memorable experiences were savored with that trike for sure. And as unbelievable as it might seem—considering my recent streak of unfortunate events— never once did I crash or even get hurt while riding it. Perhaps one could say I was discriminately conscious of my safety.

* * *

After we moved into the new house that Dad had conjured up—our trailer park palace—he had a wood burning furnace installed. Where we lived, there were no natural gas hook-ups yet, and liquid fuel was our only other option, which was very expensive to burn. But having a wood furnace meant we had to have a hefty supply of firewood on hand, which wasn't a big deal. For the cost of a few tanks of gasoline and a logging permit, we could get all the wood we needed. Dad and I would take a truck, pulling a trailer, and head up into northern Saskatchewan, where there was crown land. He'd purchase a permit that enabled us to basically log out as much firewood as we could haul. We would endure this task about two to three times each winter. Because it took all day, we'd leave extra early in the morning— like, 6:00 AM early—and get home quite late in the evening. Those wood-hauling days were hard work, but since I loved nature and being out in the wild, it was another grand adventure. These trips were a lot of fun, and Dad always bought an awesome variety of junk food to snack on. Bill sure loved his junk food. We'd even build a little fire and cook homemade garlic sausage to eat with fresh-baked buns. By the age of thirteen, I was felling trees with a chainsaw and hauling ten-foot logs over my shoulders just like any full-grown man. Quite honestly, I enjoyed those trips out to the bush.

Sometimes, however, I pushed myself too hard. At eleven years of age, as a result of over exertion, I had to undergo surgery because of a mild hernia. Once I turned thirteen, however, there was another reason I looked forward to these wood-hauling trips. Because he wasn't in very good shape physically, often times, I would get to drive partway home while Bill rested. I loved being the chauffeur and therefore welcomed the opportunity. Of course, I was underage and shouldn't have been driving. But this WAS Saskatchewan: not a lot of busy freeways to negotiate, and we were out in the sticks. Besides, farm kids were expected to drive tractors and pickup trucks on the prairies. It wasn't just a rite of passage; often, it was a necessity. Okay, I wasn't technically a farm kid! But prairie mentality, including that of the police, tended not to get too worked up over things like underage drivers. Unless you got into an accident or drove erratically or carelessly, you kind of slipped under the radar.

During the week, it was my job to chop and haul wood into the house every day after school, and to keep the wood burning in the furnace. Dad and I would take turns each night stoking the fire. He would get up one night, and I'd do it the next, and so on. Chopping wood was something I enjoyed, though. There was something peaceful about it—not to mention the fact that it made me strong as an ox. The aroma of freshly chopped wood and the crisp sound of an ax cleaving through it is a communion with nature as old as time itself. I didn't know it yet, but I would always be drawn towards working with wood.

Winter of grade eight came with a vengeance that year. We had so much snow that it just kept accumulating, with nary a melt in between. It felt like all I was doing was shoveling snow. Every day after school, it was the same old routine: The grater would go by, plug up our fifty-foot-long driveway, and I'd shovel it clean. If I didn't, Dad would come home from work, plough through the snow, and drive over it, thus packing it down and making it harder to shovel. Therefore, it was easier if I did it right away. Dad never shoveled the driveway, not even once! Not that I felt that he should have; shoveling the driveway was something I perceived as my responsibility, and I took pride in how I did it. The perfectionist in me made sure the snow banks on each side were symmetrical. Same went for the lawn and yardwork during summer. I was generally very meticulous with everything. Yes, I might have had some obsessive-compulsive disorder…but in a good way.

I was definitely earning that $35 a week I had negotiated with Mom. My parents were surely getting their money's worth. By the time I was done with all my chores, chopping wood, hauling wood, shoveling snow, and looking after Nikki, it would sometimes be eight o'clock in the evening. I never revealed to any of my friends what my home life was REALLY like, and not because I felt ashamed or embarrassed by it all. Truth is, I simply didn't want anyone to feel sorry for me or assume I was deprived or unhappy, especially when that certainly was not the case. I was a happy kid, always upbeat and positive. Having responsibilities and working hard was something I enjoyed, and the freedom that came with it was the best part. Never once did I believe my life was tough by any means, and I still don't think that way even today. After all, being a hard worker and maintaining responsibilities are all admirable qualities. Besides, the hard work was good for me. Looking back, it taught me some valuable life lessons about work ethics and likely contributed to my successes later in life.

Cue music: "Small Town" by John Mellencamp

https://www.youtube.com/watch?v=0CVLVaBECuc

CHAPTER

12

Spoiled Rich Kid

While in grade eight, I somehow started getting a reputation for being a spoiled rich kid. Me, a spoiled rich kid? I wish! If only they knew. Sure, I always had money to spend, and that was all my friends ever saw: That I always had money in my pockets. How I came by it was a product of their imagination and assumption. Adding fuel to the "rich kid" reputation, though, I would lie and say it was my allowance. Truth is, I NEVER got an allowance. My parents giving me money for nothing? That's laughable. If Mom or Dad ever handed me money I hadn't earned, it was for things like school supplies or clothing. I even paid half of the cost of the glasses I needed. At this point in my life, any money I had I worked for, and not just around the house. I worked on our neighbor's farm when he needed some extra help, and in the fall of '82, I even skirted my Uncle Tim's trailer before the snow fell. He didn't have a clue how to do it. After borrowing some of Dad's power tools, over the course of a weekend, I did it for him, and he paid me $50 to do the job. Not quite sure how I knew at thirteen years of age how to accomplish skirting a single-wide trailer in plywood, but somehow I did. Maybe it was just intuition.

The "spoiled rich kid" reputation certainly didn't come without its consequences. A couple of older kids, two grades my senior, really didn't like me much. Perhaps because of my erroneous reputation, they thought their lives were so much harder than mine…that I never worked a day in my life. Personally, not being fond of spoiled rich kids myself, I understood their dislike. Without knowing much about them or what their home lives consisted of, I can't say for sure, but it's too bad they had the wrong impression of me. Otherwise, I doubt they would've disliked me as much.

As a result of my hardworking lifestyle, I could hold my own pretty well, physically speaking. I certainly wasn't a wimpy kid. Therefore, I never faced much opposition from most of my own classmates. Confrontations would come up occasionally, as they are bound to at that age, but I wasn't afraid of anyone. Once kids get the sense you're not afraid of them, they quickly leave you alone. I wasn't known for being a fighter and often avoided it, but when the opportunity presented itself, I wouldn't back down neither. My Uncle Tim—the youngest of my mom's brothers—was exceedingly proficient in the art of hand-to-hand conflicts. Tim was only five foot seven and 150 lbs, yet anyone who knew him wouldn't dare mess with the guy. Not surprisingly, Tim loved to fight. Tim was only ten years older than I, and it would be safe to say he took a liking to me. Whenever he was in the mood, from the time I was seven years old, Tim thought it was wise to teach me strategic fight moves—to "toughen me up" as he so often put it. This included the psychological discipline necessary for street fighting as well. Over time, I definitely picked up a few useful tips and probably had far more knowledge than I ever needed in how to kick someone's butt.

One particular incident that happened early in grade eight comes to mind, when I allowed my physical side to supersede my self-restraint.

This would be one of two times throughout my life in which I would be the instigator. However, this instance involved Rene. She wasn't my girl, but because I had a serious crush on her, I didn't take kindly to anyone trying to make me look like a dolt in front of her. One of the other guys, Kevin, was chatting her up during class one day, which in itself was fine. I'm not a jealous person. But Kevin was somewhat of a "point and make fun" type of kid and on this particular day, he unwisely chose me as his victim. Kevin conjured up a little fairy tale to Rene that I was picking my nose in class, and then he even started laughing about it. Now, if he would have said that to ANYONE else, I wouldn't have cared less, but this was Rene. Understandably, I was a little more than upset. Right after class, I made sure to be one of the first kids out the door and quickly headed downstairs to wait for the little storyteller by our lockers. Kevin had somewhat of a cocky attitude that led me to believe he thought he was better than everyone. Although I certainly didn't like his attitude, this wasn't about that. Kevin was about to get a lesson in schoolyard justice.

As Kevin walked towards me, I approached him and said, "What do you think you're doing, making up stories about me to Rene?" Looking at me with complete bewilderment, he replied, "What are you talking about?" After positioning myself so that I was face to face with him, I referred to the nose picking story. That was when Kevin finally realized what it was about, and with a smirk on his face, he laughingly tried to brush it off. At this point, my uncle's tutorials on fighting were resonating vividly in my head, and I began strategizing every possible scenario while planning a tactical response for each. After carefully constructing a blueprint in my mind of what I was going to do, I offered Kevin the opportunity to make this right. I told him to apologize to me and then explain to Rene how he'd made the story up. Kevin, as I suspected, again just laughed, saying he had nothing to apologize for, that it was all just for laughs. Maybe it was to him, but it was at my expense, and it was time for some restitution. I'm quite certain Kevin wasn't expecting what happened next. I threw my books on the floor and punched him in the face as hard as I could. Then I hit him one more time before a teacher jumped in, who later described us as two roosters in a henhouse. The rooster comment was priceless and wasn't wrong either. This teacher instinctively knew eighth-grade boys, who have an excess of hormones raging through their bodies, easily get triggered into physical posturing. And what was it often about? A girl, no less!

That was my first real fight, and I can recall feeling very powerful for a brief moment afterward. At the same time, though, I also felt sorry for Kevin. Surprisingly, I didn't much like myself for what I'd done. Even though in my mind he deserved it, I actually felt guilty for hitting and possibly hurting him. He would later approach me to apologize; I did as well for my behavior. Strangely, after that incident, Kevin and I would become buddies and, later on, even close friends. I know we are supposed to turn the other cheek, and normally, I would have. As a rule, I'd have taken the high road and tried to avoid confrontation. This particular instance was different, though, so there wasn't much chance of that happening—turning the other cheek, that is.

On Saturdays, going to work with Bill at Formo's became a regular occurrence. Dad would put me to work cleaning the snow off cars, filling envelopes with thank you cards for past customers, and switching license plates between cars when he'd make a sale. Whenever I could, I'd take the keys to a nice new car and sit inside while flipping through the radio stations until finding a song I liked. There's nothing like the smell inside a brand new car. One of my favorite songs back then was "Tainted Love" by Soft Cell, an English synthpop band that came to prominence in the early 1980s. "Tainted Love" was their claim to fame, for sure, at least in North America. What made that song even more special, for me anyway, was the fact that Rene danced to it on figure skates at that year's ice show in Sturgis. Rene took figure skating, and part of that entailed participating in the annual ice show. Normally, I wouldn't have been at a figure skating event, but Nikki took figure skating that year and participated in the show as well. Rene and her partner danced on skates to "Tainted Love," and I had to admit she was awesome. Perhaps I was a tad bit biased, but even still, she was good. For me, that song has always had a pleasant boyhood memory attached to it. I think it's fascinating how our memories can attach themselves to certain things or in this case a song.

Going to work with Dad was definitely a learning experience for me when it came to the art of sales. I could easily attest to why he did so well and why people loved him. It wasn't hard to tell that some of his customers actually enjoyed buying a car from him. Many of Dad's loyal repeat customers would drive from distant parts of Alberta, Manitoba, and beyond to specifically buy from him and only him. Dad certainly had mastered the art of making people feel extra special, and his demeanor always portrayed humility. It almost seemed that some went so far as to feel bad if they didn't or couldn't afford to buy from him. He had that much of an effect on people. One of the cleverest lines in his repertoire was: "I special ordered this vehicle myself. There's nothing else like it on the lot." Because it catered to the idea of owning something unique, that particular line was brilliant. It wasn't a lie either. Dad was always very honest. Being the lead salesman, he had the privilege of choosing which vehicles they ordered and the options they came with.

My stepdad certainly had a knack for selling vehicles, especially Fords. I believe it was his natural inclination to be a people pleaser; he loved to put a smile on anyone's face. Because hard physical labor was never among his collection of favorite things to do, selling cars and trucks satisfied his niche perfectly. I've always been of the belief that every single one of us is exceptionally good at something, and coincidently, that something is usually what we love to do most. Throughout my years growing up and witnessing Bill work in different careers, selling vehicles was, without a doubt, when he was at his happiest.

The only aspect of going to work with Bill on Saturdays I didn't enjoy was after the work day was finished. Understandably, Saturdays were Dad's most successful days of the week, and he would often sell up to five or six vehicles during the single day. As expected, when someone buys a brand-new vehicle, they want to celebrate with a few drinks at the local bar. And being that Dad was such a likeable guy, he'd frequently get invited to join in after work. Dad referred so much business to one of the local establishments that he even had his own private section for entertaining clients. This particular saloon/eatery had a lounge on one side and a restaurant on the other. Obviously, I wasn't allowed in the lounge; therefore, I had to either wait in the car or sit in the restaurant by myself. At least they had arcade games to play. Consequently, after times like this, Dad was always in an exceptionally jolly mood for the drive home.

* * *

I really started getting into music at the age of fourteen, as opposed to just the one song here and there that I enjoyed. I always loved music, but spring break of 1983 was the proverbial rooster crow that woke my mind to expanding my lyrical horizons. Dad loved country music—pretty much exclusively. Waylon Jennings and John Anderson were among his more revered artists. His favorite song back then was "Tight Fittin' Jeans" by Conway Twitty. Every time it would play on the radio, he'd start singing away, and I mean really bellowing it out.

Being a fan of country music myself these days, I can see why he loved that song so much. It's a melodic combination of sexy, innocence, and humility all mixed together in a gentlemanlike style. Unlike so much of the raunchy sex-debasing lyrics we hear today. Mom leaned more toward artists such as Dolly Parton and Loretta Lynn. She liked to sing along to the radio as well. Maybe that's where I get that from—singing along to music, that is—though I'm notorious for getting the words wrong. As a fourteen-year-old, however, I wasn't much into country, but I didn't dislike it either. Because both my parents were hardcore country music lovers, I heard more than my fair share of it.

As a young teenager, my preferred music gravitated towards the rock genre. Some of my favorite songs from around that time were "It's Still Rock 'n Roll to Me" by Billy Joel, "Another One Bites the Dust" by Queen, and "I Love Rock 'n Roll" by Joan Jett and the Blackhearts. Billy Joel's *Glass Houses* album would be my very first vinyl record. And I actually bought and paid for it too. I didn't steal it! In reminiscence of that time, I can recall listening to Queen's "Another One Bites the Dust" through a high-quality sound system—something I hadn't yet acquired. Being infatuated with the heavy bass line detonating through the speakers, it gave me goose bumps every time. Correspondingly, the song is credited as Queen's best-selling single of all time. Though he'd never admit it, I think even Dad secretly liked that song. It was the one rock tune that I'd catch him lip syncing the words to.

By this time in history, home video game systems were the hot new craze. I'd hear all about them at school. There was Atari, ColecoVision, and Intellivision; they were the three main authorities of the video game industry in the early eighties. These systems were very rudimentary compared to today's gaming technology, but they were, after all, the pioneers of Xbox, PlayStation, and Nintendo game consoles. Instead of games like *Call of Duty* or *Grand Theft Auto* we had *Pac-Man, Donkey Kong,* and *Space Invaders,* to name a few. The Atari 2600 was the most popular video game console of that era, and except for me, every kid who was anybody had one. I could have easily saved up and bought one for myself. However, given my affinity for being outdoors, sitting in front of a TV screen playing video games for hours wasn't my idea of a good time. I'd have rather been outside, building a fort in the snow or, during the summer, riding my bike. Being cooped up in the house was something I wasn't fond of, which is kind of ironic compared to my life these days—especially during winter months.

On the subject of video games, I find it interesting how censorship toward what we are exposed to has changed exponentially since I was a kid. Games such as *Call of Duty* or *Grand Theft Auto*— because of their violent content—would never have made it onto store shelves. Yet somewhere over the past twenty years, we went from Super Mario, eating power pills, running on clouds, and rescuing the princess to gathering weapons, taking hostages, stealing cars, and killing human beings, all in high-definition, lifelike graphics, no less. I'm no psychologist, but whether you're an adult or a kid playing these games, that form of entertainment can't be good for the future of our race. Is it really that surprising when a teenager walks into a school and starts shooting innocent people? These video games are desensitizing them to the very violence against which we admonish.

* * *

Spring break of 1983 also marked the second time I went to visit my biological father, Roy. On this occasion, however, I was feeling somewhat apprehensive. When Mom enrolled me in grade one, after we moved to Tadmore, she did so under my stepdad's name, Perepelkin—but that wasn't my legal name. This whole time up to grade eight, I'd been using my stepdad's name. Well, that created a problem for taking driver's education or applying for a social insurance number. But everyone knew me as Perepelkin. I wasn't about to start going by a different name; that just didn't feel right. For this reason—after a discussion between Mom, Bill, and myself—we decided to legally change my name to Perepelkin. I thought about it a lot, actually. It was a big decision, after all. I concluded that because I was raised by a Perepelkin, I therefore should become a Perepelkin. Every parent raises their children a certain way. A person's character is a reflection of their teacher, just as a university is demonstrative of the quality of education a student receives. Therefore, I reasoned that changing my name to Perepelkin was a more complete representation of my upbringing. Because Bill was raising me, it made sense to take his name. After all, I did consider myself Bill's son, not Roy's. It wasn't that I resented Roy or anything like that, nor was this a form of punishing him. This decision had nothing to do with my biological father. The one hiccup, however, was that Roy would have to sign off on this. While there for my visit, I had the unpleasant task of explaining my decision to change my name. Roy didn't seem exactly thrilled about the whole idea, but surprisingly, he didn't hesitate in signing the papers. My name officially became Monte Joe Perepelkin.

My final visit as a teenager with Roy seemed really boring to me, though this was probably because of my age. And really, what is there to do in Hudson Bay, Saskatchewan? I do remember being excited about receiving the new self-titled Aldo Nova album—music always did the trick. Yeah, I was a typical selfish teenager. Buy me something, and I was happy—for about ten or fifteen minutes. I nearly wore one of the album's tracks, "Fantasy," out, playing it on my crappy little blue record player. That is the problem with vinyl: the quality degrades with each play, especially, and much more quickly, on an inferior turntable. But you just can't beat the quintessential sound it delivers to your ears—when played on a great sound system, that is. Surprisingly, even with the advancement of today's technology, vinyl still rules! At least, it does for those of us who know the difference…young or old.

This proved to be a pivotal time in my life, because Mom and Dad had decided to take in another foster child just before spring break of 1983 ended. This time, our soon-to-be-new-houseguest was a boy one year older than I. All I knew about him was that his name was Dennis and that he was also in grade eight. He was scheduled to arrive the same day I returned home from visiting my biological father. It was a Friday afternoon when Roy and his girlfriend dropped me off at home. No one was around, so the first thing I did was rip open the new Aldo Nova album and listen to it on my parents' home stereo system. Before even getting to the end of the first track, however, I looked out the window and saw Mom pull up into the driveway. I could see that Dennis was with her. Turning off the music, I headed downstairs to greet him.

Fully cognizant this would prove to be a defining moment in our relationship, I treaded lightly. This guy could either be a blessing or a curse to my life. If he was aggressive and controlling, I knew that wouldn't sit well with me. Yet if he was more laid back, not taking his position in our family too seriously or as a competition, then this could be good for everyone. It would be accurate to assume that I was both excited and cautious at the same time. Being an optimist, though, I entered the situation with that same prejudice. We met face to face by Mom's car. He was definitely taller than I by at least three inches. But that was no big deal. Dennis had a thin build with dark hair, and the way it was cut, in my opinion, resembled that of a monkey. After concluding our introductions, he seemed nice enough, very polite and even respectful towards me, as if he were saying, *I get it. This is your house, and I'm not here to ruffle any feathers.* Being easygoing myself, I wasn't interested in being in control and could tell he wasn't either. As a result, Dennis and I hit it off right away.

After escorting Dennis to his new bedroom, across from mine, I showed him my collection of vinyl albums, which wasn't much. I had Trooper, Rainbow, Billy Joel, Christopher Cross, and now Aldo Nova—given to me by Roy. That was the extent of my musical library. Dennis had a few albums himself, including REO Speedwagon. For the remainder of that weekend, the two of us hung out listening to music. I taught him how to ride our three-wheeler, and he helped me out with chores. Dennis wasn't a lazy kid by any means; he actually kept up with me, and that was surprising. He also taught me what he knew on the subject of the opposite sex, which wasn't much more than I already knew. Nevertheless, with him being a year older, I listened to what he had to say.

CHAPTER

13

Dennis the Menace

Throughout my getting to know Dennis, he confided in me a lot about his life, which led me to feel sorry for him. I don't remember the details of his family story or why he was in foster care, but I do remember likening Dennis's life to that of a Cinderella story. It seemed the poor guy was always treated as less, when really, he shouldn't have been. No one ever should. Hearing about Dennis's life made me realize how good mine was. It wasn't that I thought otherwise, but it gave me reason to feel increasingly thankful for the life I did have. In light of Dennis revealing the details of his life, I now understood where his meek and humble demeanor came from. I think the one thing that really drew me to him was how he treated my sister, Nikki. Dennis looked out for her and even went so far as to spend time playing and joking around with her—likely because he had younger sisters of his own. I could tell he was good with kids, and that allowed me to trust him. Within a short time, Dennis and I became like brothers. The following Monday—after spring break—we went to school together, and I introduced him to everyone. Dennis was well received by my friends, but with the school year only three months from being over, he never really had a chance to solidify any real friendships. Dennis would only be with us until the fall—barely five months. Once he turned sixteen, he chose to live with his mom.

My life definitely changed with the arrival of this new foster kid. The first thing that happened was Mom stayed home a lot more. She was there nearly every single day after school, causing my $35 a week deal to jump out the window in a hurry. Mom sat me down one day shortly after Dennis arrived and told me she couldn't pay me anymore because it wasn't fair to Dennis. I agreed and, quite honestly, welcomed the break from all the responsibilities, though now my spending money was gone.

Family vacation that July was somewhat unusual. Mom, Nikki, Dennis, my old Aunt Mabel, and I all piled into our big Ford LTD station wagon and headed for beautiful British Columbia. We stayed with one of Dad's sisters at Grandma and Grandpa's in Langley while they drove to Saskatchewan and visited with Dad in Tadmore. Mom brought Aunt Mabel along to get her out of the house and take her on a holiday. She was always cooped up in her little house, and Mom would occasionally take her here and there just to get her out. Taking her on this trip, however, was quite the undertaking. Aunt Mabel was in her mid-eighties, yet the old gal was still surprisingly sharp as a whip.

Now that he'd been with us for the better part of four months, I was excited about taking this trip with Dennis. He and I settled into our established roles, and I can't say—during his entire five-month stay with us—there was even one time that we had a disagreement, which was unusual considering our ages. Once we arrived in Langley at Dad's parents' place, and after a brief rest, one of our first excursions was going to Seattle, Washington. As things were considerably less expensive there, especially during the 1980s, Mom loved shopping in the U.S. All the money I had saved up for this trip was burning a hole in my pocket, and there was something very important I wanted to buy south of the border. Upon arrival in the Emerald City, let me tell you, I was chomping at the bit. And being the navigator—Mom wasn't very good at finding her way around—I was telling her where to go and exactly how to get there. Finally finding a parking spot, and with pockets full of money, Dennis and I were on our own shopping in downtown Seattle. After walking a few blocks, we found ourselves exactly where I wanted to be...the pawn shop district. Having been here once before with my parents, I remembered the deals that could be had. I just knew the one thing I didn't have but desperately wanted would be attainable for a song at one of these pawn shops. A high-fidelity home stereo system! As long as it sounded awesome, I didn't care if it was used.

These pawn stores, with stuff scattered everywhere, were more like thrift shops—very disorganized. Therefore, you had to keep your eyes sharp and scour through a lot of junk. However, I was confident there was a sound system with my name on it in one of these stores. Having previous knowledge that a person could negotiate the price much lower with relatively favorable success, I was poised and ready to pounce. You wouldn't know it, but I could be somewhat rapacious when bargaining. One store we went into, the clerk was sitting outside by the front door, as it was a scorching hot day with no air conditioning inside. No one was inside, leaving Dennis and I in there unattended. I looked around for a bit and came across this tiny old dresser. It looked very unique and possibly an antique. I'm not even sure what prompted me, but I opened the top drawer to see what was inside. Well, wouldn't you know it; the store clerk's cash box was in there, wide open, with a few American twenty-dollar bills just staring me in the face. Quickly grabbing them and stuffing them in my pocket, I motioned to Dennis for us to get the heck out of there. Once down the street a safe distance,

I revealed the little score to him. We split the money evenly between us and enthusiastically continued on.

After perusing a handful of secondhand shops, I finally found that diamond in the rough: a Marantz turntable complete with amplifier. It was an older model, but knowing Marantz was a great brand that exceled in sound quality, I was cool with it. If I'm anything, I'm about quality. Following a successful session of haggling with the owner to substantially reduce his asking price, I was one happy camper. Dennis eventually found a great tuner/amplifier at one store, and I then located a good-quality turntable for him from another old, rickety pawn shop. The thing was extremely dirty with what looked like about a hundred years' worth of dust on it. After asking the clerk how much he wanted for the turntable, the guy looked us up and down and answered, "How about three bucks?" Quickly assuming that seemed too good to be true, I piped up to enquire if the thing even worked. "It sure does!" he replied. We plugged it in, and sure enough, the turntable started spinning. Dennis gave him three dollars, and we walked out the door. Later, to complete the enduring search, we each found the perfect pair of speakers at another shop. At this point, however, I was afraid Mom might be upset with us because of all the stuff we'd bought, complaining there wasn't sufficient room in the wagon and so forth. Just being a typical mom. To my pleasant surprise, she wasn't at all upset and didn't even ask any particular questions about our purchases—questions that Dennis and I would have no doubt answered untruthfully. Good thing we had a big station wagon with lots of room.

When we drove back across the border to Canada and showed the attendant at customs the receipts for our used stereo equipment, he looked them over and said we'd have to pay duty on the turntable Dennis had bought. At this, I quickly interrupted and asked, "On three dollars?" The officer looked at that particular receipt again. Then he looked at me suspiciously with a furrowed brow and simply said, "Oh." He thought the receipt read $300.00. After that, I thought for sure this customs officer was going to ask us to park on the side like they do when they decide to go through your entire car with a fine-tooth comb, but instead, he sent us on our merry way. I breathed a sigh of relief, not because we were hiding anything, but because it's stressful when the authorities search through everything as if you're a criminal. Me? A criminal?

Upon arriving back at Grandma and Grandpa's in Langley, first thing Dennis and I did was hook up our stereos to see how they worked. Turned out, mine didn't. The turntable required an additional pre-amplifier, which wasn't a big deal. I was still happy with my purchase; after all, this was a Marantz turntable and amplifier. Dennis plugged his equipment in and hooked it all up. Then he proceeded to play a record. Unfortunately, the turntable was spinning the wrong direction. Not able to contain myself, I started laughing out loud. Dennis, however, was not impressed. "How is that even possible?" I said while giggling. After the comicality of the situation finally passed, I reassured him that there must be a way to fix it. Without tools, however, that would have to wait until we returned home.

While on our holiday, we went to visit my mom's sister Janette and her husband Russ. They lived in White Rock, another small community in the greater Vancouver area. Their son, Kelvin, is the cousin who took my bike for a spin and then parked it against the back of our moving truck. By this time, he was seventeen years old and had turned out to be a cool guy. The incident with the bike, and his denying he'd left it behind the truck, was long forgiven and forgotten. He treated us like we were his friends and even took Dennis and me to the beach one afternoon. White Rock is clustered around an eight-kilometer sandy beach and is lined by an oceanfront promenade—a little slice of paradise that is readily identified by the large white rock that sits on the beach. However, after our little spending spree in Seattle on stereo equipment and by this point in our trip, Dennis and I were both flat broke. Therefore, earlier that same day, we came up with a plan. With the idea that she must have a lot of cash on her, we decided to go through old Aunt Mabel's purse. This was before bank cards and ATM machines, so unless you had a credit card or traveler's checks, cash was your only other option. The plan we had cooked up was that Dennis would distract Mabel while I went through her purse. It worked. I found two twenties in her wallet and snagged them. One for him and one for me. I honestly don't remember who came up with the idea first—probably me—it was simply one of those "are you thinking what I'm thinking" moments.

Once we returned home from our holiday in British Columbia, priority number one was to hook up our stereos—and fix Dennis's backwards-spinning turntable. Believe it or not, we managed to repair it quite easily. All those years of taking gadgets apart finally paid off. Both of our stereo systems worked awesomely. They had fairly decent acoustic quality—I was impressed! Now that we had these high-fidelity sound systems, though, I wanted to go music shopping. There were so many albums I wanted…but no money to pay for them.

* * *

Not long after we returned from summer vacation that year, Mom decided to open a small business in the Canora mall. Because Dad had studied reflexology when Mom had fallen sick and been diagnosed with MS, he'd achieved a certificate, making him a certified reflexologist with the Ingham Institute of Reflexology. And later, Mom had taken the Ingham Institute course herself and soon became a certified practitioner as well. Her idea was to open a reflexology clinic in the mall. It was a small single-story mall, with a grocery store at one end, a hardware store at the other, and some mom and pop stores scattered throughout. Mom happened to know the owner well, and he offered her a deal on a space that was perfect for what she needed, without a lease. The mall had been struggling since it had opened— over half the place was vacant—and the owner simply wanted to get businesses in there to generate traffic. This allowed Mom an affordable opportunity with low risk. Dad kept selling cars, though, as he didn't believe the reflexology office would ever become a viable business. To his surprise, however, Mom's little idea would become a thriving success almost overnight. To keep up with all the clients she was getting, she was quick to start hiring and training people to work for her. Being the determined go-getter she was, Mom loved the success that resulted from her new endeavor. As for us kids, now three of us with Dennis, we were once again left on our own all day long at home. That, in turn, meant a whole lot of freedom during the summer. Being the teenagers we were, there certainly wasn't any objection from us.

One day, while at the new mall where Mom had her business, Dennis and I were perusing the music album selection at the drugstore. The vinyl albums were neatly stacked in a metal stand, just begging to be purchased by music lovers young and old. There was a great selection of popular music considering the small number of albums they had to choose from: two racks of about fifty—one hundred in total—if I had to guess. The albums were right near the exit, and I was quick to notice that if no one was paying for anything at the checkout, the clerk was usually near the back, putting stock away. This left the entire front of the store unattended. Dennis and I couldn't have scripted this scenario any better if we'd tried. Within a matter of minutes, I devised the perfect plan. This entailed first going to another store in the mall, where they sold crafts and art supplies. I bought a big sheet of colored cardboard—for a few bucks—and asked the clerk to put it in a big bag for me so it wouldn't get damaged. I then took the big bag with the piece of fancy cardboard in it back to the drugstore. Walking into a store with a bag from a different store wasn't uncommon—especially in a mall. And this was in an era before surveillance cameras and other security measures like barcode readers and scanners that set off an alarm if an item hasn't been scanned by the cashier. We waited for the opportune time, and I loaded up the bag with about ten albums, five for Dennis and five for me. Dennis, my partner in crime, was my lookout. We orchestrated the heist like a couple of old pros. Unbeknownst to the store clerk, I casually walked out with a bag full of albums. Dennis and I pulled that little stunt more than once. By the end of summer, we had about twenty albums each, all obtained by the five-finger discount method. A few that I can remember were by Streetheart, Nazareth, Harlequin, Styx, and Foreigner.

After getting bored during one of those long summer days while at home on our own one day, Dennis said to me, "We should go visit Aunt Mabel." At that point, I didn't know he had an ulterior motive in visiting her—not one that he'd mentioned yet anyway. I didn't think much of it at the time, and we had nothing much else to do, so I agreed. When we arrived at her house, since she lived alone and no one visited her all too often, Auntie was excited to see us. She invited us in, and we sat down at her table—she made us both some tea. I could discern by the way she had the cards placed on her kitchen table that Auntie had been playing solitaire. Therefore, I asked if she wanted to play cards with us, and because I knew how to and assumed she did as well, I suggested we play Old Maid. She agreed, and the three of us sat and played a game together. It took about an hour to finish, after which, Dennis and I left. As we were sauntering home, however,

Dennis started talking about the very thing I was thinking about… Mabel's purse, the same one we'd taken money from during our trip to BC. We had both noticed it sitting under the table, on the floor, up against the wall next to where she'd sat. We definitely had the same mentality when it came to the subject of thieving and what it really boiled down to…dishonesty.

As we walked home that afternoon, we devised a plan where we'd return the next day and, essentially, again steal money from Auntie's purse. And that's precisely what we did. Dennis distracted her while I went for her purse to look for the loot. Auntie must have just cashed her pension check, because I found an envelope with a whole wad of cash in it, which, quite honestly, kind of startled me. I took about half of what was there, folded up the bills, and stuffed them in my jeans. As we walked home, Dennis and I counted up our score. There was just over $300 to divide between us, which, by the way, was a considerable amount of coin for a fourteen-year-old in 1983 and my single largest payoff to date. It felt absolutely amazing to have that much cash in my hands from what seemed like one simple misdeed—a deed that would prove to be the pinnacle of defining moments that solidified me on an inevitable path in life. Dennis and I would return to Mabel's a few weeks later—after her next pension check—to successfully pull off another purse filching. After that, however, Auntie was getting wise to our shenanigans and began hiding her purse. Nevertheless, that didn't deter us, and we were able to pull off one more heist. Over the course of three months, we hit her up three times, and each instance, we were able to score at least $300 to divide between us. I could have taken the whole enchilada, but I made sure to leave half, more or less, of what was there. I didn't want to leave her totally broke. I may not have had much of a conscience, but I still had a modicum of fairness in me. In retrospect, by this age, I should have reached a critical point in my life when the sense of right and wrong overrode or at least influenced my ability to make decisions. Sadly, that was not the case. I just couldn't resist the instant gratification these acts were delivering. Clearly, my delinquency was escalating, even to the point where I was in blatant violation of my own misguided moral standard that stealing from a store was basically a victimless crime. Let's face it, stealing pension money from an elderly woman is no longer a victimless crime.

Looking back at this occurrence in my life has me feeling ashamed of what I did. Yet anyone who truly knew me back then knew me to be a kind, generous, and hardworking kid. I did unscrupulous things for sure, but I had a good heart to a varying degree in other aspects of my life, such as looking after my sister, the respect I felt for my parents, and especially my compassion for kids who were picked on. We often look at what a person did and judge them solely on their immediate behavior, labeling them a "bad person." Without knowing anything about my childhood, if anyone were to judge me strictly on this particular incident regarding my aunt Mabel—myself included— they would likely conclude that I was a terrible kid…maybe even evil! Analytically speaking, however, I was simply an opportunist who'd had the dishonesty component of his conscience slowly desensitized from the age of four, making it easier to ignore the fact that what I was doing was wrong. The guilt that should have been associated with each occurrence simply didn't exist for me. In terms of guilt—when it came to theft—I felt virtually nothing. I'm not making an excuse for my bad behavior by any means, but discounting a person's childhood history wouldn't be fair either.

* * *

Our family was still going strong, and business was good. We enjoyed our weekends together and faithfully participated in the

Jehovah's Witness services. Even Dennis went to the odd meeting. However, because he was a foster child, he was allowed to skip out on going. I, on the other hand, was not allowed such freedoms. In fact, Dad and I rarely missed any services, and we were still going door to door regularly. There were three meetings per week: Sundays from 10:00 AM to 12:00 PM, Mondays from 8:00 PM to 9:00 PM, and Thursdays 8:00 PM to 10:00 PM. During the Thursday night meetings, I even started taking part in the theocratic ministry school. I'd get up on the platform, read a few verses from the Bible, and then explain what they meant. It was only for five minutes or so, but I was terrible at speaking in front of a group of people. While attending all these meetings, however, I did take notice—even when I wasn't paying attention—that every once in a while, an account or biblical doctrine would get through to me, and I'd say to myself, *That actually makes sense*—not that I would apply any of this Bible-based direction in my life anytime soon. Nevertheless, whether I wanted to or not, I was definitely learning more and more about the Bible and beginning to understand WHY Jehovah's Witnesses trusted in what they believed.

There's an interesting aspect about knowledge: Once you know something, you can't go back to not knowing. It's similar to when you're a kid and first discover that Santa Claus isn't real. There's no going back to believing otherwise. It's comparable to when you diligently study the Bible and learn what it's really saying and why; it's impossible to unlearn what you know. However, at fourteen, diligently studying the Bible wouldn't be an accurate assessment of my spiritual efforts by any means—especially with the path in life I was determined to travel down. In reality, I was living a double life. The Monte that people knew at the Kingdom Hall was much different than the Monte everyone knew at school or within my friendship circles.

* * *

In late autumn of that year, Dennis and I embarked on an unsuspectingly climactic adventure, one that, quite frankly, I never imagined would lead to where it did. We decided to build a little clubhouse, or perhaps an extravagant fort is a more accurate description. We found the perfect spot to build our little home away from home a block down the street from where we lived. Problem was, although we didn't realize it at the time, where we decided to build was located on town property. And we were a little shy on materials to build it with. Dad had some two by fours and a couple of pieces of plywood, but not nearly enough for what my creative mind had envisioned. However, I remembered from when I'd worked for Peter—the farmer who lived across the street from us—that he had a bunch of plywood in one of his barns. Peter had suffered a stroke two years before and never did fully recover; therefore, he couldn't run his farm any longer. As a result, he moved away, leaving his place vacant for most of the year. His wife would return occasionally to check on the property, and during the summer months, I'd cut the grass and maintain their yard while they were away. The plywood in Peter's barn was perfect for building our clubhouse. Given our ingenuity for criminal behavior, it wasn't very difficult for us to break into Peter's barn and help ourselves to the sheets of plywood we required. They were pre-painted red with cheap barn paint, but that didn't matter to us.

Dennis and I hauled approximately four sheets out of Peter's barn and built our little clubhouse over the course of a couple days. It wasn't very big, roughly five feet wide by eight feet deep and six feet high, but it was sublime. My best fort yet! I was impressed with what we had accomplished, considering it was built—except for the few sheets of red plywood we stole—mostly with scraps. Dennis and I were proud of our new clubhouse, showing it off to every other kid in town. We tried to form a club and get other kids to join by paying a membership fee. That didn't exactly pan out. I suspect we needed to offer a little more incentive than just the prestige of being allowed in Dennis and Monte's cool fort.

Not more than a couple of days later, however, as Dennis and I were walking home from the clubhouse, we got stopped by one of the townsfolk. His name was Peter also. He happened to be the mayor of our little town that year. Peter started asking Dennis and me all sorts of questions about the clubhouse we'd built. One of the questions he asked was where we'd gotten the red plywood from? As it turned out, our town mayor was keeping an eye on the property that we took the plywood from, and during our brief communication with him, he mentioned that there was some red plywood missing, just like the plywood used to build our "shack," as he called it. He also made a point to mention, in a very deliberate way, that the RCMP was coming to investigate this. Upon hearing this, to say that we were a little freaked out would be an understatement. We both panicked. I'd never been involved with the police before and didn't know what was going to ensue. I had visions of cops swarming our house with a voice over a megaphone saying, "Come out with your hands up! We know you stole the plywood! Come out, or we'll shoot!" Dennis and I decided our only option was to run away to Melville, where his Mom lived, and stay there. I don't know how that was going to solve anything, but it seemed like a good idea at the time.

It was late in the afternoon already, and Melville was about an hour and a half drive. Our plan was to walk cross-country to one of the main highways and hitchhike from there to Melville. Late autumn in Saskatchewan can be somewhat unpredictable, but fortunately for us, the weather was considerably warm for that time of year. There'd been a heavy rain the evening before, leaving the dirt roads substantially wet and, in some areas, even muddy. It was dark by the time we made it to the highway, and the air was getting quite cool by then. I was hoping we'd get a ride pronto. Upon sticking out our thumbs at the first car that drove by, to my surprise, it stopped. I walked up to the car, stuck my head in the window on the passenger side, and saw that the car was full of Native Canadians. Being quite dark, I couldn't see inside the car very well, but a voice in the car asked where we were headed. Instead of answering, I slowly backed away and whispered to Dennis, "They're Natives." Just then, another voice from the back seat shouted in a thick Native accent, "We don't bite, eh!" Dennis and I figured, *Why not? It's better than freezing our butts off on this cold highway*, so we climbed in.

Turned out they were headed to Yorkton, which was two-thirds of the way to Melville. If I remember correctly, the vehicle was a late-seventies green Ford Monarch. Inside were what I assumed was a family, consisting of the mother and father sitting up front, and an older daughter and two younger siblings in the back. The younger two were sleeping. Dennis climbed in the back and sat beside the daughter; I hopped in the front, between the mother and father. Once we got on our way, the daughter began chatting it up with Dennis, and the parents started asking me all sorts of questions. I made up a story about how our vehicle had broken down and we needed to get to Melville to help Dennis's mom with some moving. It seemed like a believable scenario.

Eventually arriving in Yorkton, the Natives were kind enough to drive us to the other side of Yorkton and drop us on the highway leading to Melville, which was some forty-five kilometers away. They were very accommodating and friendly people; we had lucked out meeting them. After hitching another ride from what turned out to be a school teacher, it was quite late by the time we finally made it to Melville, yet another small prairie town. It was close to 11:00 PM. But seeing it was a Friday night, the streets weren't exactly quiet. A fair number of vehicles were driving around. I even spotted a few police cars patrolling the downtown core, no doubt on the lookout for late-night revelers who might be a little too rambunctious after leaving the local watering holes.

Because neither Dennis nor I had any money, we needed a plan that would lead to a reversal of fortune for us. Dennis had grown up here, so he knew his way around pretty well and beckoned me to follow his lead. We walked over to the local lumber yard, which was located on the main street. I don't remember the name of it, but it was similar to a Beaver Lumber-type establishment. Dennis, claiming he used to be able to squeeze in through the back entrance's large sliding door, wanted to try again. Fortunately for us, when Dennis pulled on it, the big door had enough play in it for me to squeeze through. Inside the store, it was pitch dark; therefore, it took a few minutes before my eyes could adjust. I'd never done anything like this before—break into a retail business, that is—but I wasn't scared. Cautious would be more accurate. I looked around to see if there was anything worth taking, but what we needed right then was money. I quickly spotted the cash register, and knowing there wouldn't be any banknotes in the bill tray, I was hoping they might have left some change and perhaps some rolls of quarters, dimes, and nickels. As it turned out, I was right. All in all, the coins added up to more or less $30. Not bad for chump change, and more than enough to purchase some food—Dennis and I were starving!

We found a little coffee shop that was just about to close. I think the owner must have felt sorry for us, because she served us anyway. Or maybe it was my big, tired puppy-dog eyes that worked their magic. The lady was cordial toward us, saying that she could serve us some leftover soup of the day. Before we'd embarked on this little escapade, it would have been wise of me to have worn a warm coat. But that would have required some thought and planning. Instead, with no consideration given to the plummeting temperatures of a late-fall night, all I was wearing was a light hoody. Being that it was late and I was cold, a bowl of hot soup sounded perfect. After we finished eating, Dennis suggested going to his mom's house to spend the night. That was the best idea I'd heard all day. I was dead tired. So far, during this fugitives-at-large little escapade of ours, never once had I thought about the consequences waiting for me back home. And even though every move we'd made seemed to have been met with some sort of obstacle, we'd been able to scrounge up transportation, food, and now shelter for the night. Thinking optimistically, who knew, perhaps there was a way out of this mess after all—or so I hoped. We walked over to Dennis's mother's house. Fortunately, she was still up, but she wasn't exactly thrilled to see me. I overheard her talking to Dennis in the other room, vocalizing her displeasure, saying it was a bad idea bringing "him" to her home and furthermore stating that I had parents who were sure to come looking for me. Nevertheless, we spent the night, and I slept on the couch. In the morning, I met Dennis's two younger sisters, who still lived with their mom. I don't remember their names, but they were cordial towards me. After eating some lunch, Dennis's mother sent us downtown with twenty bucks for a carton of cigarettes. I laughed to myself while thinking, *Hey, I've seen this movie before.* It reminded me of fetching cigarettes for my mom a decade earlier with Kelly. That fateful moment, when I'd gotten a taste for helping myself to things that didn't belong to me, had convinced me it was just another little game of life.

It was Saturday, early afternoon, and as we walked downtown, I soon realized that my running shoes were a disaster. They were wet and muddy, with big holes at the toe of both shoes. Deciding that I needed to rectify the situation, I figured that stealing new running shoes had to be easy enough. Really, all I had to do was just put them on, hide the old ones in the store, and walk out. How hard is that? First on the agenda, however, was to find a grocery store and shoplift the carton of cigarettes so we could keep the $20. Let me tell you, stealing a carton of cigarettes when you're fourteen is considerably more difficult than when you're four. You can't exactly walk out the front door holding them in plain sight—I wasn't a cute little kid anymore. That wasn't the only problem: I was drawing even more attention to myself walking about in the wet and worn-out shoes. They would squeak every time I took a step. I sounded like a walking rubber duck squeak toy. It was ridiculous. Some cat burglar I'd make. Knowing full well that I couldn't exactly stuff a full carton of cigarettes in my pocket or down my pants, I elected to rip the package open and stuff individual packs down my pants, or anywhere else I could fit them. Then I proceeded to walk out the door, strategically, on the heels of my feet so my shoes wouldn't squeak. I felt like the Michelin Man walking through an obstacle course with squeak toys taped to the bottom of my shoes. Thinking back, why didn't I steal the shoes first? That would've made this little caper a lot less blunderous. With a little craftiness, however, I managed to get out of there without raising suspicion. Maybe you're wondering why I'm ALWAYS the one doing the actual stealing. Quite frankly, I didn't trust Dennis not to get caught.

Next on the to-do list was my shoes. That was easy compared to the cigarettes. I brought a little piece of mud with me into the store to dirty up the new shoes. Compared to the rest of me, the shoes would've appeared as though they were glowing. The cross-country walk through fields and down dirt roads after it had rained hadn't exactly left me wearing clean, freshly ironed clothes.

As I suspected, stealing the running shoes was elementary compared to my last five-finger cigarettes discount. Dennis and I sauntered back to his mom's to deliver the cigarettes. She'd been kind enough to offer us dinner if we promised to return in time, which we did. Over dinner, she explained that she wanted me to go home the next day on the bus, reassuring me that she would pay for my bus fare. I thought that was mindfully generous of her, considering she wasn't exactly well off financially. The next day, a Sunday, Dennis walked with me to the bus depot. It was later in the day—the only scheduled time a bus was going to Tadmore. The bus depot was a little gas station on the outskirts of Melville. Dennis purchased my ticket and then sat with me on some chairs by the door, sort of like a waiting area. Meanwhile, Dennis, who had recently turned sixteen, negating any previous control social services had over him, told me he was going to remain with his mom from now on. Essentially, he could live with whomever he wanted. Upon hearing his decision to stay, I became somewhat melancholy. Dennis and I had become very close in a rather short period of time, and somehow I knew I'd probably never see him again. I also had a somewhat educated inclination that he was in for a tough life.

Within about ten minutes, something I was certainly not expecting occurred: A police officer walked in, looked at Dennis and me, and asked us to step outside with him. Next thing I knew, he was putting handcuffs on both of us, and we were off to the precinct, sitting in the back of a squad car. Dennis and I looked at each other with an expression that implied, *Uh-oh, what just happened?* Having never been handcuffed or in a police car ever before, this was unexplored territory for me. I wasn't freaking out or anything like that, but I wasn't exactly thrilled at this unexpected turn of events either. I started to wonder, *What does the cop know? Does he know we broke into that lumber yard? Maybe he knows about my running shoes? Even worse, maybe he knows about the stolen plywood and that we were on the run.* Still, I kept my wits and wasn't about to give up the goose just yet. Even though it WAS pretty much cooked!

As it turned out, the attendant at the gas station bus depot had phoned the police because we matched the description of a couple of teenagers who were reported to have stolen a car. Talk about an ironic situation, one that was both humorous and a sense of relief. We were guilty all right, but not of what we were being suspected of. The officer questioned us about the missing vehicle on the way to the police station, but we were adamant that he had the wrong guys. Somehow he wasn't buying it, though. Later, at the station, the officer questioned us separately, to see if our stories matched, I assumed. Being that Dennis and I were street smart enough to know there was no usefulness in copping to anything we hadn't gotten caught doing, during our interrogations, we cleverly omitted any incriminating details of the crimes we had committed. After all, as far as the police officer knew, we were just a couple of runaway teenagers. When the officer checked out our stories, he began to realize that we were, more or less, telling the truth—at least as far as not stealing the car. No doubt, the officer suspected we were guilty of something, though, for the simple reason that we probably looked guilty of something. A couple of wandering punks had to be guilty of something or another. After reaching my parents by telephone, he informed us that my mother was on her way to Melville to pick me up.

Ramona—our previous foster child and in her twenties by now—drove down with Mom. To my surprise, Mom was in a great mood and extremely happy to see me. Upon walking into the police station, she even gave me a big hug, something Mom seldom did, and said, "I was worried sick about you!" Before letting me go, the officer took me to a private room, where I had to write out a statement explaining my whereabouts for the past twenty-four ours. Yes siree, we must have looked guilty of something! At that point, the cop who'd arrested us asked me if my mom was single, to which I laughed and replied, "Why, do you think she's hot?" He neither laughed nor retorted. The guy had no sense of humor. During the ride home, I explained to Mom what had happened with the plywood and how our town mayor had told us the police were on their way. Again, Mom, with her misguided pattern of sticking up for me, confirmed that she'd suspected as much. Meanwhile, she voiced her displeasure with Mayor Peter. "He had no right to speak to you the way he did," she said. I, on the other hand, wasn't convinced that he'd done anything out of line. The fact that we knew we were guilty is what led us to run away. The manner in which Peter had confronted us had played a very small role in our decision to flee, but I wasn't about to get into a discussion about it with Mom. So far, this was going great. I just kept my mouth shut and agreed with her.

* * *

After this latest incident, which had seen Dennis exit my life, things returned to normal. It was as if nothing had ever happened. Once again, I had dodged the bullet—and it further boosted the confidence I already had in myself that I could get away with anything. Mom and Dad basically let me off scot-free. I had to apologize to our neighbor, of course, for pilfering his plywood, and continue cutting his lawn to pay for the lumber. But that was it. Our town mayor took the fall for me this time. I never discussed the entirety of what Dennis and I encountered throughout the adventure, but I gave her enough information, allowing her to remain with the satisfaction I was just a victim of circumstance. I decided it was best to let sleeping dogs lie. Mom did, however, ask how I'd acquired the new running shoes. I simply explained that Dennis's mom had felt sorry for me and bought them. Lying came pretty easy to me, despite the fact that I well knew the ninth commandment explicitly states, "Thou shalt not bear false witness against thy neighbor."

After recalling these events, I find it thought-provoking how life can take a turn in either direction by the slightest nuances, pushing or pulling us this way and that way. Most of us, while in the moment, fail to even realize when it happens. I never noticed—until now, that is, looking back with true self-reflection. It's hard not to wonder how different the next few years of my life might have been if my parents wouldn't have taken on another foster child. So far, I had more or less made an honest effort not to commit theft. As I was regularly earning $35 per week—until Dennis entered my life—I was having relative success. Now, I'm not blaming Dennis in any way for the thefts I was complicit in. After all, it WAS me who instigated most of our malfeasances—not that Dennis ever objected. Nevertheless, it seems I had many lessons to not just learn but absorb before turning the page on this phase of my life. And that wasn't going to occur overnight.

CHAPTER

14

Apprenticeship in Criminal Behavior

After the departure of Dennis, and what it felt like to have a brother, grade nine began with a solemn loneliness. I felt lost without my partner in crime. Shortly after school started, I would soon learn of certain ramifications as a result of my scapegoating Peter, Tadmore's mayor, for our running away to Melville. First thing that happened was we received a letter in the mail concerning the little fort Dennis and I had built stating that because it was on town property, the dwelling had to be removed. Then, every time I would go out on our three-wheeler, Peter would call the police. One of the officers, whom I soon got to know quite well, told us in no uncertain terms that Peter was driving everyone down at the police station bonkers with all the complaints he was calling in about me. On one lovely Sunday afternoon, we arrived home from our Jehovah's Witness meeting only to find Peter tearing out a drain culvert that Dad and I had installed years earlier across our driveway. Dad was furious and chased him away before he could finish, but that wasn't the end of it. We received another letter in the mail shortly after, citing that our driveway culvert wasn't in accordance with Tadmore's bylaws. This culvert had been in our driveway for five years or more, yet all of a sudden, it was a bylaw infringement.

Clearly, we now had an enemy hell-bent on making our lives miserable, especially mine.

Dad, meanwhile—as a result of all the trouble our dipstick mayor was causing us with the law—decided to sell our three-wheeler. I wasn't happy with that decision at all. The snow came early and heavy that fall, and I felt lost without my three-wheeler. Perhaps I didn't quite get off scot-free after all.

Later that winter, I convinced Dad to see if we could get that old Arctic Cat snowmobile going, the very one that we'd sailed through the air on, scaring us half to death. Together, we managed to get it running, and Dad's brother-in-law welded the steering shaft back together. Upon further review, the thing was a piece of junk. I rode it once or twice before one of the pistons finally let go. Somehow Dad, being the superlative salesman he was, was still able to negotiate an arrangement enabling him to eventually sell it, even with a dead piston and without lifting a finger on the machine. He made a deal with one of our JW friends in which they would repair the engine, sell it, and split the cash, minus the cost of the parts. Dad was incredibly industrious when it came to things such as this—an eternal optimist who always found a way.

With our three-wheeler and snowmobile gone, and especially with Dennis no longer bunking in the next bedroom, I was somewhat perplexed with what to do with myself. After some discerning contemplation, I came up with a plausible solution. I did the math and figured out that payments could easily be made on a snowmobile. I was still working—off and on—for our cattle farmer buddy Frank, and I knew he would increase my hours if I wanted to work more. My idea was to get my parents to co-sign a bank loan for me so I could buy a brand-new sled. And to cover repairs and maintenance costs on the sled, this gave me the opportunity to reintroduce the possibility of once again earning that $35 per week. I knew that if I ran it by Mom first, getting her on my side, this was the best course of action and path of least resistance towards success. Mom, as I suspected, loved my idea and was, unknowingly, onboard with helping me talk Dad into agreeing with my ingenious plan. The following weekend, Dad and I were off to the snowmobile dealer in Preeceville. I ended up buying a Ski-Doo by Bombardier, the people who put the snowmobile on the map. It was just a single cylinder, but it still had plenty of pep for what I needed.

Our town mayor was now calling the cops every time I rode my snowmobile. By this time, I'd had enough of his antagonistic shenanigans and reasoned it was time to correct this man's head—the Monte Perepelkin way. I bought a bag of roofing nails at the hardware store … No, I didn't have a roofing job to do. I had a statement to make. Wouldn't you know, the mayor suddenly started getting flat tires every time he'd drive his truck. Nearly everyone in town was talking about it. Understandably, Peter, being an antagonist, wasn't known to be anyone's favorite person. Therefore, most of the townsfolk were snickering about it behind his back. I'm not sure anyone even suspected me as the source of all his misfortune. Although it was quite comical to everyone else, I'm sure it was an extremely aggravating situation for our town mayor.

While Peter was mysteriously getting all these flat tires, I bumped into him one day coming out of our little town store. The town mailboxes were just outside the store, and Peter was there getting his mail. I said, "Hi Peter," dropping him one of my practiced, respectable greetings for someone I didn't particularly care for. He glared at me with a suspicious eye and his Oscar the Grouch eyebrows furrowed up as he replied, "You don't know anything about all these flat tires I've been getting, do you?" He then smiled at me with a big stupid grin on his face. At that moment, never had I wanted to punch a man in the face as badly as I did then. Remarkably, I kept my cool and calmly stated, "Well, Peter, I don't know. Who have you ticked off lately? Maybe you just need to stop being such an a**hole, and perhaps you'll stop running over so many nails. What do you think?" Then I smiled back at him as the disingenuous smirk on his face suddenly went blank and his jaw dropped to his knees. When I turned to walk away, I could have sworn the word "M-a-y-b-e" came from his mouth. Coincidently enough, the cops stopped getting calls from him around that same time. And guess what? Peter, all of a sudden, stopped getting flat tires.

February of 1984 came with an interesting development. With Mom completely engulfed in her thriving new reflexology business and Dad equally occupied selling cars, they decided to hire a live-in nanny to cook meals and look after Nikki, mostly. The nanny's name was Frieda. She was an older lady in her late fifties, if I had to guess. Frieda drove a Chevy half-ton, a peculiar vehicle for an older woman. After the arrival of our new nanny, Mom and Dad decided to cut my $35 per week in half. But since I no longer had to cook or look after my sister, I was okay with that. It gave me more time to spend on my new snowmobile. I was now fifteen years old and becoming more preoccupied with my own life anyway.

Living in Tadmore afforded me the luxury of enjoying some excellent snowmobiling country. And because a few of my cousins and uncles also had snowmobiles, we'd often go on exploring expeditions all over the scenic hills and countryside around Tadmore, Crystal Lake, and basically anywhere within the range of a full tank of fuel. That snowmobile and I put on more miles than the notorious Road Runner chasing Wile E. Coyote ever did. One of the aspects of owning a snowmobile that I seriously miscalculated when factoring operating costs was fuel. And considering the miles I was putting on, you can imagine the quantity of gas I was burning through. That created somewhat of a predicament. The gas tank in poor Frieda's truck was my first target. One afternoon, with a piece of garden hose, I siphoned her tank nearly dry, but not before getting all loopy from swallowing a mouthful of gas. I felt sick to my stomach and needed a nap to sleep off the awful hangover.

Frieda was a smart lady, though, and she figured out exactly what was going on. She even voiced her astute suspicion to Dad once. But I denied it, of course. I even felt a tad sheepish on one particular occasion when I drained her tank bone dry to the extent that Frieda had to call a tow truck to bring her fuel. After that, she began making sure to leave her tank nearly empty—now with a locking gas cap—and kept a full jerry-can locked up in the cab of the truck. That didn't stop me. With a wire coat hanger, I was past the locked door, and I stole that gas, too. I believe poor Frieda finally had enough of my stealing her gas, and she quit a couple of months later. I really was quite a shameless hooligan.

* * *

Some time had passed since Dennis's departure from our family, and so far, I was managing to stay away from Aunt Mabel's—her purse in particular. It had been more or less eight months since Dennis and I had been there last, not that I never thought about it. I simply didn't know how to pull off another purse snatching operation on my own—without getting busted, that is. However, after the snow melted and my snowmobile was just sitting dormant in our garage, I soon realized having to fork out $72 a month to pay off the thing was a pain in the butt. Unfortunately, when coming up with my ingenious plan of making payments on a snowmobile, I'd failed to contemplate the burden of making them during the summer months. Therefore,

I managed to convince myself that "one last time" was in order. The thought of not having to split the loot with Dennis this time was somewhat motivational, you might say. For this operation to work, I had to come up with a different plan. Without my partner in crime to distract Mabel—I was on my own. After venturing an educated guess that with a flat screwdriver, I could slide the deadbolt over on her front door and be inside as easy as snagging fish in a rain barrel, my decision was to sneak in during the middle of the night.

That night, I woke at 2:00 AM, put my cat burglar clothes on, and made sure I had everything I needed. Black ski mask, check! Non-squeak shoes, check! Flat screwdriver, check! And off I went. This is when I envisioned the theme from *The Pink Panther* playing in the background as I crept over towards Mabel's house. Concluding that bright clothing wouldn't have been wise, I really was wearing all black. Being seen walking around town at 2:00 AM would've been difficult to explain. I'd put some serious thought into this little B&E scheme, not my first, but the first time for a residential heist, and with somebody inside, no less. Getting through Mabel's front door was as easy as I suspected, so my first obstacle was a breeze. Next on the agenda was finding her purse. Upon moving closer to her bedroom, though, I could hear this strange noise. It sounded like a buzz saw. At first, it sort have freaked me out, wondering if perhaps Mabel was still awake. When I realized it was just her snoring, I quickly had to cover my mouth to silence the sudden reaction to burst out laughing. I'd never heard anyone snore quite that boisterously before. I could have sworn her bed was vibrating. Worrying about being quiet certainly wasn't something I needed to be concerned with; if her own snoring wasn't waking her up, nothing would. After locating that all-too-familiar yellowy brown purse of hers on the floor right beside her bed, precisely where I suspected it would be, I opened it up. Wow! I had hit the motherlode.

Because Dennis and I hadn't been around for so long, Mabel's brown pension envelope had had time to accumulate and was about an inch thick, stuffed with cash—all twenties. Being consistent, I took half and left the rest. To my astonishment, I walked out of there with $600 in my jeans. It felt like I'd just won the lottery! All that remained was to sneak back home without being detected, and then I was scot-free. In under five minutes, I was in and out of Auntie's place and casually walking home as if out for a stroll because I couldn't sleep. That was the line I would have offered any cop I crossed paths with. *Well, officer, I'm really stressed out with schoolwork and couldn't fall back asleep. After waking up, I decided perhaps a walk might calm me down.* Not sure how I'd explain the black ski mask and screwdriver, but oh well.

Finally arriving back home, I crept through the front door as quietly as a mouse through a cat house and headed for my bedroom. That's when my plan went sideways. Just as I walked through the doorway into my room, Dad jumped out and nearly scared the crap right out of me—literally! Apparently, he'd somehow heard me leave and was waiting for me to return. Needless to say, because I was holding a wad of twenties in my hand, I had to fess up to the whole caper. The first words from his mouth were "I knew it!" Sometime before this, Aunt Mabel had voiced concerns that she was continually missing money from her purse and even suspected Dennis and I were the culprits. For some reason, though, no one believed her. Everyone—except Dad—simply assumed that Mabel was just old and had likely misplaced the money or had less than she thought she had to begin with. Dad knew, though. He knew that somehow, someway, Mabel's missing money had my name written all over it. Judging by the look on his face, I could tell he was extremely disappointed in me—and not in the usual way either. He had an expression on his face that I'd never seen before...the look of disgust!

The next day, Dad stopped in at Aunt Mabel's to return the money I had just stolen and further enquire how much she thought had been taken in total since she'd begun missing cash. Mabel figured it to be about one grand. She may have been old, but her math skills were pretty much spot on. Mom had separate savings accounts for Nikki and me, in which she would deposit our monthly family allowance checks from the government. We were never allowed to spend that money. It was there for a rainy day or to contribute to our post-secondary education. I guess this was a rainy day, but not the kind one would expect to be spending the money on. Later that day, Mom withdrew $1,000 out of my account and sent me over to return the money to Aunt Mabel with a sincere apology. When I apologized to her, Auntie was admirably gracious towards me considering the state of affairs I'd made her a victim of. She even gave me a hug while saying, "As long as you're sorry." Then something strange happened. As Aunt Mabel embraced her frail arms around my body, a rhythmic flow of emotion swelled up inside me, and I wept. For a brief moment, I felt an emotion I wasn't particularly fond of...sincere remorse for what I'd done. Somewhere deep down in the depths of my soul, I did have a conscience towards stealing. Who knew!

During the short jaunt home from Mabel's, however—after concluding that guilt was an extremely undesirable emotion—I chose to modify my thinking towards a more comfortable mental state. I rationalized that after everything was said and done, all the money had been returned. Therefore, I rendered a final judgement upon myself of *no harm, no foul*. Conscience cleared. All I was left to deal with now was my parents. Surprisingly and perplexingly, Dad never did discipline me. This scared me more than anything. I remember thinking, *Just give me the strap already, so I can have some closure here.* I imagine by now that my parents were at their wits' end with me in regard to my continual pattern of stealing, and they decided on an alternative approach for this infraction. They went to a higher power and contacted the elders from our Jehovah's Witness congregation to see what they could do, concluding perhaps that the fear of God might have success in correcting my wayward ways. Hadn't they tried that approach already? Nevertheless, after Dad explained to our elders my history with theft— providing insight into just how serious of a problem this was—I met with three elders shortly after. One elder in particular was extremely upset with me and expressed his feelings quite openly. Ernie was his name. He was the father of the family we were closest friends with in our congregation. These were the folks Dad, Nikki, and I would often go to their house on Saturday evenings to visit and play board games, billiards, or cards with. Given our friendship with Ernie and his family, it would be safe to assume that he took a personal interest in me and was exceedingly disappointed in what I had done. Up until now, no one in our congregation had known anything about my constant battle with stealing. To the elders, and rightly so, this was a grave issue. After all, I was fifteen now, certainly not a little kid anymore.

When anyone from the congregation has committed a serious wrongdoing and the elders are made aware of it, procedure is that three elders from the congregation will meet with the offender to discuss the wrongdoing. The purpose of this is to keep the Jehovah's Witness organization clean in the eyes of God and to prevent unwanted influences from spreading to others within the congregation. The elders take matters such as this very seriously. When meeting with the transgressor, one of the things the elders look for is genuine repentance. They need to know that the person is truly sorry for what he or she did—while acknowledging it was wrong—instead of simply being sorry for getting caught. This is all done in a courteous, loving way, and with the use of Bible scriptures to show the individual—according to Bible standards—that what they did was wrong in the eyes of God. Then, if the offence requires, the authorities are notified.

However, at my age, I wasn't sure what to expect. They certainly didn't handle me with "kid gloves" by any means. Ernie, in particular, was quite perturbed with me. At one point, I thought he was going to throw me over his knee and spank me. He kept saying, "I don't think you're really sorry! I think you're just sorry that you got caught!" And he wasn't wrong. I don't know how many times I wished I'd left my screwdriver, ski mask, and wad of twenties stashed outside somewhere, as opposed to walking in holding the incriminating evidence in my hands. That was my biggest regret. Then I could have easily convinced Dad that I WAS simply out for a walk after not being able to sleep. Because I wasn't baptized, however, there wasn't much the elders could do in the form of discipline other than reprimand me and demote my status from being an unbaptized publisher, which they did. Something really surprised me when I met with the elders that day, though, and it stuck with me throughout my entire life. Ernie was extremely upset with me, to the point of being angry even, but after he calmed down, he asked me to look up a verse from the Bible and read it aloud. The scripture was Isaiah 48:17b, 18: *"I, Jehovah, am your God, the One teaching you to benefit [yourself], the One causing you to tread in the way in which you should walk. O if only you would actually pay attention to my commandments! Then your peace would become just like a river, and your righteousness like the waves of the sea."*

After reading those two passages aloud, I looked up at Ernie to see he had tears in his eyes. Wondering why on earth he had tears in HIS eyes, I thought to myself, *What's that all about? He cares THAT much?* Then Ernie asked what I thought the scripture meant. I answered, "If we listen to God and live our life in accordance with His advice, the result will be a better life." Even though I wasn't convinced, by any means, that the Bible was the answer to my problems and life's questions in general, I never forgot that moment. That particular scripture always stuck with me. That elder enabled me for the first time to realize that all this Bible stuff and going to meetings wasn't just in relation to learning about God. That was part of it, but there was much more to it than that. Apparently, living in accordance with the Bible promised the best possible life, now and in the future. It sounded uncomplicated enough. But was the secret to life really that simple?

Although meeting with the three congregation elders certainly didn't plant any kind of life-altering seed in me, it did reshape my perception of the Bible and place it in a whole new light. I wondered— if He existed—maybe God really does care about us. Ernie certainly seemed to care. This is not to say that I was about to set a course for the path to righteousness anytime soon. Looking back, I was just getting started down a highway in the opposite direction. All that had transpired thus far was merely an apprenticeship in criminal behavior. Whatever tiny quiver of a conscience I felt as a result of this incident was filed in a top secret compartment deep within my innermost self and labeled "things to ignore," a place where the uncomfortable feeling of guilt could easily be disregarded by means of desire and gratification, the corner of our minds where the ends easily justify the means, at the nexus of action and consequence. If there ever was, or could have been, a turning point in my life, this was it. However, instead of allowing my conscience to illuminate my decisions, I rejected it and chose the low road. Even though this spiraling descent into self-seeking behavior made it painfully obvious that my future was looking bleak and desolate, with dark, gloomy storm clouds looming overhead, the impending threat of far-reaching consequences was the furthest thing from my mind. Instead, I was hell-bent on deciding for myself what made me happy.

Cue music: "Way Down We Go" by Kaleo

https://www.youtube.com/watch?v=0-7IHOXkiV8

CHAPTER

15

The Algebra Exam Caper

Throughout my childhood, structure was never a big part of my life, other than my household responsibilities and going to JW meetings. Yet there was one strict rule that was regularly enforced on school nights: a 9:00 PM bedtime. Apparently, my parents believed sleep was important. However, by the beginning of grade ten, some unexpected developments would occur and thus alter much of what I'd become accustomed to.

With Mom's reflexology business booming in Canora, Dad decided to open an office in Yorkton—the nearest city, forty-five minutes away. By the time I was in grade ten, however, offices were up and running in Regina, Saskatoon, and Preeceville as well. That was when things began heading wayward for our family. First, Dad stopped going to JW meetings altogether, which, because I never had to go to meetings anymore, I really didn't mind at all. And except on weekends, Dad was almost never home anymore. Then, later that school year, Mom would relocate to Saskatoon in order to run the reflexology office there. My sister would go with her to attend school in Saskatoon. Meanwhile, I was once again left in charge at home, this time all by my lonesome. Even though I had an exorbitant amount of responsibility, I loved the freedom that came with it. No one was ever telling me what to do. I knew what I had to do and just did it. Perhaps in a sense, that was structure…just not supervised.

Volleyball season was always at the beginning of the school year and ran for roughly three months. By grade ten, I was becoming quite practiced at the sport, enough so that my gym teacher, Mr. Popowich, convinced me I was good enough to make the school team. Being that our school's volleyball team consisted of mostly grade eleven and twelve students, I was reluctant to try out. I thought that even if I did make the team, I was likely destined to sit on the bench for most games, especially considering that my height at the time wasn't appropriately tall—probably five foot eight at this stage in my life. However, my skills as a setter were quite useful, and I did deliver a decent serve. And with that, I made the team. Surprisingly, at least to me, I played in nearly every game. Getting to practices and games, on the other hand, proved to be a challenge, as I knew it would. Unfortunately, my parents never offered much assistance in this area of my life. I knew they were preoccupied with their new business venture by this point, but they never did take much interest in any of my extracurricular activities—even when they could have. This wasn't a Bible-based issue either. Mom and Dad just weren't interested in that part of my life. It got to the point where I no longer bothered to ask and instead simply learned to fend for myself.

Making our school's volleyball team was in many ways a big deal to me. It felt good to be part of something. However, when the team traveled to away games and then rendezvoused back at the school—where we'd all find our own way home from there—often times, we wouldn't get back until 9:00 PM in the evening. Therefore, arranging for someone to pick me up would sometimes prove to be difficult. On two separate occasions in grade eleven—in order to attend games—I elected to sleep overnight at school. No one was aware of this; it wasn't exactly something I wanted to advertise. With my parents living and working away from home during the week and my sister attending school in Saskatoon, no one was around to realize I hadn't returned from school that day. With blankets from the home economics room, a sofa in the student lounge to sleep on, and food in the cafeteria, I made myself comfortable, and no one was ever aware of my little overnighters. The student lounge even had a color TV. My dinner consisted of potato chips, chocolate bars, and ice cream, but I wasn't complaining. To acquire said snacks, I had to pull the pins off the door hinges to break into the cafeteria, but that was child's play for me. I'm sure there were other options I could have considered to avoid sleeping at school, but I didn't want to bother anyone. And quite honestly, I was somewhat embarrassed that my parents were not there for me. For that reason, I kept it to myself and did what I had to do. Besides, the school sleepovers were kind of fun.

On one occasion, I had a close call that could have left me roaming the streets of Sturgis for the night. Normally, after returning from our game, Mr. MacDonald, our coach, would head straight home while the few of us who were left waiting for our rides sat in the front lobby area of the school. This time, however, he sat with me as I pretended to wait for someone to pick me up. *Okay, this isn't good*, I silently concluded. If Mr. MacDonald decided to wait this out—knowing that once I walked out the front door it would lock behind me—I was in a bit of a conundrum. Not at all confident that I could break back into the school, I was starting to get concerned. Finally, the coach said to me, "I have to go! Will you be okay here on your own until your ride comes?" His question was music to my ears; I stifled a sigh of relief. "Yeah, no problem! My dad probably got hung up and should be here any minute," I convincingly lied. Good thing he didn't realize he was dealing with a streetwise kid who knew the ropes of survival and, most importantly, how to keep his cool. Otherwise, my visions of spending the night in a cold vacant bus over in the school parking lot would have become reality.

Perhaps saying that my parents never took an interest in any of my after-school sports isn't entirely accurate. I do remember a time Dad drove me to a badminton tournament at one of the neighboring schools on a Saturday. Nikki came with us to cheer on her big brother. They stayed long enough to watch me play my first game, and then went shopping for a new BBQ. I won every game I played that day, thus winning the men's singles division in the tournament. I'd be lying if I said my parents not taking much of an interest or supporting me in my school sports activities didn't hurt my feelings. However, being a person who doesn't particularly enjoy feeling sorry for himself, I quickly brushed off the negative emotions and didn't let it diminish my resolve. It was what it was, and I dealt with getting to games and practices the best I could. I always found a way to make it work, even though some of my solutions were at times unscrupulous.

Sometimes, when I speak of my parents and how they raised me, it feels like I'm pointing out all the mistakes they made. However, that's not my intention. They made mistakes, and they know they did, just like I know that I made mistakes raising my kids. We've all made mistakes in raising our children. That's a part of life. Learning from our mistakes is what really matters. I love both Mom and Dad very dearly and appreciate that they did the best they could with the skills they had. That's all any of us can do. I'm certainly in no position to judge anyone. Besides, learning to fend for myself has served me well throughout my life.

* * *

For shop class, our teacher, Mr. Keller, had us designing and building dust pans that year. We were learning sheet metal. Our shop teacher was unlike any teacher I'd ever known. He told you exactly what was on his mind and didn't mince words going about it. Half the time, because his expressions were so out of left field, I didn't know for sure if he was serious or just kidding around. After tracing out the dimensions of my dustpan on to a piece of sheet metal with a metal scribe, I cut the pattern out with a pair of tin snips and proceeded to drill the rivet holes. I did all this in a matter of roughly fifteen minutes—unsupervised. Finally, after making his rounds inspecting the other boys work, Mr. Keller walked over to my work bench, took one look at what I had done so far, and barked, "Are you a f****** idiot?! What the hell is that thing? A bloody shovel?" This was one of those times when I couldn't tell if he was angry with me or kidding around. Turned out, he was kidding around—I think. Admittedly, my dustpan was quite big, but I'd made it that way on purpose. Before walking away, Mr. Keller patted me on the shoulder and quietly said, "At least you were smart enough to overlap your rivet joints." As it turned out, that crazy dustpan would become very useful in a future phase of my life.

Earlier on, towards the end of grade eight, I became friends with a kid named Craig. He lived on a farm, and I could tell his parents weren't exactly well-to-do. But they were hard working, salt-of-the-earth kind of people. Craig was a stocky kid who could easily hold his own in any situation. He was by no means a wimpy teenager—a good friend to have. Craig would come with his parents to Jehovah's Witness meetings once in a blue moon, and I believe that's what initiated our friendship in the first place. As time went on, Craig and I soon became best friends, but our friendship certainly wasn't based on our love for the Bible, that's for sure. It was as if we had an unspoken agreement between us that we would never talk about God, the Bible or being a JW. It would also be safe for me to speculate that both Craig and I leaned more towards what I would describe as "the ungodly ways of life." Perhaps we did this subconsciously to prove to our friends that we weren't really JWs; just our parents were.

By the end of grade eight, Craig and I created a school ritual that we agreed to partake in every year thereafter. For one of the last days, when we had an afternoon off, which meant we had to take a final exam during the morning, we'd bring alcohol to school. My mom and dad always had a healthy supply of liquor on hand, which they rarely kept track of. Craig and I would go to the fairgrounds and drink said beverages. In grade ten, however, instead of having an afternoon off like we usually did in the past, we had the morning off. Our shop class final exam was scheduled for the afternoon. In the spirit of not wanting to abandon our school tradition of celebrating the year's end by getting somewhat intoxicated, we did it anyway. Which meant taking our exam under the influence of alcohol. If I remember correctly, we both passed. After all, it was only shop class, and woodworking, no less—a trade that I was naturally gifted at.

Craig and I certainly shared some entertaining memories together because of our year-end tradition. Not particularly attracted to alcohol as much as some of my friends were, I drank strictly for social reasons, with the odd infraction of overindulgence here and there. And since drugs were never of any interest to me, my need to rely on substances for a good time, thank goodness, never got the best of me. My friends all smoked weed and ate magic mushrooms, and the offer was always there for me to partake, but I declined. Peer pressure never influenced my resolve. I'm not sure why—at such a young age—I was opposed to trying recreational drugs. Something inside me was simply dead against them. I wish that same resolve had been in me when it came to stealing. My early years might have been a whole lot easier.

Sometime during grade nine—1983/84—heavy metal music began making its way into mainstream popularity. I believe it was the thick, excessive sound, characterized by highly amplified guitar solos, emphatic beats, and overall loudness that attracted me to the genre. Craig was into heavy metal as well—another ingredient that contributed to our friendship. Coney Hatch, Quiet Riot, Iron Maiden, Kick Axe, Wasp, Keel, and Krokus were some popular metal bands I gravitated towards. However, my favorite band was none other than M□tley Crüe. It was during this era that Crüe came out with their *Shout at the Devil* album. And being adamantly opposed to the Devil—if he actually existed—the Crüe's title track, "Shout at the Devil," was one of my favorite songs. I'd often listen to music on my Walkman during the boring bus ride home from school to pass the time. I found music to be a great escape from reality.

* * *

My sister Nikki always had a tough time in school. I don't recall her ever having or mentioning any close friends. She wasn't gregarious and confident. Nikki was quiet and shy around kids at school. She mostly kept to herself. Early on in grade ten—my sister would have been in grade five—Nikki came to me after school one day, complaining about being picked on constantly by this one boy in her class. This would have been shortly before my mom moved Nikki with her to Saskatoon. Considering how I already felt about bullying, upon learning that it was happening to my little sister, you can be certain that nothing was going to stop me from doing something about it. The only person who was allowed to pick on and tease my sister was me, something I did plenty of. The next day, I walked over to Nikki's school during lunch hour, and she pointed the little thug out to me from afar. After waiting a few minutes to observe the little hoodlum—to monitor his interaction with other kids—sure enough, he was picking on another poor kid by the swing set. I walked over and said to him, "You and I have a problem." He looked at me and replied in a cocky tone, "Yeah, what's that?" In a stern voice while dominantly peering into his eyes, I asserted, "You see that girl over there?" I pointed to Nikki. "She's my sister, and from now on, I don't want you to talk to her or even LOOK at her ever again. In fact, if you see anyone else picking on her or treating her badly, I want YOU to protect her from now on. Otherwise, I'm going to have to come back here again. Are we clear?" Just as I finished giving my little lecture to the young man, a bunch of his schoolmates, mostly girls, started clapping. It seemed that this kid had been picking on many others as well. I went on to explain how he should be ashamed of himself for picking on girls. It seemed my little scare tactic worked; Nikki later informed me that he never bothered her again.

During the winter of grade ten—shortly after Christmas—Craig and I planned a sleepover at my house. He would come home on the bus after school with me and then return to school with me the next day. Well, wouldn't you know, that night, a blizzard hit the area, causing our school bus not to run the next morning, leaving Craig and I home all alone for the entire day. The snowstorm that hit us that night was conspicuously convenient, almost as if we'd planned it. Being left home all alone, we helped ourselves to the opportunity and went on a little journey by snowmobile to Canora. I'd never gone that far on my snowmobile before, but with all that fresh, powdery snow on the ground, it was as if the universe was begging us to go out and enjoy ourselves. Who am I to argue with the universe? By snowmobile, Canora was roughly fourteen miles away. I know that doesn't sound like much of a journey nowadays, but in 1985, for two sixteen-year-olds, it sure seemed like it. Our target destination was the mall, where we parked near the rear entrance. We had lunch in the mall restaurant and then headed to my favorite drugstore to buy a newspaper—the one where Dennis and I shanghaied all those albums. You're probably wondering why on earth a couple of sixteen-year-olds would want to read the newspaper, but hey, I was somewhat culturally inclined. Is it that unusual for a sixteen-year-old boy to want to read the newspaper? Okay, maybe it is, but not if there's a copy of the latest porn magazine inside it. Best part was it only cost thirty-five cents; that was the cost of the newspaper. As for how the porn magazine found its way inside that particular copy of *The Globe and Mail*, old habits die hard.

* * *

The end of grade ten would soon arrive, and with it final exams—something I never studied for. I can't remember ever studying for an exam, ever! The only subject I was concerned about not passing was algebra. Some aspects of math and algebra I would breeze through, while other sections not so much. My biggest downfall was not paying attention in class. Therefore, in order to ensure a passing grade, I came up with the brilliant idea of stealing the algebra final from our algebra teacher, Mr. Fadek. I was surprised at how easy it was for us to pull off this little stunt. When I say "us," I'm referring to my friends Craig, Nolan, and Kevin. After contemplating when our best option for success was, we executed our devious plan over the noon hour, when Mr. Fadek walked home for lunch. Nolan was my main lookout at the entrance to Fadek's classroom while the other two watched the exits at each end of the hall. Our trusting algebra teacher didn't even bother to lock his classroom door. This was far too easy! The exam was in the top drawer of his filing cabinet, also unlocked, just sitting there waiting for me. It was like stealing the proverbial candy from a baby. I took the exam home that night and used Dad's photocopy machine to make several copies of it, returning the original exam the next day right where I'd found it, hoping our naïve algebra teacher hadn't noticed it missing yet. I gave copies to my partners in crime, and within a few days, the exam was passed around to nearly everyone in grade ten. To keep suspicions at a minimum, I discreetly kept telling everyone— especially my mathematically challenged classmates—not to get too many questions correct. However, despite my efforts, eyebrows were raised when the lowest mark for the algebra final was around eighty percent. A definite red flag! But I wasn't too concerned. When considering this plan, I'd reasoned that if orchestrated properly—no matter the outcome—it carried minimal risk. Being that it was the end of the school year made it difficult for the faculty to put any pressure on anyone to find out who was responsible. And if everyone used the cheat exam, it would be counterproductive for anyone to spill the beans. Besides, other than the four of us actually involved in purloining the exam, I doubt anyone had any knowledge of exactly who was behind the caper.

But there's always one detail that gets overlooked and has the power to throw a monkey wrench into even the most perfect of plans. In this case, it was a kid named Michael. Rumor circulated that it was none other than Michael who'd spilled the beans about a copy of the exam floating around. Word had gotten around that Michael was upset with the results of his algebra final. Choosing not to use the cheat test, he'd had one of the lowest marks, which I already mentioned was still in the vicinity of eighty percent. For many a lesser student, it would have been a high mark. For brainy Michael, however, it wasn't. Being the academically intelligent kid that he was, I can surmise that having one of the lowest marks must have been a tough pill to swallow.

Perhaps my recollection of these events suggests I'm drawing a negative caption over Michael. On the contrary. I think it was incredibly ethical of him not to use the cheat test, and I can't help but respect him for that. It really does characterize his integrity. Besides, when I have to face the music, I face it. Dealing with the fallout of the stolen examination questions, however, wasn't a big deal anyway. It is a troubling fact, though, to know that out of roughly sixty grade ten students, there were only a select few, if that, who chose to take the exam on a level playing field. Not that I'm judging anyone. I have no doubts that back then, I was likely the most dishonest of them all. After all, I was the instigator who perpetuated these events. My point is that honesty doesn't seem to come natural with people. In fact, it would be fair to suggest that honesty is an arduous task to maintain throughout one's life. It seems the only difference among us is the level of honesty we are able to maintain. It's simply a matter of perspective. For example, if you have ever knowingly gone over the speed limit in your car, that is dishonest. Yet many who consider themselves to be honest people have certainly been guilty of that infraction. We don't think of this as being dishonest, though; we're just in a hurry. Or if you have ever eaten a grape at the grocery store without paying for it. No big deal, right? It's only one grape. Still, it's stealing, no matter what spin you put on it—like you were only tasting the grape for its sweetness factor to determine if you wanted to buy a bunch. For many people, honesty has a price tag attached to it. If someone offered you a million dollars to steal a candy bar, would you do it? Many would likely commit the same infraction for a lot less, or just to not have to pay for it, but does that make them less honest than the person who would only do it if a million dollars were at stake? I don't believe honesty works on a sliding scale. A study by Robert S. Feldman, a psychologist at the University of Massachusetts Amherst, revealed that sixty percent of adults lie once every ten minutes during a conversation.

As for the algebra exam caper, other than a small number of us having to rewrite the final, there were no further repercussions. I was questioned about the incident, of which I pretended to know nothing and therefore had nothing to say. Perhaps the school's hierarchy wrote off the caper as a simple student prank, one that taught teachers a lesson: Keep exam questionnaires under lock and key! Our algebra teacher, on the other hand, considering that he had to compose a new exam and then spend even more time marking them all over again, was understandably not a happy camper. I'm sure he had better things to do than spend a nice day in July at school, babysitting the few of us while we retook the test. Summer holidays had already begun by this time. I was somewhat curious, however, as to how they came up with a formula deciding who had to retake it and who didn't. On the other hand, Mr. Fadek was an algebra teacher, and mathematical formulas were his specialty. All in all, considering this could have seen me kicked out of school, once again, I got off lucky!

As for my final mark on the algebra retake, other than the fact that I failed, I honestly don't remember. But I do believe Mr. Fadek purposely made the retake exam extra hard. Can't say that I wouldn't have done the same if I were him. Pass, fail...I really didn't care. Perhaps if I had heeded my own advice to the others and not scored too high on the exam, I would have escaped suspicion. Maybe not. Be that as it may, learning algebra had about as much value to me in the real world as knowing that liquid nitrogen boils at -196 degrees centigrade and freezes at -210. Some of us are born to be blue collar workers, and some are born for university and white collar jobs. Society needs both. By this age, I was well aware of where my future ambitions and employment lay.

And Michael? After learning that everyone had found out that he'd spilled the beans about the cheat exam, for fear of getting beat up, rumor had it that Michael was apprehensive about returning for grade eleven. And during the summer—between grade ten and eleven—his family conspicuously moved away. I don't know if it was true or just a stupid rumor, but I did think it was all rather ridiculous and completely blown out of proportion.

CHAPTER

16

Crystal Lake

With the Algebra Exam Caper behind me and yet another school year over, my favorite time of year was at hand: summer holidays! And this wasn't just any summer. This was the summer of 1985. I was sixteen years old and had acquired my driver's license. For a teenage boy growing up in secluded farming country, obtaining one's driver's license was a right of passage. If you didn't have your license, you just weren't cool. Having booked the appointment far in advance, I took my driving test on January 9th; the day I turned sixteen. Completing the test in Mom's little white Chevrolet Chevette standard transmission car, I passed with flying colors.

Turning sixteen was a monumental time in my life, as I'm sure it is with most males and females. I could literally feel my body changing and beginning to fill out in areas I never noticed before. Growing like a weed and gaining approximately twenty pounds of mass that year, my muscles began to develop substantially. Dad said I ate like a horse. My hormones were raging at an astronomical level, thus generating an entirely new perspective on girls. Meanwhile, impulse control was at an all-time low—not that I ever had a whole lot to begin with. This primal state of affairs appropriately reminds me of an old Robin Williams joke I once heard: God gave men enough blood to run either their brain or their penis, not both!

With Mom and Dad still preoccupied with running their thriving reflexology business, they weren't at home a whole lot—a common theme by now. As a consequence of their new enterprise escalating to the point where they couldn't keep up, it began eroding their marriage and our family unit. With Dad abandoning his JW faith altogether, my parents' union—unbeknownst to me at the time—was in shambles, leaving me basically on my own for the entire summer to look after the house, garden, yard, and anything else that popped up. In light of how busy Betty and Bill were, it's interesting that Mom had still found time to plant a huge garden earlier that spring. I had to look after said garden, needless to say. Nevertheless, I loved it…all the freedom that is.

Considering the fact that I had my driver's license, my one complaint is best articulated in the words of my sixteen-year-old self: *It totally sucks not having a car to drive.* Short of taking public transit or hitchhiking meant I was pretty much confined to a pedal bike. Be that as it may, my home WAS in close proximity to Crystal Lake—a two-mile bicycle ride. Therefore, I practically lived at the lake all summer. Unlike most guys my age, I loved to play golf. Back then, the sport hadn't caught on yet with the younger crowd, but for me, I enjoyed the peacefulness of walking through beautifully landscaped fairways. With Crystal Lake having a nice little nine-hole course, I played a considerable amount of golf that season. I even saved up enough money to buy a membership that year. With all that practice, I was parring the course nearly every time—even shooting a couple of games under par. And astonishingly, I did something I never believed was actually possible: a hole in one! Twice, no less, both times on the seventh hole, once with Dad and then once by myself. Playing golf with my dad was quite comical at times—he detested losing. Whenever I beat him on a hole, he'd get all quiet, with this solemn look of discontent embedded into his face. The best part was watching him get all frustrated after making a terrible shot. He'd mumble curse words under his breath and say, in a self-absorbed feeling-sorry-for-himself tone, "I can't golf worth a damn today! Shoulda just stayed home!" There were other words too, but I'll leave those out.

Although I did golf a considerable amount throughout my teenage years, hitting the greens was the perfect cover as to why I would be at the lake all day. Crystal Lake was a popular resort, with cabins and homes encircling the entire lake, and families would come and spend weeks at a time to enjoy their summer vacation. And because many of these families had teenage daughters, it dramatically raised my interest level. This, in turn—given my adjacency to the lake and the opportunist that I instinctually am—led me from ages fifteen through nineteen, to engage in several close friendships and even a few relationships with said females.

Let me just clarify that these teen romances—if I can even call them that—were certainly not the result of me being this irresistibly attractive guy or a Casanova by any means. Sure, I did okay in the looks department and took care of my grooming, etc., and was sociably inclined, but that was about it. My Crystal Lake relationships were entirely based on opportunity and a very simple strategy: realizing that when it comes to meeting girls, as long as you don't come off acting like a complete nincompoop, just about any girl at that age will talk to a boy. That's not to say I never got rejected. I did more times than not, but that never broke my spirit. After all, to me, it was a numbers game; *You win some, and you lose some* was my mentality. I was good at concentrating on the wins and had a short memory for the losses. Truth be told, all any guy needs is an opportunity, and I had plenty where I lived. Most of these encounters were short in length, sometimes a day or two and even just an afternoon, while others lasted up to a month, which is an eternity when you're young. All of this was on the down-low, of course. Dad would have probably kicked me out of the house if he'd known about my assignations with these young ladies. His mentality was that a person shouldn't enter the dating scene until they were looking to get married. Being a hormone-raging teenager, however, I thought that was ridiculous. But now that I'm older, I can understand his reasoning. As Rod Stewart sings, "I wish that I knew what I know now, when I was younger."

* * *

I'll jump ahead three years in my timeline to describe my favorite encounter at Crystal Lake, which was at the opposite end of the relationship scale from what I was used to. It was August of 1988. I was nineteen and did have a car. No, it wasn't a Ferrari, but a 1987 Chevrolet Camaro, a decent sports car nonetheless. Having a car makes an exponentially huge difference when it comes to girls.

Anyway, during the month of August that year, I began spending a considerable amount of time at Black's Beach Resort located on the east side of Crystal Lake. Black was the surname of the man who owned the resort and beach, hence its name. There were two beach areas at Crystal Lake; the west area was known as Johnny's Beach. Want to hazard a guess why I was spending all my time on Black's side of the lake? Her name was Margo! Margo was one of Black's granddaughters, who would come every year to spend an entire month—during summer holidays—at the lake with her family. They were from Winnipeg, Manitoba. I had previous knowledge of Margo from meeting her two years before, when she was fifteen and dated a guy I knew from school.

In 1988, Margo was seventeen and even more filled out than the last time I'd seen her. She was a gorgeous blond with a killer body, and I'm really not exaggerating these details for my benefit—she really was!

As I've identified, Margo was the reason for my hanging out on Black's side of the lake, but I wouldn't have guessed in a million years that I actually had any chance with this girl. As we've already established, I wasn't overconfident by any means when it came to girls. Though my experiences convey the impression I did generally well in that department, it never seemed like it at the time. When around males my age, I was a confident, cocky teenager for sure. But that attitude completely changed around females. I became a soft-spoken, chivalrous romantic, opening doors for them and that sort of thing. Apparently, girls like that kind of guy.

One afternoon, while hanging out with Margo and her cousin, they asked me if I'd give them a ride to the other side of the lake. Apparently, they were bored with always being stuck at their grandpa's. Well, they didn't have to ask me twice. It was only about a mile by car, but I guess the girls didn't feel like walking, or maybe there was more to this than I thought.

We hung out for about an hour on Johnny's Beach, mostly talking about what there was to do around there for fun. I told them about the drive-in theater, which they already knew about, and then disclosed the whereabouts of some nearby towns. Truth is, there really wasn't a whole lot in terms of excitement for people our age, especially for someone like Margo, who hailed from Winnipeg, the capital city of Manitoba, no less. There was a local Friday night party spot dubbed "the foundation" that I informed them about, and they were both suddenly curious about what that entailed. I further explained that "the foundation" was an old, abandoned cement house foundation, minus the structure, located out in the bush about a mile from the Crystal Lake garbage dump. Access to this infamous party spot was north from where the black top ended on Black's side of the lake, after which you turned down a couple of unmaintained old dirt roads. All the local kids would congregate there after dark on Friday nights and build a big bonfire in the bottom of the old basement foundation. We'd sit or stand around the foundation and party with music blasting from whoever had the best car stereo—sometimes it was mine. We'd usually party there until almost dawn. I went on to tell Margo and her cousin that on a good night, there could be as many as fifty kids at the party, so it did get pretty wild at times. The boys in blue would come around occasionally, usually asking yours truly if anything was getting out of hand, but they never did shut us down. Reminiscing about this place reminds me of a popular Jason Aldean song: "Dirt Road Anthem."

I could tell, after describing this place to the girls, they were both equally excited about attending one of these parties. As we drove back to the other side of the lake, Margo asked me if I'd like to take her to the drive-in that evening. "I'd love to!" was my enthusiastic response. She said that permission from her mom was needed first, but she ensured me that it shouldn't be a problem. Margo's mom, however, insisted on meeting me first. Being that I was a clean-cut guy with good manners and a nice car, getting mom's approval was a shoe-in—with the condition that her cousin came with us. Come to think of it, the mother of every girlfriend I ever had adored me. Funny thing about that, if any of them had really known me, I suspect they'd likely have chased me away with a pitchfork.

Somewhere during those few hours with Margo, however, I must have done something right, because she and I became boyfriend and girlfriend after that first date. We spent a considerable amount of time together that month, going for walks, movies, attending a foundation party, and just hanging out at the lake. We held hands and kissed, of course. But surprisingly, we never did become intimate with each other. It's not that our relationship lacked passion by any means, and we certainly had every opportunity if we'd really wanted to. In fact, surprisingly, those thoughts weren't really ever on my mind. Okay, maybe once or twice.

Once summer holidays were coming to their end, however, the time arrived for Margo to leave. It certainly wasn't easy for either of us to let go of what we'd started. She and I had become somewhat connected to each other. That final afternoon, while reluctantly saying our final goodbyes, we sat on a bench facing the lake and held each other tightly. Both of us knowing this was farewell, we barely spoke a word. She was going back to Winnipeg to begin grade twelve, and I needed to search for a job. Sensing the mutual sentiment that our relationship felt like much more than simply a summer romance, neither of us wanted to let go. For at least an hour, with our legs intertwined, the two of us just sat there in each other's arms, with the culmination of emotion welling up between Margo and I perfectly in sync with the waves washing up on shore.

To break up the monotony of sadness, Margo's mom walked up to the beach area and summoned Margo in an irritated tone, telling her to get ready. They were leaving soon. Even though I didn't want to accept it, I knew this was where our fork in the road began and it was time for us to part ways. Upon leaning in to kiss her one last time, I could taste the bittersweet flavor of our tears mixed in with her flavored lip gloss, thus creating a never-forgotten sensation on my palate. With my emotions escalating and becoming far too intense, I needed to leave. Before somehow finding the courage to let go and walk away, however, I whispered in her ear, "It'll be okay." Then, as Margo held on to my left hand, I stood up and pulled away slowly to feel her fingertips gradually slip through my hand.

Not wanting to succumb to the emotions chained up inside me, I hurriedly walked towards the parking lot. I couldn't deny myself one final look, however, and with tears steadily streaming from my eyes, I paused for a moment to gaze back and drink in one last farewell vision of her silhouette sitting on the wooden bench, facing the water. Motionless and silent, with golden-blond hair draped delicately over her shoulders as if frozen in time on a painted canvas, a memory was forever forged.

Upon arriving at my car and listening to music for a few minutes to reflect on our time together, I realized this was the first time in my life that I'd had feelings for a girl without engaging in physical intimacy. And even though I know we both felt it, neither of us ever once said that we loved each other. My experience with Margo—without the distraction of sexual gratification—unknowingly taught me a valuable and mature understanding as to what a meaningful relationship might feel like. That was a first for me, and I liked how it felt. Be that as it may, because of an already prominent pattern of promiscuous behavior, old habits die hard—especially for yours truly.

After waiting in my car for the effects to dissipate from saying goodbye to Margo that afternoon, I locked the shifter into drive, tromped the pedal to the floorboards, and burned a 180 in the sand parking lot—as if to intentionally leave my mark. And with a heavy heart, I headed for home. Margo and I never saw each other or spoke to one another ever again. And to this day, I haven't set foot on Black's Beach since our final farewell.

Cue music: "Young Blood" by The Naked and Famous

https://www.youtube.com/watch?v=0YuSg4mts9E

CHAPTER

17

Red Flags

As I sit at my keyboard, reflecting on the events and the encounters I participated in at Crystal Lake, they almost feel like a set of well-composed fantasies right out of a romance novel. Yet at the time, those wistful acquaintances didn't seem as glorious as they sound or may appear written in a book. It's not until I think about these memories that I am reminded of how wonderful it was to be young, healthy, and full of energy. Not recognizing what a great time it is to be young until we grow up seems to be a common theme among adults. More often than not, it's not until real life begins that we reflect on such memories, often realizing we took them for granted. It's sad, really, that life ends up that way. It kind of makes you want a second chance at being a teenager, or at least being young again.

Once I returned from the hospital after my spinal cord injury, I couldn't count how many times I dreamt of making a full recovery and regaining that same youthful spirit I'd once had. It's interesting how a person's mind can manifest lifelike dreams that seem more vivid than reality itself. In the dream, I would simply decide to get up and walk, and I would. It seemed like such a simple solution. I'd even wake up with the same enthusiasm, only to fade back towards the reality of my situation. Sometimes it felt like the perfect escape, while, other times, it felt like a cruel joke. Apparently, to find oneself walking around in a dream is not uncommon to people who have suffered a spinal cord injury. But regardless of how real the dream may feel, reality is always there waiting when you wake up.

When I first woke up at Chris and Anne's place, where I stayed before moving into the group home, 4th Dimension, I felt a little disoriented, wondering where I was. This, of course, is not unusual either when sleeping for the first night in a new environment. For the most part, my stay with Chris and Anne—before moving into the group home—was awesome! Catering to my every need, they took me to the mall, movies, and out for dinner on a regular basis. Since becoming paralyzed, this was all new to me—rarely did Nicole and I go out in public. While out and about with Chris and Anne, however, I was quick to take notice of how uncomfortable most able-bodied people were around me. When passing people on the street or in a mall, most wouldn't even make eye contact. And the few who did—usually elderly folk—had expressions of pity written all over their faces. Since feeling sorry for me was probably the one sentiment I hated most, that really bothered me. Many times, I had to bite my tongue from saying, *The pity written all over your face is far worse than this injury actually is. So please stop it.*

Little kids, however, were, and remain, my favorites. With no hesitation, they would walk up and start rattling off all sorts of questions: What happened to you? Will you ever get better? How do you drive your wheelchair? Meanwhile, mortified by their child's inquisitive nature, the parents stood by with looks of absolute embarrassment written on their faces. And afterwards, they would apologize profusely. I'm not sure why they were so apologetic. After all, their children were simply asking questions that everyone was wondering anyway. The best, or perhaps most awkward moment for the individual, was when someone would mistakenly reach out to shake my hand. I would smile and respond, "That's why I drive with my chin. My hands don't work." After which, their face would turn fifty shades of red. Yeah, I'm bad, but a guy has to have SOME fun. Over time, I began to enjoy the art of people watching and studying human behavior. Not surprisingly, you can tell a lot about a person just from observing their mannerisms. Even people who knew me before my injury were at odds with what they might say. Perhaps afraid they might offend me by asking how I was doing, many chose to keep their distance. *I'm paralyzed! How do you think I'm doing?"* was likely what they might have feared would be my response. In retrospect, if the situation were reversed, I might have elected to keep my distance as well.

Getting out in public was a major breakthrough in the overall healing process. As a result, I proved to myself that I had adjusted quite well to this new life. No question, I was a different person, and there were a few wrinkles that needed to be worked out. But for the most part, I had returned to the person I was, just modified a little bit from the "walking" Monte. The old gregarious, comical, and often times cocky Monte had come full circle. And it wasn't long before being physically challenged was something I forgot about. No longer looking back at what was lost, my focus shifted to the future and where life might take me. Instead of viewing every activity as something I could no longer participate in, I searched for solutions and found new activities to enjoy. Hellen Keller told us, "Life is either a daring adventure or nothing at all." Being blind and deaf did not inhibit her from living life to the fullest. Why should I allow paralysis to inhibit mine? Finally deciding once and for all to view this new life as an adventure, I adjusted my thinking to acknowledge the challenge of finding enjoyment in the journey. After all, I always did possess a willingness to experience things most people would never dare to. In retrospect, this life has certainly fulfilled that niche of my personality… and then some! Having said that, there were still a couple of obstacles that did occasionally get the best of me.

As a result of living with Chris and Anne, and then of dealing with the hustle and bustle of moving in to the group home, I was conveniently distracted from living apart from my children. The impact didn't hit me until my first evening alone at the group home. So far, I'd managed to soldier through being paralyzed from the neck down, losing nearly everything I owned, and saying goodbye to the woman I once loved more than life itself, and I'd come out on the other side with a smile on my face. Most days, that is. However, being disconnected from my daughters while taking up residence in an assisted living facility among strangers was an aspect of this new life that I wasn't prepared for. Consequently, the dark shadow that had seemingly been cast over my life suddenly became dauntingly inescapable. That very first evening at the group home, I can remember sitting next to my bed as the sudden urge to weep uncontrollably began to suffocate me. Quite frankly, I don't know that a worse living nightmare could have been scripted, other than the one that caused all this in the first place. This adjustment was seemingly a tad more than I could bear.

* * *

Fortunately, I envisioned an eventual escape from this reality, one that didn't allow my mood to wander too far towards the depths of depression. After our acreage sold, Nicole and I split the proceeds fifty-fifty. This was more than enough for a healthy down payment on a small house in Calgary. In other words, get the heck out of this place, which I thought would have been my refuge. Sure, it had helped me bridge the gap from losing my wife, being more or less estranged from my children, and having to give up my dream home, but there had to be more to it than saying, *Well, here I am. Now what?* For me, acquiescing to this group home, once I lived there, was like throwing in the towel for good and limiting the possibilities of functioning in the outside world again. With that mindset, I focused on using the opportunity to become more independent and saw the group home for what it was: the perfect transitional bridge to living independently. Besides, after getting acquainted with a couple of the residents and nursing staff, I soon realized the group home wasn't half bad. With my own private suite, a perfectly situated desk to accommodate my computer, a wall-mounted television, and a pullout sofa for my daughters to sleep on when they visited, I had everything I needed. Of course, being Monte, there was also a certain female who helped brighten my mood considerably as well.

While living with Chris and Anne, they were kind enough to set their computer up for me to use. Around that same time, one of the girls I had often chatted with online from CareCure was becoming of certain interest to me. Her name was Priscilla; she was twelve years my junior, and she was quite beautiful. Paralyzed from the waist down, her injury was significantly lower than mine, and therefore, she had use of her upper body, arms, and hands. But the major obstacle between us was that she lived in the United States, in Texas, no less—not exactly a short road trip away. As is so often the case when two people become romantically involved online, we really wanted to meet in person. Accordingly, deciding it was probably easier for her to fly to Canada, we set a date and booked the flight. Fortunately, the group home was gracious enough to allow Priscilla to stay with me in my room.

Considering that I'd been in a committed relationship for the past twelve years, however, my dating repertoire had become a tad rusty. As a consequence, picking Priscilla up from the airport had to be the most nerve-racking experience I had ever encountered—while dating, that is. Nevertheless, after one look into those gorgeous, big green eyes of hers, suddenly, just like riding a bicycle, it all came back to me. A memorable moment during our time together in Calgary occurred while on a stroll through Confederation Park—a stone's throw from the group home. We were sitting side by side in front of the duck pond when Priscilla reached over and held my hand. This was the first time since my injury that a female had touched me in such a way. Although I couldn't feel her physical touch, to my delight, the warm sensation of affection was still dominantly perceptible. Surprisingly, I could feel the emotion that her touch produced. In turn, I learned a valuable lesson in regard to physical intimacy. Understandably, because we were both paralyzed—I more than her—the act of physical intimacy was determinately minimal. Yet to my surprise, it didn't seem to detract from our relationship. In fact, it drew us closer. Through words and a strong mental connection, we discovered new non-physical ways of expressing and satisfying amorous emotions. That was when I first began to recognize how powerful and adaptive the human mind truly is. After often wondering if I would ever again be able to experience the pleasure and passion that went with making love, Priscilla's heartfelt embraces gave me optimism.

The two of us spent nearly every moment of that entire week together, and it was a period of time that I never wanted to end. Unfortunately, as uncontrollable as destiny can be, future circumstances would have us headed off in separate directions. As a result, shortly after that paradisiacal encounter with Pricilla, we amicably parted ways. Our time together, however, was of great benefit in helping us individually adjust mentally to our new lives. Becoming trusted confidants, we were able to express freely to one another about the loss and hardship of dealing with our injuries—a mental activity that served us both well. We also thought it was rather serendipitous how our injuries had occurred exactly seven months apart—not that I believed in that sort of thing. If nothing else, knowing we were still desirable to the opposite sex was an encouraging byproduct of our romantic friendship.

While living in the group home, Danielle would often have weekend sleepovers with me. Nicole would drop her off on Friday after school and pick her up on Sunday afternoon. Haylee was a little too young for that yet. Danielle and I would go for walks in the park and feed the ducks breadcrumbs, play games on the computer together, and go for rides on my wheelchair. But our favorite thing to do was watch sappy movies together. Danielle's most treasured motion picture was *Titanic*. She'd sit on my lap, feeding me popcorn and wiping the tears from my eyes with a Kleenex—after wiping her own. She's a softy as well.

* * *

During my getting comfortable at the group home, Nicole purchased a house in Calgary with one of her sisters. There were seven siblings in her family: four girls and three boys. She was the second youngest. Nicole and I, having parted ways amicably, began, over the course of the next few months, confiding in each other. After being married and having two children together, I would suspect that was normal. While conversing one evening, she disclosed the particulars of a date she'd gone on with a guy—her first since we'd parted—and how, over the course of their date, she'd noticed something was awry with the fellow's posture; instead of simply turning his neck to look at something, he'd turned his entire body. Nicole, not afraid to ask awkward questions, enquired about his abnormality. As it turned out, the young man had recently broken his neck and had three vertebrae fused together just like I did, though he wasn't paralyzed. Considering the irony, the two of us couldn't help but find the situation conspicuously amusing. After all, what are the odds that the first guy she dated after me had also suffered a broken neck?

After regrouping and putting her own life back on track, Nicole would also become a more regular visitor. As a result, we came to realize that there were still strong feelings of love between us, and we decided to give our relationship another try. To say that I was excited about the prospect of her and I working things out and staying married would have been an understatement. I was ecstatic! Eventually, if all went well, our long-term plan was to buy a bungalow together with a suite in the basement that would accommodate a live-in caregiver. But for the time being, we were taking things slow and being cautious. In the meantime, Nicole enrolled in the nursing program at Mount Royal College. Getting her nursing degree seemed like the logical career choice, and I was very proud of her.

A fellow quadriplegic, Jason—whom I had befriended while in the hospital—invited us to his house for a New Year's Eve 2001 bash. In the spirit of the festivities, I rented a nice hotel room for Nicole and me to spend the night after the party. Having talked about it beforehand, this was going to be the first time since my injury that she and I would attempt physical intimacy together. Accordingly, I wanted to make the occasion as special as possible. I even had a caregiver pick us up at Jason's place and take us to the hotel, where he assisted me with getting into bed. When we're able-bodied, we don't think about the process of retiring for the night or timing it: We simply undress and slip into our nightwear, or nothing at all, lie down, and pull the covers over us. When you're paralyzed, it's a process that with somebody's assistance, takes about twenty minutes or more. Although I was certainly excited about the possibility of experiencing this milestone with her, at the same time, I was somewhat uncertain of what might or might not happen. Normally, I wouldn't be apprehensive about such proceedings, but considering the circumstances—being paralyzed—this was different...very different!

When it was over, I wasn't sure how to feel. Without sensation, the experience left me both confused and annoyed. Nicole seemed to enjoy herself, however. Through no fault of hers, I was left feeling like a water balloon that didn't break after just being thrown at someone. And being a typical man, of course, I wasn't prepared to talk about it either. Instead, I lay there waiting for the frustration to eventually subside and went to sleep, hoping maybe next time it would be like the good old days and I'd have my own release. Of all the obstacles there was to conquer in regard to my injury, I never would have guessed sex would be such a difficult one.

* * *

When spring of 2001 arrived, feeling comfortable with giving our marriage a second attempt, we embarked on the lofty endeavor of finding a place for us to live. Our plan, once we found a suitable bungalow with an acceptable basement suite, was to renovate the home and make everything accessible for my wheelchair. Then, while Nicole attended nursing school, I'd stay home with the nanny/caregiver and raise our children—a complete role reversal. Nonetheless, it was an adventure I was looking forward to. Considering their attitude toward me after I became paralyzed, all of this was met with heavy protest by the majority of Nicole's family. We were on our own. After enduring an entire day of driving around and looking at multiple properties, the ideal bungalow was a block from where the girls were going to school—half a block from where Nicole was currently living. Located in the mostly family-oriented district of Southwood—about twenty minutes from downtown—it was considered inner city. Coincidently, it was also the very first property we viewed that day. The home was owned by an elderly woman who'd recently lost her husband. And thanks to our realtor, we were able to purchase the property $10,000 below market value. With a private, self-contained one-bedroom suite in the basement and three bedrooms with an ensuite on the main floor, all within our meager budget, this place couldn't have been more perfect. Life was good!

After taking possession of the house, I took advantage of living at the group home and used the opportunity to have the home completely renovated—making everything wheelchair accessible being front and center. This included raising the sunken entrance and building a permanent ramp up to the front door, widening the hallway and doorways, creating a barrier-free shower, designing and constructing a customized desk for my computer, and expanding the exterior walkways to accommodate a wheelchair. Fortunately, because of my extensive background in home renovation, I was able to design and draw blueprints on the computer for the entire project and be my own general contractor. This saved us a substantial amount of money. Two brothers, Frank and Tony, one of the builders I used to subcontract with, pitched in to help with the demolition and framing. Considering my picky attitude, when it came to interior woodworking, I was pleased when Peter Issler offered his services to handle the finishing carpentry for me. Being the best carpenter I knew, Peter's willingness to complete the woodworking was a considerable relief. Taking into account a huge falling out we'd had five years earlier, Pete's gesture was a humbling experience for me.

By August 15, 2001, the house was ready. Moving out of the group home had to be the happiest day of my disabled life so far. This is not to say that it was a horrible place to live. On the contrary! Living at 4th Dimension was a pleasant and helpful experience. I met some wonderful and compassionate people during my eleven-month stay there. Some of them I'm still friends with to this day. The independence of living in my own home, though, with my children, was where my happiness rested. Besides, for a person with my mindset and disposition, permanent life in a group home would have been a psychological death sentence. In the spirit of not wanting Nicole involved with any of my personal care, I took advantage of the opportunity of having lived in the midst of several professional caregivers and hired the part-time services of three people who worked at 4th Dimension. For the remainder of my needs, we hired a live-in nanny, who took up residence in our basement suite. Her name was Nikkita. She was of Eastern European heritage and had a ten-year-old daughter, Kimberly, who lived with her as well.

Although everything appeared as if it were falling perfectly in to place, there was something very unsettling about this situation. After interviewing several candidates for the nanny position, I was surprised that Nicole's first choice was Nikkita, a twenty-nine-year-old attractive blond ex-model and showgirl—one of her previous occupations had been as the scantily clad girl who holds up the board at boxing matches indicating which round it is. Nikkita was the best interviewee, of course: She was immaculately groomed, appeared well put together, and had previous nanny experience. But in light of the fact that Nicole would be attending nursing school all day while I was left alone with the attractive nanny, the decision was completely out of character for my wife. Normally, she would have been extremely jealous in this type of situation. Surprisingly, Nicole didn't even bat an eye. It wasn't that I ever thought an attractive, able-bodied girl would be interested in me—a quadriplegic. Quite honestly, as hard as it may be to believe, the thought never even crossed my mind. My sole focus was on keeping our family together. Nevertheless, in regard to our marriage, it proved to be the first red flag of danger being waved at me.

After a couple of weeks went by, we all settled into our designated roles. Danielle, by now seven years old, was attending grade two. Haylee, four, was home during the day with me. Nicole attended nursing school, and I was busy with my *MXP* magazine writing assignments. A typical weekday would consist of a caregiver coming in at 7:00 AM to get me up while Nicole looked after our daughters and then left for classes. Once I was finally up and finished my morning routine of eating breakfast and keeping Haylee occupied, it was time to start thinking about what to prepare for lunch. Danielle walked home the brief distance from school during the noon break. Having her split up my day like that was something I actually enjoyed. Mornings, by far, were the most hectic. The remainder of the day was spent looking after Haylee, instructing our nanny on what chores to do, and having dinner cooked and on the table by 5:00 PM. I was your typical stay-at-home dad. I was loving life!

Nicole, who had to get up at 6:00 AM every school morning, would be exhausted by day's end. We soon learned that going back to school wasn't quite as easy when you're thirty-two years old and raising two young daughters. Throw in one parent who was severely disabled, and it wasn't by any means a walk in the proverbial park, not to mention constantly living in and around caregivers and a nanny all day long. Personally, I was handling the situation quite well. Nicole, on the other hand, not so much. Nevertheless, for the first month, everything appeared to run smoothly. That is, until I tried to initiate said husband-and-wife activities. Despite the enjoyable tryst in the hotel room on New Year's Day, my wife now wanted no part of it. I understand that she was probably exhausted, but I waited until the weekend and even let her sleep in on Saturday morning—I wasn't completely insensitive. Now I had two warning flags waving in the back of my mind. In the spirit of wanting to confront this situation before it progressed, one day in early October Nicole and I had a heart-to-heart talk. That was when she revealed that her love for me had evaporated and she wanted to separate—but not in the traditional sense. She wanted to set up a bedroom for herself in the other half of our basement and move downstairs. Meanwhile, we would maintain our current living arrangements—without husband and wife stuff, of course. Although heartbroken, I was still desperate to keep our family together, so I reluctantly agreed to her request.

After about a week of living with this new arrangement, which clearly wasn't working for me, my emotions began to spill over into anger. Which, admittedly, made our situation worse. Pretending we were just friends while watching her come and go as she pleased, all the while wondering if another man might be involved, was driving me to madness. I soon came to the realization that living under the same roof with my wife, who I still deeply loved, while she was with someone else was something I just couldn't bear. I'm not implying she was, but the thought of it was painful enough. Living away from my children didn't seem any less painful. Besides, where would I go? The group home filled my bed the day after I moved out. And an old age facility—as I stated earlier—would be nothing short of a mind-numbing death sentence. On top of that, I'd used up every cent of my lifetime disability allowance and all the government grants available on renovating our house. Therefore, buying another house wasn't, and likely never would be, an option, which meant that if I stayed in the house, my children, who had just finally settled into their new home—a block from school, no less—had to once again become uprooted and move. No part of me wanted them to go through that again, and I didn't have the means to raise them on my own. If that wasn't bad enough, because Nicole had spent the majority of her cash helping to purchase our house, having to move meant a huge financial loss for her as well. Every scenario seemed inescapably hopeless.

After looking closely at the situation and mulling it over in my head for several days, the problem solver in me came up with a justifiable answer. In living up to the sentiment of loving my family more than life itself, this answer seemed like an appropriate choice. I reasoned that the only formula that made any sense for anyone was to take me out of the equation. My family could remain uninterrupted in the house, and I wouldn't have to suffer with living apart from them. Nicole, being an attractive girl, would surely find a decent, able-bodied man to fill my place. And my children, being young enough, would likely get over my absence fairly quickly. After all, I never missed my biological father after my parents split up. All I needed was to figure out how a quadriplegic might go about doing such a thing—as painlessly as possible, of course. My only concern at this point was whether or not being separated from my daughters was something I could bear—even in death.

Cue music: "Looking too Closely" by Fink

https://www.youtube.com/watch?v=qoWRs7lXtYE

CHAPTER

18

Opportunity Comes Knocking

After the summer holidays of 1985 came to an end, I entered grade eleven. By this time, while continuing with high school, I was basically living on my own at home. With Mom residing in Saskatoon, three hours away, and Dad in Regina, also three hours away—a recipe for disaster in any marriage—my parents drifted even further apart. I'd see Dad on most weekends, but Mom rarely came home anymore. Therefore, going to school was becoming a struggle, and I began losing interest completely. It was quite obvious that virtually everything we were learning at this point would be useless to me in the real world. The majority of it was an introduction to post-secondary education, and knowing that university certainly wasn't my destination, the only things keeping me in school were volleyball, badminton, and my friends. Even though I did want to graduate, the next two years hardly seemed worth it. I was hanging on by a thread.

There was one favorable aspect of living on my own at home during grade eleven: I was given the freedom of choosing my own groceries. This, in turn, afforded me the luxury of electing what to have for school lunches. Unlike when Mom was in charge of that department, I finally had some decent snacks for lunch every day.

As a consequence, however, one of my close friends at school was constantly asking for part of my dessert—the best part—everyday. Kevin, the kid I'd punched in grade eight, was my lunch-scavenging friend that year. Being the type of guy who has a hard time saying no to a friend, I was getting frustrated with continually giving a portion of my lunch away every day. Now I knew how the kid I'd stolen lunches from in grade five must have felt—funny how some things in life end up coming full circle back to us—which kind of makes me feel guilty for what I did next. After getting sick and tired of putting up with reluctantly giving part of my lunch away on a daily basis, I decided it was time to fix Kevin's little red wagon. In a manner of speaking, I was going to flush this problem down the proverbial toilet once and for all. On the way home that day, I bought a package of chocolate Ex-Lax from the store, and then I melted it down. After finding Mom's candy-making trays in the shapes of fish, teddy bears, and whatnot, I poured the melted chocolate laxative into them. I let them cool and then packaged them up into a nice little baggy for Kevin. Sure enough, the following day, along came my unsuspecting lunch-scavenging friend, asking me for another handout. I enthusiastically offered him my chocolate treats. "Here, Kevin, I'm too full and don't think my stomach can handle these chocolates. You have them" is precisely what I said. Kevin, eager to accept such a generous handout, gobbled them up before I even had a chance to feel remorseful. Now normally, when an individual is feeling as if things might be moving a tad slow in that particular area, one of these chocolates would suffice, but my hungry friend ate all eight of them. As a result, Kevin wasn't at school the next day. Coincidently, he never asked me for food ever again. I love it when a plan comes together!

* * *

Near the beginning of March that same year, with the volleyball and badminton season all sewn up, I'd finally had enough—of school, that is. Four months shy of finishing grade eleven—I quit high school. One would assume that leaving a secondary education behind would be a scary thing to do—especially with no real prospects lined up as far as employment was concerned—but at the tender age of seventeen, I was ready for the real world…or so I thought. These days, not having a high school diploma puts one at a serious disadvantage, but back then, you could still cut it without a scroll of paper. If you were good at reinventing yourself, a quick study, and resourceful—which I believed I was—you had a chance to still make something of yourself. Even though I wasn't the quitter type, it really wasn't a big deal for me to quit school and never look back. Dad, however, was furious and made it clear that if I wasn't going to school, then there was no way I was living at home. That didn't seem unreasonable. Quite frankly, I'd expected as much. That was simply his way of attempting to keep me in school, but there wasn't any possibility of that happening. Once my mind was made up, there wasn't much chance of anyone changing it, even if it meant getting kicked out from home. Besides, in anticipation of Dad's reaction, I'd already made plans to move in with my cousin Kimberly and her boyfriend Dwayne. They lived just down the block from us in Tadmore. For the time being, I took a room in their basement that they were kind enough to let me rent for free!

Being the calculated strategist that I am, and was, one would assume I must have had some sort of stratagem laid out for myself. After all, it seems rather short-sighted to simply quit school and move into a cousin's basement with, other than the occasional odd job here and there, no financial assistance. Truth is, I didn't have a game plan. A positive attitude and a hardworking spirit combined with the genuine conviction that something would eventually turn up was my only solidarity. Surprisingly, I wasn't wrong. After barely a month of being a basement dweller, opportunity came knocking. Dad came home to Tadmore one weekend in April and asked me to come over to the house for a chat. I had no idea what he wanted and was somewhat skeptical of what this "chat" entailed. I was expecting a long lecture about the importance of staying in school, which, quite frankly, I didn't want to hear. Nevertheless, after deciding to indulge myself and listen to Dad's torturous lecture, I was completely in disbelief of what happened next. He sat me down and offered me a job. He wanted ME to run the Canora reflexology clinic. I was speechless! All I could think was *Really? Me working on people's stinky feet every day?* When deciding to quit school, that hadn't exactly been the dream job I'd had in mind.

Over the years, since Dad began studying reflexology, he would always get me to work on his feet—in other words, give him a reflexology treatment. While I would do this, Dad was, in effect, teaching me everything there was to know about reflexology in terms of technique, pressure points, and mapping of the feet in correlation to each body part. Dad eventually became certified to teach reflexology. Over time, I started giving treatments to Mom as well. By this time in my life, I had logged a considerable number of hours in reflexology experience just from working on my parents' feet. Apparently, I was quite good at it too. Mom even went so far as to say that I was better than Dad, but he didn't like hearing that very much. Personally, I always believed she said that simply to get him to do a better job on her feet—it wasn't unusual for Dad to be somewhat distracted by watching a hockey game while he worked on Mom's feet.

The offer Dad made me was a very reasonable and attractive proposal. Basically, I got to keep every cent the clinic made...after overhead expenses. Being that my employment compass wasn't pointing towards any future job prospects whatsoever—and given that my current residence was my cousin's basement—I figured why not give this a shot. I accepted the job offer. What I didn't know, however, was the sorry state of affairs the Canora clinic was in. One of the things I really loved about Dad was that he always saw everything with a glass-half-full type of attitude. Sometimes, though, he saw the glass being half full when, really, it was bone dry. I didn't know it yet, but this was definitely one of those times.

I moved back home, and Dad rounded up a vehicle for me to drive back and forth to work every day. One of my parents' employees was driving a company vehicle 1974 Ford Elite, but the transmission was in the early stages of failure, so dad parked it. Nevertheless, I knew this old clunker—a very cool car in its day, based on the Ford Torino—would suffice for the time being. Other than the fact that the vehicle felt like you were driving a boat down the road, and one of the doors alone weighed as much as a Smart Car, it handled like a Cadillac on the highway. Problem was, it burned fuel as if there was a hole in the gas tank too. For the first week—being convinced there had to be a hole in the fuel tank—I kept looking under the car, checking for a puddle of gasoline. There was no leak. The car was simply a beast when it came to fuel consumption.

My first day on the job, I met George, a thirty-something registered massage therapist who was from Czechoslovakia—the country would later split into the Czech Republic and Slovakia. In addition to reflexology, clients had the option of a massage. That was George's department. I looked after the feet. Wearing a white smock over a dress shirt and a pair of dress pants, I looked and played the part quite well. It seemed acting professionally came natural to me somehow. And with a little creativity, I came up with a solution for the stinky feet dilemma as well. After buying the perfect-sized basin and some strongly scented soap, I filled the basin with warm water and had every client soak their feet for ten minutes before I started. My explanation was that the warm water softened their feet and made the treatment more effective. My reasoning wasn't completely untruthful, and it beat telling them the real reason. In essence, I was washing everyone's feet.

Whenever Dad drove home for the weekend from Regina, we'd hang out, going fishing or golfing. Guy stuff. One weekend, while we were golfing at Crystal Lake Golf Course, he made a terrible tee shot, and then, out of frustration, the F-word came bursting from his mouth. Quite honestly, it startled me. Up until then, I had never heard him say that word before. I had seen him get plenty angry on numerous occasions—usually at me—but that type of profanity was never part of his repertoire. What further had me wondering about Dad was that he paid George, our massage therapist, under the table. It was around this time I began to notice my father was no longer the same man who'd raised me. His personality was different, and his morals had started to slide. Bill had changed. Considering I wasn't the most stand-up guy in the room, I certainly had no right to judge him. I kept my observations of the new Bill to myself, but to be perfectly honest, I liked my old dad better.

* * *

My first week of working at the clinic—concluding it was a good opening line to stir up interest—I spent every spare moment phoning old clients to introduce myself as the owner's son and the new reflexologist, only to learn that the majority of these clients were very dissatisfied with the service they received. I began to see what the problem was. The people my parents had left in charge to run this location didn't have a personal interest invested to care enough about doing their job properly. Clients were complaining about not getting proper treatments. These same clients had received reflexology from my mom and dad, so they knew what a legitimate treatment felt like, not to mention the results and benefits that would be missing from a mediocre treatment. As a result, many of these clients were quite upset, vowing never to return. I had my work cut out for me. To make matters worse, one of the reflexologists my mom had trained opened up her own clinic in the same town. In essence, she'd learned the trade while working for us and then opened her own business and stolen our clients. It was a pretty clever idea, really—have to give her an A for effort. Can't say that wasn't something I might have thought of myself. The only problem with her plan: There wasn't enough business for both of us to survive, especially with all the dissatisfied clients from previous lackadaisical, couldn't-care-less, employees my parents had hired to run their business. Nevertheless, I was giving this reflexology thing an earnest effort, and within a couple of weeks, my clientele began to mildly increase. Somehow, I had a natural inclination when it came to running a business. I paid the rent, took care of all the bills and expenses, washed sheets and towels at home every night, and even completed the janitorial services within the establishment. I was running the place all by my lonesome. The money wasn't great, but like Dad, I had high hopes.

The old 1974 Ford Elite I was driving back and forth to work, however, was beginning to show signs of unreliability. One evening, while driving home from Grandma's house after her kindly feeding me dinner, I noticed the transmission beginning to slip—a problem both Dad and I already knew existed. Nevertheless, as long as I didn't accelerate too abruptly, the beast was getting me to and from work every day—for now.

Within the first month of taking over the business, it became quite apparent that there simply were not enough clients to justify paying

George by the hour. Therefore, instead of laying him off, I offered George a client-based pay schedule, which he quickly realized meant he would be taking a significant pay cut. Consequently, he declined my offer and quit, which, quite honestly, was the outcome I was hoping for. Because the majority of my clients just wanted reflexology anyway, and with George costing me more than he was bringing in, I really wasn't risking anything. Besides, with Mom having studied and taken various courses throughout her life on different massage techniques, she'd taught me plenty over the years. I was confident enough to perform the odd massage here and there myself if need be. Accordingly, I was convinced this was a smart business decision

Being only seventeen, however, it certainly felt a little weird when women would get fully naked on the massage table. I'll never forget one particular experience. She was a regular client who always got "the works": foot and full-body massage. If I had to guess, this gal was likely in her early thirties and somewhat attractive for what I considered then to be an older woman. Upon walking into the massage room for the first time, there she was, lying on her stomach COMPLETELY nude. *No problem! I can handle this*, I said to myself. After working my magic on the backside of her body, I instructed the well-proportioned lady to turn over, placed two clean towels on the table—thinking she'd use them to cover her breasts and privates—and left the room for a moment, allowing her some privacy to do so. Returning after about two minutes, I walked in the room only to find her, once again, lying totally nude on the massage table with the twins pointing straight up. Without skipping a beat, I confidently proceeded with no hesitation or nervousness whatsoever and simply did what I knew how to do. Then, after completing her front side and announcing as much, the nude woman pleasantly voiced her affirmation by saying, "You have the most amazing hands of any masseuse I've ever had." To which I replied, "Well, thank you. It was my pleasure."

I'd be lying if I said that experience didn't lighten my day. And to hear a woman compliment me, well, that felt pretty good for my ego as well. Not that I needed any encouragement by any means. Coming for weekly massages and never missing an appointment, the perky-breasted lady became a regular client of mine. In case you're wondering, nothing ever happened between us. Our relationship was strictly professional, with no sexual undertones with regard to my massaging her. She was a married woman, and call me old-fashioned, but being older and supposedly much wiser, I would have to say that I most certainly would not want my wife getting a nude massage from anyone...but me.

* * *

The next dilemma to challenge my enthusiasm was the transmission in my car. As expected, it was becoming intermittently more unreliable, to the point where I finally had to drive all the way home in first gear one Friday after work—the transmission would slip in any higher gear. It took me an hour to drive fifteen miles. Fortunately, I didn't get a ticket for driving too slow, which I'm sure would have been a first for a policeman too: a teenager not speeding. The one good thing is that Dad was coming home that weekend. I didn't know it yet, but he and Mom had discussed and agreed to help get me a new car. The plan was that Dad was taking me to Yorkton that weekend to help me pick out some new wheels. How's that for timing? He'd co-sign a loan with me, assisting me to buy a new car. Dad was excited for sure with what I'd done so far in terms of mildly increasing business at the clinic. And being the eternal optimist that he was, he had exceedingly high expectations of what the future held for me there in Canora.

When Mom was running the Canora clinic, she was netting over five K a month. In 1986, $5,000 a month was a healthy paycheck for anyone, especially in a little town like Canora, Saskatchewan.

That Saturday, Dad and I drove to Yorkton, and being that Dad was a Ford man through and through, we headed straight for Royal Ford—the number one Ford dealership in Yorkton. At first, I was thinking modestly and speculated a Ford Tempo would suffice, as it was cheap, reliable, and easy on fuel. I took one for a drive, and it was okay but gutless, doing a quarter mile in ten minutes instead of ten seconds. Then, after seeing the unimpressed look on my face, the salesman said, "I have the perfect car for you, and it just so happens it's on sale." The car was driven by another salesman as a demo, so it only had about five thousand kilometers on it. We took it for a drive, and yeah, this particular automobile was DEFINITELY more my style. It was nothing less than a Mustang Cobra GT, charcoal gray, with a five-speed short-shift manual transmission and a V8 302 fuel-injected motor. It even had T-tops! The thing was literally a race car. In 1986, this particular automobile was, other than the Chevrolet Corvette, the fastest North American factory-built muscle car on the market.

Problem was, I only had a grand to offer as a down payment, which wasn't typically sufficient to secure a car loan back then. But dear old Dad, being the smooth talker he was, negotiated with the salesman to write up a deal where I'd give them $1,000 as a down payment and another ten thousand dollars within six months. The dealership would then carry the debt for me until I paid the ten-K balloon payment, allowing me to finance the balance as if the balloon payment had been made at the time of purchase. This would make my car payments more affordable. I wouldn't have been able to afford the payments on the full loan otherwise. Back then, the best interest rate you could get on a car loan was ten to twelve percent, which would have made my payments in the neighborhood of six hundred a month. Money wasn't cheap to borrow like it is today. We wrote up the proposal in the salesman's office, after which, the dealership owner had to sign off on it before the car was mine. Never imagining in a million years this was going to pan out, I went outside and started looking at Ford Tempos again while we waited for an answer.

Meanwhile, Dad went into the owner's office to have a chat with him. After sharing a solid business relationship that dated back over ten years from when Dad was selling cars, he knew the owner quite well. This obviously improved my chances of this working out. About fifteen minutes later, Dad came outside, and as long as I live, I'll never forget what happened next. He walked over to where I was scouting the endless supply of Ford Tempos they had on the lot and said, "Would you rather drive a Tempo?" I laughed and replied, "No! I'd rather drive that Mustang, but there's no way they're going to agree to this deal, so I'm just being realistic." Dad looked at me, smiled, and said, "You should have more faith in your Dad, then, because they approved the deal for you on the Mustang. But if you'd rather drive a Ford Tempo, I'm okay with that. Personally, though, I think you'd look pretty good driving that Mustang."

While walking briskly—I wanted to run—back to the office to sign on the dotted line, I was imagining in my mind the fun I'd have with that car and the girls...all the girls! What teenage girl can resist a bad boy in a hot car? I was on cloud nine all day after that, with a permanent smile etched into my face for about a week. I went to sleep at night with a smile, only to wake up in the morning, look in the mirror, and see the same smile permanently molded onto my face. How could I not? I was a seventeen-year-old high school dropout driving a brand spanking new Mustang Cobra with a racing engine. I'd pinch myself sometimes just to make sure this wasn't a dream.

http://montejperepelkin.com/photos-8

As the perfect celebratory ending to an awesome day, during the drive home from Yorkton in my new car, Dad suggested stopping in for a round of golf at the Canora golf course. Upon arrival, we went inside to pay our green fees. Then, on our way toward the tee-off spot, this attractive female walked by. She was probably about twenty-five and wasn't wearing a bra under her excessively tight t-shirt. Being the hormone-raging teen I was, it was hard for me not to stare. I couldn't help noticing that Dad witnessed this woman's chesticles as well. Cognizant that we'd both observed this woman's indiscreet appearance, an awkward moment ensued. That was until Dad cracked a huge smile and said to me, "It's normal for a man to notice things like that, son. But when you look, remember that it's like looking at the sun. If you stare, it will burn your eyes." Hey, perhaps that's why I needed glasses in grade eight.

To be sure I understood his metaphor. Dad then went into a brief conversation about the whole attraction element and man-versus-woman instincts that we all have. It was interesting, really, to hear his perspective on the matter. I thought a lot about Dad's analogy afterward and concluded that he had a healthy, intelligent view on the matter. Basically, it's natural to look at and be attracted to the opposite sex. If you dwell there for too long, however, your thoughts soon lead to desires that become difficult to control. Dad was right that it's a normal instinct to notice, and let's face it, every guy looks even if it's just a glance. It's like radar in our brains, and I don't know that it can be turned off. Fact is, as long as there are women who find it necessary to adorn themselves provocatively in public, unfortunately, that's the world we're forced to live in. Perhaps if women realized the type of nasty thoughts some men are capable of, that would persuade most of them to reconsider their attire. Because, rest assured, the thoughts that most men are capable of are not innocent little whimsical fantasies. Besides, even as a teenager, I certainly would not have wanted my girlfriend to dress in such a manner. Not in public.

CHAPTER

19

Mustang Monte

A few weeks after procuring my new set of wheels, I decided to go to Crystal Lake Drive-In to meet with some friends, and my cousin Candace caught a ride with me. She was meeting some friends as well. Crystal Lake Drive-In was an infamous party place for teenagers during the summer months. Back in the mid-1970s, this little drive-in even made national news because of a riot that broke out between the police and a bunch of rowdy partygoers. I remember hearing about the incident when I was a kid. What made this venue so popular was its unique location, being situated smack-dab in the center of four different school districts: Canora, Norquay, Sturgis, and Preeceville were all within roughly a twenty-minute drive. It also was the only operating drive-in theater for at least a hundred miles, making this place the ultimate carousing and party destination. It wasn't uncommon for the younger generation to be walking around, partying during the entire set of movies. Showing courtesy, so as not to disturb the people who were there to actually watch the movie, we'd usually park in the back rows. However, if you were there to party, then that meant you smuggled alcohol through the gate. On any given weekend evening, there'd be cars lined up halfway around the lake, waiting to get into this venue. The boys in blue would sit at the entrance, checking every car that entered for contraband, but they weren't very thorough. I simply removed my spare tire, thus leaving the compartment empty and making it the perfect hiding spot for smuggling alcohol.

After the evening's festivities came to a conclusion around 2:00 AM, Candace and I hopped in my Mustang and began our two-mile journey home. Knowing that I had to drive, my alcohol consumption for the entire evening had consisted of two beers; therefore, my ability to operate a vehicle certainly wasn't impeded by any means. I was tired and ready for bed, perhaps, but fully cognizant of my surroundings. Taking the closest route home, I was traveling west on the narrow two-lane paved road, approaching the bridge that crossed the Assiniboine River, about a mile from Tadmore. Candace was sitting next to me in the passenger seat. Being somewhat elevated from the road, there was a rather sharp incline leading up to and away from the bridge. The bridge itself was only about seventy-five feet long, but it was elevated enough that you couldn't see the road on the other side until you were on the deck of the bridge. And because it was somewhat abrupt, most people would slow to about 50 km/h and ease over the incline. However, with my driving behavior gravitating towards fearless and reckless, I discovered that if I hit the approach of the bridge at precisely 130 km/h, I could smoothly and perfectly jump my Mustang from one end to the other. Attempting this little stunt in any other vehicle would be suicide, but this was a sports car with fairly rigid suspension and could therefore handle the g-out on landing—according to my reasoning anyway. In mid-flight, my car was only about a foot off the ground, but it felt a lot higher. Upon reflection, I do realize that if my calculations had been off even slightly, that crazy maneuver could have, at the very least, destroyed the front end of my precious little Ford muscle car.

At any rate, I approached the bridge at my usual 130 km/h while my cousin Candace—somewhat intoxicated—sat in the passenger seat next to me. This is where things got a tad eerie, and just thinking about it has the hairs on the back of my neck standing up. Right when the car landed smoothly on the decline of the bridge deck, I couldn't believe what the headlights of my Mustang suddenly revealed to my field of vision. Sitting right smack dab in the middle of the road, roughly fifty feet in front of me, was a large concrete culvert—the size of my car! Any sleepiness I might have previously felt was instantly converted to a state of absolute readiness. However, traveling 130 km/h meant I had less than half a second to react. To this day, I'm not sure how, but without panicking, I instinctually took evasive action and simply swerved around the large object, miraculously avoiding it completely. In doing so, because the road was narrow with no shoulders to speak of whatsoever, the right side of the automobile was in the grass. Upon steering the car back toward the road, I could feel the rear end fishtail slightly before catching traction again on the pavement. Because of the abrupt course correction, Candace immediately sat up straight and said, "What happened?" To which I expressively replied, "DID YOU SEE THAT?" I quickly looked in my rear-view mirror to see if what I had seen was actually there and not a figment of my imagination; it was there all right, a big cement culvert sitting right there in the middle of the road. My heart pounded out of my chest from the sheer terror of what could have happened, and I was ecstatic that we were still alive. While shaking my head in disbelief, I whispered, *"What the hell!"*

Not being able to stop thinking about what had happened, the next morning, I drove back out to the bridge to inspect the situation. And sure enough, burned into the grass, I could see where my car had fishtailed, but there was no cement culvert to be seen anywhere. It was gone! Upon closer inspection of the situation, I was in complete disbelief as to how we'd survived with nary a scratch on my vehicle. There were absolutely no shoulders on this little highway, and the road was just wide enough for two vehicles to pass by. How I'd managed to maneuver around an object that had taken up more than half of my lane, was beyond me. After explaining to a few of the townsfolk the unusual happenstance that had nearly killed Candace and me, I enquired as to why a concrete culvert might have been at the bridge. But no one knew anything. If you lived in this little town, you'd know that everyone knew everything about anything that was ever going on. It's hard to believe this massive culvert simply rolled itself onto the path of my vehicle at 2:00 AM in the morning while strategically concealing itself from my field of vision due to the architecture of the bridge. There were no people around and no flares or pylons to signal danger of a construction zone either. If I were to believe in such things, it seemed as though someone or something was trying to do away with yours truly. I do understand that perhaps I just needed to SLOW DOWN and drive the speed limit like a normal person, to which I would answer, "Touché!" However, that doesn't answer the question as to why a massive concrete culvert had been strategically positioned on the deadliest section of road at that late hour, only to vanish as though it had never been there. One thing I am certain of: I didn't imagine what I saw, and I certainly swerved around something that evening.

Growing up in Tadmore, I knew several people who had migrated there from Europe, where hundreds of years of folklore and superstition were rife. There were a multitude of tales regarding curses and spirits constantly passed around. I generally chalked these up as great entertainment around a campfire in the dark. Even though I had heard and seen what appeared to be a spirit or some kind of unexplained phenomenon when I was thirteen, I'd never actually believed it was possible to put a curse on someone. However, at this point, I was beginning to rethink my skepticism. Considering that neither Candace nor I were wearing our seat belts—I know, not very bright—how I managed to avoid such a large obstacle at that speed in the darkness of night still scares the hell out of me to this day.

Switching roles from weekend party guy to reflexologist by day, the following Monday morning, during my drive to work, I had yet another mysterious near-miss incident that could have ended ugly. While heading down the double-lane main drag that went through Canora, an elderly driver in a four-door sedan decided he wanted my lane. With no signal, no shoulder check, nothing, the old fellow just abruptly moved over. Fortunately, at that exact moment, I happened to be passing by the entrance to an Esso service station on my right and immediately adjusted course for this entrance to escape what would've been a collision to the left front quarter panel of my shiny new Mustang. Because of my speed, however—yes, I was speeding and not wearing a seatbelt again—I wasn't able to turn sharp enough or stop in time to avoid two power poles that didn't appear wide enough to negotiate my car between. Preparing for the worst, I clenched my teeth and braced for impact. To my amazement, somehow I managed to graciously squeak narrowly between the two poles. Other than the impressions of my fingertips embedded into the steering wheel— from the death grip of terror—there was no damage to my sweet little Mustang whatsoever. I was utterly in disbelief, so much so that I drove around the block to have a second look. The car fit all right. Barely! It was so tight that while attempting to drive between these same two poles—at the speed of a turtle, no less—I couldn't do it without one of my mirrors touching. Yet at 80 km/h, I had somehow managed to successfully dart off the road, avoid what certainly would have been a collision, and successfully maneuver my vehicle between these very same poles. While standing outside my car, sizing up the situation, a younger teenager who'd been pumping gas just as the incident had happened walked over and mumbled something about me having horseshoes where the sun doesn't shine. Horseshoes? This kid didn't know the half of it!

* * *

Sometime after the bridge incident and narrowly maneuvering my Mustang between the two power poles, in an effort to make some kind of sense from it all, I began contemplating what these butt-clenching, *Twilight Zone* experiences were all about—these were simply two of many similar incidences that seemed to keep happening to me around this time period. Quite honestly, something felt awry. That was when a strange discovery I'd made behind our house while doing a late-spring cleanup a few years prior came to mind. The area hadn't been maintained for quite some time and was becoming somewhat of an eyesore. The grass was nearly eight inches high, and I, being somewhat of a neat freak, wanted to spruce up the place. As our deck was at least eight feet off the ground, the space beneath it made for a great place to store various items. Most of the stuff that had found its way there was junk, however, which should have gone straight to the garbage dump.

Dad had lumber stacked next to the house, along with a couple of sheets of plywood leaning against the wall. Not wanting to hit anything with the lawnmower, I combed through the tall grass and found a few pieces of rogue lumber strewn about. That was when I noticed one of the sheets of plywood had fallen over. It was lying flat on the ground, with grass grown in around it, indicating to me that this plywood had been there for quite some time. After one final sweep of the area, I decided to pick up the sheet of plywood and lean it back against the house. Upon leaning forward to lift the plywood, I observed an unusually large number of strange insects crawling around on the ground, some of which were rather beastly in appearance. Nevertheless, not making a big deal out of it, I lifted the plywood off the ground. While doing this, a black snake came darting out and scared the crap out of me. Although I'm the kind of guy who isn't afraid of too many things, I'd have to say that snakes are at the top of my list of creepy creatures to avoid. I jumped back and let the creature slither on its merry way.

After leaning the sheet of plywood back against the house—now wearing gloves—I could ascertain where all the mysterious insects were coming from. There was a dead cat decomposing under that piece of plywood. It was a disgustingly gross discovery, to say the least. Not really thinking much of the encounter, I immediately went to retrieve a garbage bag, along with a shovel to dispose of the dead feline in a proper grave. Upon scooping up the dead animal, I noticed it was missing something…its head! That was when a cold shiver traveled up my back and I could feel my body shudder in horror. Nevertheless, soldiering on, I shoveled the abhorrent creature into the garbage bag and decided to look around for the missing body part. After all, I certainly didn't want to hit THAT with the lawnmower. I'd seen enough horrific images for one day and wasn't about to add hitting a cat's head with a lawnmower to the list. My search, however, was to no avail, and that left me somewhat perplexed. At the time, I wondered, *How can a dead cat with its head cut off find its way under a sheet of plywood?* I concluded that someone had to have put it there…minus the head. But who? Even more bewildering to me was why. A practical joke perhaps? It all seemed rather occultist and cryptic—things I never paid much heed to—but it certainly was not very funny, regardless of how it had come about or what it was supposed to mean—if anything!

Upon remembering my unpleasant discovery of the headless cat, I was beginning to draw a sinister conclusion about the recent stroke of weird incidents that could have cost me my life—all of which began shortly after turning thirteen years of age. This had me wondering if someone might have cast some kind of sinister curse against me. Was that what the dead cat was all about? If so, why? And who? Being a skeptic when it came to such mumbo jumbo, I kept the gory details to myself. After all, if someone had related the story of this dead, headless cat stashed underneath a sheet of plywood story to me, I would have thought he or she was a couple of cards short of a full deck. Regardless of my skepticism and belief systems, I was kind of spooked by all this. Psychoanalyzing myself, I concluded that maybe I was just a tad paranoid and that there was a logical explanation to be had, like dodging the bullet while driving like a maniac was just one of a series of self-imposed coincidences that only sheer luck—linked with a bit of good driving—had gotten me through. And maybe the cat had simply lost its head in some kind of accident after using up its nine lives, and its owner had dumped its body where I'd found it, minus the head. Who knows? But the more I reflected on these strange occurrences, the more I realized how desperate I was to put Tadmore in my rear-view mirror and move to Saskatoon. There was just one hitch: I was committed to running the reflexology clinic for my parents.

Nevertheless, with each close call I survived, a deluded sense of invincibility began to materialize inside me. This, in turn, caused me to subconsciously embark on a dangerous mission of testing the limits of what I could do in an automobile. For instance, I'd speed down the highway at 140 km/h and then swerve in a precise manner while pulling the E-brake, which, in effect, would put the car into a four-wheel slide rotation or drift. Then I'd quickly downshift into third and accelerate abruptly to spin the rear wheels. Because of the positraction rear end, the car thus continued rotating around 360 degrees, all in one smooth motion. *Poetry in an automobile*, I called it, a sentiment that only fellow thrill seekers would likely appreciate. Yes, I definitely had speed in my blood. That little stunt, however, being extremely hard on the transmission, eventually broke something in the gear box. Fortunately for me, Ford covered the costly repair under warranty.

* * *

Even with the mysterious experiences I encountered, I'd have to say summer of '86 ranks up there as one of my top three of all time. That Mustang and I embarked on many interesting adventures together. While some were a bit precarious in nature, others were extraordinarily enjoyable. One late Sunday afternoon, after cruising around the lake, I was hoping to meet up with a girl I'd met the day before. I parked and waited. Feeling somewhat mellow, I was listening to The Outfield on my car stereo. The pop/rock band from Manchester, England, enjoyed some commercial success in North America during the mid-1980s. While inaccurately lip-syncing the words to the band's signature song, "Your Love," some guys I knew from Sturgis pulled up on either side of me. One of them, accompanied by his girlfriend, was driving a brand-new baby blue IROC Z-28 Chevrolet Camaro. A totally sweet ride! Apparently, there was a rumor going around that he and I had raced our cars and I had totally annihilated him with my Mustang. Like a lot of rumors that make their rounds, it had some basis in reality, but it had nothing to do with the guy driving the baby blue. Yes, I had raced a car just like his in Yorkton about a month earlier, but it had been a yellow IROC. And yes, I had annihilated that car and its driver. Nonetheless, to set the record straight, Baby Blue wanted to race me. It's kind of amusing how rumors take on a life of their own.

My racing challenger told me to follow him out to a section of highway popular for such occasions that was not far from Crystal

Lake, where the road was freshly paved, flat, and straight for several miles. He and I lined up our cars side by side while the third guy, Harvey, signaled the start for us. Baby Blue, I guess trying to impress his girlfriend, had her along for the ride. On GO! I hastily dropped the clutch and sat there, spinning my tires like an idiot, as he pulled away from me. By the time my rear wheels hooked up, he probably had a one-hundred-foot lead. Well, that just made it more of a contest, and I had every intention of redeeming myself for the botched start. Putting the potent Cobra through its paces, meticulously clutching and pouring on the gas, I passed Baby Blue like he was standing still. In short order, I pulled away to the point that I almost felt sorry for him. Upon returning back to the starting point, he wanted to race again, and then again, and even again. The guy wouldn't let up, refusing to accept that his car wasn't going to beat mine. He tried starting in a different gear. Then he wanted me to keep going for a couple of miles, thinking he might catch up. And then he wanted me to have a passenger sitting next to me, because his girlfriend was in the car with him. None of these tactics made any difference in the outcome, but I was a good sport and played along. I thought about saying to him, *Let me go hook our boat on the back of my car. Then you might have a chance.* In the end, it was all in fun, and we were just boys being boys.

Looking back at myself, it's apparent to me now that I might have come across to some guys as being extremely arrogant. However, I didn't mean to, and it's not like I ever believed I was this super-cool guy by any means. I'll admit, however, I was definitely sporting an attitude, and as time went on, I began to realize how that car, combined with my presumptuous demeanor, was painting a target on my back. After attending a few local parties and dances where guys were trying to provoke me into a fight, I soon came to the sobering conclusion that I needed to watch my back. In retrospect, after quitting school and buying a super-fast car, which everyone likely believed my parents had bought for me, it was no wonder there were a couple of guys out to kick my butt. If the situation were reversed, I might have shared their sentiments. After all, who likes a spoiled rich kid who has everything handed to him on a silver platter? Truth be told, by midsummer, I was barely making ends meet. And because I wasn't able to save up any of that $10,000 lump-sum payment—now due in two months—it was simply a matter of time before the spoiled rich kid had his car repossessed.

* * *

After roughly four months since taking on the reflexology challenge, for the most part, I was doing quite well. Even with business being somewhat stagnant, I was able to pay the bills and generate enough income to survive. My only disappointment was that I wasn't getting ahead. And all the speeding tickets I was acquiring certainly weren't helping the situation. I swear the cops would just sit and wait for me to drive by. It wasn't long before I got to know each officer on a first-name basis. Finally wising up, I bought myself a radar detector, which paid for itself after the first week. Learning to be somewhat creative at arguing my way out of many of those tickets in court didn't hurt either.

Despite my efforts, thus far, it was becoming clear how significant my predecessors had damaged the reputation of the reflexology business in Canora. When Mom had started this venture all on her own, she'd built up a solid clientele base that had resulted in a thriving operation. She'd helped many people improve their health, and word of mouth, being the best advertising at zero cost, had brought new clients into her waiting room on a regular basis. After she'd left, however, the business had basically gone to hell in a handbasket. Regaining the trust of so many dissatisfied clients was proving to be an impossible task. I was becoming weary of the whole thing, and I had an expensive car—basically owned by the bank—hanging around my neck like an albatross. Maybe that Tempo would have been a wiser car to buy. I was learning fast—well, at least as far as car payments, maintenance, stops at the gas pump, and insurance were concerned. A muscle car has its ups, but it's the downs that were overwhelming me.

If that wasn't enough, another wrench was thrown in my gear box by the fact that it was now prime-time farming season in the heartland of Saskatchewan's agricultural belt, the main industry in that province. With the majority of my clients being farmers, aches, pains, and moderate health issues were put on hold as their attention was primarily focused on making a living. This was understandable, as the farming season provided their income for the entire year. As a result, my appointment book was left with less and less ink on it as each week went by, which, in effect, played right into my affinity toward extracurricular activities. After all, instead of working on people's smelly feet all day long, I'd much rather have been out cruising around in my beautiful Mustang, chasing girls. Truth be told, I was simply no longer interested in pursuing this reflexology venture any further—not to mention that I was just seventeen and this wasn't exactly what I had in mind as my "dream job." Although feeling somewhat downtrodden by my failure to save a single red cent towards the ten-K down payment I needed in order to keep my car, I also saw a silver lining on the horizon in terms of an exit strategy.

Deciding it was time for a change of scenery, I called Mom—who was living in Saskatoon—on the phone to explain the business situation I was dealing with in Canora. After a lengthy conversation, Mom agreed that closing the clinic was a sad but inevitable reality. And me moving to Saskatoon in search of a job was a viable option. Truth be told, I couldn't have quarterbacked my discussion with Mom on this matter at a better time. She was in the process of moving the following weekend and wanted my help. Besides, I think she missed me. Dad, on the other hand, wasn't exactly pleased with our decision. Misguided optimist that he was, Dad had high hopes of me being a part of the family business. He still believed the Canora clinic could once again become a thriving business. Being the happy-go-lucky guy that he was, however, Dad eventually accepted our decision.

Another reasonable conclusion as to why this business failed could be that I was simply a kid who undoubtedly lacked the knowledge, as well as experience, to manage a reflexology practice successfully. In terms of giving a proper reflexology treatment, did I even know how? Not to mention, I'd been pleasantly distracted since acquiring my new ride. I can't deny that any of these factors didn't play a small role in contributing to the dissolution of the reflexology practice. I can attest, though, that there were more than a few regular clients who loved my treatments. There's no doubt in my mind that I knew what I was doing, and I never lacked confidence in my ability to do reflexology. As for the business side of things, I was extremely capable when it came to paying the rent, opening on time, and maintaining a professional relationship with clients, all of which somehow came natural to me—or maybe it was simply a matter of what I considered common sense. As eager as I was to turn the page on this chapter of my life and move to Saskatoon, after building up a solid repertoire with a number of clients, when all was said and done, a definite sadness came over me from the realization that I'd likely never see these people ever again. Truth be told, however, I still had some growing up to do, and I seriously needed to mend my affinity towards breaking the law.

Whatever the case, this venture simply wasn't paying off, and it was time for me to take that next fork in the road. Accordingly, after placing a CLOSED INDEFINITELY sign on the front window one Friday afternoon, I got my act together to split town. I packed up a few things from home, took the T-tops off my car, and headed west—literally into the sunset—for Saskatoon, the cultural and economic hub of Saskatchewan. The Guess Who, one of Canada's best mid-sixties to early seventies rock bands, and one of the first to find major international success, wrote a catchy tune about the city called "Running Back to Saskatoon." It was released in 1972. I may not have been running BACK to Saskatoon, but no doubt about it, I was running from something: the rather tedious and limited life Tadmore and its environs had to offer, a misguided business venture, a checkered reputation…and perhaps a demon or two.

CHAPTER

20

Strike One

Arriving in Saskatoon, I immediately began packing and moving boxes for Mom. Betty was relocating from a two-bedroom apartment into much larger digs, which, conveniently for me, had three bedrooms. This allowed me to have my own room—not to mention a place to live. The apartment was literally a stone's throw away from the reflexology practice Mom ran in Saskatoon. It enabled her to walk back and forth to work each day in a matter of about thirty seconds. She could be home for Nikki when my kid sister came home from school at lunch time.

Within a week or so of living in Saskatoon, my cousin Doug landed me a job working with him at Ackland's—a decision he would later regret. The job was a warehouse position that barely paid minimum wage. However, beggars can't be choosers, and it was a paycheck nonetheless. Ackland's was the main warehouse supplier that provided all the Bumper to Bumper stores in northern Saskatchewan with product. For anyone who's not familiar with Bumper to Bumper, they sold mostly tools and automotive aftermarket parts. If you needed a water pump for your vehicle, you could purchase a rebuilt one and save substantially on the full price of an OEM replacement. My job entailed pushing a shopping cart around a huge warehouse all day long, filling orders, an excruciatingly mind-numbing task. A monkey could have done what I was doing. After just two weeks at that place, I wanted someone to shoot me already.

The only thing keeping me going was the weekends. I'd drive back home to Tadmore right after work every Friday to party with my homeys. The trip normally took three hours traveling the speed limit, but I'd do it in under two—a bit over the speed limit in my Mustang. On more than one occasion, I could see red lights flashing in my rear-view mirror, but I never stopped. When traveling nearly three times the posted speed limit, stopping didn't seem like an option. The cops would have locked me up and impounded my car for going that fast. The RCMP doesn't take kindly to people traveling at 260 km/h. Fortunately for me, they were never able to catch me, probably because they were understaffed. Otherwise, I would have been intercepted down the road by fellow redcoats whom they had radioed ahead to about a maniac speeder.

In one particular instance, failing to notice him until it was too late, I sailed by a police cruiser sitting by the side of the highway. He was just finishing up with another offender on the oncoming shoulder. Taking note that my vehicle was clearly traveling way beyond the speed limit, even though he didn't have me on radar, the cop flashed his lights and pointed right at me—in a rather stern manner, no less—signaling to pull over. Not wanting to ruin my weekend plans by spending the night in lockup, however, I simply waved back to him, smiled, put the pedal to the floorboards, and kept going. Since I was traveling at warp ten, I speculated that unless he had laser-vision eyesight, he hadn't been able to see my license plate number. And dashboard cameras had not made the scene yet. Being it was a busy highway, by the time the poor cop got turned around and up to speed, I was likely more than two miles ahead of him already. He never had a chance. Again, I was just lucky there wasn't another police cruiser for him to radio ahead to further up the road.

* * *

It was during one of these weekend trips back home that the next phase of my life began and eventually culminated with my first head-on collision with reality. Understandably, driving back and forth from Saskatoon every weekend to Tadmore was costing a considerable amount of money, more than I was making at Ackland's. I desperately needed to supplement my income. One day, while pushing my shopping cart around the warehouse, collecting orders like a monkey picking bananas, I got a bright idea. Although it was quite clever, it was very illegal. One of the details I was quick to observe while working at Ackland's—given my propensity for shoplifting—was how awfully trusting this place was of their employees, especially considering the slave-labor wages management was paying us. Most warehouse jobs in the city paid considerably more. I'm not implying that this was a viable excuse for what I had in mind. Being an employee of Ackland's, I received a fairly substantial discount on everything they sold, so I bought a big box of Kimberly Clark toilet paper. Why on God's green earth would I buy a big box of toilet paper? Well, I wasn't planning to sell toilet paper to everyone I knew. These boxes were huge, two feet high and three feet square. After my discount, the paper only cost $35. In other words, for thirty-five bucks, I had myself a massive storage bin, able to hold anything I could fit into it. But first, I needed to establish whether or not the guys at the front counter would pay much attention to this large box as I wheeled it past them on a dolly out to my car. Sure enough, they didn't even bat an eye. You can bet the farm my next box wasn't going to be filled with toilet paper.

All I needed now was someone to sell the expensive merchandise I was going to fill the next box with. That was where one of my friends back home came in handy. He and I got to talking one weekend, and as it turned out, he had the perfect connection. After meeting with his contact, it was agreed I would get fifty percent of the retail price of anything I could pilfer, which my friend and I would split fifty-fifty. I could have nickel-and-dimed him to less of a cut, but I'm not a nickel-and-dimer; and without him, I would have still been looking for a fence. My friend made it easy for me, at least for the time being, and I trusted him. Trust was worth an even split to me. So in essence, I would net twenty-five percent of the retail value of everything I stole from my employer. That was still better than one hundred percent of nothing or the risk of flogging the stuff on my own.

The first order from my friend's connection was mostly for automotive tools. The thing about wrenches and socket sets is that they're extremely heavy, especially a big box full of them. Nevertheless, after dumping the toilet paper into the dumpster, I found a nice, quiet corner in the warehouse and filled my first box to the brim with tools, tools, and more tools. I even had room in there for a few tools to start my own collection. Trouble was, this large box now weighed about 200 pounds. Although it seemed like a good idea at the time, I was freaking out about how on earth to get this mammoth-sized cardboard chest of tools—that now squeaked and jangled with every bump the dolly rolled over—past the front counter without raising suspicion. To top it off, I was afraid the box might fall apart on the way. Committed to this endeavor, however, I decided the lunch hour was likely the most opportune time in which to facilitate my devious scheme. And I went for it. Fortunately, I was a likeable guy and therefore had a great rapport with the guys working the front counter. As I wheeled the heavy box through the side door and out to my car, no one suspected a thing. One of the fellows even ran over to hold the door for me. A helpful chap he was. My heart was nearly pounding out of my chest as he held the door, though, hoping he wouldn't hear the strange noises jingling around inside the box every time I hit a bump with the dolly. Nevertheless, I made it to my car without incident and completed my first sale the following weekend.

Every couple of weeks after that, I'd buy a box of toilet paper. And I even had the perfect cover story for what I was doing with all the butt-wipe. It was simple, really: Mom ran a reflexology clinic, and I was doing her a favor by supplying the clinic with cheap toilet paper. In turn, Ackland's felt like they were doing me a favor. It got to the point where they expected me to buy a box of toilet paper on a routine basis and payed no attention whatsoever to what I was hauling out the side door. In no time, my income suddenly tripled. Being the entrepreneur I was, over time, I found a few buyers of my own. This was definitely more profitable, not having to pay my friend his cut on these solo ventures. One such instance, I loaded up a toilet paper box to the brim with piston ring kits. Considering these kits were nearly weightless, retailed for $150 each, and I could stash over fifty of them in the box, this was the perfect score. After carefully selecting kits that fit the most common engines—thinking they'd be easier to sell—I approached a local dealer back home with a somewhat believable story, explaining how a relative of mine from British Columbia had passed away after owning a little parts store for years and these piston ring sets were simply left over from the auction we'd had. I'm not sure he actually believed my story, but when all was said and done, the store owner paid me fifteen hundred for the entire box. It wasn't exactly fifty percent of the retail value, but it was a quick and easy score—equal to six weeks' pay, no less! This was just one instance of many that no one ever knew of. I never told a soul of my extracurricular activity at Ackland's.

With all the extra money I had to throw around as a result of this unscrupulous business venture I had going on, life was great! And it wasn't long before I successfully managed to accumulate a full shop of quality tools for myself as well. Not being one of those freeloaders who lived off their parents, I helped Mom out with extra cash and always paid her rent money. As my parents' once-promising reflexology business was headed for bankruptcy, I knew Mom needed the financial help.

I'd known full well that the day was fast approaching—the six-month period of grace to cough up the $10,000 was nearing its end—when the Ford dealership where I'd bought my Mustang from was going to repossess my car, but there wasn't a thing I could do about it. I had money, sure, but not ten-K kind of money. To be in that disposable cash bracket, I would have had to break the law in bigger ways than what I was doing. I wasn't quite up to that. Near the end of November, they did just that; repossessed my sweet ride and that was all she wrote. Let me tell you, having your car repossessed is extremely depressing, even more so when it's a car like a Cobra GT. Nevertheless, after racking up over 60,000 kilometers on the odometer in just six months, that little Mustang and I had some great, memorable adventures together. I mean, can you even envision me recounting the exploits I pulled off with the Mustang if I had bought that lame Tempo? Not! Besides, in addition to the car payments, I knew it would also have cost me a pretty penny on garage bills to repair the wear and tear I had subjected the Cobra to. I hadn't exactly babied the vehicle.

Okay, so my cool car was history. No point crying over spilt milk. I had to deal with it and move on. I needed to replace the Mustang; sadly, it would have to be replaced with a lot less flashy and powerful automobile. George, the massage therapist who had worked with me at the reflexology clinic, proved to be the solution to my problem. He owned a 1985 Dodge Colt that he wanted to get rid of. Although it also carried the name of a horse, the Colt was a huge step down from my beloved Mustang, but at least it wasn't some old clunker. I made a deal with George to buy the Colt. He agreed to a down payment of one grand, with the rest being paid off at two hundred a month for two years. In all honesty, in 1986, that was more than a fair deal. I was mobile again, albeit not in the grand style I had grown accustomed to.

Since my vehicular dejection, however, life took a sudden lane change to the slow-moving avenue of the real world, a tough transition for sure. And if I'm honest, it was a somewhat embarrassing one as well, kind of like moving from a penthouse to an outhouse. I went from going zero to sixty in six seconds to pretending the Colt wasn't really my car, often referring to my new set of wheels as a "puddle jumper." Nevertheless, it was a decent little car and very cheap on fuel too. In hindsight, I should have never owned that Mustang in the first place. A Dodge Colt would have been the ideal first car for a seventeen-year-old. And in all honesty, a cheap, efficient car was all I ever expected.

* * *

Snow soon fell in late fall, making this the first winter since I was six years old that I lived away from Tadmore. Other than the fact that I'd been constantly surrounded by gossiping neighbors and narrowly escaped a number of experiences that could have ended my life prematurely, I kind of missed the place. Chopping and hauling wood, looking after the garden, shoveling snow or cutting the grass, and even looking after those stupid chickens were all things that might have seemed like nuisances at the time, but now that they were gone, it felt like something was missing from my life. Being a country boy through and through, it wasn't long before I realized city life was for the birds.

Another facet that I found myself out of sorts with was that I missed my grandma—Betty's mom—not to mention her home-cooked meals. Her name was Ada, but most of our family called her by the nickname Hank. I'm not sure what earned her the handle, but out of respect, I always called her Grandma. She was a good, kind-hearted woman who believed the way to anyone's heart was through their stomach. Anytime you were over for a visit, she would always put food in front of you and say with a thick Ukrainian accent, "C'mon, eat! Eat! You have to eat, because you never know when you might be hungry." Let me tell you, that woman made the best homemade soup, so good you couldn't stop eating it. Grandma was quite generous in terms of keeping me fed while living on my own. In turn, I was always more than willing to help her with any chores she needed done. While growing up in Tadmore, during periods my parents weren't around, I had grown somewhat close to my grandmother.

The snow blew in that winter, which made living in Saskatoon—already a difficult transition—even worse. The previous winter, I had traded in and upgraded my snowmobile to a 1985 Yamaha Phazer. Though I'd bought the machine slightly used, it was a beautiful snowmobile nonetheless—especially compared to my previous, single-cylinder Bombardier. Considering that this awesome snowmobile was sitting in our garage back home while I worked at my mind-numbing job in the city, this metropolitan lifestyle was beginning to wear on me. I'd much rather have been blazing the trails around the countryside back home on my slick Yamaha snowmobile.

Around this same time, to water down my boredom of city life, I began hanging out with my cousin Duane, who was born and raised in Saskatoon. Duane is the younger brother of Doug; they were the two cousins whose family we stayed with when attending JW conventions in Saskatoon. Duane, a year older than I, knew all the hot spots in

Saskatoon for kids our age, and he was a great guide to making the best of city life. One of the things Duane and I had in common, other than our lack of morals, was that he was also an avid snowmobile enthusiast. It wasn't long before I resumed my weekend excursions back to Tadmore on weekends, but now I was accompanied by Duane as my sidekick and snowmobiling partner. And because our relatives in the area also had snowmobiles, this led the way to plenty of enjoyable and picturesque trail rides touring the countryside around Tadmore.

Meanwhile, I was still supplementing my income with car parts and tools-filled toilet paper boxes, which enabled me to afford driving back and forth to Tadmore on the weekends—especially in my fifty-miles-per-gallon little Dodge Colt. While hanging out in Tadmore every weekend, Duane and I would make our rounds to each relative, hoping to score a free meal here and there. Fortunately, if we just happened to be there around dinner time, our family was quite generous and more than willing to feed our sorry butts. During these freeloading visits, however, Duane and I would get a chuckle out of how they all talked about one another behind each other's back. We'd go to one uncle and aunt's house for coffee and listen to them talk about the relative we'd just come from, and vice versa. Neither Duane nor I could relate to their gossipy behavior, but it sure was entertaining. We knew they were kind-hearted people who all loved one another; therefore, we simply played along. For a good laugh, we may have instigated the conversations now and then. Nevertheless, all of my aunts and uncles are genuinely good, hardworking people whom I sincerely owe a debt of gratitude to for helping me out as much as they did while growing up. I just wish they'd gotten along better with one another.

The only inconvenient aspect of snowmobiling with Duane every weekend was that I had to double him on the back of my machine everywhere we went. Surmising that two snowmobiles would be far more enjoyable, we began to problem-solve this inconvenience. However, with Duane not having a job, he certainly couldn't afford to buy one, and I wasn't in any position to buy a second snowmobile. Nor did I want to. What were we to do? That was when Duane brought it to my attention that a friend of his had once stolen a sled from the city and kept it hidden on the family farm for years without anyone ever knowing. After some strategizing, it seemed reasonable to conclude that if we stole a snowmobile from Saskatoon and brought it all the way back to Tadmore, no one would be the wiser. Who was to say that we hadn't bought it. We further concluded that as long as we did any repairs on the stolen machine ourselves, which I knew how to do, there really was no way to EVER get caught. It seemed like the perfect crime.

In the meantime, concluding it was simply a matter of time before I got busted stealing a toilet paper box full of expensive merchandise from Ackland's, I needed a long-term solution. Besides, my attitude towards working at Ackland's was becoming increasingly insipid. It simply was not my kind of job and led nowhere but a dead end—other than being promoted to another dead-end job if you toed the line, kissed butt, and showed a proprietary interest in the business. I definitely did not fit that description. Needing an occupation that challenged me intellectually, I decided to search for more gainful employment. However, in order to acquire a second snowmobile, my new job quest was temporarily diverted while Duane and I spent every spare minute we had scouring the outskirts of Saskatoon for the ideal target.

Interestingly enough, at that same time, the perfect employment opportunity fell right into my lap. This new occupation opportunity just happened to be right up my alley: a carpenter's helper. And it offered double the pay I was receiving from Ackland's. Turned out one of Mom's reflexology clients was a successful contractor and he'd happened to mention that he was looking to hire someone. I couldn't have asked for a more perfect situation, not to mention the increase in pay. It would afford me the luxuries in life without having to supplement my income by means of stolen goods. After a quick interview with the contractor, he hired me on the spot. My boring job at Ackland's was history. It seemed like I had it made in the shade, and I considered myself extremely fortunate to walk away from Ackland's virtually unscathed—not to mention with a garage full of every possible automotive tool that even Tim "the Tool Man" Taylor would have been envious of. My only regret at this point: It was too bad Ackland's didn't sell carpentry tools.

Meanwhile, dedicated as we were to this new endeavor, it didn't take Duane and me long before we located the perfect mark. Our lengthy search found an almost brand-new machine sitting on a trailer—just waiting for us—in the alley behind some poor schmuck's house. There were no locks, chains, or anything to stop us. All we had to do was back up, hook the trailer to my car, and drive away. Easy as 1-2-3! After locating our target, that same evening, the two of us went to Canadian Tire, bought a hitch for my car, and I installed it in Duane's parents' garage. The next day, we scouted out some backroads leading from the victim's place to the highway. We definitely wanted to avoid pulling the machine through the city. All we had to do was wait for Friday and hope the snowmobile was still there.

Having to wait until 1:00 AM in the morning, hoping everyone in and around our target's home was asleep and not looking out their windows, was a drag, but everything went exactly according to plan. However, it was one heck of a nerve-racking three-hour drive to Tadmore. And I couldn't dare speed either. The unnerving thought of the cops pulling us over caused my poor heart to thump like a jackhammer. For the duration of our entire trip, I spent more time peering into the rear-view mirror than ahead on the road. Finally, we arrived in Tadmore. I was suddenly able to breathe a much-needed sigh of relief. Now it was time to enjoy the spoils. Wound up tighter than a snare drum from the intensity of the situation—even though it was 4:00 AM—I wanted to take this machine for a rip. Sleep was the last thing on my mind. After enthusiastically jumping on the snowmobile—still sitting on the trailer hooked up to my car—I reached to grab the start cord. *"What the...!"* The start cord was missing. Immediately lifting the hood to inspect why there was no pull cord, to my dumbfounded amazement, THERE WAS NO ENGINE!

In light of the circumstances, I started to chuckle just as Duane sauntered over and asked what was so funny. I replied, "You can have this machine!" Did we ever feel stupid. Apparently, the rightful owners of this snowmobile had removed the engine for repairs of some nature. If that wasn't a sign that stealing a snowmobile was going to end badly, I don't know what was. In the spirit of not wanting anyone around town asking questions, we quickly hid the machine while hoping no one had seen us drive in with it hooked to the back of my car. A short time later, during the wee hours of morning, Duane and I pulled the engineless machine with my snowmobile to the Crystal Lake garbage dump, where we torched the evidence, speculating that no one would ever find the incinerated snowmobile out there in the middle of a garbage dump. And to be sure, we even covered it with a bunch of rummage and debris to help conceal what was left of it.

Surprisingly, the following summer, someone actually found the sled and recovered the serial number. The police were knocking on my door in no time. I, of course, denied any involvement whatsoever. Would you believe they asked me to take a lie detector test? "Really? For a stolen snowmobile?" I asked the officer. Crime must have been a tad slow, or maybe they just wanted to try out their new lie detector on me. Without needing to call a lawyer, I knew they had no evidence to charge me. If they did, I'd have been in handcuffs already. However, because of my inquisitive nature, I was curious to know if that contraption they called a lie detector actually worked or if it could it be beaten. Nevertheless, as enticing as this precarious situation was, I went with the wise choice and declined. Just as I'd suspected, I never heard about the incident ever again.

Stubborn as we were, and not willing to give up just yet, Duane and I were quick to target another sled in Saskatoon. This one was opportunely more accessible and convenient than the first one. When Friday finally arrived, the two of us repeated what we had so flawlessly pulled off the first time around. This time, we made sure the snowmobile had an engine. This particular sled was a brand-new Yamaha Phazer, just like my snowmobile, the one I'd actually paid for. Then, ironically, on Friday, March 13, 1987, I backed up my little Dodge Colt to the snowmobile sitting ever so conveniently on a small trailer out on the street in the suburbs of Saskatoon while Duane hooked the trailer to my car. Even though it WAS Friday the 13th, the trip went as smooth as silk, and once again, we arrived in Tadmore unscathed—not that I was ever inclined to believe in that crazy superstition in the first place, though I suppose the people we stole the snowmobile from that night may be apt to believe otherwise.

* * *

Duane and I thoroughly appreciated having a second machine that weekend. But it was now mid-March and the weather was getting warmer. Our precious snow was slowly beginning to melt. Guessing we might have only one or two good weekends of great snowmobiling left, when Sunday arrived, the two of us were already making plans for the following weekend. After all, not having to share my snowmobile or double Duane on the back was much more enjoyable—for both of us. After a nearly perfect weekend of snowmobiling, there had to be a fly in the ointment. Late Sunday afternoon, I discovered a rather unsettling set of circumstances. Because the weather was quite warm that afternoon, the snow had melted a considerable amount. Upon returning to home base after riding that afternoon, I noticed some fresh vehicle tracks in our driveway. Then, with the use of my tracking skills, I detected a fresh set of footprints leading from said vehicle to the hitch of the stolen trailer that had come with the snowmobile we'd just sniped. I could tell that someone had stood in front of the hitch for a moment or two before returning to their vehicle. The unsettling part was that the serial number was located on the hitch of the trailer, and whoever had been standing there had rubbed it clean—likely in an effort to read it clearly. After quickly piecing this together in my mind and concluding that two plus two always equals four, my heart instantly began racing. I didn't want to believe it, but my street-smarts intuition was telling me the tracks had been made by none other than the RCMP. At this point, the only thing I didn't know was how all this was going to play out. You know that sinking feeling you get when you just know your goose is cooked? Multiply that by two, and that was how I felt.

Be that as it may, not able to do anything about it, we drove back to Saskatoon that evening, and I went to work the next day. Having worked two weeks at my new job so far, I was loving it! However, for the next four days, not a moment went by that I wasn't wondering what was going to happen next. Everywhere I drove, my eyes kept roving about, expecting to see the police following me. Finally, on Thursday, Mom got a phone call informing her that the RCMP had obtained a search warrant for our residence in Tadmore and searched our entire house. From what I heard, they'd had the entire cavalry meandering through every inch of our home. They'd found all my precious tools from Ackland's, most of which were still unopened in their original packages, and taken them all! They'd even taken a lot of things that hadn't been stolen.

The police, aware that I worked at Ackland's, became suspicious when they found all these brand-new tools, many of which had serial numbers on them. With due diligence, the cops phoned Ackland's and determined that I'd never paid for any of them. The only thing Ackland's had a record of me purchasing were boxes upon boxes of toilet paper. After work on Thursday evening, I called the RCMP in Sturgis to inform them that I was returning to Tadmore on the weekend, and the officer on the line instructed me to contact them once I arrived so we could clear this up—in other words, arrest me. At least they were kind enough to allow me the dignity of turning myself in—two days later, no less.

Upon returning to Tadmore—after a worrisome sleep—Saturday morning, I decided it was time to pay the piper and made the consequential phone call to the Sturgis RCMP. An officer was immediately dispatched to our home in Tadmore. Dad was home that weekend, and surprisingly, he didn't display much emotion either way. He simply shook his head while saying in a somewhat disillusioned tone, "You've got a lot to learn, son." I'll never forget that while the cop leaned me against his police car to cuff my hands behind my back and read me my rights, I turned my head to look up and see Dad watching this unfold from our living room window. I wondered what he was thinking as he watched his eighteen-year-old son being arrested. And for a brief moment, from the look in his eyes, I felt my conscience stir towards remorse.

After a lengthy questioning process at the Sturgis police station, I was transferred to a holding cell in Yorkton for the remainder of the weekend to await court on Monday morning. Was that ever a long two days. Even though he was just as guilty as I was, I refrained from implicating my cousin Duane in any of this—not to mention the fact that the idea of having a second snowmobile was more for him than me in the first place, as I already had my own sled. Conceding in my mind that there was no point in both of us going down for this, I solely took the hit and crafted my statement in such a way that wouldn't incriminate my cousin. I did omit a few details when confessing to my crimes. These involved the thousands of dollars' worth of tools and parts I had sold. I didn't see the point. I was a sinking ship anyway. Adding a few more kilos to the wreck would have made no difference, and I would have been pressured to name any accomplices in the sales I'd made of the stolen booty, something I wouldn't have done; it just would have complicated things.

Just before court that morning, I was taken to a little room, where a lawyer met with me to discuss my case. This wasn't some inexperienced Legal Aid lawyer either. I could tell he was a well-seasoned defense attorney. After looking over my case, he was adamant that he could easily get me off scot-free on a procedural technicality. When the cop had retrieved the serial number off the stolen snowmobile trailer, he'd been trespassing on private property. Therefore, this lawyer wanted to argue that the evidence was not admissible. Nevertheless, though it was unlike me to pass up on an opportunity to get away with something, I still wanted to plead guilty. In my mind, I was caught and guilty of much more. I likened this scenario to a game of hide-and-seek; when you're caught your caught! There are no technicalities. Whatever the outcome, it was time to face the music and get it over with. Well, this lawyer was not happy with my decision, even having me sign off on a statement declaring as much. Perhaps it would have been a feather in his cap to win a case such as this by getting the charges dismissed.

I'm not exactly sure why I didn't take the easy way out of this situation. Upon reviewing my life during this particular time, I was all about taking the easy way. Considering the circumstances—the reasoning behind prompting me to plead guilty—a person could glean what may have been the underpinnings of integrity. Who knows? On Monday, March 23, 1987, I pled guilty in front of a judge to my first criminal conviction. He sentenced me to one day in jail, which was considered time served, as I was already in custody. He also gave me a $400 fine, along with one year of probation. Upon his gavel pounding the desk, I was free to go. All that I received in terms of punishment was a minor fine and one year of probation. After assuming I was definitely going away for a while and doing jail time, I could not believe my ears. Talk about a slap on the wrist.

* * *

Immediately after the judge's sentencing, in an effort to put the past behind me, I hightailed it back to Saskatoon and went to work the next morning. With the joy and reward I was experiencing from my new job, I focused on the positives in my life. Learning about carpentry, and the considerable increase in the amount of my paycheck, was icing on the cake. In view of being arrested and expecting to spend an extended period of time at the crowbar hotel, life was still looking rather awesome.

Not letting any rust gather on my positive outlook, I came to conclude that an upgrade in my current mode of transportation was now affordable. It was time to trade in that ugly Dodge Colt for something a little more my style. After calculating how much of a car payment I was able to realistically afford while still paying Mom rent and George the payments on the Colt, I began shopping around all the local dealers. Three days after getting out of jail, I traded in my little puddle jumper for a brand-new red Pontiac Firebird without George's knowledge or consent. As far as I was concerned, there was no need for him to know. I had every intention of paying off the debt I owed him. The Firebird wasn't anything like the Mustang in terms of horsepower, but it was still a sweet ride nonetheless. Barely a week since my arrest and the associated drama and trauma it had entailed, I was once again feeling on top of the world. Life was good! Little did I know trouble was brewing for me in paradise.

George didn't exactly agree with my decision to trade in the car I was still paying him for. In hindsight, I can understand why he was a little ticked off. As long as I still owed money for the car, technically, it was as if there was a lien against the vehicle. Then a few days later, during my coffee break, my boss took me aside. I knew from his demeanor that the other shoe was about to drop. He explained that after meeting with my former boss, he knew about the details of my arrest and goings on at Ackland's. Because my new employer had no way of otherwise knowing what happened or any reason to contact my previous employer, especially nearly a month after hiring me, I suspected he must have read about it in the newspaper. Surprisingly, after begging him not to dismiss me, which was rather a humbling experience for me, he didn't fire me. Instead, he decided to give me a second chance. I'm not sure if he saw something good in me or if, perhaps, it was the fact that I was an assiduous employee who was dependable and capable of handling any job he threw at me that played a small role in his decision not to fire me. I seriously liked this new job. Being stuck in some warehouse, factory, or office all day wasn't my cup of tea. I thought with this carpentry job, I had found my niche.

The next morning, during my coffee break, I walked over to the snack truck and noticed my car was gone. Bewildered as to the whereabouts of my pretty red Firebird, I hurried to our break area to enquire if anyone knew anything. Apparently, someone from the dealership had come by to pick it up, leaving instructions for me to phone them ASAP. Needless to say, I had a bad feeling about this situation. When trading in my Dodge Colt, I'd purposely neglected to tell the finance department that I was still making payments on the vehicle. As it was a private arrangement between George and myself, I'd reasoned that the dealership didn't need to know. And I really believed George wouldn't care. As long as I kept making the payments, then what did it matter? Well, as it turned out, I was dead wrong. George had contacted the Pontiac dealership, and in the end, they took back the Firebird, and George canceled our deal on the Dodge Colt, leaving me with no vehicle at all. The day got even worse before it ended. My boss, suspecting something was awry, decided to venture off to the Pontiac dealership that afternoon and get the skinny on what was going on. Not being thrilled with the situation, the blokes at the dealership were all too happy to share the details with him. As I was leaving to go home after the work day, my boss handed me my walking papers, but not before giving me a long lecture about life and what kind of a man I was supposed to be. SIGH! Life suddenly wasn't so good.

In hindsight, I can't say that I blamed him for letting me go. After all, who wants a freshly convicted criminal working for them? Over the course of an eight-hour day, I went from having a great job that I thoroughly enjoyed and a sweet ride to drive to work, to losing both. I was now jobless, with no vehicle and a criminal record, and left to contemplate my uncertain future. Needless to say, I was totally ticked off at George. If he had just kept his mouth shut and accepted my monthly payment in good faith, this new twist to my life might very well have been avoided. In hindsight, that was just shifting the blame for my own shortcomings onto somebody else instead of taking responsibility. Adding insult to injury, seeing it was her reflexology client who'd hired me, Mom was quite upset with me as well. But I couldn't really blame her for that either. I'd caused the poor woman so much grief in my eighteen years that it was just a matter of time before she reached the point of being fed up with me.

Feeling completely dejected, I decided a return to Tadmore was in order. With my tail between my legs, I hopped on the next Greyhound bus and headed for home to lick my wounds and seriously contemplate my next move. As I sit and write about these events, it's difficult to accept that this actually was my life.

Cue music: "Life of My Own" by 3 Doors Down

https://www.youtube.com/watch?v=jeCcFdng7EY

CHAPTER

21

Lost in Paradise

Returning to live in Tadmore, the very place I was eager to distance myself from, was a humbling experience. Up until this point in my life, I can't remember ever feeling as low as this. Adding another layer to the mix was the discovery that it was someone from Tadmore who'd ratted me out to the police. Suspecting that Duane and I might have stolen the snowmobile, they must have thought it was their civic duty to inform on me. Coming for a brief visit shortly after my return to Tadmore that spring, I learned of this information from a police officer who had befriended me. For some reason, this man of law enforcement had taken a liking to me and, in view of my most-recent disadvantaged lifestyle choices, wanted to know how I was doing. Truth was, I kind of liked him as well. He didn't mince his words and said it like it was, and I respected that about him. To me, that's what real friends do—they tell it to you like it really is. Although not saying outright exactly who it was who'd informed on me, the policeman hinted towards the individual, and I received the message loud and clear. In a sense, he was telling me, "Watch your back!" Before leaving that afternoon, the officer said to me, "You're a good guy, Monte. It's just too bad everyone has to keep their valuables nailed down whenever you're around. You need to change that about yourself."

I wasn't surprised that it was someone I knew who'd turned me in to the cops. The way the officer had shown up on that particular Sunday out of the blue hadn't been random. At least I knew exactly who the rat was. However, I never confronted them or ever told a single soul what I knew. But I knew. Revealing who this individual was serves no value to anyone. In fact, I consider what they did a colossal favor. Knowing full well that sooner or later everyone gets caught, it was better that I took my licks and learned my lessons as a teenager rather than much later in life. Besides, that entire situation eventually taught me much about consequences. After all, since moving on from Ackland's and working a new job in construction, my life had experienced a definite uptick in terms of income and overall happiness. I finally loved my job, was learning a trade—something I considered useful—and could see a future in that career. But then the consequences of my past and present actions collided with reality, causing me to literally lose it all in the blink of an eye. As if I couldn't have felt any worse, another mammoth consequence as a result of my symphony of misdeeds was revealed when Mom informed me that my cousin Doug was also none too pleased with me. In all honesty, I hadn't even considered the effects my entanglement with Ackland's would have had on my cousin. After all, he was the one who'd recommended me for the job. Doug had stuck his neck out and vouched for me; therefore, he had every reason for being upset.

Apparently, since my arrest, the bigwigs at Ackland's had been interrogating poor Doug relentlessly, trying to find out if he was in on any of my thefts. The hierarchy, being especially curious as to how I'd managed to get all that product out of their warehouse undetected, wanted answers. Mistakenly presuming I had to have had help, this made my cousin their number one suspect. Since I'd been charged with possession of stolen property, the details of how I'd come to acquire all their merchandise had never been revealed. Surprisingly, because the police already had me dead to rights on possession—and possession is nine-tenths of the law—they hadn't been overly concerned with how all those tools found their way into my garage.

The fact that Doug and I were somewhat close in terms of friendship had me feeling terrible for what he had to go through as a result of vouching for me. With everyone at Ackland's knowing Doug and I were cousins, it had to have made the situation awkward for him, not to mention embarrassing. Considering what he was getting paid—a few cents above minimum wage—I was surprised that he didn't quit his job and look for employment elsewhere. In hindsight, however, quitting likely would have solidified everyone into believing he was, in fact, guilty of something, thus never really clearing his name in terms of a reference either. Strangely, the only remorse I could identify with hinged on how my actions affected Doug. The fact that I'd stolen thousands of dollars' worth of merchandise and two snowmobiles never even phased me. I did, however, learn an important lesson through this experience in terms of recommending anyone or giving a reference. Just because I know a person or, as in this case, am related to someone, it doesn't oblige me to vouch for them. It goes the other way as well: When a person vouches for my character, I'll do well to remember that my actions reflect upon the person who recommended me in the first place. Food for thought that I'm sure we should all ponder on.

Nevertheless, there I was, eighteen years old, broke, jobless, and with a fresh new criminal record, no less. In my temporary broken-down state of mind, I began listening to music that seemed somewhat relevant to my mood. "Someday" by Steve Earl and "Workin' Man (Nowhere to Go)" by the Nitty Gritty Dirt Band were a couple of songs that spring to memory. Yes, that's right, country music.

Fortunately, over the course of the previous few months, while my cousin Duane and I were traveling back and forth between Saskatoon and Tadmore on weekends to snowmobile, we spent a considerable amount of time at our Uncle Jim and Aunt Linda's. We'd go there for coffee quite often as well as to sponge the occasional meal from them. Duane and I even raided their pantry—in the five-finger discount kind of way. I'd never seen a pantry stocked with so much food before; you'd think they were preparing for the apocalypse or something. Loading up on cookies, puddings, and Fruit Roll-Ups, we'd take the grub back to my house for something to eat. However, because they were so generous with us, we only did that twice before I put a stop to it. Feeling guilty, I later snuck a twenty-dollar bill into one of their kitchen drawers to compensate for our misdeeds.

During this period of time, however, being in the sorry state of affairs I was in, Jim and Linda took me under their wing, so to speak, and kept me from going hungry. In turn, I did what I could to help them out around the house while Jim worked for the CN Railway away from home during the week. Because my parents were off living in different cities, trying to keep their business afloat, Jim and Linda sort of became my second family—something I badly needed. Since I no longer owned a vehicle, nor could I afford one, they kindly offered me their old truck to drive and use as my own. It was an orange 1972 Chevrolet half-ton. The truck was a rust bucket on its last dying breaths and burned about as much oil as it did fuel, but it was something to drive. My uncle was generous enough to offer me the vehicle, and I was grateful to accept. Quite honestly, considering where I was in life, that old truck suited me to a T. And as humbling an experience as it was to drive that ratty old vehicle, surprisingly, I wasn't embarrassed by it at all. The best part was that the old Chevy only cost me $56 to insure…for the entire year. Surprisingly enough, even though I'd been canned from my previous job, I somehow qualified for Employment Insurance. As it turned out, because of my increase in pay as a carpenter's helper—compared to what I'd been earning at Ackland's—my EI checks were paying more than the job with Ackland's had. Things were looking up.

* * *

Not long after getting accustomed to living in Tadmore once again, I soon learned that my uncles, Tim and Keith, were going to Watrous, Saskatchewan, to have their wax read. Still being somewhat suspicious of my most recent unexplained near death experiences—especially the cement culvert episode—I jumped at the opportunity and went with them. This well-known wax reader, whom our family referred to as Greba, lived in Manitou Beach, Saskatchewan, just outside of Watrous. Apparently, he was quite effective at revealing and circumventing any curses that might have been cast onto a person. Others from our family had visited this particular elderly gentleman from time to time, and they spoke highly of his qualifications as a seer. Not convinced by any means there was in fact a curse placed on me—nor was I inclined to believe in such nonsense—I figured because a reading only cost $20, what could it hurt to give this a try. I thought if nothing else, it could be good for a laugh.

While waiting for my turn in a small reception area, I can remember sitting, reading a magazine. In light of the situation, Tim, in his typical fashion, was cracking jokes, making scary ghost sounds, and laughing the whole time. The place was a quaint little house that—with some renovations—had been converted to a place of business similar to that of a small doctor's office. When it was finally my turn, I was taken to a room and told to sit on a chair and wait. A short time later, Greba came in and, after a brief conversation, proceeded to pour melted wax into a bowl of water—while holding it over my head.

When the wax hit the water, however, I felt two especially powerful heart-pounding thumps inside my body. I also heard them. Quite honestly, it scared the crap out of me! My immediate reaction to this was "Whoa! What was that?" Not saying a word, Greba hurriedly left the room in a panic and never returned. There was no reading...no nothing! I guess old Greba was spooked by something, or else he was a great actor. He had me spooked as well, regardless of my disbelief in occultism. It sure was an unsettling experience and not really good for a laugh. Eventually, one of my uncles came to get me, and we left.

During our trip back to Tadmore, I questioned Tim and Keith about whether this guy had said anything to them about my reading, but they didn't appear to know anything either. In the end, that entire situation left me more confused than I had been to begin with. I couldn't help but wonder, *Was something revealed by my wax reading that he didn't want to tell me? Was it that bad?* Sheesh! The next day, after dismissing from my mind any notion of being under some kind of curse, I decided to concentrate on the things in my life that I was able to control...myself! My mindset was: *Whatever is going to happen will inevitably happen.*

Having a strong affinity towards taking things apart and fixing them, the next little project I occupied myself with was right up my alley. After concluding that it was cheaper than buying all the oil that old truck was burning—not to mention the smoke trail left behind everywhere I drove—rebuilding the engine seemed like a fun adventure. And with nothing more than a few wrenches Dad owned, some borrowed tools, and a conglomeration of verbal advice from various sources, I tore apart the motor right down to the crankshaft. Then, piece by piece, I rebuilt it with new pistons, rings, and bearings. And yes, I returned the tools after I was done with them. After reconstructing the engine on the old girl, surprisingly, she ran pretty good and no longer burned a drop of oil. I even painted the engine block bright orange, installed a set of chrome valve covers, a chrome air filter housing, and neon spark plug wires. No argument, the truck itself was a rust bucket, but the engine looked pretty rad. Hoping, of course, that the motor wouldn't eventually blow up on me, I was cautiously optimistic of what I had accomplished. After all, unless you're a skilled mechanic, rebuilding a complete engine is certainly no small undertaking. In turn, the accomplishment felt extremely rewarding. It seemed that understanding elementary mechanics and working with my hands somehow came natural to me. Furthermore, it gave me the confidence to do a valve job on my Uncle Tim's truck and replace a head gasket for another relative, a skill that would later serve me well racing dirt bikes.

Despite my natural skill with engines, however, I soon realized what didn't appeal to me about automotive mechanics was always having grimy, oil-stained hands and black grease under my fingernails. I disliked that to the max! Not very sexy. Now in possession of a somewhat-reliable vehicle that wasn't sending smoke signals everywhere I went, my focus shifted towards finding work that was perhaps a little more in my wheelhouse: carpentry! After putting the word out to everyone I knew in the area, I soon had some offers to put my woodworking ability to use. First, I framed my Uncle Larry's basement, assisted by Dwayne—my cousin Kimberly's boyfriend. Next up was my Uncle Tim's basement, which I framed on my own. After that, I designed and built a cool set of bunkbeds for my young cousins, Lindsey and Kristen, Uncle Jim and Aunt Linda's kids. As far as getting paid for these jobs, well, it wasn't very much. However, the amount of food they fed me while I worked more than made up for it—I ate like a horse. Plus, I was getting plenty of experience in the carpentry trade.

By late spring, with not much else to do, I also had my parents' yard looking immaculate. I put my old truck to good use, hauling load after load of rock to top off our driveway. And because Dad kept parking on the lawn, I built a little fence to separate our yard from the driveway—preventing him from further ruining the grass. The next project I took on, admittedly, may have been slightly out of my league. One afternoon, while visiting with Grandma to see the new silver Toyota she had just purchased, I could detect how excited she was about her new wheels. Just prior to this, poor Grandma had gone through a rough patch with automobiles—she kept crashing them. During the course of our conversation that afternoon, I suggested that she should have a garage to park her new vehicle in. In that markedly thick Ukrainian accent of hers, she said, "I'd love to have a garage for my new car, but who's going to build me one?" Enthusiastic at the opportunity, I piped back, "Grandma, if you pay for the material, I'd be happy to build you a garage." She was ecstatic with my offer and offered to pay me, but I refused, mentioning that with all the meals she had fed me over the years, it was the least I could do.

Despite not having any real experience how to even build a garage, I managed to do a somewhat proper job of it nonetheless. With all this time and energy I was bequeathing to others, I began feeling good about myself. It was a new experience for me, as I was usually on the taking end. Working for food, with virtually no cash reward, felt pretty good. Besides, I was collecting unemployment insurance at the time. During this short interlude of my life, I can without question attest to feeling the rewards from doing good for others as well as recognize the inner satisfaction my conscience was enjoying. Although I didn't put these experiences into perspective at the time, they can easily be likened to the popular adage: "What goes around comes around; karma." Or biblically speaking, "reaping what one sows."

The basic definition of "karma" is action, work, or deed. It also refers to the spiritual principle of cause and effect, where intent and actions of an individual (cause) influence the future of that individual (effect). Good intent and good deeds contribute to good karma and future happiness, while bad intent and bad deeds contribute to bad karma and future suffering. The practical explanation of karma is quite simple, really. No, it's not some invisible personality who directs to whom good things or bad things will happen. It's simply positive energy. Everything in our universe is made up of energy, even us. And positive energy attracts positive energy, and likewise does negative energy attract negative. Therefore, to attract positive influences into your life, you must first exude them. When someone does a kind act for you, doesn't it make you feel good? It might even change your mood to a more positive one, which, in turn, may cause you to do something nice for someone else and so on. Therefore, the act of doing something good for another person, in essence, perpetuates the act forward and becomes a centrifugal force. In other words, it gains momentum. Our world would be a much easier place to live if everyone did that every day. At this stage in my life, however, this knowledge was unknown to me.

In the wake of bequeathing my services toward helping others, something extraordinarily positive just fell right into my lap. Well, two things, actually. First, while over at Uncle Jim's one Saturday afternoon, helping him diagnose a small carburetor issue on his 1980 Ford LTD—a vehicle he'd recently purchased with the hopes of flipping for a quick profit—I made him an offer that benefitted both of us, and he accepted. I was confident I could make the repair on my own and then sell the vehicle for substantially more than what my uncle wanted, and our agreement was that anything over and above what he'd originally wanted was mine to keep. In the end, after making the small repair, I quickly sold the car and netted myself a cool 700 bucks. As a result, considering how quality tuneage can make even the least-desirable vehicle a little easier to bear, the first thing I purchased with part of my spoils was a stereo for my old truck. A cheap Canadian Tire sound system was all I could afford, but it sounded awesome and was definitely better than nothing. I purchased the brand-new John Cougar Mellencamp album *The Lonesome Jubilee* shortly after installing the stereo in my truck. Instantly relating to and thoroughly respecting the lyrical emphasis that went into Mellencamp's music, I was extremely drawn to that album. It had a small-town feel and nearly every song had a story I could relate to—even learn from. I completely wore that cassette out, playing it everywhere I went in that old truck. The second extraordinary thing to come along was Uncle Tim getting me a job. I suddenly found myself working with him for K-Line Construction, installing underground telephone cable all over Saskatchewan. The hours were long—essentially working five days a week from dawn till dusk—but the pay was far superior to any job I'd had thus far. And the job was much to my liking. I was outdoors and not confined to an office with four walls and a roof caging me in.

* * *

It would seem that perhaps I was now pointed in the direction and heading towards redemption, ready to change my wayward ways. Sadly, that was not the case. Getting through life the easy way without considering the consequences, unfortunately, was still intrinsically ingrained within me. Quite simply, even with this temporary feeling of peace and contentment I'd encountered as a result of these most recent good deeds, the easy way was still my favorite path. Since acquiring my new job—in order to ensure getting to and from work on time every day—I needed a few parts replaced on my old truck, one of which was the rusted-out driver's side door. With hinges that were both bent and worn out, it was simply a matter of time before the door fell off the truck.

A few years before this time period, during bailing season, my cousin Kelly and I would often work for Frank the cattle farmer, loading and hauling square bales all day long. On one particular day—while taking a break—Kelly showed me a vacant farm adjacent to the land Frank was leasing. Located on this vacant farm were several older model cars and trucks parked in rows, maybe fifty in total. If I had to guess, it seemed that whoever owned this place was running a small-scale auto wreckers, yet there was never anyone around. Now that I was in desperate need of a new door for my truck as well as a few other parts, this place immediately sprang to mind. And with the hopes of there being a half-ton similar to mine, I hopped in my truck and drove out to the site. I knew that the odds that a truck exactly like mine being there, with the parts I needed perfectly intact, were slim, but I had nothing to lose. To my amazement, among the now much larger wrecking yard, there sat an orange 1972 Chevrolet half-ton—the exact same model and color as mine, no less. It was too good to be true. This truck had no rust on it, and the doors were in great condition. There was only one disparity between my door and the doors on this truck: Some wording painted on the outside indicated that at one time or another, the vehicle had been used for business.

Up until this point, since my arrest and conviction just over three months ago, I'd been living my life on the straight and narrow, even helping others in the process. All I had to do now was contact the owners of this property and purchase the needed parts from them. However, this is where any good karma I might have accumulated through my most recent good deeds likely evaporated. Once again, I regressed to an all-too-familiar course of taking the easy way. Before driving out to this place on the off chance of there being a truck with the right working parts, I had taken the initiative to bring some tools with me. Clearly, contacting the owners to legitimately purchase the parts was never part of my plan. Instead, I instinctually resorted to my ingrained methods and climbed over the barbed wire fence. A sign was clearly posted and read: PRIVATE PROPERTY, KEEP OUT. In my mind, however, that didn't apply to me. I proceeded to strip the parts off said truck as fast as I could and hightailed it out of there. The door ended up fitting perfectly on my old jalopy.

Not long after the door-swapping caper, Dad and I went to Canora one Saturday, and for some reason, we elected to take my old truck. Upon arriving at our destination—a local automotive parts store—I parked on the street, and we went inside. A few minutes later, as we were walking back towards my truck, I noticed some people standing around my vehicle. And this would be the precise moment when "whatever a man is sowing, this he shall also reap" came busting down my door—literally! I, in my infinite wisdom, hadn't bothered to paint over the lettering on the truck door that I'd stolen, thus leaving these distinctly identifiable markings visible to everyone, including the rightful owners. They were standing around my truck, waiting for the police, whom I soon found out they had called. Poor Dad, in his dismay, once again just shook his head and never said a word. For a somewhat street-savvy kid, I wasn't as bright as I thought I was.

This was quite the conundrum. Facing criminal charges while still on probation wasn't going to end well. I could end up going to jail…for an old truck door, no less! Requiring a plausible yet believable scenario to explain where I'd gotten this door from—without admitting that I'd, in fact, stolen the damn thing—I needed to think fast. The police came just minutes later, and the officer had me follow him in my truck back to the station, where I was questioned. Being a quick thinker, I said that I'd found the old truck door at the Crystal Lake garbage dump with one of my uncles a couple of weeks ago. Once I finished writing out my statement saying as much, the constable left me to wait all alone in his private office. After sitting there unattended for roughly fifteen minutes, wondering what was taking so long, it finally dawned on me what was going on. The officer who'd taken my statement was standing in the reception area, talking on the phone to the Sturgis RCMP office while an officer from that detachment drove out to verify my story.

Upon realizing what they were doing, and without speaking to my uncle before the cop did, I knew my goose was cooked—not that I expected my uncle would actually lie for me anyway. However, right in front of me on the desk was a telephone. All I had to do was pick up the receiver, press "line two," and dial—the constable was using line one. Because I could see through the open doorway that his back was turned towards me, I quickly dialed my uncle's number. To my surprise, he was home. Then, after a very brief conversation—in a quiet voice—indicating what I needed him to say, I quickly hung up the phone. He was none too pleased with my asking him to lie for me. Considering the circumstances, however—needing to get off the phone—I didn't exactly have time to have a conversation about this. Therefore, I hung up without any conformation that he'd actually follow through. I wasn't out of the woods just yet. All I could do at this point was hope for the best. As it turned out, not more than a few minutes after I hung up the phone, a constable from the Sturgis detachment was knocking at my uncle's door. And yes, my uncle totally saved my bacon that day.

I've often pondered the events that took place, leading up to and including that day. The question I can't help but ask myself is: Why didn't I simply contact the owners of the truck and offer to buy the door from them? I'm sure they would have been more than happy to sell the parts to me. What would I have paid for an old truck door like that? Maybe $50? Was such a minimal amount worth the stress and embarrassment I incurred over this stupid ordeal? Hardly! And this doesn't even take into account the legal consequences that could have ensued, along with the fact that I put my uncle—knowing he was an honest man—in a tough spot by asking him to lie for me. At the time, however, the common sense I've just explained never even occurred to me. As for my decision to steal the truck door as opposed to acquiring it honestly, this was a classic case of taking the easy way. In hindsight, though, the predicaments I found myself in by taking the easy way hardly seem like the easy way at all. Paying for the door and having a clear conscience would have been the easy way and the right way.

After the police released me that afternoon, with instructions to either return the door to the rightful owners or purchase it from them—within forty-eight hours—I breathed an overwhelming sigh of relief. *That was a close one!* The next day, while at my Uncle Jim's, I learned that he'd gone to school with the fellas who owned the property from where I'd stolen the old truck door. Even though Uncle Jim wasn't the uncle who covered for me with the police, word travels fast in that town; therefore, he already knew everything about my close encounter. As a result, Uncle Jim wasn't particularly happy. I can still vividly recall him shaking his finger, with a displeased expression on his face, as he scolded me in a rather serious tone for what I had done. As it turned out, if I had taken that OTHER path—the honest road— and contacted the owners to legitimately purchase the parts, I would have learned of the relationship my uncle had with these people and gotten the door for free. Besides, thanks to my well-paying telephone cable installation job, I certainly could have afforded to buy that old truck door.

If I were to believe in such things, it was as if a higher power conveniently provided exactly what I needed to fix my truck. All

I had to do was choose the right course of action. I have come to realize that throughout this life, whenever something specific you truly need suddenly comes into your life, it is rarely a coincidence. True, coincidences do happen. But how many times does something need to happen before it stops being a coincidence? It's as if the exact same model and year truck as mine was conveniently provided in the perfect situation to test my slowly ascending conscience to see if it would win out over the one that had lent itself so well to my string of misdeeds. If that was the case, I definitely failed.

* * *

The following Monday morning, I woke at 5:00 AM and drove to my job, working for K-Line. Truth be told, since driving was my only means of getting to work, I needed a slightly more reliable vehicle than the old clunker my uncle had given me. The motor ran smoothly, but it was simply a matter of time before something else conked out on the old beast. I thoroughly enjoyed my new job with K-Line, and it more than satisfied my love for the outdoors, with plenty of fresh air and exercise. Walking up to fifteen kilometers per day behind the caterpillar, picking flags that marked our course while making sure the cable continually funneled through the plow in an unobstructed fashion, kept me busy, non-stop, all day long. I also had to hook and unhook the heavy cable from the tow caterpillar that helped pull the plow caterpillar through sloughs and swamps. Working in such close proximity with equipment of that magnitude—the plow caterpillar was a D-9, a large track-type tractor with 475HP and weighing fifty tons— was a learning experience in itself. I had to keep my head up and stay alert at all times. There was no room for goofing around on that job. It was mandatory that we wear hardhats and work boots all day, and my poor feet paid the price. The first month was somewhat painful, as my feet went through an excruciating break-in period. I had blisters on top of blisters. Once the boots were broken-in and I'd mentally adjusted to the physical labor, my job actually became very satisfying

One of the more memorable experiences during my long days of walking behind the plow was the many exquisite aromas emanating from beneath the metal tracks of the caterpillars after they'd trampled over the earth and everything in their path. The exorbitant amount of weight of these machines would grind away at whatever vegetation grew in their wake, thus exuding a bouquet of the most pleasant odors I've ever encountered—the earth's natural perfume, you might say. Even the scent of good ole Saskatchewan farming soil had a surprisingly pleasant fragrance to it. One of the things about laying underground telephone cable, once a heading was established, we would follow those little flags in a straight line for miles, often times right through the center of a slough or swamp. Rarely did we deviate from the trajectory. That was when my job got ugly. Having to drag the heavy tow cable through the middle of a slough in water up to my chest and then hook it to the plow's hitch—which was underwater—was no easy task. First thing I learned in that situation was: NEVER drop the cable! Otherwise, you're diving for it—in murky water, no less.

Another element of my job was assisting in the maintenance of these heavy machines; cleaning the tracks, changing the oil, and greasing the rollers. As a result, I was becoming somewhat familiar with how they operated, which, in turn, offered me the opportunity to occasionally finagle my way into the driver's seat. Somewhat successful at selling myself, I managed to convince our crew boss into letting me operate the tow caterpillar when circumstances permitted. This would usually be during lunch break. After quickly wolfing down my food, I'd be out packing the last mile of trench all by my lonesome in a quarter-million-dollar piece of machinery, each time getting more and more acquainted with piloting the heavy equipment. Meanwhile, everyone else sat, relaxed, and ate their food. Because operators earned substantially more money, my inclination at the time was to graduate one day from a general laborer to the position of an operator. With my quick reflexes and sharp learning curve, I surmised that becoming an operator wasn't out of reach. After all, everyone has to learn from somewhere. Little did I know, for an altogether different reason, this experience would become extremely valuable later on in life.

By the time late August rolled around, my old jalopy of a truck was beginning to show signs of being worse for wear. With the transmission in early stages of deterioration and an exhaust system that desperately needed a new muffler, I had to start looking for a more reliable set of wheels. After saving most of my paychecks and selling my snowmobile, I found an immaculate short box half-ton that just had a brand new engine and transmission installed. The truck was a black 1976 Chevrolet Scottsdale. After a bit of negotiating with the salesman, I purchased it for $2,600. The following weekend, after stripping all my tricked-out parts off the old rust bucket, I installed them on my new Scottsdale. Last but not least, I transferred my rockin' Canadian Tire stereo over as well. The old truck, having seen better days, was no longer drivable. I pulled it out to Uncle Keith's farm, where everyone in our family laid their junkers to rest, sort of like a cemetery for automobiles. As grateful as I was to Uncle Jim for giving me the truck, I felt no sadness whatsoever waving goodbye to the old girl.

* * *

Knowing full well my job was seasonal, once the calendar finally rolled over to October, I received a layoff slip from K-Line. The timing wasn't too favorable: I was still four weeks short of qualifying for Employment Insurance. Not even five minutes after receiving my layoff slip, however, I learned that K-Line had just won the bid on a big construction project in northern Alberta. My boss asked if anyone from our crew wanted to go, informing us the job would extend our employment by another month. This extra month seemed heaven-sent. It was precisely what I needed to qualify for EI over the coming winter. I jumped at the opportunity and took the job. The contract entailed installing underground fiber optic cable from Cold Lake, Alberta, to the province's capital city, Edmonton. I was positioned on a work crew whose job it was to clear a fifty-foot wide swath through any wooded area. The path was created to facilitate a thoroughfare for the lead caterpillar, which laid the cable. Alberta, having stringent rules when it came to clearing bush, meant we had to fell the trees by hand and then cut the logs down to eighteen inches and stack them up in piles. It was hard work, with twelve-hour workdays, seven days a week…no downtime except for short coffee breaks, lunch, showering, dinner, and sleeping. As labor intensive as it was for some guys on my crew, after my wood-hauling days with Dad, I handled it quite comfortably. The seven-day grind wasn't easy by any means, but I was nowhere near my breaking point. Getting up at 5:45 AM, I'd shower, get ready, and be out the door by 6:00 AM. If you weren't on time at the departure point, the truck left without you. I never missed that truck. At the end of the day, we would get back to the motel around 7:00 PM—in the dark—shower again, change clothes, and head over to the restaurant for dinner. By the time I was finished, it would be well past 9:00 PM. That was when I'd head to bed.

Being the type of work this was, it put me in the company of some seasoned alcoholics. These guys would often stay up all night drinking and then go straight from the bar to work in the morning—with no sleep. Their watering hole of choice was conveniently located next door to our motel. Sadly, I witnessed some individuals drink their entire paychecks away. Never understanding the logic in working that hard only to spend all your earnings on booze, the entire scenario seemed counterproductive and didn't make ANY sense to me whatsoever. Seeing these guys blow their entire wages in the bar was a good, up-close lesson for me in terms of what the effects of substance abuse can have on a person.

We were stationed in Elk Point, halfway between Cold Lake and Edmonton. Like many northern towns in any of the Canadian provinces, Elk Point dates back to the glory days of fur trapping. With a population of roughly 1,400 inhabitants, there was somewhat of a nightlife available in the small town. As I was the only guy who'd elected to drive up in his own vehicle—everyone else had driven up in company trucks—I had my own means of transportation. Although not inclined to drinking all night long as some of these fellows were, I definitely was into girls. The first Friday night after work, a few of us piled into my truck and headed for one of the nightclubs downtown. It was a country bar that played live music and was supposedly a hot spot in Elk Point. This is where I met Jaylynn. My evenings of going to bed early were coming to an end. Jaylynn was a year older than I, nineteen, brunette, and quite gorgeous. We experienced one of those moments where both of us noticed that we were looking at each other. Therefore, with confidence, I sauntered over and struck up a conversation with her. The two of us chatted for only about five minutes before she had to head home, but during our brief conversation, I did learn that she used to work at the restaurant next to the hotel where my crew was staying. That was all I needed.

The next day after work, I went to the restaurant for dinner, banking on the fact that since Elk Point was a small town, everyone knew everyone. I asked the waitress serving me if she might know who

Jaylynn was. My assumption was correct. She knew her. I asked if she might have Jaylynn's phone number. "Let me go check and see if we have it on file" was her reply. I guess she felt comfortable giving me her number, which I received a few minutes later. After acquiring Jaylynn's phone number, I headed back to my room and immediately dialed the number. Extremely curious as to how I'd acquired her number, the first thing Jaylynn did was probe me for answers. "I have my ways" was all I said. Considering all I'd had to go on was her first name and that she used to work at the restaurant next door to our motel, I believe my resourcefulness might have impressed her. We chatted on the phone for over two hours that evening. I learned she was single, had a two-year-old daughter, worked as a kindergarten teacher, and lived in an apartment building not far from where I was staying. Surprisingly, the fact that Jaylynn had a child didn't faze me at all. For some strange reason, it made her more attractive.

Over the course of the next month, Jaylynn and I spent nearly every spare moment we had together. On more than one occasion, we stayed up and spent the entire night talking, meaning both of us went to work the next day on no sleep. This led to some long, hard days working in the bush. Considering my affinity for children, I soon became quite fond of her daughter…and I was definitely falling for Jaylynn. Once my job ended and it was time for me to leave, however, I wasn't sure how this was going to play out. An honest perception of our relationship—at this point—would have been that my feelings for her were stronger than hers were for me. On the other hand, enjoying the chase, I preferred it that way. Besides, if it ever came down to ending the relationship, I'd rather GET hurt than inflict it. The day finally arrived when the job was completed and I had to return to Saskatchewan, but I didn't want to give up just yet. Upon saying our goodbyes that afternoon, I promised to call her every night at midnight—long distance charges being far more reasonable after 12:00 AM. It's always been interesting to me how our memories can store vivid details of certain situations—for no apparent reason. I can distinctly recall Jaylynn sitting on the kitchen counter as I stood between her legs and kissed her goodbye. She had a favorable look in her eye that told me she wanted to see where this would lead, a look that also said, "You better call me!" I left that afternoon with a pleasant feeling of both enthusiasm and optimism.

After doing the phone thing every night for about two weeks, I was getting the sense that Jaylynn was coming around in the feelings department. Anxious to see each other, we planned a trip to Saskatoon during a weekend that my mom was back in Tadmore, giving Jaylynn and me the opportunity to be alone. I'd drive up to Elk Point—Jaylynn didn't own a vehicle—pick up her and her daughter, and then drive back to Saskatoon, where we'd stay at Mom's apartment for the weekend. From our conversations on the phone, and from the tone and enthusiasm in her voice, it was evident that she was excited about spending time with me. There was a certain degree of anticipation in her, and I could definitely identify that she was missing me. Because I really liked this girl, her eagerness to visit me left me feeling pretty good.

I drove up to Elk Point on Friday in my usual double-the-speed-limit fashion and arrived around 6:00 PM. It was December and already dark outside in northern Alberta. This would be where I got lost in paradise, and those old habits that die hard would, unfortunately, get the best of me. While working for K-Line, I ended up acquiring a master key to the motel rooms. My bunkmate had our room key, and one night, I returned to the hotel and found myself locked out of the room. A young girl around my age working at the front desk gave me the key so I could get into my room. She mentioned she wasn't supposed to give it to me, as it was a master key. "Make sure you give it back, okay," she said when she gave me the key. I never did give it back and had it with me the night I went to pick up Jaylynn. Instead of heading straight to her apartment, I pulled into the back of the motel. I should have dropped the key off at the front desk, but instead, I used it to enter one of the rooms and steal a brand-new color TV, complete with remote control—a very sought-after accessory during the eighties. After placing the TV safely in the back of my truck box on a towel, I drove to Jaylynn's.

Seeing each other for the first time after nearly a month, we were both somewhat excited. The three of us piled into my truck and hit the road for the return trip to Saskatoon. With the Nitty Gritty Dirt Band's "Fishing in the Dark"—one of Jaylynn's favorites—softly emanating from the stereo speakers—it wasn't long before she fell asleep nestled up against my shoulder. That was when my mind couldn't stop thinking about the TV I'd just stolen. And somewhere along the way, it seemed my conscience was getting more defined. The fact that I'd just stolen this TV was seriously weighing on me. As a result, I kept hearing that little voice in the back of my mind continually admonishing me and telling me that I was bad news for this girl. She had a two-year-old daughter to think of. I wasn't boyfriend material. I realized that before seriously becoming involved with Jaylynn, or anyone for that matter, I had some serious issues to resolve first. Consequently, for the entire weekend, I was withdrawn and clearly not myself. Extremely unlike me, I never even attempted intimacy with Jaylynn during our time together that weekend. As I was nowhere near the charismatic guy I was capable of being, Jaylynn sensed something was off. She asked what was bothering me, but I just danced around the subject. I wasn't about to confess to her I was a thief and totally wrong for her and her little girl.

Not long after that weekend, she wisely broke up with me. I didn't have the heart to end the relationship myself. Part of me was glad she did, because I really didn't want to mess up her life. She definitely deserved better than me. Despite the pain of a heavy heart, in cold-turkey-like fashion, I never spoke to her again. My parents never said anything, but I could tell they were relieved that my relationship with Jaylynn was over. It wasn't difficult to ascertain that the idea of their son dating a girl with a child wasn't sitting well with them. Little did they know I would have likely been far worse for her than she ever would have been for me, especially considering my affinity for breaking the law. I later pawned the stolen TV for a disappointing $50, and that made me feel even worse. I felt like such a loser. For the rest of December that year, I laid low to let my wounded heart heal. That was my very first broken heart, and it was really devastating. How was I ever going to be a man worthy of a good woman while navigating the twisted road I was on? I knew I had to change my ways. But that remained easier said than done.

Cue music: "So Far So Good" by Thornley

https://www.youtube.com/watch?v=SMjEOCkdJbM

CHAPTER

22

Strike Two

December of 1987 was an awfully cold month. And as is the case when going through a painful transition, the grains of sand once again appeared to fall through the hourglass in slow motion. In an effort to consolidate my emotions and vent some frustration, I went outside in the frigid temperature one afternoon and chopped wood for four hours non-stop. Nothing like good, hard work to soothe the soul. Considering I wasn't paying any rent, and figuring it was the least I could do to help save my parents some dough, I kept a hefty supply of firewood stocked up and always had wood burning in the furnace. Mom and Dad were still living apart in separate cities; they were struggling. I didn't know it at the time, but this was the lowest point in their marriage, and Mom was even considering the possibility of divorce.

After working for K-Line and earning a decent income, my EI benefits were more than enough to live on, especially with no real living expenses to speak of other than food. Believing it would help me find respite from the temporary dispiritedness of losing Jaylynn, I began dating a girl named Sheri—one of my cousin Candace's friends. Having known for about a year that Sheri had a major crush on me, and as she was kind of cute, it seemed like the perfect solution to filling an undesirable void that had been left in my life. Although she did invoke a sense of comfort to my broken-heart situation, unfortunately, because this was a classic rebound scenario, our liaison lasted less than a month. In the end, I felt incredibly guilty for using the poor girl.

The calendar flipped over to 1988, and nine days later, I turned nineteen. Finally, I was of legal drinking age in Saskatchewan—not that my age had ever stopped me. With Dad having a table saw and a few rudimentary woodworking tools in the garage, out of sheer boredom, I decided to build some furniture. After a trip to the lumber yard to grab some material, I bought some wood and built two night tables for my parents' bedroom and a stereo cabinet for mine. Having a tendency to lean toward perfectionism when building anything, my woodworking efforts turned out quite well. Even I was somewhat impressed. To this day, those end tables still sit next to my mom's bed.

Later that spring—April of 1988—Mom decided to move from the apartment into a duplex. I once again journeyed to Saskatoon in my truck and helped her move. However, in expectation of K-Line calling me back to work soon, I didn't stick around and headed back to Tadmore immediately afterward. By the middle of June, I had not received the anticipated back-to-work call from K-Line. Discouraged and wanting to pursue new adventures, I decided another trip to Saskatoon was in order. After throwing a few things in a duffle bag, I jumped in my black Chevy half-ton and headed for Saskatoon.

Taking my usual back-way to the highway from Tadmore meant traveling on gravel roads for roughly five miles. In Saskatchewan, after a couple of days without rain, because of the dusty, dry conditions, you could literally spot me coming from a mile away. The truth about dust is that a person gets accustomed to living in and around the stuff; it literally becomes a part of one's life. As annoying as dust is, it's amazingly beautiful when it colors the sky as the sun begins to set, or when each particle becomes distinctly visible when a ray of sunshine peeks through the shades of a dimly lit room—revealing a miniature universe to the beholder. Since I normally kept my vehicles spotless—always having fresh Armor All on the dash—once I finally turned on to the highway, it was hard not to notice the amount of dust that had already accumulated inside my truck. In memory of feelings once felt, with my finger, I wrote Jaylynn's name in it up on the dashboard.

While passing through Yorkton on my way to Saskatoon, I spotted a very unique-looking car sitting outside on the show rack at a dealership. This automobile was a 1987 Chevy Camaro, silver in color, with red interior, an automatic transmission, and a 305 cubic-inch V8 engine. It was not nearly the powerhouse my beloved Mustang had been, but nevertheless, it was plenty of muscle for me. Although a dime a dozen back then, this Camaro had a very distinctive red digital-effects aftermarket decal all the way down the side of the car. Whoever decided to put this decal on the car was a designer genius, because it made what would otherwise be an ordinary Camaro extraordinary. At least, in my opinion, it did. I can't exactly describe what I was feeling after seeing this car other than to say *it had my name all over it*—it was me! The car simply popped. Besides, the IROC (International Race of Champions) stock car series used identically prepared Camaros during the 1975–1980 and 1984–1989 racing seasons. If it was good enough for that, it was good enough for me.

Not exactly having thousands of dollars saved in the bank or stuffed in my mattress meant applying for a bank loan. Considering the fact that EI was my only source of income, I knew getting approved for financing was going to be a challenge—not to mention this would be my first loan without a co-signer. With my parents' business struggling and them having filed for bankruptcy, they were in no position to help me. I was on my own with this one. Nevertheless, after the salesman and I agreed on a price, with the trade-in value of my half-ton as the down payment, the bank miraculously approved the loan. My car payments were $356 per month at twelve percent interest for five years. Upon waking up that morning, I never would have guessed in a million years that I would be buying a new car that day. After signing on the dotted line, just like that, I was driving to Saskatoon in a swanky new Camaro while "Money for Nothing" by Dire Straits blasted through the crappy GM factory speakers. Considering this WAS a Camaro, I couldn't believe all it had for a sound system was a radio with cheapo speakers. Being the music lover I am, and quite particular about how it sounds, that little dilemma needed to be rectified sooner rather than later.

http://montejperepelkin.com/photos-9

The very next day, Saturday, I woke early and went straight to Crazy Kiley's in Saskatoon. Kiley's—one of those popular stereo shops that constantly advertised about having a "once-in-a-lifetime blowout sale" every month—seemed like the perfect destination. Wouldn't you know, they were having one of their famous sales that very weekend. By day's end, for a cool $2,000 and an easy payment plan, I had an awe-inspiring Alpine compact disc stereo system installed in my new ride, complete with four brain-piercing speakers and two body-thumping Bazooka sub woofers. That sound system rocked…literally! At only half volume, the car actually shook, and the music was so powerful you could feel your hair moving with each beat. First tune I listened to was "Lunatic Fringe" by Red Rider. Sporting a week-long permanent grin on my face once again, I was on cloud nine. Or was it life number nine?

Still collecting a hefty EI check every two weeks, I wasn't overly concerned with my financial situation. Because any job available to me in the city wouldn't have come close to equaling that pogey check, I reasoned that it was counterproductive to even bother looking for a job—at least not quite yet. Alternatively, my first choice would have been to return to K-Line. But that didn't happen. Nevertheless, with six months before my EI cash cow ran out, I was sitting pretty well. Other than my car and stereo payments, food and entertainment were my only expenses. And when you're nineteen, six months seems so far away. Since my EI checks were being delivered to our mailbox in Tadmore, however, this meant a trip there every two weeks, which proved to be a waste of my time, not to mention gas money. Near the middle of July, I decided to spend the remaining summer days in Tadmore, hanging out at Crystal Lake. That was when I met Margo—mentioned earlier. Having learned quite early in life that opportunities always seemed to have a way of presenting themselves around me, I wasn't overly concerned about my future. My only mistake with most of those opportunities was choosing the correct manner in which to take advantage of them.

* * *

Two days after arriving in Tadmore—just long enough to get our yard in tip-top shape—Dad called me up on the phone. Apparently, his parents were coming for a visit, and he wondered if I wanted the four of us to go on a four-day fishing trip to Flin Flon, Manitoba, taking our boat along to do the fishing. Only problem was that Dad drove a Ford Ranger, which meant we'd have to take my Camaro.

Nevertheless, I was game. After installing a hitch on my car, the four of us were off to northern Manitoba—roughly a four-hour drive—on a fishing expedition. Perhaps it was the simple fact that I was now an adult, but this fishing trip—for whatever reason—was one of the best visits I ever had with Grandma and Grandpa. For once, instead of as a kid, they treated me as an equal. Most often in the past, whenever Dad and Grandpa had been together, I'd felt like their little slave. All they'd ever done was yell at me and scold me for one thing or another. But this time was different. It was a welcomed change.

Once September rolled over on the calendar, I once again journeyed back to Saskatoon and reconnected with my cousin Duane. The problem with us hanging out all the time was that we were TOO much alike! And not in a good way. In terms of dishonesty, neither of us had the inclination to consider the implications our lawbreaking deeds had on others, nor the dire consequences we were provoking on ourselves. Dishonesty became so pervasive in our lives that it was second nature to us. Except for the occasional twenty-dollar bill that he'd finagle from his parent's, Duane rarely had any money. This left me always having to pay for everything when we went anywhere.

Feeling somewhat discouraged by the fact that summer was nearly over, and because it was a warm day, Duane and I decided to spend one of the last hot afternoons at the waterslide park, where there were always plenty of girls in bikinis. While lying on a towel soaking up the last bits of Saskatchewan sunshine, my old buddy Shaun from high school spotted me and came over to say hello. Having not seen each other for quite some time, we chatted for a few minutes catching up on things. However, considering the attendance at the water park that afternoon consisted mostly of older moms with their kids, the scenery was somewhat undesirable, and our enthusiasm quickly withered. Accordingly, Duane and I decided to throw in the towel and leave. That was when Shaun asked if I'd give him and his friend a ride. I obliged. Later that evening ended up with me throwing a Frisbee around with Shaun and his buddy at Kiwanis Park along the river downtown, at which time, unbeknownst to me, Shaun's buddy put his wallet in the center console of my Camaro—for safekeeping.

About a week later, Duane found the very same wallet in the center console of my Camaro. It had an ID, driver's license, library card, and an Esso credit card inside. Neither of us recognized the ID; it was a different name than Shaun's friend. Therefore, Duane and I had no clue who this wallet belonged to, and being the opportunists we indeed were, I immediately headed for an Esso station. We filled up my tank with fuel, picked out a bunch of snacks, and handed the credit card to the cashier. To our surprise, the card worked! Quite honestly, it couldn't have come at a better time. Paying Duane's way everywhere had seriously been putting the screws to my bank account. A few days later, Duane came up with the brilliant scheme of using the ID in the wallet to rent a Super Nintendo game console, along with some games to go with it. We had no intention of ever returning said items, as the cash they could bring superseded anything else. Super Nintendo was the most popular of all the video game consoles during the late 1980s, with *Super Mario Bros* being the number one sought-after game of its time. After acquiring the Super Nintendo entertainment system, Duane and I would stay up until 5:00 AM some mornings at his parents' house, playing the stupid game, attempting the arduous task of rescuing the imprisoned princess, after which we'd sleep until noon.

* * *

For the next month and a half, our lives consisted of playing tennis, hanging out at various parks, sun-tanning, going to movies, going to clubs, playing video games all night, and using the Esso credit card to fill my fuel tank and buy tons of junk food, all while collecting EI from the government. I had become a certified bum. As a result, I could literally feel—because of all the junk food we were eating—my body beginning to wear down and my energy level becoming exceedingly deficient. In light of where I'd been a year ago, my self-worth had diminished considerably. Doing hard physical labor for K-Line while earning some decent dough felt great. Now I felt disgusted with myself. To top it all off, I was using a stolen credit card. I was fully aware that sooner or later—if we kept using the card—getting caught was an inevitable reality leading to undesirable consequences. Each time I used the card, I kept telling myself, *Just this one last time. Then I'll cut the card up.*

Earlier in my life, I'd equated stealing with an addiction, and although I'm not familiar with substance addiction, using that credit card certainly had one very distinctive characteristic: I simply couldn't resist using the darn thing, even while knowing full well what the consequences would be if we got caught. Here we were, two guys who weren't violent, didn't ever get involved with drugs, both raised by decent families, and we weren't purposely malicious by any means. But when it came to dishonesty...well, it seemed as if we just couldn't help ourselves. Even though common sense tells us that the easy way in life is almost always the wrong way and inevitably ends up being the hard way in the end, somehow we trick ourselves into believing that the knowingly harmful action we're doing will be okay this one time or "one last time." That goes for everything, whether it's stealing, lying, cheating, overeating, abusing drugs or alcohol, adultery, and every other vile deed under the sun. Perhaps that is the difference between men and boys: men see the big picture, and boys only see themselves in the picture. In other words, men see the full consequences of their actions, whereas boys only see the instant gratification in each choice they make. Clearly, I was the latter.

Towards the end of October, I began noticing a creaking sound coming from the front end of my car whenever I took a corner fast. After parking one wheel up on a curb, I crawled underneath and determined that the bushings in the front control arms were both worn out and needed to be replaced. Conveniently for me, there was an Esso station, complete with service bays and skilled mechanics, just two blocks from Duane's parents' house—allowing me to easily walk back while they replaced the bushings. Fully comprehensive in my understanding that I'd exceedingly pushed my luck with this credit card, I was determined that this was going to be the very last time I'd ever use it. After calling ahead to make an appointment, the mechanic put my car up on the hoist and showed me what the problem was— which I already knew. This mechanic, however, with gray hair and a permanent scowl built in to the creases on his face, was a cantankerous old fellow. He said to me while pointing at the worn-out parts, "These bushings are completely worn out, and this car is barely a year old. This isn't a Porsche! You can't drive it like a bloody race car!"

Who did he think he was, my dad? Nevertheless, ignoring his condescending attitude, I gave instructions to go ahead with the repairs. He quoted me a price, but what did I care? I wasn't actually paying for it. Before leaving, the cashier asked how I was going to pay for the repairs. When I answered, "Esso credit card," she asked for the card, wanting to take an imprint of it for the work order. This was slightly before the era of chip cards and instant computer transactions. A few stations had card readers, but the majority of them still did it the old-fashioned way. Nevertheless, while taking an imprint of the credit card, she also asked for my license plate number—which I quickly answered by giving her a fake one, of course. I wasn't stupid!

Upon walking back to Duane's, I distinctly remember how fortunate it was that she'd ASKED me for my license plate number instead of checking for herself. With my actual license plate number on the work order, this transaction could have easily been traced back to me. *That was a close call*, I silently reproached myself, further fortifying my resolve to destroy the credit card after this final transaction. A few hours later, I headed off on foot with the Esso card in my back pocket. During my five-minute journey, it was hard not to reminisce on how awesome getting free gas was. I hadn't even cut the card up yet, and I was already missing it. Arriving at the station, I walked up to the counter only to be pleasantly greeted by a new cashier. She was probably in her late twenties early thirties, but still a very attractive female nonetheless. Upon handing her the credit card, however, to my dismay, this little honey began to read me my rights. Then another undercover cop snuck up behind me and handcuffed my hands behind my back. Utterly in disbelief, my heart instantly began to beat like a horse galloping for home. In my mind, I thought…*here we go again*!

The two undercover cops walked me over to an unmarked police car and placed me in the back seat, after which, the interrogation began. Already fully aware of Duane and his involvement, the first question they asked me was "Where's the other guy?" As with the snowmobile bust, I wasn't going to give my cousin up, and I said, "What other guy?" Apparently, these two detectives had been shadowing Duane and me around for over a month. We had reached the end of the road; the show was over for both of us. I figured if they wanted him, they could find him for themselves. Turned out the cantankerous mechanic lecturing me about how I drove my car had somehow noticed that the license plate number I'd given for the work order didn't match the one on my car and immediately alerted the police. To top it off, my car wasn't even repaired. They were simply holding it until the detectives could get set up to arrest me. It was all one big charade.

During the ride back to the station, the attractive female detective said to me, "How does a good-looking, clean-cut guy like yourself get wrapped up in this kind of thing? And this isn't even your first time either." All I could do was reply, "Good question." As it was near rush hour on Friday afternoon, the ride to the police station took about twenty minutes. On the way, the two detectives were very lighthearted in their conversations. I think they kind of took a liking to me. I even flirted with the female officer, explaining that she looked far too young and beautiful to be a detective. From the look I received in the rear-view mirror—she was driving—I could tell she enjoyed the compliment. However, my perspective quickly deteriorated when she told me about being married and having two kids.

Once we arrived, and I finished writing out my statement—confessing to everything—it was about 6:00 PM. By this time, I was starving. This is where my flirtatious compliment toward the female cop might have earned me some favor. After explaining how I hadn't eaten all day, she brought me two burgers, fries, and a Coke. She even let me eat the food in her office before taking me to my cell. After being escorted to my holding cell, the sound of the guard slamming the iron door shut to lock me in echoed an ominous tone throughout the entire area. That sinking feeling began to once again settle in around the pit of my stomach. A few minutes later, the same guard walked Duane to his metal cage. Again, the iron-barred gate slammed shut. My cell had a sink, stainless-steel toilet, and a single—very uncomfortable—metal bed bolted to the floor, with those scratchy gray blankets that irritate your skin to keep you warm at night. Seeing that it was Friday evening, this would be where Duane and I would spend the next three days, eating MacDonald's for breakfast, lunch, and dinner. Nutrition at its best! Having cells to ourselves—side by side—allowed Duane and I to communicate. But we didn't talk much at all. Sitting there with no windows or visible daylight for the next sixty-plus hours, every moment feeling as if it could have been 3:00 PM in the afternoon or 3:00 AM in the morning, caused minutes to pass by as hours. The only visible light was the fluorescent glow that invariably painted the concrete wall across from my cell. This truly was a dungeon. I had plenty of time to contemplate my dire situation…and I wasn't too thrilled with myself.

Monday morning finally dawned. The calendar said it was October 24th, 1988. I stood before a judge and pled guilty to the charge of theft over $1,000. My second strike! Before the magistrate sentenced me, however, he looked up and asked me how I liked spending the weekend in jail. "It was horrible, Your Honor," I replied. The somewhat sympathetic judge next queried me if I'd learned my lesson yet. "Yes, absolutely, Your Honor!" I answered, with as much sincerity as I could muster. Deep down inside, though, I wasn't as sure as I sounded or thought I did. I was just hoping against hope that the bottom wouldn't completely drop out of my life. "Well, we'll see about that," he replied. I didn't know if that was good or bad. After looking over some papers on his desk and doing some calculations on a calculator, the magistrate sentenced me to thirty months suspended sentence. That was definitely good. I had figured on jail time, for sure. He ordered me to pay $60 per month restitution until the financial encumbrance I'd caused was fully compensated. That was less good…but far from bad. And that was it. I was free to go. Sitting in the courtroom were Duane's mom and my mom—two sisters whose sons were criminals. I'm sure at some point one of them must have said to the other, with a measure of sarcasm, "Are you as proud of your son as I am of mine?"

Following my release, Mom drove me back to my car, which was parked behind the Esso station where I'd been arrested. During the drive—expecting a long lecture—I was surprised she didn't have many words to express about what had just happened. All she had to say was "It seems whenever you and Duane are together, the two of you just end up in trouble. I think you guys should stay away from each other from now on." There certainly wasn't any argument from me with Mom's advice. She wasn't wrong. However, it was a moot point. Duane was leaving for New Zealand in a few days to play ball for the next six months. Quite frankly, for our own sakes, I wasn't at all sad he was leaving. As Mom approached the area where I'd been arrested, fully expecting to find my Camaro broken into with my precious Alpine sound system gutted from the dash, I held my breath. However, by no small miracle, everything was completely and surprisingly intact. A huge sigh of relief escaped from my lungs. First thing on the agenda was to drive straight to Mom's and have a long-overdue, much-needed hot shower.

While standing in the shower, appreciating the hot water running over my body, I contemplated what it meant to be a free man. I doubt many of us realize how fortunate we are to possess the luxuries and freedoms our western lifestyle bequeaths us, becoming so blindly acclimatized to this way of life that we presuppose even the smallest of comforts: hot running water, the freedom to choose what we eat each day, a private bathroom with a door on it, a warm, comfortable bed with a variety of linens to choose from, and let's not forget soft toilet paper. Take even one of these simple amenities away, and you'll suddenly acquire an entirely new perspective towards modern living. Unfortunately, this type of insight can rarely be fully understood without firsthand experience. In order to appreciate their true value, one must first feel their absence.

By this time, surely one would think I had reached the point where the pendulum of life finally reached its pivot point and began to swing the other direction toward consequential living, the moment when a person takes stock of their behavior and decides to make changes. Truth is, I had every intention of doing just that. Unfortunately, any momentary culmination of personal reflection and individual refinement I might have experienced was forgotten within a few hours. And any lesson in consequences I should have learned as a result of these most recent misdeeds was quickly lost in the subterfuge of my mind in favor of the all-too-familiar lifestyle to which I was accustomed.

Cue music: "All Fall Down" by Thornley

https://www.youtube.com/watch?v=Iq3_Vn4rl_E

CHAPTER

23

Choices

Less than twelve hours after receiving my sweetheart sentence from the judge, plans were already in motion to spend that evening with Duane at Esmeralda's, a popular night club located within the Saskatoon Inn. Although I had agreed it would be best to stay away from my cousin and partner in crime, I and a few of Duane's friends had previously planned a little send-off party for him that evening before he left for New Zealand. As Duane was leaving in two days, I figured I'd have plenty of time not to hang around with him once he was gone.

After picking my cousin up later that evening, we headed for the Saskatoon Inn. Upon arriving at the club—because it was a warm autumn evening—there had to have been at least fifty people standing in line waiting to get in. As I've already established, I most often considered Duane to be somewhat of a freeloader. Don't get me wrong, he was a likeable guy, but when it came to paying his way, my cousin turned in to a sponge. Every now and then, however, he did come in handy; this would be one of those times.

Duane, being the amiable character he was, went to school and was friends with the bouncer behind the velvet rope guarding the entrance to this particular club. Like rock stars, we walked right past the long line to where the big, muscular doorman—wearing black dress pants and an Esmeralda's club shirt—was standing. And after a quick glance at who we were, he gave us the usual head nod, unhooked the velvet rope, and let the two of us walk right in. Upon walking by, I could hear the bouncer click twice on the counting device attached to his belt, keeping track of how many people were inside the club. Just that morning, I'd been in police custody, standing before a judge—feeling like I'd spent the weekend in a dumpster—pleading guilty to some fairly serious charges. Yet here I was, barely twelve hours later, wearing designer jeans, an Armani dress shirt, and my favorite Polo cologne and being treated like a celebrity.

The time was near 11:00 PM, and the place was jam-packed with people; many of them were attractive females, which was definitely part of the attraction at Esmeralda's. We settled in at the bar, and I ordered my favorite drink, which, ironically, was a tequila paralyzer. Little did I know I was about to meet an attractive brunette who would eventually alter my life's trajectory.

After ordering my drink, I looked across the circular bar, and there she was, sitting with another not-so-bad-looking female. Glancing over every once in a while, I was quick to pick up on her eyes, which were giving me some scrutinizing attention. I couldn't resist flashing her a smile to see if she would mirror it. She did and responded in kind. There was no mistaking the mutual attraction between us—it almost felt magnetic, not the usual bar boy-girl type of pull. Besides, the alcohol factor hadn't set in yet. I mustered up enough courage to walk over to say hello and ask her to dance. I introduced myself—she introduced herself. Her name was Nicole…none other than my future wife. Wearing a pair of jeans that fit just right and standing at five foot six, with brown eyes, long, dark, curly hair, the most beautiful smile, and curves that went on forever in all the right places, Nicole was an extraordinarily attractive girl. We danced to a couple of songs and then headed back upstairs to hang out with her girlfriend. Nicole later declined my offer to drive her home that evening, which I totally respected; she obviously was not a one-night-stand type of girl. But she did give me her phone number.

I wasted no time and called her the next day. I had no intention to play the waiting game or any other games. I wanted to see her again, sooner rather than later. We made plans for a date at Max's Diner—a trendy little restaurant where mostly the younger generation hung out. It was not a place you'd go for a good meal, but it was great for a drink date and chatting. We had an enjoyable evening at Max's, although Nicole had arranged for another one of her friends, whom she introduced as Shari, to meet us there. Like Nicole, Shari was easy on the eyes, and I didn't mind her hanging out with us. Three was company on that particular night. I would continue dating Nicole for roughly two weeks. Then she dumped me. Ouch! Quite honestly, I was probably coming on too strong for her liking. While lying in bed that evening, feeling confused and a tiny bit crushed by her rejection, the little voice we all have inside of us said to me, "Don't worry, eventually you're going to marry her." After laughing to myself and thinking, *Yeah right,* I turned over and went to sleep. Even though Nicole WAS gorgeous and I did like her, breaking up with me after just two weeks certainly wasn't the end of the world. Being a regular subscriber to the platitude "There are plenty of fish in the sea," I quickly moved on. Besides, with my EI soon to run out, I needed to find a job before a girlfriend. Looking back, however, I can identify with this particular moment—at nineteen years old—as the first time in my life feeling the serious desire to have a steady girlfriend with an eye on one day getting married.

In anticipation of receiving my next employment insurance check, and deciding it was time to fix my Camaro, I headed back to Tadmore. I definitely couldn't afford to pay a mechanic four or five hundred dollars to replace a couple of bushings, so I elected to do the job myself. I made a quick stop at the local car parts store and purchased said bushings for $60. Then I borrowed the required tools and did the repairs on our front lawn. After roughly four hours of strenuous labor, bleeding knuckles, and having used plenty of expletives known in the English language, I finished the job. And after a trip to a local garage for a $69 wheel alignment, VOILA! My Camaro was fixed for under $150. Without even the power of perfect hindsight, it's easy to conclude I should have done the repairs myself in the first place. As hard-headed and set in my ways as I was, however, this little educational cul-de-sac, sadly, still wasn't recognizable quite yet.

* * *

After returning to Saskatoon, I landed a job as a delivery driver for Panagopoulos Pizza, a Canadian delivery and take-out chain that began in 1986 but was rebranded as Panago in 2000. Currently, the franchise has over 180 locations across six Canadian provinces. In 1988, I worked at the location off 8th Street, on the east side of Saskatoon—just blocks from where my mother lived. When not out on deliveries, they had me slicing meats and vegetables or making pizza dough. The money wasn't great, but the added bonus of tips every night compensated for the negligible wage—not to mention the free food. The tips more than kept my gas tank full while affording me a constant stream of spending money. Because Mom always took up residence on the east side, I had vast knowledge of that particular quadrant of the city. Knowing it like the back of my hand, I quickly became the take-out restaurant's number one delivery driver. Often taking two or three deliveries at a time, I'd return before other drivers who'd taken just one. Another reason for my speedy delivery times might also have been due to my fast car.

About a month into working at Panagopoulos, the owner planned to open a second franchise—to be managed by his son Trent—and he wanted me to move over to the new location. Being on Broadway Avenue, the location of the new franchise would divide the east side between the two locations. From a marketing standpoint, it would prove to be a disastrous business strategy. Nevertheless, with preparation for a grand opening being a huge undertaking, it offered me the opportunity to step up and establish myself as a reliable, responsible, and very capable employee. Trent soon promoted me to assistant manager. In reality, other than the addition of a few added responsibilities and a salary instead of an hourly wage, I was nothing more than a glorified pizza delivery guy. The promotion did mean full-time employment, though, and the ability to choose which deliveries I went on, free pizza, and a set of keys to the store. Trent, a few years older than I, was a fairly decent boss. It wouldn't be inaccurate to say that he and I became friends.

Not long after being promoted, Trent's dad offered me a regular gig driving a large truck to northern Saskatchewan on the first Wednesday of every month. In addition to two pizza franchises, the old boy also owned a beef jerky company in La Ronge named Hero Bros. The truck would deliver raw meat up to the plant in La Ronge, where the jerky was made, and then on the return, it would haul packaged product to their distribution warehouse in Saskatoon. The trip there and back took roughly ten hours, for which he offered to pay me $50. Considering the weighty responsibility involved in this endeavor—not to mention the obligation he was entrusting me with—fifty bucks certainly was not a generous payday. Nevertheless, I took the job—mostly for the adventure and free beef jerky.

During my first trip to La Ronge, I couldn't help but observe how beautiful northern Saskatchewan actually was. The northward region of the province consists mostly of lakes and wooded area, providing truly magnificent scenery, especially during late autumn. Deer, moose, coyotes, and even bears could be spotted along my journey. With the autumn air being cool and dense, the sweet, decadent aroma of decomposing leaves was distinctively recognizable. At one point, I couldn't help myself and pulled over to take a brief walk through the forest. The sound of leaves crunching and branches cracking beneath my feet strangely reminded me of my biological father Roy and the walk he and I had once taken in the woods. Getting back on the road, this being my first trip, I was extra attentive to keeping a sharp focus on driving. The truck itself wasn't difficult to drive, but as it was the largest-capacity hauler it could be without needing an air brake license to operate, it certainly took some getting used to. In hindsight, for a nineteen-year-old kid who could easily be considered underqualified, I handled the large hauler quite well. For some reason, I had been blessed with a natural ability to operate motorized vehicles. Maybe it was because I had almost been crushed by one as a toddler, providing me with some strange machine/human bond.

* * *

With my regular hangout buddy Duane in New Zealand, I started hanging out with a guy named Rod, one of Duane's friends. Complete with long black hair to about the center of his back, looking like a rock star, he was an interesting character to say the least. Our friendship consisted mostly of going clubbing together. One night, we were out carousing, and I bumped into Shari. In Saskatoon, the nightlife scene was indeed a small world. We all seemed to be doing the same circuit back then. Sometimes I would even run into Nicole and her new boyfriend Kevin. On those occasions, we just said hi but didn't interact further. Shari and I, on the other hand, shared a few dances at one club or another, since Nicole had dumped me. But because she was Nicole's best friend, I never considered that I had a shot with her, naturally assuming there was some kind of "girl code," where I was considered off limits. During one cold night in December, however, Shari asked me for a ride home. Of course, being a gentleman, I couldn't say no to a beautiful damsel in distress. One thing led to another, with us ending up at my mom's apartment, where I was still living while holding down the pizza delivery job in Saskatoon. With Mom and Nikki gone to Tadmore for the weekend, Shari and I had the place to ourselves. At this point, I never dreamed in a million years that Nicole would ever be back in my life. Therefore, when this opportunity presented itself, I truly didn't see the harm. We ate some Panagopoulos pizza and watched a rental movie, *The Lost Boys*, with then relatively unknowns Kiefer Sutherland and Jason Patric. *The Lost Boys*, basically a comedy/horror flick aimed at a youth demographic, helped shift popular culture depictions of vampires and set the stage for a slew of "cool" vampire movies and television series. At the time, I had no idea what this flick was even about, nor did I care. I don't recall if Shari or I picked it off the shelf. The movie was incidental anyway. The mood that night was comfortable, and it felt intrinsically natural being with Shari—as if the two of us had been in a long-term relationship. Nothing seemed unfamiliar with Shari at all, and we spent the night together.

When dropping Shari at her home in the morning, she gave me her phone number and said she'd had a very nice time with me. I replied that the feeling was definitely mutual, and with every intention in the world of calling her, I drove away. On more than one occasion,

I can recall holding Shari's phone number in my hand, contemplating on whether or not to call. Yet for whatever reason, I never did. It's not like I was shy or afraid, and confidence certainly wasn't an issue—I knew we both felt the same strong connection. She never called me either. Our one-night affair ended as a one-act play. I can't help but wonder, though, what would have happened if I had called her. My liaison with Shari was definitely one of those mysterious forks in my journey through life. The path I did choose, however, led me to have two beautiful daughters whom I wouldn't trade for anything. As for my evening with Shari—as is the case with most extracurricular activities of this nature—it didn't come without consequences, but I'll get to that later.

* * *

Christmas of 1988 rolled around. Mom put up a tree and decorated the house in Saskatoon to the nines with holiday spirit. She went all out that year. Being that it was against JW beliefs to celebrate any pagan holidays, this was a first for me. Even Dad was taking part in the festivities. That's when it became clear: not only had my parents abandoned their Jehovah's Witness faith completely, they were ignoring the very principles once held dear to them. I later found out they had both been disfellowshipped from the JW organization. To be completely honest, I can't say it bothered me at all. In fact, I was quite content with them abandoning their faith. Being a JW—especially as a kid—felt unnecessarily restrictive. From my warped perspective of enjoying life to the fullest—no matter the cost—it seemed like everything fun had been taken away. Deciding to let sleeping dogs lie, I never enquired as to why they'd turned away from being Jehovah's Witnesses.

Mom made a big turkey dinner, and we exchanged gifts, played Christmas music, and drank eggnog. Our family did everything I'd thought we were missing out on all those years. That was the first time since I was a young boy that I'd celebrated Christmas. I will admit, even at nineteen, there was a certain degree of excitement associated with opening gifts, and it was nice to spend time with my family, but I could have done without all the Christmas paraphernalia—it seemed a tad excessive. I remember hauling three huge bags of trash out to the garbage bin that evening. After all was said and done, with all the hype about what the spirit of Christmas was supposed to entail, I couldn't help feeling extremely disappointed. After all those years thinking how much fun I was missing out on, in the end, it wasn't that big of a deal. And the gifts—well intended that they were—weren't anything I particularly wanted or even liked.

On January 9th, 1989, I turned twenty. It goes without saying my teenage days had been spent in search of a good time that led to staying out late, chasing girls, loud music, and driving fast—and even some serious drinking for a guy who wasn't really into drinking. I definitely had an affinity for pushing the limits. With the inclination that it was cool to break the rules, I had no qualms with violating the law. By now, I had maintained this calamitous lifestyle for some sixteen years and was fully cognizant of having experienced more than most teenagers ever could—at least in my circle of friends and acquaintances—and lived to tell about it. However, there was this indisputable awareness inside me affirming that sometime before my twenty-first birthday, I was in for an awakening, probably a rude one. Somehow, I recognized that turning twenty would mark the beginning of a transformation stage in my life.

Although I had, over the years, grown accustomed to not celebrating my birthday while a Jehovah's Witness—now a former one, having joined my folks in their exodus from the organization—I was in the mood to paint the town red on my twentieth birthday. Rod and I decided that Esmeralda's would be the perfect place to commemorate this milestone—in other words, an excuse to party a tad more than usual. There were no gifts, no cake, and no one singing Happy Birthday, all stuff I could do without, but I did meet a girl named Michelle at Esmeralda's that night. Being exceptionally beautiful, she really caught my attention…and she was the one who approached me, not the other way around. Nicole was there too, but without her boyfriend. We chatted for a few minutes, but that's as far as it went, not because she proved to be indifferent towards me, but because I was in the mood to mingle. That was when Michelle entered my life.

Meeting this gorgeous brunette, who was a "ten" if there ever was one, caused my heart and soul to light up like the northern lights against a dark sky. The two of us danced and drank all night long; before we knew it, we were both too inebriated to drive. Lucky for me, Nicole was a good sport and offered to drive all of us home in my car. I must say I was kind of blown away by her gesture, which I accepted on everyone else's behalf, making for a full carload. We stopped for submarine sandwiches on the way, and by the time everybody got dropped off, including Rod, I had sobered up enough to drive. Michelle was still in the car, and after we got to Nicole's place, I got behind the wheel and drove her home. I wasn't expecting to go inside, just to give her a goodnight kiss and ask if I could call her the next day. To my surprise, she invited me in. When I asked Michelle if she was sure about me coming inside, with a twinkle in her eye and a mischievous grin on her face, she responded, "Hurry up before I change my mind."

In the morning, when I woke, Michelle was already up and in the shower. After quickly getting dressed, I went and sat on her couch—waiting to give her a goodbye kiss before leaving. While sitting there—having not actually seen this girl in daylight—my mind began to wonder: *Is she really as beautiful as I thought, or was the alcohol skewing my perception last night?* Turned out she was every bit as beautiful as I thought and had a personality to match. Later, I learned she had done a significant number of local modeling gigs. I was already imagining the good-looking kids we could bring into this world, but that flight through fairyland would soon come crashing down. After the long-awaited goodbye kiss that morning, Michelle brought me face to face with an abrupt reality check: She prudently began explaining there was a certain boyfriend in her life. Convinced he was cheating on her, she reassured me they were on the verge of breaking up. *Like you just cheated on him with me,* I thought to myself. To say that I was disheartened would be an understatement of immense proportions. It seems puerile now to have felt that amount of sensitivity after just one night, but I really liked Michelle. At that point, I seriously wanted a genuine girlfriend— and true, everlasting love.

* * *

Working at Panagopoulos was fun, for sure, but certainly nowhere near my dream job—if there was such a thing. Truth be told, within a matter of a few short months, I'd learned everything there was about running the place. No longer challenging me intellectually, I was becoming bored with working at the pizza joint. I finally came to the conclusion that I needed to make some drastic changes in my life. I had no clue where to begin, however. Perhaps it does for some, but turning twenty didn't exactly mean that the floodgates of wisdom, direction, and true fulfillment would open up for me. At this point, it felt as if I had absolutely no control over my life.

My third time driving the beef jerky truck to La Ronge was in early February of the new year. With the temperature dipping down in the nether regions of -40° Celsius, it was an extremely cold day. You'd get frostbite simply walking from your house to start the car.

But being a person who enjoys contemplating the deeper things in life, I always looked forward to this trip. The peace and serenity of this journey through northern Saskatchewan afforded me time to do just that…think! During the drive on that cold day in February, I recall pondering on what I truly wanted out of life. Much of it was identical to the boyhood version I'd had on that day in Tadmore at thirteen years old, when I'd presumably had a conversation with God—the day before seeing the unexplained image on our garage door that had swirled into a ball and shot off into the sky. Yet those dreams of living the perfect life seemed as far as east is from west compared to where my life currently was.

Slowly crouching towards La Ronge—about an hour away—the traffic was becoming increasingly scarce. Even though I had the heat on full blast, the side windows were completely iced up—that was how cold it was! In the process of stopping a couple times to scrape the windows in order to see my side-view mirrors, within those few seconds, I could feel the tips of my nose, ears, and fingers beginning to freeze already. Saskatchewan winters are certainly not for the faint of heart. With northern Saskatchewan's landscape consisting mostly of wooded areas, the highway began to weave through the bush with the odd clearing here and there. In consideration of how frigid it was, the tires felt as if they were made of plastic, and as a result, I could feel every crack in the highway. Approaching the next sweeping corner, there was a visible clearing in the trees just ahead. Therefore, in an attempt to compensate for the wind catching the truck as if it were a sail, I steered to the center of the two-lane highway. Sudden wind shear can easily push a big truck straight into the ditch. Sure enough, as soon as I entered the clearing, the truck immediately shot over to the right roughly four feet. Just as this happened, I could feel the front wheels break loose—as if there was ice—and lose traction for a brief moment. I was headed for another close encounter of the almost fatal kind.

At this point, the truck seemed to have a mind of its own and veered off towards the ditch. Being an inexperienced truck driver, I overreacted and turned the wheels abruptly in an attempt to avoid driving off the road. In light of what happened next, I should have simply driven into the ditch. As a consequence of my knee-jerk reaction to turn the wheel, the entire truck slowly began tipping over. That was when the eerie feeling of knowing something bad was about to happen became entrenched within me. In a desperate attempt to correct the situation, I steered out of the roll, but with a full load on the back, it was too late. At that point, there was no stopping the truck from tipping over. Next thing I knew, while hanging on to the steering wheel for dear life, standing on the side window—not wearing my seatbelt, of course—the truck was sliding down the highway on its driver side. Upon looking down at my running shoes planted on the glass, I could see sparks flying everywhere from the cab of the truck scraping against the pavement. Suddenly, the realization hit me that standing on the glass probably wasn't the best idea, and I quickly repositioned my feet onto the frame of the door—immediately after which the glass that I'd just been standing on suddenly exploded between my legs. My first thought was *Wow, that was close!*

The truck finally slid into the ditch and stopped. Gathering my senses, I turned off the engine and climbed up and out of the cab through the passenger side door. Once outside, the dead silence of the cold air brought home how serious this situation indeed was. The last car I had encountered had passed me over forty-five minutes ago. It felt as if I were on the moon, with not a soul around for thousands of miles. If circumstances weren't bad enough—in alignment with the risk-taker in me—my outerwear consisted of nothing more than jeans, a sweatshirt, running shoes, and a skimpy jacket. I wasn't prepared for this type of scenario at all. Within seconds, I was feeling frostbite on my ears, nose, and fingers. This was not good. Then, all of a sudden, a vehicle appeared from around the corner—a half-ton truck with two guys in it headed back in the direction I'd come from. They were kind enough to give me a ride to the nearest town. After a brief explanation of what had happened, one of the fellows said to me, "It's a good thing we came along when we did. There isn't a whole lot of traffic around these parts, you know, especially this time of year. The way you're dressed, young man, you'd have frozen to death." In all likelihood, those two gentlemen saved my life. Needless to say, that was the end of my truck driving gig. Surprisingly, however, my boss wasn't noticeably upset with me.

The Friday following my daunting brush with death, in celebration of surviving the ordeal, Rod and I got all geared up for a night of debauchery at the clubs. This ended with neither of us in any position to safely drive. Fortunately, Nicole again happened to be at the same club. She was accompanied by her boyfriend Kevin. I couldn't believe she offered to drive us home...again. Unceremoniously ditching Kevin, she walked out with us, got behind the wheel of my Camaro, and off we went. She dropped Rod off first and then proceeded to take me to my mother's residence.

During the drive, I took the opportunity to turn the stereo down low and ask Nicole how things were going with Kevin. Being a quick study of people, even though my brain was absorbed in an exorbitant amount of alcohol, I could still sense by the tone of her answer that things weren't all that great between them. That was when I took advantage of the favorable circumstances—under the camouflage of being intoxicated—to make it known that I was still quite fond of her. I even got around to telling her I'd been somewhat heartbroken when she'd ended our relationship. Following my confession, it wasn't hard for me to discern that Nicole took a certain delight in hearing me expose my feelings. Upon rolling up to my place, with the premise that she'd return it in the morning, Nicole dropped me at the curb and drove off in my car. Trusting my Camaro to wander off without me in it was completely out of character for me. I obviously trusted this girl a great deal. After that particular evening, Nicole and I would periodically keep in touch with one another—just as friends.

* * *

Meanwhile, as the calendar flipped over to March 1989, I had to make a quick overnight trip to Tadmore for something important. Coincidentally, Nicole happened to call me the day before this trip. During our chat, she revealed that she had broken up with Kevin and was thinking about moving to Calgary. In turn, I gave her the "you're better off without him" consolatory speech, and as any friend would, I offered my services to assist her in moving. During this same conversation, I mentioned about going to Tadmore and offered her the opportunity to come along for the ride, affirming right up front that we'd be spending the night. I expected her to pass on the offer, but to my surprise, she was game. Neither of us was aware at the time, but this particular trip to Tadmore on Wednesday, March 15, 1989, would become a benchmark day in both our lives.

Even though we ended up crossing the boundaries of an innocent friendship during this trip, I never suspected Nicole might be interested in dating again. Therefore, without putting any thought into why she'd chosen to come with me in the first place, upon returning to Saskatoon the next day, I dropped her off at home and went to work at the pizza place. Tossing any expectations out the window, I simply chalked the event up as a couple of fun days with an attractive girl. I didn't even bother to call her the next day. Quite frankly, in light of my most recent experience with Michelle, my attitude towards women was becoming jaded.

Within a few days, however, Nicole rang me up on the phone, and from her tone I could distinctly sense she wasn't too pleased about my not having called. However, using the old philosophy "fool me once shame on you, fool me twice shame on me," I brought her up to speed on the details of how she'd dumped me last time and therefore didn't believe the onus was on me to initiate anything between us. Surprisingly, Nicole understood and agreed with my point of view. When does that ever happen? Then she responded in kind by making it clear how much she'd enjoyed our trip to Tadmore and further invited me to do something with her on the weekend. Interesting how in the absence of my calling, Nicole all of a sudden seemed noticeably more attracted to me.

As intriguing as this sudden turn of events with Nicole was, there was still the issue of my involvement with Michelle. Hoping she might break up with her boyfriend, making her available for a relationship with me, I was sending her flowers every Wednesday after we'd met. And the two of us would hang out regularly, strictly as friends. I now had somewhat of a dilemma on my hands and wasn't sure how to proceed. Although I liked Nicole and could tell she was all of a sudden interested in me, how did I know she wouldn't just dump me again? On the other hand, waiting for Michelle to break up with her boyfriend seemed even worse. Part of me wanted to tell them both to go to hell. Instead, I kept my cool and waited to see how this played out. Besides, technically, I wasn't dating anyone yet, and in the spirit of letting this play out, I made plans with Nicole for Saturday night.

When Friday rolled around, however, something totally unexpected happened. Michelle popped in to surprise me at work.

Saying she had something exciting to tell me, she gave me one of those long, dynamite kisses that I hadn't received since the night we'd met. Then she left. Being that I only worked until 7:00 PM on Fridays, we agreed to meet afterward. Then, not ten minutes later, Nicole dropped by for a quick hello, gave me a kiss on the cheek, and left. Considering both of these incidents transpired in the customer area of the pizza joint, the girl working our front counter said to me in a jesting manner, "Shame on you, Monte." Except, it wasn't like that. I wasn't officially dating either of them. Nevertheless, the fact that I was visited by two separate potential girlfriends ten minutes apart didn't sit well with me. A decision needed to be made soon before this got out of hand.

When 7 PM rolled around, I went home, showered, and headed to Michelle's. The exciting news was that she'd finally broken up with her boyfriend. Considering how long I'd been waiting for this day, you'd think I'd have been extremely overjoyed. But for some reason, I wasn't. After wanting this commitment from Michelle for the past two and a half months, I'd envisioned feeling much different then what I was. She was planning to go over to her ex-boyfriend's house that night one last time to pick up a few things that were left there and asked if I'd drive her. During the drive—he lived in a little farmhouse outside the city—Michelle intertwined her fingers with mine and held my right hand like that for the entire trip. Being pitch-dark outside, I remember the red effervescent glow of the dashboard in my Camaro, painting us in a romantic hue as music played softly in the background. This was what I'd wanted all along, and because touchy-feely women appeal to me, it felt intimately comfortable being with her in that manner. We talked a considerable amount during the drive there, and that's when the subject of why she'd finally dumped this guy came up. As it turned out, Michelle was right; he WAS cheating her. On a hunch, she'd driven out to his house one evening and caught him with another girl. After which, she'd dumped him on the spot.

Once we arrived at his house in the country, Michelle ran in to grab her stuff. She wasn't in there more than five minutes, but that was long enough for the gears in my head to start turning. *Let's back up the infidelity train and analyze this situation for a moment*, I thought to myself. Michelle finally wanted to be with me because she'd caught her boyfriend cheating. In other words, if he had been faithful, she would've stayed with him? That meant I was her second choice. That didn't sit well with me. I didn't like finishing second place at anything, especially my girlfriend! All of a sudden, that intimately comfortable feeling I'd felt with Michelle just moments ago was gone, replaced by the sensation of my heart being squeezed. As a result of this, during our drive back to the city, I wasn't very communicative. Michelle, sensing something was wrong, asked if everything was okay. Still in the process of digesting my newfound understanding of the situation, I didn't let on that anything was awry.

Arriving back at her place around 11:00 PM, even though I wasn't exactly thrilled with the circumstances under which this had all come about, having a weakness for gorgeous women, I accompanied her into the house. However, while what we did that night would normally have been considered a consummation of a relationship, instead, it wound up being an act of farewell. I never even spent the night. The only vivid memory from that evening was driving away from Michelle's feeling like I was her second option. That was when the choice to walk away from Michelle became crystal clear. My only regret was that I never told her—I just stopped calling. And the two of us would drift off into different fates.

At this point, Nicole and I hadn't committed to anything, and I didn't know for sure if we ever would. All the same, my decision with

Michelle had nothing to do with Nicole. This wasn't about choosing. Shortly after this last rendezvous with Michelle, Nicole and I did begin a relationship, and the details of how that evening transpired are still theatrically alive in my memory. Up until this particular evening, Nicole and I had been hanging out off and on, but except for the night we'd spent in Tadmore, nothing ever happened between us to indicate we were dating. We hadn't even kissed since that trip. It felt like we were just friends. While sitting on Nicole's sofa waiting for her to get ready—we were going out to a club that night—all of a sudden, wearing a pair of jeans and with a swagger in her hips, she strutted towards me looking as if auditioning for the "Looks That Kill" Mö tley Crüe MTV rock video. Dressed in a white cotton blouse, a pair of long white leather boots with tassels, and your typical 1980s high-volume hair style, she definitely would have gotten the job. If her aim was to impress me, mission accomplished! Then she sat next to me on the sofa and wanted to talk about "us." If it were up to me, we'd have headed straight for the bedroom and partaken in activities that likely would have destroyed her perfect hairdo. But fair enough, communication was good, so we talked.

Nicole wanted to know if I considered her my girlfriend and was curious as to how I was feeling. Then she informed me that she was falling for me. Quite honestly, I was completely caught off guard with the level of maturity and mental posture she demonstrated by wanting to talk about and define our relationship. Usually, it was always me revealing my feelings first. This was kind of nice for once. After explaining that I was still being cautious, I did reciprocate a mutual sentiment toward her. That was when she REALLY kissed me. Wow! I hadn't seen this side of Nicole before…ever! Now I really wanted to go into the bedroom. That didn't happen, however. Instead, we stuck to our plans and headed out to meet with her friends and eventually my buddy Rod for a night on the town.

* * *

Not long before Nicole and I restarted our relationship, however, a string of events would be set into motion that would impact my future…and my past played a crucial role in the entire scenario. Because there were now two Panagopoulos locations in the east end of Saskatoon, what had previously been one big territory for just one franchise was divided in half. It doesn't take a mathematician to understand that this cut revenue in half as well. Consequently, both franchises were struggling to make a profit. To make matters worse, someone was stealing money from our till. Every night, when we'd cash out and add up the evening's receipts, the till would almost always be short twenty to thirty dollars, sometimes as much as fifty. Someone was stealing cash directly out of the cash register. As hard as it may be to believe, it wasn't me. This was a frustrating situation, and I'm sure Trent was distrustful of nearly everyone. A video camera above the cash register likely would have solved everything. Except, this was 1989, and that sort of technology was quite expensive back then, making it somewhat unaffordable to a measly little pizza joint.

Upon arriving at work one Monday afternoon for my regular shift, I was surprised to see Trent there. My boss wasn't normally around on Mondays, and with a locksmith rekeying the front door, I knew something was up. Nonetheless, in my usual manner, I began prepping for the dinner rush. Within a few hours into my shift, Trent approached and requested that I go out on a delivery. This wasn't out of the ordinary—managers went on deliveries now and then, even Trent. Upon returning from the delivery, as soon as I walked through the front door, Trent pulled me aside to accompany him next door to the coffee shop. After a brief sit-down, he made it clear that I was his number one suspect regarding the theft from the cash register, and therefore, he had to let me go. In other words, he fired me. Can't say I was surprised, though; even without anyone stealing, the place had been bleeding cash every single month since it had opened. Considering my deep commitment to that little take-out franchise to succeed, and how hard I'd worked at it, I was disappointed with this turn of events. Nevertheless, with somewhat hard feelings, I went to the back office, gathered my belongings, and left peacefully. Knowing I had three or four work shirts at home—the franchise supplied custom embroidered polo shirts for us to wear—I returned a short while later to drop them off.

After the dust settled in my head, I was somewhat glad in a way to move on from the pizza joint. Being a manager isn't all that it's cracked up to be. The pay—without tips—after all the hours I'd spent trying to help build that place into a successful franchise wasn't even equivalent to minimum wage, which quickly taught me the downside of getting paid a salary as opposed to a set hourly wage. After further contemplation, I couldn't help but wonder if Trent had done a background check on me and, after learning of my criminal record, which was coincidentally in line with the issue in question, had decided to avoid the risk of having me around. In hindsight, I likely would have fired me as well. It was just taking care of business. Within a few days, I found another job earning twenty percent more income for a lot less hours—at a car wash, no less.

CHAPTER

24

A Selfishly Selfless Act

We all make decisions every day that affect the course of our lives, with each choice taking us down a different path. The problem with many of us is that we don't have a destination picked out. Without a goal or a purpose, we make snap decisions based on immediate circumstances instead of longevity and future consequences. As a result, our number one concern centers on solving temporary problems. After all, how can we make decisions that benefit our future when we don't have any kind of future in mind? I know for myself, after moving in to our newly renovated bungalow and becoming somewhat accustomed to life in a wheelchair, I was ignorant to the consequences of my immediate decisions.

Nevertheless, with my living quarters now completely accessible, it definitely made life in a wheelchair easier to endure. Everything was strategically designed and positioned perfectly. The remote controls for my stereo and television were Velcroed to the wall, allowing me access with the custom mouth stick I had made. The desk I'd designed, where my computer sat, was at the precise height for efficient use thanks to Peter Issler's exceptional carpentry skills. The ensuite in my bedroom, though quite modest in size, was set up with a wheel-in shower and accessible sink in case I ever wanted to wash my hair in the morning. An automatic door opener with a remote switch positioned on the chin control of my wheel chair was installed. This allowed me to open and close the front entry door. Our entire yard was wheelchair friendly, giving me full access to everywhere my daughters were. Even our rear deck was accessible for me to enjoy the Alberta sunshine. And finally, after learning early on how important drinking water is for quadriplegics—it prevents bladder infections—I had a special station built in to the design of our kitchen. The counter overhang was just enough for me to access a one-gallon (3.78 litres) water jug with a straw attached to it.

In addition to everything else, with some careful planning and because of the L-shaped architecture of the house, I was able to design an open concept living room, kitchen, and front and rear entry, thus enabling easy access to the entire property, including each of my children's bedrooms, all within the confines of a humble 1,400 square foot bungalow. This house really couldn't have been more perfect and was a joy, if that is the right word, for me to live in. On top of that, to make transportation a tad more comfortable, just before moving into this home, we sold the old beater van and purchased a new minivan. Then, thanks to an Alberta government grant, we had the vehicle converted to accommodate my power chair, a process that entailed lowering the floor eleven inches (27.94cm), installing a side entry ramp, which remotely slid out from under the van, and removing the passenger chair—as well as the middle row bench seat—allowing me the ability to wheel in and sit next to the driver. Accordingly, this new van afforded me the comfortable freedom to go anywhere I wanted at any time, as long as there was somebody available to drive it. I may have been disabled, but thanks to all kinds of advancements to aid wheelchair-bound people, I wasn't a prisoner to my immediate environment. The

Tetra Society of North America—founded in 1987—an organization dedicated to assisting people with disabilities in living an independent and fulfilling life, helped me build one contraption that I'd come up with. It sits on the table and has metal prongs that stick out—like skewers—allowing me to grab food off it using just my mouth. I don't and never did use any high-tech gadgets, such as voice recognition equipment to turn on lights or type on my computer. I prefer doing everything with a mouth stick.

Finally, because of my stubborn will to become independent, I came up with a crazy idea to design a special bowl that rested on the chin control of my power chair, which would allow me to eat snacks such as chips or popcorn without anyone having to feed me. With the bowl literally inches from my mouth, I was successfully able to grab said snacks with my tongue and mouth. It's surprising how many things a person can accomplish with just the use of one's neck, mouth, and tongue. By the way, the human tongue IS the strongest muscle in the body. Quite honestly, with all these adaptive conveniences, life as a quadriplegic really isn't so bad.

Nevertheless, after thorough contemplation, I just couldn't justify living in the house while my family was forced to move again. Putting my personal comforts before the well-being of theirs wasn't something I could live with. And since living in a facility for the rest of my life wasn't any better an option, I proceeded towards what I considered a justifiable solution: suicide. Did depression play a decisive role in my thinking? Well, other than experiencing short intervals of sadness, guilt, or heartache, I can't say that I have ever encountered feelings of hopelessness or depression for any prolonged periods at any time during my life. As difficult as that may be to believe, it's the truth. And this wasn't a cry for help either. This was simply a misplaced effort to solve a complicated situation.

As cold and calculated as my final solution sounds, it didn't come without a heavy heart and streams of emotion—which I successfully concealed from everyone. Nearly every night before falling asleep, I would run different scenarios through my mind, imagining my daughters at an older age being happy and enjoying life. My only dilemma rested in the fact that by ending my life, I wouldn't get to participate in or witness theirs. However, as heart-wrenching as it was, I also believed it was a justifiable and a necessary sacrifice for the welfare of my family. To me, it was the lesser of two evils.

In following through, I researched on the internet extensively and learned that an extreme overdose of a high-strength sleeping pill would allow a person to essentially fall asleep and not wake up again—a seemingly perfect method to facilitate a peaceful exit. I immediately set in motion the necessary steps to obtain a suitable prescription from my doctor. That was when—after looking back at this instance—something occurred that could be considered conspicuous in its timing. I had just finished making a phone call to make an appointment to acquire said prescription, when the doorbell rang. Danielle was at school. Haylee was watching cartoons. Nikkita, the nanny, was preparing lunch in the kitchen. Upon maneuvering my wheelchair over to answer the door, I found two Jehovah's Witnesses standing there with smiling faces. Before I could say hello, one of them dove right into giving me a brief presentation concerning their newest piece of literature. *What else is new?* I thought to myself. They were always coming up with different excuses to knock on people's doors. Not exactly in the mood to shoo them away, however, I simply sat there and waited for him to finish. When he finished his pitch, the gentlemen said, "Here, I'd like you to have this." He placed a brochure under my hand and left. On the cover was a question asking if God really cares about us. By this point, I was pretty much convinced there was no God. After all, considering my immediate circumstances, how could there be a God who cared about me?

After the Witnesses left, Nikkita and I had a brief discussion about JWs in general. Apparently, she'd had an encounter or two with them herself. I don't remember all the details of our conversation, but I got the distinct impression that Nikkita wasn't very fond of Jehovah's Witnesses, at which point, surprisingly enough, I found myself sticking up for them and their way of life. Always knowing them to be sincere, trustworthy, and joyful people who knew their Bibles inside and out, I remember saying to her how it was hard not to like anyone with those qualities. Nevertheless, I couldn't see how they or God—if He existed—was going to be of any benefit to my current predicament. Therefore, into the trash can went the brochure. At this juncture, nothing was going to prevent me from fulfilling my exit strategy. Or so I thought.

Getting the meds from my doctor was a piece of cake. After making up a story about experiencing severe sleeping issues, she was more than happy to write out a three-month prescription for me. Truth was, I generally slept like a baby. While filling out the prescription at the pharmacy, I requested the three-month supply all at once in one bottle. Grandstanding, with my best impression of a pathetically helpless puppy dog on my face, explaining it would help simplify my life by not having to return each month, the pharmacist was more than happy to oblige. I thanked him and left, secure in the knowledge I had enough pills to fulfill my plan.

I chose Saturday, October 27, 2001, as the day to say goodbye to this world. In the spirit of wanting the last day with my family to be remembered as a happy one, I suggested going to McDonald's for lunch. After that, we took the girls to an indoor play center for young children. The entire day, I concentrated on soaking up and savoring my daughters' every movement, gesture, and mannerisms. And with a perpetual smile deeply ingrained upon my face, my mood consisted of genuine contentment. Convinced that everything was about to be perfect for everyone, I wasn't faking it either. After enjoying what I considered was the perfect day to end a well-lived life, I set the final steps of my plan in motion. This was when I did something I will regret for the rest of my life. As a result, writing about this is extremely difficult for me to articulate. Before she went to bed, I had Danielle place the plastic pill bottle containing my ninety powerful sleeping pills, with the cap removed, on top of my water jug in the kitchen. Then I followed Danielle to her bedroom to say goodnight to her and Haylee for the last time.

Upon tucking my daughters in—metaphorically speaking—and telling them one of my famous good-lesson bedtime stories about the porcupine who befriended the mischievous rabbit, I gave them a goodnight kiss and left them to sleep. With the next two hours to myself—the caregiver arrived at 10:00 PM to put me to bed, and Nicole left for a much-deserved evening with one of her sisters—I used those two hours to finish writing a final letter to Nicole and left it conspicuously on the center of the desktop of my computer. In the letter, I expressed sincere feelings of how much I cherished our time together and apologized for how it had ended. I gave her specific instructions on how to proceed financially and explained why I felt this decision was best for everyone. Then I conveyed the love I felt for Haylee and Danielle, as well as what I wanted her to tell them, and closed with a heartfelt goodbye.

Before embarking on this journey of living with a spinal cord injury, I'd definitely been one of those people who never thought in a million years—no matter what life threw at me—that anything in this world could ever break ME. I'd thought that people who succumbed to such drastic solutions were weak. For instance, when I'd been told that the young man who'd visited me in the hospital had committed suicide, I'd felt little sympathy. After all, I was the one lying in a hospital bed paralyzed. My reasoning at the time came down to *What could he possibly have been experiencing that would even come close to what I am experiencing?* Clearly lacking compassion toward anyone who buckled under the pressures of life—even after my injury—I wasn't very sympathetic. Apparently, in order to understand what could possibly drive a person to such drastic measures, I required direct contact with the intricacies of what seemed like one of life's unsolvable situations. As a result, the experiences I had lived through, beginning with my arenacross accident, certainly humbled and taught me that valuable lesson. Admittedly, it was a lesson I needed to learn. And in being consistent, not surprisingly, I had to experience it firsthand in order to do so.

When my caregiver arrived at 10:00 PM, she began getting things ready in the bedroom. This was my cue to cross the rainbow bridge. I unhesitatingly headed for the kitchen, grabbed the pill bottle between my lips, and shot my head back in order to empty its entire contents in my mouth. Then I twisted my neck abruptly to fling the empty container onto the counter and proceeded to take a big swig of water. It took a couple swallows to down that many pills, but I got them down nonetheless. Next, I headed to the bedroom. Knowing full well that after swallowing that many sleeping pills, I'd likely be out in a matter of minutes, I instructed my caregiver to skip our usual routine. After explaining how dead-tired I was and that I just wanted to hit the hay, she quickly removed my clothing and put me into bed. Then, to save the paramedics from having to deal with it, I had her remove my indwelling catheter and not bother hanging a night urine bag next to my bed. By this point, I remember feeling excited about permanently saying goodbye to that nuisance of a thing, as well as all the other baggage associated with this complicated life. Within minutes, my caregiver left, and I was all tucked in, awaiting my journey into the unknown. While lying there, feeling sublimely at peace with myself, my final thought was *I hope there is a God.* And while holding on to the love I felt for my family, I drifted off into oblivion.

The next morning, Sunday, October 28, around 11:00AM, I began to feel the first sense of consciousness. At this point, I didn't really know what this consciousness entailed: *Am I dead and waking up to face my final judgement?* I opened my eyes to a foggy blur of a church sitting off in the distance at the end of a snow-covered road. At the top of its steeple was a barely legible image of a cross. Upon gaining full cognitive abilities, I looked around the room to quickly realize it was a painting on the wall across from my bed. There I was, once again, lying in a hospital room…paralyzed! Then, like an unstoppable tidal wave, every unwanted memory from the past thirty-two months came flooding back to my mind. And at the top of my feeble, paralyzed lungs, I yelled out, "Why won't you let me die already!" Extremely angry with the situation and with nowhere else to turn, I summoned God for answers: *Why won't you just let me die already? What do you want from me? This isn't fair!*

At this point, a nurse came running in to my room asking if everything was okay. Apparently, my yelling wasn't all that feeble after all—they'd heard me all the way down to the nurses' station. Following my abrasive inquiry as to what had gone wrong and why I was still alive, she informed me the resident doctor would be in to talk with me shortly. Once the nurse left, I lay there, stewing in a pot of self-prepared discontent, wondering, *Now what am I going to do?* Within a couple of minutes, the doctor walked in, stared at his clipboard. Then, while looking me square in the face, he put his hand on my shoulder and with a noticeable Indian accent said, "It's a miracle you're still with us." Rolling my eyes at him, I wasn't in the mood for expressing gratitude for said miracle. Upon instructing me to follow his moving finger with my eyes, the surprised doctor kept shaking his head in disbelief.

Apparently, after swallowing the amount of sleeping pills I had—aside from causing death—at the very least, my brain function should have been reduced to that of a vegetable, especially since the drugs had been in my system for over five hours before reaching the hospital. Nicole, arriving home that evening around 3 AM, for some strange reason had chosen to use the bathroom in my bedroom instead of the one down the hall before heading to bed. In doing so, she'd happened to notice the night urine bag wasn't hanging beside my bed. Knowing how important it was for me to have the proper drainage system setup during the night, she'd lifted my blanket to discover I didn't have a catheter in place. She'd tried to wake me up, and upon failing to get any kind of response from me, had dialed 911.

The doctor who attended to me that morning was definitely one of the most compassionate physicians I'd ever met. Instead of a lecture, he tried to put himself in my shoes and further expressed empathy for how difficult my situation must have been. After a brief discussion, he asked if I had any children. Upon learning that I had two young daughters, he kindly suggested I think of them and how they might feel about losing their dad. He shared a statistic with me that indicates children of parents who commit suicide are far more likely to succumb to the same fate. Not having weighed any of those consequences, I found myself in an all-too-familiar room inside my head asking the question: *What was I thinking?* The mindful doctor then asked me if I believed in God. I answered, "Not really." Explaining that we all live for something, he recommended I find something to live for and suggested, "How about living for your daughters. I'm sure they love you. I've only known you five minutes, and I already like you." Considering I didn't like myself very much at that moment, feeling guiltier than I ever had about anything in my life, I just stared at the ceiling. But he was right; if for nothing else, I had to live for my daughters. And then I thought about how difficult it would be to face them both, especially Danielle, who, despite her young age, was old enough to grasp that her daddy had done something he shouldn't have.

Before leaving my room, the doctor explained about seeing what he could do to get me home as soon as possible. Normally, after someone attempts suicide, they hold the person for at least seven days for evaluation—to make sure they're not in danger of trying again. Bearing in mind my circumstances, he was willing to break protocol. Later, a nurse sympathetic to the fact that I couldn't get out of bed and didn't have a television in my room, brought a radio for me to listen to. After requesting that she tune the dial to my favorite radio station, CJAY 92, the first song I heard was "Further Again" by Staggered Crossing. In light of how my carefully orchestrated attempt to abruptly terminate this journey through life had just failed, the title, lyrics, and even tone of this song seemed appropriate. Headed further down life's road than previously anticipated, I couldn't help associating my situation to the song.

While lying there for the remainder of the day, it was difficult not to stare at the painting of a church with a cross atop its steeple. It was, after all, directly opposite my bed. Fully aware of the words recorded in John 3:16, I acknowledged what the symbol stood for and wondered how Jesus might have felt while enduring such an excruciating experience. In effect, this kind of gave my situation some much-needed perspective.

Two days later, I was released from the hospital. Nicole, furious with me for resorting to such drastic measures, certainly wasn't throwing me a welcome home party. As she was the one who'd wanted to end our marriage, I believe her anger was more fueled by guilt than anything else. The most excruciating moment of my entire life, however, wouldn't arrive until Danielle walked through the door from school, at which point, my precious seven-year-old daughter—not able to find the words—just stood in front of me for several seconds with the saddest expression etched into her face. Then, in a barely audible tone, she finally said, "Are you okay, Dad?" While wrapping her tiny arms around me, she began to weep uncontrollably, in a way I'd never seen before, and she wouldn't let go. That was when the little room inside my head—the place I'd go to seek refuge when I didn't like myself very much—suddenly became too small to hide in, and a tidal wave of emotion tore through me unlike anything I've ever experienced. In that moment, as if forged from red-hot iron, the memory of my firstborn child succumbing to such distressing emotions became permanently branded into my mind. Haylee, thank God, was too young to understand what had happened. I understood then that I had sought out a permanent solution for a temporary problem—without giving any consideration to the life-altering effects it would have on my daughters. Having said that, I don't believe it was by coincidence or luck that I survived. God apparently knew something about me that I had forgotten about. I had a commitment to fulfill. And to do that, I needed to continue on this journey and take care of the business of doing all the things that still needed to be done in order to remember what that commitment entailed.

* * *

During the course of our lives, we experience a varying degree of obstacles, large or small; no person is immune from them. Most have a simple solution, but some are a tad more complicated. The one thing most solutions have in common is they come with either sacrifice or consequence—sometimes both. During the process of arriving at the decision to sacrifice my life for the greater good of my family, I neglected to comprehend the immediate impact this would have on Danielle, who was and remains very close to me, an element of my life today that I wouldn't trade for anything.

While writing about this account, I sit at my desk reflecting on my past. In doing so, it's easy to revisit my cross-country and motocross career. To the left of me, on the mantle of my fireplace, sit a significant number of trophies. Then, behind me, on the wall, is a memorable poster of me with an impressive racing resume printed on it. Around the poster is a conglomeration of plaques and medals commemorating my racing accomplishments. I would often look at that picture of myself and wonder: *Where exactly did it all go wrong?* I wasn't a terrible person. I loved my family. I was a good provider and really did straighten out my life considerably. Accordingly, once the dust settled from attempting to end my life, and for many years after, I would struggle to understand why this had happened to me.

I have some old pictures of myself from a photoshoot posing for a spot as "Sunshine Boy" in our local *Calgary Sun* newspaper before a race. Admittedly, it's difficult not to look at those images of myself flexing for the camera without a certain degree of fondness. What I wouldn't give to have that body back, and how I'd live my life differently if given the chance. But then there's the other element of that guy I don't miss, the guy whose life revolved around racing and making unwise decisions to be successful at it, the guy who often had a hard time being humble. That guy sacrificed far too much. And for what? Certainly not for money. He already had plenty—more than he ever made from racing. For a top-ten ranking in Canadian motocross? His name in the sport's history books? His face on the cover of a magazine? Maybe it was all of the above. Truth is, I have never been able to answer that question. The one thing I am certain of is that God didn't do this to me. As for the guy in the poster on my wall, yeah, he still comes out every once in a while. But after reminding him that he's the reason we are sentenced to this chair, he goes away. And these days he rarely shows his face anymore.

Cue music: "Hurt" by Johnny Cash

https://www.youtube.com/watch?v=4ahHWROn8M0

CHAPTER

25

Strike Three

During my soul-searching journey for a better life, as I suspected, 1989 proved to be a definitive year for me. Turning twenty would mark a time in my life when I finally realized I was headed to a place of no return if I didn't slam on the emergency brakes and make an abrupt 180-degree turn. Nevertheless, it wasn't easy by any means to address the conflict in my mind, but I knew if I didn't change, my future was going to be seriously compromised.

By mid-April, 1989, I was getting comfortable with working 8:00 AM to 5:00 PM at the car wash. One thing was certain: I definitely enjoyed having my evenings free. Nicole and I—now seriously dating—settled in to a nice routine where I'd pick her up from work every evening after her shift, which ended at 10 PM, and we'd go out for something to eat. This was where my reflexology talents would earn me some serious boyfriend credentials, and it happens to be one of my fondest memories of when we were dating. Nicole, having worked a waitress position, was on her feet during the entire shift. Therefore, every night, while waiting for our food, I'd massage her aching feet under the table. Needless to say, she loved it! And I loved doing it for her. Yes, I had my moments.

On April 24, having just returned from New Zealand, Duane and I were at Esmeralda's on a Monday night. We just couldn't seem to avoid hanging out together. Sure, my inner voice kept telling me that I really needed to not associate with Duane for both our sakes, but I convinced myself I had things under control. Nicole was working, but she was aware of my going out that evening. Normally, I wouldn't be at a club without her, but these were special circumstances. Sipping on soda with nothing other than ice in our glasses, Duane and I basically talked the entire evening about his experiences in New Zealand for the past six months. At one point, he headed off to the men's room to use the facilities while I sat and waited for him to return. Within a couple minutes, my duplicitous cousin returned from the restroom, sat down, and inconspicuously leaned in towards me to indicate that he'd just found a wallet in one of the stalls. And guess what, there was a credit card inside. Now, one would think that by this juncture in our lives, Duane and I would have learned our lesson with credit cards. And the honorable thing would have been to hand the wallet over to one of the servers. However, naturally gravitating towards committing lawlessness whenever we were together, that thought never even crossed our minds. In fact, we argued about who was going keep the credit card, an argument that I won—though it turned out to be one that I WISH I would have lost.

Two days later, on Wednesday, April 26th, I left my car wash job during lunch break and drove down the street to Tiger Automotive with the hopes of using the credit card for the first time. After browsing around and picking out a few items—all of which were absolutely nonessential—I walked up to the checkout, handed the credit card to the cashier, and watched him swipe it through the machine. Then, after a brief pause, the cashier asked me to hang on a second while he phoned the credit card company. Following a brief chat on the phone, the cashier then asked me for my mother's maiden name. That was when I knew the jig was up. Not having a clue what to say, I simply stood there, shrugging my shoulders, After which, as inconspicuously as possible, I hightailed it out of there. Of course, the cashier, not having been born yesterday, cleverly wrote down my license plate number as I pulled out of the parking lot. In hindsight, because it was only a few blocks away, I should have simply walked back to work and picked up the car later in the day. One would think that exposing myself to this amount of stupidity—using the credit card and driving away in clear sight—was actually scripted, and I was just an actor following directions. It would make for a more interesting movie if anybody was watching. But this was me, embarrassingly enough, in real life, thickening the plot to my own life.

After returning to work, within an hour, three police cars swarmed the car wash. And I could tell by the way they approached—from all angles—these cops were expecting me to run. Where was I going to flee, Mexico? Grab my go-bag stuffed under the dash of my Camaro and abscond to another country? I was caught, and I knew it! Once again, it was time to face the music. Therefore, in peaceful fashion, I surrendered, and they escorted me away in handcuffs. Talk about learning the hard way. I've heard that some of the smartest people have made the most mistakes. And how wisdom comes from experience, and experience often comes from failure. If that's true, I should've been a freaking genius by then. I wasn't smart enough, however, to conclude that after two days, the rightful owner had likely noticed he'd lost his wallet and canceled the credit card. Given my vast amount of street knowledge, it's hard not to wonder why I couldn't figure that out. Clearly, I was a lousy criminal!

Thursday, April 27, 1989, the morning after my subsequent arrest, I was being held in lockup at the Saskatoon courthouse, awaiting my arraignment. Feeling somewhat disheveled after having slept the night in jail and wearing the same clothes they'd arrested me in, my brain felt bruised, and my body ached as if a dump truck had run over it. Although I'd spent the majority of the past twelve hours engaged in true self-reflection, my biggest concern was whether or not Nicole would stick by me though all of this. Fully aware of the fact that this was my third strike—I was still under the thumb of the suspended sentence from the last mishap—I concluded it would take nothing short of a miracle to keep me from going to prison this time. Although it had only been less than a month since we'd started dating seriously, during my evening of psychoanalyzing myself, it became clear that I had serious feelings for Nicole. This was my eleventh hour, and I made my one and only phone call…to her. After explaining my disheartening predicament, it wasn't hard to discern from the tone of her voice that she was extremely disappointed. This left me acutely uncertain as to what my future might entail with her—especially facing the prospect of having to go away for a while. The only question was for how long?

Finally, a guard came to unlock the solid-steel sliding cell door, looked down at his clipboard, and read the next name on the docket. Stumbling through the pronunciation, he called out, "Monte P-e-r-a-pelican." Sitting in a large holding cell with roughly fifteen other prisoners, I was in an extremely bad and uncharacteristically arrogant mood. A considerable lack of patience for anything was the end product. I should have been feeling remorseful, humble, repentant, and submissive, but I wasn't. Walking up to the guard, I said, "That's me." And because of his mispronunciation of my name, I whispered under my breath, "Idiot. Can't even read properly." In an authoritative manner, the guard asked me what I had just said and to repeat it out loud. "My name is P-e-r-e-p-e-l-k-i-n," I replied, sounding it out slowly for him to wrap his brain around it. This, of course, incensed the big brute, causing him to grab my arm and shove me down the corridor while grumbling about my disrespectful attitude. Weighing in around 250 pounds, standing about six foot five, and built like Arnold Schwarzenegger, this guard was a big guy. You'd think I'd have been a tad more respectful if not thoughtful. I usually knew better than to antagonize someone with authority. Instead, my reply was, "You don't have to get your panties all knotted up. It's not my fault you don't know how to read."

After the irritated officer finished escorting me to the courtroom, the prosecutor was in the process of reading out my name, pronouncing it perfectly. Turning around to look at the guard standing behind me, I reiterated, "See, the prosecutor can read." Glaring back fiercely, while pointing to the judge, he replied, "Eyes front, you little punk!" My charges were read aloud, after which, the judge directed his attention specifically at me and asked how I would plead. "Guilty, Your Honor," I said. I mean, how else could I plead? The game was up. While His Honor took a few minutes to examine my résumé of past criminal activity, I looked over at the people in attendance to see Nicole sitting with her sister. The expression on her face was of utter horror. She was white as a ghost. In effect, it suddenly reminded me of the seriousness of this situation. Seeing Nicole in the courtroom forced my mind to cascade across a multitude of possible scenarios. Upon realizing that each realistic outcome was worse than the next, my emotions began to redline. With each granule of sand inside the hour glass of time seemingly paused, the agony of truth and reality colliding proved to be almost more than I could bear. Desperately wanting to get this over with, I silently debated, *Just let me go already, and I promise to be good from now on.*

Further attempting to cling to and hope for that miracle, my mind reached out: *I've been in this exact situation twice before and gotten away with slaps on the wrist. Why should this be any different? And this little infraction is the smallest of them all.* But I instinctively knew this time was different. With this being my THIRD strike—not unlike baseball—I wasn't going to get a fourth chance to redeem myself. Standing in the tiny defendant's pew, awaiting my fate, I began feeling generously terrified, anxious, and nervous all at the same time. My hair felt gross, and I hadn't washed my face or brushed my teeth in over twenty-four hours. The inside of my mouth tasted like a toilet, and all I wanted to do was to go home, brush my teeth, and take a hot shower. Yes, this definitely was a déjà vu moment, one that I could have and should have avoided. After a long, hard night of deep contemplation, with the added mental exhaustion from attempting to sleep with one eye open while worrying about the possibility of my cellmate feeling the desire to rape me in my sleep, I was coming apart at the seams. And to top it off, my stomach felt like one gigantic cluster of knots. I just wanted this nightmare to end already: *If only I'd let Duane keep that credit card. I wouldn't even be here.* Truth is, I deserved getting busted…and then some!

* * *

Many people live their entire lives in denial, never having the courage to see the true reflection of who they really are in the mirror. Instead, they lie to their conscience and justify their decisions by deceiving themselves. And when they are finally caught in the act, rather than owning up to the consequences, they become enraged by their own guilt. At that critical moment, when a person should be humbling themselves before their actions, they choose to live a life of anger, hatred, and blame. How do I know this? Because in this particular situation, I was that person. Yes, I was my very own self-perpetuating victim of circumstance.

Before Trent fired me from the pizza joint, the truth is I did feel extremely underpaid for my work there. Therefore, to compensate myself, every now and then, I would deliver a pizza without ringing it in to the till, pocketing the money for myself. And after disposing of the paper trail, I left no evidence of the transaction ever taking place. Hence, the till should never have come up short. Someone else was obviously stealing as well. So the fact that Trent fired me without actually catching me was somewhat aggravating. As a result, when a split-second opportunity presented itself, I took advantage of it. The day I was fired from Panagopoulos, when collecting my belongings from the office, I noticed Trent's keys lying on the desk. The new key that had just been made for the front door was on the chain. Knowing that I'd be returning shortly to hand in my work shirts, I took his keys and made a copy of the new front door key. Then, upon delivering the garments, I unobtrusively returned his key ring to the desk. Okay, so what would be the benefit of having a key? Break in during the middle of the night and whip myself up a pizza? Not exactly! Being an ex-manager, I was aware that on Sunday nights, before locking up, we always hid the deposit bag containing Friday's, Saturday's, and Sunday's revenue in the walk-in refrigerator. The reasoning behind this was to avoid taking that much cash home at such a late hour—the owner had decided it was safer to leave it hidden overnight. Therefore, my plan was to sneak in after closing on a Sunday—there was no alarm system—and swipe the deposit bag full of cash.

However, because of my previous friendship with Trent, and the fact that I had found a new job right away, I'd decided against going through with the plan. That is, until we had a verbal altercation that turned violent in the parking lot of Esmeralda's. This was shortly after getting canned. Although I saw many of the same people time and time again at the night club, this was the first time I'd run into Trent there. Nicole and I had just arrived and were about halfway across the parking lot when she realized she'd left her ID in my car. Therefore, we started to quickly double back across the parking lot to retrieve it. This is where things took a bizarre twist. Trent and a buddy had just arrived too and were heading to the entrance of the club. Upon seeing us deviate from our heading, he also turned back and hotfooted towards us. Next thing I knew, he was literally in my face, accusing me of intending to vandalize his vehicle while he was inside—which never once even crossed my mind. Hearing the allegations spewing from his mouth, I just couldn't let it go. Seconds later, Trent was lying on the asphalt with a bloody nose. With all the pent-up frustration from being fired and then Trent being confrontational for no just cause, my fuse had been lit. Fortunately, the aggression ended quickly, with Trent wisely deciding not to retaliate. He didn't call the cops either. Seeing that I had his blood splashed all over my shirt, Nicole and I left and called it a night.

Two days after the parking lot incident, I went ahead with my original plan to use the key and steal the hidden deposit bag. Somehow, I now felt justified in liberating my former employer of some money. I had absolutely no qualms with fulfilling my mission. There ended up being roughly $2,200 of cash inside the deposit pouch. After placing the wad of bills into a brown paper bag, I stuffed it under the dash of my Camaro. Then, a few days later, I found myself standing before a judge, facing prison time for an incident that I was certainly intelligent enough to know had an extremely low probability of success—and for an assortment of merchandise I had no real use for, no less. Seemingly, I'd subliminally wanted to get caught.

* * *

Only upon true and honest reflection of these occurrences during that night in lockup did it become genuinely clear who I truly was. Not surprisingly, I didn't like what my conclusions were yielding. Even worse, coming to terms with the fact that serious changes were needed wasn't something I was ready to accept, which explains my uncharacteristic insolent attitude with the guard. However, the powers of universal justice can be awfully persuasive. While awaiting my fate in the courtroom that morning, the somber judge, after gazing over my file, finally looked up and asked if I had anything to say. With hopes of swaying his rendering towards letting me off with another slap on the wrist, as respectfully as possible, I explained my current status of maintaining a full-time job. His Honor seemed totally disinterested in my pitiful ploy or any pathetic job I had. The stern look on his face said enough. His words articulated the rest: "You don't seem to be learning your lesson, son." With a furrowed brow, he peered directly into my eyes and asserted, "Maybe six months will teach you something. I sentence you to six months in Saskatoon Correctional!"

The whack of the judge's gavel echoing through the courtroom felt as if the very hand of God himself had just reached out and smacked me across the face. My heart actually stopped beating for a brief interlude before starting up again, pounding at 200 beats per minute. The reality of my actions finally intersecting with consequences caused the chronological order of time to synchronize with my emotions, tripping out at ten on the Richter scale of life. And as the gravity of this situation became very sobering, any sense of cockiness that had been present just minutes before evaporated completely. Contemplating the realization of prison time reduced me to a comatose state of mind. With no idea what the next six months of my life would entail, I began reeling for mercy. Bowing my head, I whispered in an undertone, *"Dear God, please help me."*

Cue music: "Running Blind" by Godsmack

https://www.youtube.com/watch?v=t0LQLO4oVg4

CHAPTER
26

An Unexpected Turn of Events

Considering how well I hadn't learned my lessons, it did, after all, seem inevitable that prison time was in my future. Having journeyed down some dark corridors throughout my life, worst of those being the times I found it difficult to live with myself, the epilogue in the parking lot with Trent and the theft at Panagopoulos hovers at the top of the list. My encounter with Trent—and my subsequent behavior, hitting him and stealing from him—is something I not only avoided relating to anyone, but I tried blocking out of my own mind as well. Sitting in my wheelchair, writing about these details years later, it isn't any easier. Without question, that particular theft bothered my conscience the most. As is the case with anyone I've wronged in my past, my apologetic appeal for forgiveness is all I can humbly request, and I only hope that absolution is in the aggrieved one's heart.

* * *

While being escorted back to a holding cell by the big burly guard, he commented in a rather salty tone, "Not so cocky now, are you!" I couldn't argue the point. The sobering reality of my six-month incarceration caused any reluctance to accept that my life was in desperate need of a serious course correction to reverse course. This was a reality check to end all reality checks. No, I wasn't cocky at all. Within thirty minutes of being sentenced, I was walking single file with seven other convicts, all of us in handcuffs, to a transport vehicle that was slated to take us to our new home, Saskatoon Correctional Center. Although this was the reality I'd created for myself, the entire experience felt remarkably surreal. Never had my heart pounded so heavily in my chest. During the twenty-minute drive—to absorb my last remaining fragments of freedom—I peered through the side window of the corrections vehicle, watching people going about their lives without a care in the world. The weighty realization of spending my life behind bars for the next six months had a deeply profound effect that reached far into my soul. It caused me to seriously question who I really was, as opposed to who I wanted to be. The only countermeasure at this point was acceptance.

Upon arriving at the crossbar hotel, armed guards escorted the eight of us, single file again, to a bleak-looking admittance room. Here, we were immediately told to strip off every stitch of clothing and stand with our backs to the wall, and then we awaited further instruction. Then a guard wearing rubber gloves and holding a long black flashlight called us one by one to step up and follow his directions explicitly. Well, wouldn't you know, my name just had to be first. Considering how unnecessarily bright it already was in this room, right about then, I was seriously concerned with what this corrections officer could possibly require a flashlight for. Actually, terrified would be a more accurate adjective. Nevertheless, as courageously as possible and not showing an ounce of fear, I stepped forward—with my privates swinging in the open air—into the center of the room as seven other naked men and three armed guards watched. The rather large-fingered corrections officer instructed me to stand with my legs spread apart, nice and wide, lean forward, and pull my butt cheeks apart. Even though it went against every fiber of my being, I closed my eyes, gritted my teeth, and did what was instructed of me. Feeling him grab onto my scrotum and penis and move them to and fro while shining a flashlight into each crevice, had me shuddering in repugnant disgust.

After inspecting every inch of my entire body—even between my toes—he sent me back in line and proceeded with the next guy. Not wanting to watch this horrifying display, I stared intensely at the ceiling. Following the completion of my admittance agendum, one of the guards privately escorted me through a series of heavily locked doors that would slam shut behind us with a deafening metal-on-metal clang—sending shivers down my spine—thus driving home the full meaning of incarceration. Finally, we arrived at a big room resembling a gymnasium, except it was filled with rows and rows of bunk beds. Following a brief scan of the room, I concluded there had to be a hundred convicts sitting around. And it wasn't difficult to distinguish that being Caucasian, I was certainly among the minority. Apparently, the prison was overcrowded, and this was the overflow area.

The guard handed me a blanket and pillow and then assigned me to a bed, where I sat wondering, *Now what? Am I supposed to sit around on a bunk bed visiting with other convicts for six months?* Sure enough, within minutes, another inmate—about my age—came over to introduce himself. He was a clean-cut guy not all that dissimilar from me. Well, he was Caucasian. After sharing his story as to how he ended up in jail—breaking and entering—I conceded mine. Upon learning this was his second time in Saskatoon Correctional—with the objective of educating myself—I used the opportunity to ask as many questions as possible. I could discern that he wasn't all that bad of a guy. Like me, he'd simply made a few bad choices that had ended up derailing his life. Upon catching sight of my eyes roving about—I was keeping constant surveillance of my surroundings—he added, "You don't have anything to worry about. You have a certain look that says *don't mess with me!* You'll be just fine." The two of us were well built—physically speaking—but settling into the notion of getting through the first night unscathed, and keeping my guard up at all times, seemed like the prudent thing to do for now.

By late afternoon, surprisingly, I was actually getting hungry and beginning to wonder when dinner might be served. Then something rather extraordinary happened. A corrections officer walked in and called out two names, mine and my new friend's. The two of us were told we were being transferred to a work camp. This camp, located just outside the prison fences, had no locked doors, gates, or fences. Arriving just in time for dinner, I walked in, sat down at a large table— where there were roughly twenty others already eating—and consumed a lovely full-course meal. Talk about a drastic change in circumstances! There was a pool table in the entertainment area, a weight room, and each inmate had private quarters with a shower. Getting up early every morning to participate in whatever work detail we were assigned to for the day was part of the curriculum. But I had no qualms with that.

I was unsure if perhaps they saw me as a clean-cut, first-timer white boy who deserved a break. Or maybe a small miracle had just happened. Either way, I was quite pleased with the upgrade in accommodations. The next morning, I woke early, showered, and headed out on a bus with five other convicts. We were driven to a lake resort near Saskatoon, where we picked up garbage all day long. When we got back to the facility, another awesome dinner awaited us. Although my living arrangements had become somewhat more pleasing, there certainly were plenty of reminders to prevent me from forgetting the fact that I WAS doing time. We had a strict daily regimen to follow. Being late for anything—even a meal—earned you a demerit. Three demerits got you sent back to the main prison. Living in the company of several seasoned veterans of prison life was another helpful example as to why my life required change. It gave me a glimpse into a life I definitely wanted to avoid.

The weekend arrived, and that meant two days off from picking up garbage. In other words, relax and lounge around. On Saturday, I decided to write Nicole a letter describing my sincere feelings for her. What prompted me to write this letter was a dream I'd had the night before. It had entailed me putting a ring on her finger, but I'd only been able to get it halfway on. Not ever having been the type of person who subscribes to interpreting dreams, I never tried to deconstruct any deeper meaning from it. There was one distinguishable piece of information within the dream that couldn't be ignored, however: marrying Nicole. It was something I could easily see myself doing—eventually.

Sunday afternoons from 2:00 to 4:00 PM were designated for visiting hours at the camp. As much as I was desperately looking forward to seeing Nicole, there was some apprehension within me as to how she might respond to my current state of affairs. Surprisingly, she came with my mother, and they stayed for the entire two hours. Mom wasn't nearly as disheartened by my incarceration as I expected her to be. At one point during the visitation, shaking her head, in a jesting yet serious tone, she said, "Monte, how do you get yourself into these situations?" I paused for a moment before disclosing the particulars. "You need to get your act together. Otherwise, it's going to be a lot more than six months next time," she replied in an astringent tone. In an effort to hold back my emotions, I sat in silence for a few seconds, gazing downward at the table between us, but my watery eyes gave me away. Looking up, in a strained voice, I said, "Yeah, Mom, I know."

After we got things that needed to be said out of the way, my mother was thoughtful enough to leave the visitation room, allowing Nicole and me some time to ourselves. We held hands across the table as we talked and exchanged an emotional interlude, but that didn't last long. Nicole wasn't a very touchy/feely type of girl. In hindsight, it seemed I was the "chick" in our relationship when it came to affection. Her mood that afternoon was surprisingly joyful and even sarcastically entertaining. At one point, she explained—in a reassuring way—that her dad had gone to prison during his misspent youth as well. This gave me the impression that Nicole somehow accredited my going to jail as a sign that I was THE ONE for her. Feeling more content and confident with our relationship, I revealed to her the $2,200 I had stuffed under the dash of my car. I asked her to use the money to make my car payments. Ironically, the six car payments of $356 totaled $2,136. I never divulged the truth as to where the cash had been acquired. Thankfully, she never asked. I suppose the right thing to do would have been to anonymously return the money to Trent, but I decided to let sleeping dogs lie. Besides, I didn't want to lose my car. I promised myself to change my ways and let bygones be bygones. The stolen money was a part of a past I was going to put behind me.

At the end of our visit, with tears in my eyes, I reached out and handed Nicole the letter I had written. She took it without showing any anxiety, which I interpreted as a good thing. For all she knew, it could have been a goodbye letter. Upon taking the letter and depositing it in her shoulder bag, she assured me, "Don't worry, everything will be okay. We'll get through this." Sensing that we were earnestly committed to each other through thick and thin, that particular visit was a turning point in my life—perhaps in both our lives. I could feel that we truly did love each other. However, I was also attentive to the fact that cleaning up my act and consistently becoming a responsible adult was paramount. In order to look in the mirror and like what I saw, serious changes needed to be made.

* * *

By this stage in my life, even though I wasn't completely convinced God was there or listening—I did on occasion say a prayer before going to bed. And before I went to sleep that evening, the contents of my prayer included asking for the strength to help me be a better, more honest man.

The next day—Monday—after returning from my work assignment, I was greeted by an older gentleman wearing a suit, who invited me to sit with him for a moment. Having no idea what this was about, I was unsure how to feel: excited or afraid? Turned out he had an interesting proposal. After a brief question-and-answer session, this distinguished gentleman went on to offer me an opportunity to finish the remainder of my sentence—with the possibility of earning up to forty-five days of early release. It involved my living in a halfway home—located in the city—where they would find me a job and attempt to rehabilitate me. This meant the ability to earn evening passes and eventually qualify for overnight weekend passes as well. Quite honestly, I couldn't believe my ears. With no convincing necessary, I was game! There was only one caveat: I had to agree to obey their stringent rules. Otherwise, I would be sent back to prison "so fast my head would spin," as the gentleman delicately worded it.

By Wednesday morning—seven days after my arrest—I was working at a temp job, loading a meat truck by hand for four hours every day. I commuted to and from my part-time job, unsupervised, by public transit. Eventually, the halfway home landed me permanent full-time employment at a small pallet building business. If I thought working at Ackland's was the most mind-numbing job I'd ever had,

I was wrong about that. This pallet job made working at Ackland's feel like Mardi Gras. Putting aside that it was monotonously boring, it was quite dangerous to boot. Workplace safety was not a high priority; cost-cutting measures were. Because pallets are in most cases made of wood, building mass quantities of them in any particular size required a large number of boards that were exactly the same size. Instead of cutting the boards one at a time, the owner had devised a conglomeration of various assembly-line type contraptions that would quickly cut several pieces of lumber. Envisioning the loss of another finger or, worse, a hand, I REALLY did not want to work at this place. But it wasn't like I had a choice. I was extra careful and on guard at all times, and managed to survive my employment unscathed. The first opportunity that presented itself for me to leave this job, I was out of there!

* * *

As part of their attempt in rehabilitating their inmates, the halfway home would bring in an array of experts in a variety of fields. This would take place on Tuesday evenings. Most of the information was on the topic of drug abuse and alcoholism, yet there were a couple of presentations that I did find extremely beneficial. One was about the repercussions theft and fraud had on society in relation to how they affected everyday common people. I had never had the consequences of my misdeeds explained to me with such intricate detail before. And I'd be lying if I said it didn't have a lasting, profound effect on me. I'd never realized how much my actions as a criminal affected the very fabric of our society, right from government down to homeless people walking the streets. In a sense, through my absolute disregard for right and wrong, I was in effect contributing to the lack of assistance available to people who were truly in need. Saskatchewan's rehabilitation program had actually gotten through to me.

While residing at the halfway house, I made an effort to be friendly with each correctional officer who worked there. Subscribing to the old adage "You get more bees with honey than vinegar," I was hoping my approach might garner some favor when it came to early release. At one point, towards the latter part of my stay at the halfway home, I had an interesting conversation with one of the custodian officers on the topic of religion. How that topic came up was in response to my claiming to be a Jehovah's Witness, even though that was not exactly the case. Okay, so I still had some work to do as far as being truthful at all times. But this lie came with a couple of angles. The rehabilitation programs offered at the home came with a mandatory attendance. The majority of these programs were on the topic of alcohol and drug abuse. I wasn't a druggie, and although it might be said I wasn't shy of alcohol, I wasn't an alcoholic. I knew my limit, and I didn't drink on a daily basis. My drinking of alcohol was pretty much limited to social occasions. With the anticipation of being exempt from attending these particular meetings, I took it upon myself to make it known that I was a JW and, as a consequence, didn't ever drink alcohol or use drugs, although, if anyone there had actually known anything about JWs, they'd have known that drinking alcohol wasn't against JW beliefs. After all, even Jesus drank wine. Nevertheless, I was permitted to skip any meetings or lectures pertaining to alcohol and drug abuse. My plan worked!

My second angle—knowing that JWs are generally regarded as trustworthy people—was that it might award me an advantage in terms of gaining trust and perhaps contribute to taking full advantage of the forty-five-day early release program. No one had ever received the maximum forty-five days—the most any of my predecessors had acquired was thirty-nine—I wanted to change that. Granted, it sounds rather pretentious trying to earn trust while serving time for credit card fraud, but if I could come across as a clean-cut religious white boy who'd made a few missteps here and there but wanted to mend his ways, then why not? Besides, it was true, except for the religious part. I was committed to a sincere path on the road to redemption and wanted to put my criminal behavior behind me. During my exchange with the custodian—on the subject of what JW's believe— he somehow knew that Jehovah's Witnesses didn't recognize the cross in their worship, which wasn't incorrect. You'll never find a true JW in possession of a cross. Naturally, this fellow wanted to know the full extent as to why. The custodian further reasoned, "Christ died for our sins, didn't he? Then what could be wrong with honoring what he did by at least hanging one cross on our wall?" After a quick appraisal of the situation, it wasn't difficult for me to determine this corrections officer wasn't going to let up. In all fairness, the guy had made a valid point. Being the sort of person who doesn't give up easily, and in the interest of not wanting to blow my cover, I kept my first response simple, stating there were several scriptures in the Bible condemning the use of any sort of idols in our devotion to or exaltation of God, whether directly or indirectly a representation of Him. But that didn't satisfy the guard: He wanted to know where these verses were in the Bible, leading me to silently question, *What did I get myself in to*?

Not exactly sure why he was so adamant about this particular topic, I wondered if perhaps this might be a test to confirm that I WAS indeed a Jehovah's Witness. Or was I simply using this as a ploy to avoid participating in the drug and alcohol programs. Unable to back out of this little conundrum, I finally had to tell this guy that some research was required on my part before I could accurately answer his questions. Sure, I remembered some things from my childhood years as to why

Jehovah's Witnesses didn't participate in popular religious traditions practiced by other faiths, but I had no idea where the reasoning for their beliefs was found in the scriptures. After some digging around in the Bible, I did find three passages to support why JWs don't use idols or carved symbols in their worship. My only concern was hoping that this information wouldn't offend the corrections officer. Last thing I needed was a person in his position insulted by me. However, after concluding that these verses could be read from any translation of the Bible, he couldn't fairly take this out on me. The next day, this same fellow was sitting at his desk in the front office of the group home when I came home from work. Upon knocking on the half-opened door, I walked in, asking if this was a good time to answer his questions regarding the cross. He told me to sit down and enquired about what I had to say on the subject. I shared the info I had gleaned from the Bible. He pulled out a Bible from one of the desk drawers and looked up the three scriptures I had written down on a sheet of paper. After reading them silently from his own Bible, he thanked me and told me I had given him something to think about. I never did ask what religion he belonged to or if, in fact, he was religious at all.

Not long after the sit-down with the custodian regarding his theological question, I submitted my paperwork for early release to him. When handing him the documents, I enquired as to what my chances were of getting the full forty-five days. He simply informed me that I would likely have an answer within a few days. In the end, I received forty-three days off my six-month sentence and was released on Thursday, September 14, 1989. They awarded me four more days than anyone else had ever earned. In the end, I never spent a single night inside a real prison.

CHAPTER

27

Turning the Page

After my release from prison—not that what I served could be justly considered prison time—I made a resolve not to end up in such a predicament ever again. This time, I had learned my lesson. I had been given a second chance, and I had more than one reason to make the best of it. Nicole never wavered in her support for me during this difficult time, and I knew she was the real deal and I was fortunate to have her in my life. Therefore, not only did I owe it to myself to walk the straight and narrow...I owed it to her as well.

First thing on the agenda was to find new employment. With my affinity towards owning nice things and living an above-average lifestyle, the five dollars an hour I earned working at the pallet shop wasn't exactly going to provide that. And considering that anything illegal was off the table, I knew that I needed to find a viable solution. Going back to school seemed like a place to start, but that wasn't the answer. I had never liked school, and I wasn't about to delude myself into thinking that I might. I needed to bank on the talent and skills I had...and harness the innate drive I possessed to let me become a success in my own right, doing something I liked doing. I didn't have to dig deep to figure out what that was: working with wood! It really was a no-brainer. I didn't know it yet, but my stint at the pallet shop would prove to be fortuitously beneficial. Because pallets are fastened together using air nailers and staplers, I became familiar with using these pneumatic power tools, acquiring valuable experience and proficiency with how they functioned. Furthermore, working with and maintaining every kind of saw one could imagine had given me knowledge and understanding that would prove to be a godsend for the next stage in my life.

After becoming frustrated with the employment opportunities available to an uneducated—in the scholarly sense—twenty-year-old who'd just gotten out of prison, a new approach was needed. I decided to put an ad in the classified section of the *Saskatoon Star Phoenix* newspaper for odd carpentry jobs. Getting desperate, I was willing to try just about anything—within the law, that is. On day one of my ad running in the paper, the telephone started ringing off the hook. My very first job proved to be the installation of a Whirlybird turbine roof vent for an older gentleman. The acquired experience from shingling the occasional roof with Bill over the years made this little job a piece of cake. Next, for a different client, I built a new set of steps. From building stairs, more than once, with my stepdad Bill, it was another task I had obtained some knowhow to take on. These were small, menial tasks, but job after job kept rolling in. I was earning more money in one hour than working all day at the pallet shop, where I was still putting in forty hours a week.

Taking my time with each project, making sure it was done right, I began to experience a strong sense of confidence from my efforts. I quickly recognized that selling myself to potential customers was something I had a knack for. Maybe some of Bill's salesmanship had unwittingly rubbed off on me. Before long, my determination grew, resulting in the realization that this occupation was perfect for me. Whenever anything came up where I wasn't quite sure on how to proceed, there was a multitude of books available explaining everything

I needed to know. In doing these various carpentry jobs, I observed that when customers inspected my completed work, it was the little details that put smiles on their faces. Being a person who strived for perfection, this aspect shone brightly toward enabling success. Learning very quickly that word of mouth was the most powerful marketing tool of all, common sense dictated that if my customers were happy, they would recommend me to others. That was exactly what happened!

Soon it was becoming more and more difficult to squeeze these jobs in after work and on weekends. Confident my new endeavor was a sustainable source of income, I finally gave my notice at the pallet shop. I felt liberated...again! It wasn't unlike leaving the penal system behind, except this was a decision I made for myself. I had found my niche in life and the confidence to pursue it wholeheartedly. My first big project was to paint the exterior of an entire house. After I finished— impressed by what I had done so far—the same family contracted me to develop their entire basement...start to finish. Granted, at this point, a complete basement development was probably a tad out of my league. I got through it nonetheless. And for a beginner contractor, I did a fairly decent job at it too. The homeowner was a friendly guy, helping me out now and then when I needed an extra pair of hands. Carrying on, I soon became comfortable tackling larger projects, and learned a valuable lesson early in my career as a contractor—a lesson that actually stuck! If you're going to build something, build it well, build it once, and finish it completely. This, by the way, is also the secret to getting paid when the job is completed...usually.

* * *

Remember when I stated that my extracurricular activity with Shari during that cold night in December didn't come without consequences? Well, one evening after Nicole and I returned from a night at the movies with Shari and her new boyfriend Chester, those consequences came looking for vengeance. Driving home from the movie, in the middle of a conversation and completely out of the blue, Nicole said to me, "Why didn't you ever call her?" She was referring to the fact that I'd never called Shari after the evening we'd spent together. Being somewhat caught off guard by the sudden subject change, not to mention incredibly uncomfortable talking to my girlfriend about being with another woman, I kept my answer simple. "Something just didn't feel right," I answered. Then came her next question: "So, how was she?" Of course, me, in my infinite wisdom, incorrectly presumed that girls who were best friends told everything to each other about that kind of stuff. Therefore, I mistakenly concluded that Nicole was already fully aware of the details surrounding Shari and me from that evening in December. And in the spirit of being truthful, with exceptionally poor judgement, I answered, "Pretty good." Yes, we have a new king, and we shall call him, **Lord of the Idiots**.

Of all the available words in the English vocabulary, I'd chosen "pretty good." Without question, in my forty-seven years of life, that was the dumbest thing I've ever said! Needless to say, after learning about my extracurricular activity with her best friend, that put the kybosh on Nicole and Shari's friendship—not to mention that Nicole was about ready to break up with me, again! Truth was, never in my wildest dreams had I believed Nicole would ever be back in my life. That's the problem with consequences: you never know when they will come back to bite you.

Nevertheless, once the dust from all my little hiccups finally settled, Nicole stuck by me. While I was committed to doing something positive with my life, Nicole certainly made it easier to persevere, offering plenty of moral support and encouragement. Failure wasn't an option anymore. It wasn't just about me; it was about her as well. Since I had been granted my freedom, Nicole and I saw our bond grow exponentially. One of the things we did as a couple was acquire a puppy from the litter of my parents' Giant Schnauzer. We named her Skye. Being of mixed breed, Skye wasn't a big dog, but she had the energy level of a fusion reactor. Nicole and I loved that crazy pup as if she were our first child. Skye went everywhere with us. With the strong bond between us, and Skye a part of that unit, we had all the makings of a family. We decided it was time to start down that road and make it official: On July 7, 1990, we were married.

I couldn't help but remember how, a little under two years ago, after she'd broken off our short two-week relationship, I had told myself I was going to marry her. Maybe I'd been half-joking, maybe I'd been hopeful, but whatever the case, we became husband and wife. I felt like I had it all: my dream job, my dream girl, and a profound sense of dignity, something I had never managed to attain before turning over the page on the old Monte. Roughly one hundred people attended our merrymaking event that day in Saskatoon. Even my biological father, Roy, came to share in the joyous occasion. For our first dance, we danced to "Living Inside My Heart" by Bob Segar. But the true highlight of the day was Nicole, who looked absolutely gorgeous in her white wedding dress. I was continually captivated by her the entire day. Having bankrolled the entire wedding on our own and despite efforts to keep the celebration modest, after all was said and done we were $5,000 in debt.

The following Monday, we rented a U-Haul trailer, pulled up stakes, and moved to the booming metropolis of Calgary, Alberta. As the center of Canada's oil industry, it was a city enjoying an upwardly mobile curve. Steeped in the western culture, Calgary had earned the nickname "Cowtown." This culture is still evident in the Calgary Stampede, a summer rodeo and festival that grew out of the farming exhibitions once presented there. We rented a modest yet well-maintained bungalow in the Bankview area of South Calgary. Sporting a heated double-detached garage in the backyard, which made for a great workshop—this place was perfect for my new construction business. Within one year, we went from living in her parents' ant-infested basement to renting an apartment and then to a full-sized house in Calgary. Pouring my heart into this new entrepreneurial endeavor was certainly paying off. Working hard and earning a respectable, honest living felt great. Looking back, over the course of turning twenty-one, it was almost as if I had become a different person. Well, I did become a different person in many ways, all for the better.

After moving to Calgary, my business literally took off overnight. The contrast between working for people in Saskatoon verses people in Calgary was like night and day. The options for work were endless, and in most cases—when it came to giving estimates—price was no longer an issue. Instead, the more important question was how soon can you get it done? It was as if I had discovered the land flowing with milk and honey, and I soon realized the harder I worked, the more money I made. And the more money I made, the more I wanted. Success became an aphrodisiac, and not wanting to turn down profitable opportunities, it wasn't long before I was working twelve-hour days, seven days a week. Being able to visualize, with intricate detail what a project would look like before it was built gave me valuable insight in the design process. Meanwhile, possessing a unique understanding of procedural aspects within the construction industry afforded me the ability to give accurate estimates.

My first full year working in Calgary as a contractor, I grossed 180 grand. The only problem was having TOO much work! This resulted in me running around like a chicken with his head chopped off, trying to keep each client happy. As a consequence, it often took twice as long to finish a job than it should have. I finally reached the point where I went to bed in the evening completely exhausted, and dreamt about projects that didn't exist, only to wake in the morning not knowing what was real and what wasn't. That was when the realization hit me:

I needed to slow down and streamline my efforts more efficiently. I rationalized that it was better to keep my sanity and maintain happy customers than it was to be mentally exhausted while dealing with dissatisfied clients every day—not to mention getting half as much accomplished. If that meant turning down work, then so be it. Besides, never having been the type of person who enjoyed driving around all day supervising and telling everyone what to do, I preferred and took pleasure in the hands-on aspect of building with my own two hands.

With all this money rolling in, a new problem arose. I needed to spend some of it—or pay a hefty tax bill. Never in my wildest imagination had I foreseen ever having that problem. And to think I'd accomplished all that without stealing a cent. First thing on the agenda was a new full-size work truck. Since hauling tools around in my Camaro wasn't the ideal situation, a few months before moving to Calgary, I purchased an almost-new red Chevy S10 truck. However, for the type of contracts I was now becoming involved with, my little quarter-ton simply wasn't big enough. A full-sized truck was necessary. I am not the type of person who enjoys the rigmarole of going through the excruciating process of buying a new vehicle, nor could I afford the time, so on my way to a job one day, I stopped in at a GMC dealership and quickly test drove a 1991 GMC Scottsdale half-ton. An hour later, I drove off the lot in a blue and white half-ton. A few days later, a professional decal company tastefully installed my business name across each side of the truck. I even designed my own company logo. My next purchase consisted of a complete set of pneumatic equipment, which included an air compressor and an assortment of fasteners. Then, to complement the dream garage, I acquired a high-powered table saw. Having enjoyed watching *The New Yankee Workshop*, with Norm Abram on PBS, every time I saw Norm use a new woodworking tool on his program, I'd run out and buy it. It wasn't long before I owned virtually every sort of woodworking tool known to man.

For Nicole's twenty-first birthday, I made her a cedar wood chest complete with rounded lid and locking latch. It was roughly eighteen inches deep by thirty inches wide and twenty-four inches high. Fashioning it after an old pirate's treasure chest, it even had some sentimental words engraved into a brass plate fastened to the front. Considering it important to remind the people you love that you think about them often, before heading to work in the mornings, I would often leave little notes lying around for Nicole to find.

Shortly after moving to Calgary, I purchased one of the earliest cellular phones Motorola had on the market. This thing was the size, shape, and weight of your typical masonry brick. The only options it came with were call display, call waiting, and voicemail—no texting or internet yet. This not only kept me in touch with Nicole, it also facilitated taking care of business. I wondered at the time, *How did we ever get along without these things.* We've taken huge technological leaps since then, but having a cell phone in 1990 was fairly unique.

* * *

Around the same time of purchasing the new work truck, I made another acquisition of a more personal nature, something I'd LITERALLY dreamed of owning since I was thirteen years old. It was inspired by the hit drama *Night Rider* on the NBC broadcasting network in 1982. The series aired from 1982 to 1986, with the infamously acclaimed David Hasselhoff playing the lead character, Michael Knight. Knight drove an artificially intelligent, self-aware black Trans-Am while solving crime. Contemplating on getting rid of our Camaro, on my way home from work one day, I decided to pop in at the Pontiac dealership just down the street from where we lived to see if anything might pique my interest. Nicole, who generally did not show much interest in these types of decisions—perhaps I didn't care to ask—left me to make them for us. I would have bought her anything she wanted, but Nicole wasn't a high-maintenance or materialistic girl and never asked for much. Upon walking into the dealership that afternoon, there it was, sitting on the showroom floor, looking as beautiful and stylish as any automobile I had ever seen: a brand-new 1991 black Pontiac Trans-Am, fully loaded, with black leather interior and complete with a 350 Corvette engine under the hood. This sweet ride was the very definition of pristine. It might not have been AI equipped, but it was all I imagined it would be. Although I had loved my Mustang and Camaro, this car had attitude written all over it. With great anticipation, the next day, Nicole and I picked up our new sports car. As expected, it was fast and a real pleasure to drive. All it needed was a proper sound system. When all was said and done, every time I sat in the cockpit of that magnificent machine, there was a perpetual smile engraved into my face. Loving this new lifestyle, success was suiting me just fine.

The following summer, Nicole and I drove that beautiful sports car through the mountains on our way to Victoria, British Columbia. We were finally taking our postponed honeymoon. At one point, while driving through the Rockies, Nicole was sleeping in the passenger seat, wearing sunglasses, a slinky white tank top, and a pair of shorts. The sun was shining in such a way that it reflected off my bride's shades, lighting up her entire body as if she were glowing and thus accentuating the beauty of her gorgeous physique. Gazing in fondness, I thought to myself, *I'm the luckiest man on the planet. Life can't get any better.* During this trip, Nicole and I stopped in to see Grandpa and Grandma Perepelkin, who still lived in Langley, British Columbia. We had a nice two-hour visit with them, ate some Russian borscht, and then got on our way. Grandma Perepelkin made awesome borscht. I didn't know it at the time, but that would be the last time I would see my grandpa alive. He died sixteen years later in 2007. The plan was for Nicole and I to spend a week honeymooning on the West Coast and then return for a week of camping with some new friends. After a few days sleeping in a fancy hotel, however, we were bored out of our minds. We couldn't wait to go camping in the mountains. Besides, there's only so much time even a newly married couple can spend naked between the sheets. Nevertheless, the two of us stuck it out in British Columbia as long as we could, sightseeing and pretending to be tourists, before deciding to return home two days earlier than scheduled.

Shortly before our honeymoon to Victoria, Nicole introduced me to Andrea, one of her friends from work in the cafeteria of the Foothills Hospital. Turned out Andrea had a boyfriend, Jason, who wanted us to go camping with them. There was a caveat attached to their invitation: We had to bring dirt bikes. Well, that sounded like fun. Requiring no persuasion whatsoever, I walked in to Bow Cycle and purchased two brand-new dirt bikes: a Honda XR100 for Nicole and an XR200 for me. The salesman was desperately trying to sell me one of their Honda CR250s, a two-stroke, but considering my having virtually no experience riding motorcycles, something told me to stick with the much tamer XR200. Other than the little 80cc motorcycle Dad had let me ride a few times when I was a kid, I hadn't been on a dirt bike since. Considering that we were going riding in the mountains, I speculated that the smooth power band of a four-stroke was the wise decision for both of us, at least for the time being.

As soon as we got back to Calgary, we prepared ourselves for our camping trip with Jason and Andrea. We were headed for Burnt Timber Campground, near the small village of Waiparous, some seventy kilometers west of Calgary. The campground was accessible only by a forestry trunk road, and you really felt you were in the middle of nowhere—though to say nowhere would do injustice to this grand slice of nature along the eastern edge of the Rockies. Once we arrived at our destination, we set up our tents in a pristine location. I learned that this area was actually ground zero for several off-road racing events. The entire region was host to Canada's National Hare Scramble and Cross-country Series, as well as Alberta's provincial series. Other than the occasional race in British Columbia, every cross-country event in Canada was never more than a three-hour drive from Calgary. Being a couple of twenty-two-year-old newlyweds simply out for a week of camping and riding in the mountains, Nicole and I had no inclination whatsoever that this would mark the beginning of what would later become a pro career for me in racing motorcycles.

During this pivotal camping trip with Jason and Andrea, I met up with two guys, Ken Voutier and Dennis Bennett, who were camped next to us. They were friendly enough to ask Jason and me to go riding with them. Ken had been riding this area for years and was therefore a local guru as to the whereabouts of some spectacular trail rides. The places they took us that afternoon were scenically breathtaking. Being that I love a challenge, the best part was that these trails were extremely difficult to ride. Ken was roughly twenty years my senior, while Dennis was my age. Ken effortlessly rode his Honda XR350 darn near anywhere. I think he got a kick out of watching a guy twenty years younger struggle on trails that he had no problem negotiating. But hey, I was a complete beginner at this! After that first ride, I would head out to the mountains with Ken and Dennis every Sunday until the snow fell. Seemingly all I ever did was work. And being a high-testosterone type of guy, this new adventure provided a much-needed outlet to release some pent-up aggression.

* * *

My new hobby of riding with the boys every Sunday, however, was NOT going over well with my new bride. Within the confines of our marriage, we certainly had our problems, but this added a whole new level of complications to our nuptials. At one point, just to get some space, our situation became so tense I had to spend a couple nights in a hotel—all because of going riding on Sundays. I wanted my marriage to work, of course, and knew that Nicole did too. But riding with the boys once a week felt like something I really needed in my life. It provided an outlet where I could release some frustration. From my wife's perspective, however, going riding every weekend was interpreted as an escape from her. Barely having passed the threshold of our teenage years, we didn't have a clue as to what a healthy marriage consisted of. At the same time, both of us possessed admirable qualities that contributed to our devotion to one another, and I know we loved each other deeply. It's hard not to look back on this time of my life and wonder what might have happened if I'd simply given in and quit riding every weekend.

I had no idea just how much Nicole was in despair until one terrifying night after a hard day's work. Dead tired, I went to bed around 11:00 PM and was out like a light. At this point in my life, once I was asleep, there was nothing that would wake me—that is, until the blaring echo of the clock radio pierced my ears at 6:00 AM. Uncharacteristically, something woke me on this particular night at about 2:00 AM. I looked at the clock and thought to myself, *Thank God I still have four more hours to sleep*. Gazing across the bed, however, I noticed Nicole wasn't next to me. Wondering if she was in the washroom, I called out her name, but there was no answer. I called out again, this time much louder, so that she'd hear me throughout the entire house. Again, there was nothing but silence. Getting out of bed, I put on a pair of jeans and searched the house high and low, but to no avail. Wide awake now and becoming ever more concerned with every minute that passed by, I headed out to the garage to see if she was there.

Upon entering the garage, a billowing cloud of exhaust fumes rushed towards me, instantly stinging my eyes. With my heart in my throat, I clawed my way through the smoke and found Nicole sitting transfixed in the driver's seat of our car. Both windows of the now-ominous-looking black Trans-Am were rolled down, and the engine running. Barely able to breathe, I opened the car door, picked her up, and carried her lifeless body swiftly into the house. After placing her on the sofa, I could see that she was white as a ghost. To my relief, she was somewhat conscious and taking shallow breaths. Not wanting to take any chances, I picked up the phone to dial 911. Nicole, who suddenly seemed to snap into the moment, realizing what that entailed, insisted she was fine and begged me not to make the call. Concerned about what her family would think, not to mention everything she'd have to go through after attempting suicide, she pleaded with me to hang up the phone. I gave in and respected her wishes. After throwing up in the toilet, her cognitive abilities seemed normal. Be that as it may, I stayed up the rest of the night to make sure she was alright. There was no way I was going back to sleep after that. To this day, I know for a fact it was no small miracle that I woke up during the middle of the night to save her life that evening. And I wonder if it's just irony or coincidence that some years later, she would end up saving my life in a similar way.

If attempting suicide wasn't enough, the next thing that happened between Nicole and me proved to be the clincher, convincing us to get help with our marriage. This occurrence took place during another heated argument, when Nicole threw a half-full bottle of wine and smashed it against the wall. I was so angry with her that I could literally feel my temperature rising, as if the blood within me was boiling. Knowing full well it was paramount to her safety that I get some respite, my plan was to go for a walk and seek a bit of solitude. As I went into the bedroom to put on a shirt, Nicole, not wanting to let calmer heads prevail, followed me, verbally escalating the situation. While in the bedroom, standing by the bed, pulling my shirt on in a hurry to get out of there, Nicole, who was clearly agitated and not willing to back off at all, cornered me on my side of the bed. To make my exit, I would either have to climb over the bed or push her out of the way. Unwisely, I chose the latter. Upon reaching out to push her out of the way, not surprisingly, she assumed I was about to strike her. In the end, my head connected with her cheek bone. We collided hard enough that even I had a considerable bump on my head. Meanwhile, Nicole was left with a noticeable welt under her eye.

Even though I knew what had happened had been an accident, I felt guilty and immediately apologized after the collision. But in her mind, what I'd done was intentional. In the past, there had been times that we'd given each other a shove now and then, but never had anything like this occurred. In any event, the truth is, I had been extremely angry and what had happened shouldn't have happened. The situation had escalated beyond my control, and I'd acted aggressively. Shortly after the incident, Nicole left to stay in Sylvan Lake with her sister.

After analyzing the events that had taken place over the last couple of months, with the culmination being this final altercation, it wasn't difficult for me to decipher what was really going on between us. Nicole and I certainly had issues that we both needed to work on, but this was much simpler than that. We were both feeling resentful, lonely, sexually frustrated, and undesired by each other. After a long day of deep contemplation about our marriage, I concluded that the only way to salvation was to make this relationship work. In light of everything that had happened, even as unhappy as I was, the fact that I loved Nicole more than the expanse of our universe never changed. That was when it became crystal clear that we needed help…professional help. The next day, I called Nicole at her sister's place and begged her to come home. Amazingly, she had the same idea, and she agreed to come home if we pursued counselling. After a few sessions with a psychologist—to my surprise—our relationship rapidly improved. Almost overnight! It was as if we became two different people in how we handled situations. Even our sex life was enhanced. Without question, Nicole and I had reached a milestone in our marriage. The fighting virtually stopped, and although our relationship wasn't perfect, we were both noticeably happier.

In hindsight, it's easy to understand why our marriage improved to the degree it did, and it certainly wasn't because our therapist was some kind of relationship magician, as many in this world claim to be. Other than the practical advice she offered, our success had nothing to do with the psychologist. The answer to the concealed mystery of what it takes to sustain a happy marriage lay within our very own attitudes. Nicole and I attended every counselling session with one synonymous goal: to do whatever it took to make our marriage work. Both of us accepted the fact that changes needed to be made in how we handled situations, and neither was concerned about whose fault it was or playing the blame game. Aware that each of us was equally imperfect, we recognized there were issues. Our common goal now was to deal with them together. After all, if you truly do love one another, that mutual mindset seems like a no-brainer.

* * *

Less than a year later, we began planning a family—apart from our pet, Skye. Our first child was conceived on February 14, 1993. Because we were still renting a house, one of our first priorities was to buy our first home. Before our baby was born, we searched and searched for months, looking for a suitable home. But being a contractor, I had fairly high standards as to what was and wasn't acceptable. My goal was to avoid buying something that I would have to completely renovate. With a baby on the way and my contracting business in overdrive, I had not time for that. And living on the outskirts of Calgary was an option neither of us wanted to consider. Therefore, buying a brand-new home was out of the question. Eventually, we found the perfect home in the Huntington Hills district of northwest Calgary. The owners had just finished a complete renovation on a beautiful 1,500-square-foot bungalow and then decided to divorce—go figure! Conveniently for me, it had a perfectly sized double detached garage for my construction business in the backyard.

However, with all the wonderful changes going on in our life, these changes wouldn't come without at least one sacrifice, one that was by far the most difficult for me. I had to sell that beautiful black Trans-Am. What's even worse, I later replaced it with a MINIVAN! Nicole went into labor on the morning of Tuesday, November 16, 1993. I drove her to the hospital at around 5:00 AM and never left her side through the entire process. During the course of the next thirty-six hours, Nicole and I bonded in a way that only having a baby together could accomplish. While watching my wife endure each contraction as she held my hand, it was as if I felt her pain in real time. The love I felt for the mother of my child through that remarkable experience impressed upon me a magnitude of which nothing of this world could seemingly ever transcend. Our first baby girl was born at roughly 5:00 PM on November 17, 1993. We named her Danielle Wenzday Perepelkin. I came up with her middle name. When the doctor handed me the scissors to cut the cord, I was so overtaken with love and emotion that I shook my head and said, "No, you do it. I don't want to hurt her." Admittedly, my opinion is extremely biased in my sentiments on this, but Danielle was the most beautiful creature I'd yet to witness of all God's creations. My heart, overwhelmed with love that exceeded all human comprehension, caused a steady stream of tears to flow continually down my face. Upon gazing in fondness at my wife as she held our baby girl, I was delighted to see the experience equally moved Nicole as well.

After becoming a father, something changed inside me. It was as if my heart and the love I was able to feel increased substantially the moment I laid eyes on my newborn baby girl in the delivery room. In my wildest dreams, I never imagined being capable of feeling that much love for another human being. The fact that neither Nicole nor I had experienced exemplary childhoods made the task seem even more daunting. Fortunately, Nicole was a dedicated mother and soon began reading a multitude of books on the subject of competent parenting to get us through the formative years.

Cue music: "Love Is a Battlefield" by Pat Benatar

https://www.youtube.com/watch?v=D0EysM1iNMk

CHAPTER

28

Putting on My Race Face

My very first experience with the world of racing occurred in May of 1992. It proved to be a momentous event that would forever shape my future and those close to me. Since I'd started the weekend hobby of riding dirt bikes every Sunday—less than a year earlier— Ken, Dennis, and I had established a morning ritual of stopping to enjoy a big, hearty breakfast before heading out to the mountains. The adventurous trail rides we would indulge ourselves in were long and physically demanding; therefore, loading up on calories was essential. Over the course of the previous year, Ken and Dennis had slowly introduced me to people within the amateur cross-country racing scene. Often times, we would meet up and ride with these same amateur riders. As my riding skills progressed, the subject of racing kept coming up more and more. I was informed that there was a Sportsman division for beginner riders. At my first sanctioned race, I would be told over and over not to push myself, just to finish the course and receive a T-shirt. It was explained to me that just finishing the race and receiving a T-shirt at one of these events was a challenge in itself. However, telling me not to push myself was like telling the sun not to shine. Some of the newbies would take up to eight hours or more just to complete a race—if they even finished at all. I knew I had to do better than that; as it turned out, I would do a lot better than that.

The first race I chose to test my skills at was the Porcupine Hills Alberta Provincial Cross-Country on May 24, 1992. This discipline of dirt bike racing—within Canada—was exclusive to Alberta and select areas in British Columbia. The majority of them were held on the eastern edge of the Alberta Rockies, starting in an area that spanned roughly two hours northwest of Calgary, then south along the rugged foothills all the way down to the U.S. border. Most of this area—known as crown land—was open to the public for off-road use and was the largest of its kind anywhere in Canada. As it was both remote but close enough to small and large towns, this region was ideal for staging Canada's cross-country and hare scramble national and provincial races. The Porcupine Hills riding area—where this particular cross-country event was held that year—is nestled among the foothills roughly two hours straight west of Lethbridge. As tenting in the mountains wasn't exactly all that favorable to Nicole and me, we upgraded our accommodations to a tent trailer with a heater and a hot shower. With bikes loaded in the back of my work truck and a brand-new tent trailer in tow, we were off to the races. I raced the Sportsman class that day and finished in first place. I was hooked! Awakening the next day, however, every muscle in my body ached; even my eyelids were sore. I may have known how to ride a bike and was physically fit due to the demands of my job, but my muscles certainly were not conditioned for the demands of hardcore racing.

For the uninitiated, the intricate details of what a cross-country race entails begins with choosing the desired brand and size of dirt bike you want to ride. The most common cross-country bike of choice in our area at that time was a 250cc two-stroke. However, my first race was on a Suzuki DR350 four-stroke. These days, everyone is on four-strokes. The most notable difference between the two—to the person riding the motorcycle—is in the delivery of horsepower to the rear wheel. A two-stroke engine has an enormous burst of power, but only at higher rpm, whereas a four-stroke has a more even and consistent, less-abrupt, power delivery, which makes a four-stroke motorcycle, although heavier in weight, much easier to ride.

Typically, there is a cross-country beginner class known as Junior. Then a step up from there is Intermediate. After Intermediate, if you're qualified, you advance to Expert and then on to Pro. Some regions and sanctioning bodies don't have an Expert class. Instead, you advance from Intermediate straight to Pro. When I was racing, under sanctioning of the Canadian Motorcycle Association (CMA), they did have an Expert class. There was also a Veteran class for competitors over thirty and forty years of age. At any given race, there could be up to 150 rider entries in total. The start of a race consisted of each competitor lining up with their respective class, engine off, at the designated start area. The Pro riders would line up first, wait for their cue—the sound of a starting pistol—and then start their bikes as quickly as possible, and off they went. After a few minutes, the Experts went next, and so on down to the Sportsman class last. A normal race would generally take the fastest riders a minimum of three hours to finish. It would cover anywhere from one hundred to 140 kilometers—sometimes more—of a marked course through all sorts of trails. The terrain varied from tight tree trails—sometimes so tight that you couldn't fit your handlebars through without straddling them—to wide-open cut lines and river crossings. Further challenges included riding over logs, up or down rock slides, and having to go places a mountain goat would have trouble…up or down hills so steep you couldn't walk them. All of this combined with a vast amount of super-cool trails that were generally a lot of fun to ride. However, not everyone rode the same course. Beginner riders often had a less difficult and shorter race.

The tricky element of this particular discipline of dirt bike racing is following the course markings. This was something I often had issues with. The racecourse was marked with orange or pink ribbons; blue ribbons indicated the turns. When going fast, it is easy to get sidetracked, following the trail instead of the ribbons. Deviating from the designated racecourse is a mistake that can be extremely frustrating—and costly when you're chasing a championship. Points are awarded based on the position a rider finishes in their respective class. Throughout the course of a race, each competitor passes through a series of random checkpoints—to ensure that no one cuts the course. These checkpoints are heavily marked with white ribbons so that a racer doesn't blow by so fast he fails to see the check—missing a check means an automatic DNF (Did Not Finish). National races would often have live checks, meaning a person was actually there to record your plate number as you passed through. But not all race organizers subscribed to this standard. Dead checks or unmanned checkpoints were commonplace in this sport back then. Instead of a trail marshal, a handheld hole punch would hang by a chain from a clearly identified tree. After the competition trail card—zip-tied to your person or handlebars—was punched, the hole it left was unique to the punch used, assuring no cheating occurred.

Cross-country racing has an inimitable element to it that sets it apart from almost every other form of motorcycle racing. You're trying to go as fast as you can on a course that you've never ridden before. Therefore, you have no idea what is around the next bend or over the next hill, all the while attempting to keep an acute focus on the course markings. This makes the sport not only physically demanding, but also mentally. Any rider who makes it to the Pro level in this sport assuredly has exceptional peripheral vision, razor-sharp mental focus, and lightning-fast reflexes, as well as possesses extraordinary riding ability—not to mention is in peak physical condition. It is commonly purported that the two most physically demanding sports are soccer and motocross. I've competed in both and would argue that cross-country motorcycle racing may be a tad more physically demanding, or should at least be mentioned in the same sentence. A Pro motocross race consists of two thirty-five-minute races on a closed, familiarized circuit, with a fairly lengthy recovery break in between. A cross-country rider is not afforded that luxury. He or she will race just as hard for over three hours on an open, unfamiliar circuit…with no break!

* * *

Needless to say, after winning my first race, I had crossed the threshold of no return. Nicole was with me at the race that day. Other than a "way to go, Monte" remark, she didn't seem too overjoyed with my success. Not being entirely fond of my new hobby, I'm sure she was cynically thinking: *That's just great!* With my first bona fide cross-country competition experience behind me, I quickly realized why nearly everyone chose to race a two-stroke motorcycle over a four-stroke. Two-strokes are considerably lighter in weight and therefore easier to maneuver, especially after three hours of racing. I decided to trade in my Suzuki before the next race for a shiny new Kawasaki KDX200 two-stroke. In 1992, the KDX200 was probably the most popular off-road motorcycle of its generation. It was slightly heavier than its motocross KX125 or KX250 counterparts, but it was the perfect step forward in the evolution of my riding career.

The next race on the schedule that year wasn't until July 5th at Moose Mountain—located roughly two hours northwest of Calgary. Unlike the first race I'd competed in, Moose Mountain was a national event and notorious for being one of the more difficult races on the schedule. At this juncture, I knew that if I was going to keep racing, I HAD to get my wife onboard. By this time, Nicole and I had gone camping and trail riding together enough times that she was becoming quite an avid rider herself. She still had the Honda XR100, which she rode every time we went camping. As circumstance would have it, at every cross-country event, there would be a race for the ladies as well. The women would race on Saturday—guys always raced on Sunday. With a little coaxing and a few inspiring words, I convinced Nicole to enter the ladies' race on her little XR100. She finished in fifth place in her very first race. After the race, I recognized that all-too-familiar look in her eyes. She was hooked too! I listened to her intently as she went on and on about each experience she'd encountered throughout her race. It was really quite adorable. My strategy had worked. Now Nicole also couldn't wait for the next race. For the remainder of the 1992 season, we went to and entered every single race on the CMA schedule. As for me, I also finished fifth at the Moose Mountain National in the men's Junior Division, earning five points in my very first amateur national.

I would go on to win my very first amateur event two races later. I won the last race of the series as well. I finished the points chase in fourth overall in the Alberta Junior Cross-Country Championship, despite having missed the first two races of the series. Nicole, meanwhile, raced at every event as well, soon becoming a consistent top-three competitor among the ladies. Camping in the mountains was a blast, and racing added the icing to the cake. Even our dog, Skye, was having fun. We were loving life!

At the last showdown of the 1992 season, I met a rider who had also raced that day. His name was Peter Issler. Pete, as he preferred to be called, was a sponsored racer and consistent top-five provincial cross-country contender in the Pro division. Being impressed by his riding ability, it wouldn't have been a stretch to say that I looked up to him. I found it difficult to fathom how fast these pros could actually maneuver their motorcycles through the varying degrees of what I considered extremely difficult terrain. Earlier that year, at one of the events, a train of pros had flown by me at incredible speed, leaving me behind in their dust. I'd concluded they must have ridden a different segment of the course before having to ride the amateur section. I had not expected anybody to be passing me, one by one, like I was standing still. I'd tried to keep up with them, but I just couldn't cut the mustard. All I could do was dream of one day being that good. Over the course of the next few months, Pete and I would become close friends.

* * *

Pete, a finishing carpenter who also lived in Calgary, worked for his dad, Hans, who subcontracted from several reputable home builders in the city. Hans would handle the finish carpentry contracts on upwards of 200 homes per year, which was more than he could actually complete himself. Therefore, he subcontracted the rest to other finishing carpenters. This ended up being a windfall for me. In January of 1993, Pete, on behalf of his dad, offered me a house to do on my own. I had hung the occasional door and done some minor finish carpentry while doing various renovation projects, but I had never done an entire house before. This meant hanging the doors, casing the windows, building a fireplace mantle, stair capping or railing, shelving, baseboards, and any other custom cabinetry that the homeowner requested. Realizing what an amazing opportunity this was to learn and advance my skills as a carpenter I eagerly jumped at the chance. Because I already had all the tools necessary to undertake a project of this scope, there was no need for me to invest a dime in this step-up in my career.

When I met Hans at the house to go over the work details, I could tell right away that he was a meticulous kind of guy when it came to his work. Being that I considered myself meticulous as well, I welcomed this challenge as an opportunity to measure myself against a thirty-plus year veteran of the trade. I was curious to see how good I actually was. The first house I completed was a smaller home, and therefore, I finished it in three days. When Hans came to inspect my work, the one and only complaint he had was that the clearance gaps in my doors were a little too big. He explained that the doors often shrink over time, thus creating even larger gaps. Well, I couldn't argue the point with him, as I had no expertise in this area, and wondered if I had failed the acid test. I didn't have to wonder long. Sensing my anxiety, he gave me a fatherly slap on the back and asked me if I wanted to do the two houses next door, which were ready and waiting. "Just keep an eye on the door gaps," he said, giving me a sly wink. Although Hans never said so, I think it was safe to say he was mildly impressed with the first job I did for him. I began working for the Issler's nearly full time, taking on bigger, more complicated houses as time went on. Along the way, I was awarded the privilege of working side by side with Hans and Pete on different occasions. They were more than happy to share their trade secrets with me, teaching me the intricacies of being a skilled finishing carpenter. Strangely enough—as much as I learned from them—much of the techniques I observed them using were exactly what I was already doing. If I believed in such a thing, I would have concluded that I must have been a carpenter in a previous life.

One of the major builders the Issler's worked for, Stepper Homes, was noted for their exceptional interior craftsmanship, even receiving awards, so I considered myself extremely fortunate to have the opportunity of working side by side with the best. The experience gave me the confidence of knowing that my workmanship met their high standards of excellence. I felt right at home doing finish carpentry, so much so that I'd actually look forward to going to work every day. I absolutely loved my job and credit Pete and his dad for that privilege. That shovel-sized dustpan I'd built in high school just happened to be very useful for collecting debris when sweeping up after myself. That very dustpan would forever become a staple in all my carpentry endeavors.

Although we were very busy keeping up with the construction boom happening in Calgary, it wasn't all work and no play. Pete convinced me to race the 1993 ice racing series with him that year—January through April of 1993—and even supplied the bikes for me to ride. I took to ice like a fish to water and won the Alberta Provincial Ice Racing Championship in the Junior class. Ice racing was exhilarating and certainly beneficial to my riding career in that it made me feel comfortable going fast in corners while teaching me the art of drifting. All in all, I wasn't a big fan of racing in minus thirty-degree Celsius weather and never did it again. One season had served its purpose: It helped me become a more skilled rider for my cross-country aspirations, one that would see me move up one class.

http://montejperepelkin.com/photos-10

Spring finally arrived, and I couldn't wait to get back on the dirt. I was bored racing on ice. Going around in circles for three minutes while freezing your butt off wasn't exactly my cup of tea. In March, I bought a brand-new 1993 Honda CR250 and couldn't wait for the first race of the season. Pete showed me how to properly set my bike up for racing cross-country. This consisted primarily of how to build and install handguards to avoid whacking your knuckles on tree branches.

Because I'd won two races in the Junior Class the previous season, the CMA bumped me to the Intermediate Class, and I welcomed the challenge. Before the snow was even completely melted, Pete and I would go riding together on a regular basis. The first secret I learned in how to become a faster rider was to ride and practice with guys who are better than you. It forces you to push yourself in order to keep up with them. Unbeknownst to Pete—or maybe he knew—he was mentoring me in the art of becoming a more advanced racer. I credit Pete as a major contributor to my success in cross-country racing. He taught me more than anyone about the mechanical side of bikes and, more notably, how to ride one—not to mention the start he gave me in a career of being a bona fide carpenter. The fortuitous circumstances of meeting and befriending Pete certainly made a huge and positive impact in terms of my future.

Before the first race of the season even began, I somehow got the crazy idea in my head that no matter what, I was one hundred percent certain that I would win the Intermediate Provincial Cross-Country Championship that year. The first race was in April at Lake Koocanusa, British Columbia. The terrain in and around Lake Koocanusa is sublime, with beautiful tree trails that are more open than a regular Alberta cross-country race. The soil is loamy, with the perfect mixture of sand to it, making this venue my favorite race of the circuit. Lake Koocanusa has an extraordinary feature: the lake itself is a reservoir formed by the damming of the Kootenay River with the Libby Dam in 1972 between the Canada-United States border. Every spring around the time of this particular race, the reservoir would be conveniently empty, thus allowing off-road connoisseurs such as ourselves to enjoy riding on the moist sandy soil of the lake bed. The current that flowed through the reservoir while it was full created almost sand-dune-like terrain for us to ride in. During the race, however, I broke my rear brake pedal and finished the race in a dismal tenth place, accumulating just one lousy point.

Moving on to the next race, which was Porcupine Hills, where one year earlier I'd won my first ever race, I got my first DNF of the year. It rained the entire day, creating a sticky soil compound that could only be likened to peanut butter, thus making it very difficult to negotiate a bike. Over half of the entries that day DNF'd, so I didn't feel completely defeated. After collecting just one point after two races, my confidence wasn't shaken by any means. It was a long season, with seven races still remaining in the series, and I was still unwavering in my resolve that I would win that championship. The third contest and first national round of the series that year was Moose Mountain, the biggest, most prestigious race of the season. It was there that I would finally redeem myself, netting my first win in the Intermediate Class and, at the same time, my first-ever national victory. Crossing the finish line that day, I experienced a feeling that can only be described as pure euphoria, not just because I'd won, but because I'd proven to myself that I could. I remember having tears in my eyes—hopefully no one noticed—when I walked up to receive my award at trophy presentation that day. Nicole hugged me afterward and told me she knew I could do it. Even my parents were in attendance on that momentous occasion. They attended the odd race now and then, and it felt refreshing to see Mom and Dad taking an interest in my endeavors. As for my sister, Nikki, since my moving to Calgary, she and I had drifted apart to the point where we almost never saw each other anymore. I wouldn't say that we were estranged, but somehow time, distance, and life just seemed to have taken precedence over the once-close brother-and-sister bond that we'd shared. If there was such a thing as do-overs in life, maintaining a good relationship with Nikki is definitely something I would like to have tried harder at.

http://montejperepelkin.com/photos-11

Of the six remaining races in the series that year, I would go on to finish the season with one fifth-place finish, three second-place finishes, and two more wins. As it turned out, the single point I'd acquired at the first race of the season, where I'd finished tenth, won me the 1993 Intermediate Championship with 88 points.

The year of 1993 was definitely a turning point in my life. If I hadn't met Pete, I don't know how my career as a finishing carpenter would have even begun. Sure, I had the skills and had dabbled with interior woodworking earlier in life, but working exclusively in that particular industry had never been on my radar. Although I didn't exactly look forward to going to work every day as a general contractor, I was quite content and did extremely well at it, with no desire to change anything. But after discovering the trade of interior woodworking, I felt my overall attitude towards life in general had changed dramatically for the better. I once read a quote by Confucius that said, "Choose a job you love, and you will never have to work a day in your life."

How true those words are, indeed. Interesting how, throughout our lives, certain people that we meet become paramount in shaping our future—usually without us even realizing it.

* * *

As dirt bike racing was becoming a bigger part of our lives, and because of our new baby girl, Danielle, Nicole, and I decided an upgrade in our camping accommodations was in order. Before the 1994 season began, we traded in our tent trailer for a brand new twenty-two-foot holiday trailer. Being substantially more comfortable than our previous accommodations, it made camping a lot more fun, especially on rainy days.

After claiming the Intermediate Championship in '93, I was advanced to the Expert class for the '94 season. And after having trained all winter and being in the best physical condition of my life, I was as ready as I had ever been. With a dismal tenth-place finish at the first race exactly one year ago, I was dead set on kicking the new season off with a win.

The first cross-country race of the year was slated for April 3, 1994, which again saw the opening round take place at Lake Koocanusa. At this particular event, everyone…Beginner, Intermediate, Expert, and Pro started at the same time. Therefore, getting a bad start and having to carve your way through all the slower riders is something you wanted to avoid at all costs. As many as 150 competitors fired up their engines and began the race by speeding across a dry lake bed, headed towards a smoking fire, usually a couple of miles away. At that point, the course flags began guiding racers up the steep embankment of the reservoir, continuing on through various tree trails.

When I arrived at the end of the lake bed, I followed the course markings up the embankment leading into the trees. I was in second place overall and right in the rear fender of the pro rider in front of me, who was none other than former Provincial Pro Cross-Country Champion, Julien Cerny. Given the latitude of this momentous experience, the proceeding events remain crystal clear in my memory. After following him for what seemed like roughly five minutes, I decided to set him up for a pass in the next turn. I managed this with surprisingly little effort and even started pulling away from him. I was riding the race of my life! My bike, a 1994 Honda CR250, was dialed in exactly to what I needed for tackling the terrain.

A short time later, I began to recognize the landscape heading back towards camp, allowing me to conclude that I was about to pass back through the starting area. This meant I was already twenty minutes into the race, yet to me, it felt as if the race had just begun. There were several spectators lined up on either side of the course as I approached. Adrenaline now pumping at maximum capacity, I rode my CR250 off the three-foot embankment, jumping onto the wet sand. Spectators were enthusiastically giving me the "number one" signal with their index fingers—indicating that I was in first place overall. Seeing that I had an unobstructed racecourse in front of me with a long, sweeping bend through camp, I was looking for more speed. With my right hand holding the throttle wide open, I engaged the clutch slightly while simultaneously pulling up on the shifter pedal with my left foot to upshift from second to third gear—without ever backing off the throttle. When the sudden burst of mechanical energy was transferred to the rear wheel, I gripped the handlebars firmly with both hands as the raw horsepower of two-stroke energy pulled and stretched out the muscles in my arms and shoulder blades. Clenching the bike tightly with both legs, I held my body in the sweet spot of the motorcycle and balanced the front wheel of my CR250 about six inches off the ground while tearing around the long, sweeping corner through camp. Feeling the raw adrenaline course through every vein in my body, I took a deep breath and harnessed the seemingly uncontrollable aggression to focus on riding smoothly yet swiftly, after which I headed out—with an all-star lineup of exceptional talent hot on my heels—onto the next segment of racecourse.

The experience of riding through camp at the head of the freight train that day was one of the most exhilarating moments in my life. Next to the birth of my children and marrying my wife, it was the greatest feeling in the world.

After leading the race for roughly the next thirty minutes—knowing there was an all-star lineup of lightning-fast pros behind me—with no one catching up to me, I began to get worried. I'd never been in this type of situation before, and considering my history of not following race flags very well, I started wondering if maybe I had taken a wrong turn somewhere. Yet there were clear, bright orange ribbons hanging from the trees, indicating that I was definitely following the designated racecourse. By now—what felt like an hour into the race—I was expecting someone would have caught up to me. *I'm fast, but not that fast,* I thought to myself. While in the next long, straight section of racecourse, I slowed considerably to look back and see if anyone was behind me. There wasn't. When you're riding a motorcycle—especially at race speed—it's impossible to hear a bike behind you unless they're practically on top of you. I decided to stop completely—turn my engine off—and listen for bikes. Two-strokes are loud and can usually be heard from up to a kilometer away. After sitting on the side of the marked trail, for what seemed like an excruciatingly long time—in reality probably no more than fifteen seconds—all of a sudden, I could hear the thundering sound of several bikes coming towards me. In the mere moments it took me to re-start my CR250 and get back up to race speed, there were four pro riders on me. In no time, I found myself in fifth place. How demoralizing! I felt like a complete idiot for stopping.

I was still the lead Expert rider, however, as the four riders now in front of me were all in the Pro division. But I wasn't going to take this lying down, and I poured on the gas. Within minutes, I passed one guy, then another, and before I knew it, I was back in front. I tried to pull away, but there was no shaking any of these guys off my tail. They were all quite capable of riding my pace. At the finish line, I would record second place overall on the day and first, by a long shot, in the Expert class. Although I didn't nail down the coveted overall win, I was ecstatic to finish second among a long list of seasoned pro riders. The pro that finished ahead of me that day was Pete Degraaf, a veteran of the sport. I was still an amateur; two years before, I hadn't even entered my first race. A year before that, I hadn't even thrown a leg over a bike since I was thirteen years old. Five years earlier—almost to the day—I'd been sitting in a prison cell, contemplating a six-month jail sentence. Yet somehow, with nothing more than a grade ten education, I was four years into consistently earning a six-figure income. My business was flourishing, my marriage to Nicole was excellent, I was the father of a beautiful baby girl, and I was excelling in a sport that I absolutely loved. At twenty-five years of age, life was perfect!

* * *

I had no championship goals in mind for the 1994 season, choosing instead to broaden my horizons. Early in the year, I decided to attend the International Six Day Enduro (ISDE), which would be held in Tulsa, Oklahoma, that year. This was only the second time the event was going to be held on North American soil. The iconic race has been held annually in Europe since 1913—except during the WWI and WWII years—and remains a supreme test of rider and machine. Over the six days, and upwards of 1,250 miles, competitors must contend with stringent rules regarding time allowances and restrictions on mechanical replacements all while carrying out his or her own motorcycle repairs. The ISDE can attract entries of more than 500 riders worldwide, together with thousands of support crew and spectators. Usually referred to as the Olympics of Motorcycling, trophies for best six-rider national, four-rider junior national, three-rider women's national, three-rider club national, and three-rider manufacturing teams are awarded. Gold, silver, and bronze medals are awarded on an individual level. The medals are typically presented based on percentage of finishers or relative to the best individual performance in the event within their specific class. Individual gold medals go to participants who finish within ten percent of their class's top competitor's total elapsed time, silver medals are awarded for those who finish within twenty-five percent, and bronze medals are awarded to any rider who finishes all six days within their time allowance.

Expecting to turn pro the following year in cross-country, I determined that competing in and finishing this event would solidify me as a contender for a Canadian Pro National Cross-Country Championship. My ultimate goal was a gold medal in Tulsa. However, a considerable amount of preparation was necessary before competing in an event of this stature. Therefore, legitimately vying for the Expert cross-country title that year was unrealistic. But I did finish second in the championship point standings, with two wins on the season. The Tulsa ISDE was held September 20–25, 1994. A week before the event—in an effort to become acclimatized to the humid Oklahoma weather—I and three others drove down in my work truck, pulling a holiday trailer. There was Paul, aka "Spodey," who worked for me at the time as an apprentice, Craig, and Jeff. Paul was competing in the event, while Craig and Jeff went along as support crew. My wife, as much as I wanted her to come, elected to stay home with Danielle.

With the Tulsa ISDE being in such close proximity to Canada, there was an onslaught of Canadians who wanted to participate. Only thirty spots were available to Canadian competitors, however. Due to the huge North American interest in the '94 ISDE, two pre-qualifiers were held in Canada during the months leading up to the Enduro. One of these was held in Kamloops, British Columbia, while the other was in eastern Canada. I attended the Kamloops qualifier, finishing in the top ten…with a flat tire, no less! I had to stop and fix the tire out on the trail, with limited tools, and this betrayal of rubber cost me 600 seconds on my time card. Basically, in ISDE competition, the rider with the least number of seconds on his time card wins. Nevertheless, as much as I was disappointed with my overall finish, I was certain it was adequate to represent Canada. My only fear at this point was that I might actually make Canada's official Trophy Team. Secretly, I wasn't overly enthusiastic about being on the Trophy Team, especially with this being my first ISDE. Six days of riding ten hours a day is a long time to spend on a motorcycle, and anything can happen. I wanted to ride for myself. My goals were to finish the event and have fun doing it. This wasn't about patriotism or anything like that. When the official announcement was released with my name on the list but not on Canada's Trophy Team, I was relieved.

The opening ceremonies were quite the spectacle, with a parade, fireworks, and even a marching band. When the Canadian entries came in wearing the country's official red and white ISDE attire, the fans went ballistic. I believe the Canadian group of riders received the loudest cheers of any other country. Americans seem to love Canadians. I felt like a rock star, I think we all did that day. Making the ISDE cut is something I consider one of the highlights of my dirt bike racing career.

The first day kicked off on Tuesday, September 20, 1994; my start time was right around 8:00 AM. The day began with my motorcycle having to undergo a tech inspection; upon passing it, the bike was stored in an impound area, along with everybody else's. At this point, no one could touch their machine until it was time to start. You were given roughly ten minutes each day to do maintenance...with no assistance from anyone. During this time, a rider would normally change both tires—using the same rims—change the oil, and clean the air filter. Try doing all that in under ten minutes with only hand tools. It certainly is possible, because I managed it. Before setting off for the day, everyone was provided with a time schedule, which was zip-tied to your handlebars. Upon leaving the start area, each rider was given an equal number of minutes to make it to the first checkpoint, then the second checkpoint, and so on. If you were late, every second counted as one point against your total score. I found that riding at about seventy-five percent of race speed would get me to each check with a few minutes to spare.

The competition side of the event came into play in the form of special tests, of which there were two each day. Throughout the course of a day, while riding from one checkpoint to the next, you would come upon a sign that read "Test Section Ahead" or "Special Test Ahead." Then you would see a timing official sitting at a desk station, recording your plate number as you rode by with a laser-guided time device. After that, each competitor would ride as fast as possible to the next time station—which was usually within five to ten minutes. The faster each test was completed, the lower your overall score was. Special tests consisted of varying degrees of terrain, including motocross-style grass tracks, rocky trails, technical off-camber trails, and anything else they could come up with. The goal was to test a rider's abilities in every terrain imaginable.

After the first day, I was riding gold-medal pace, but I was so exhausted I actually began to wonder if I had it in me to finish five more days. Every muscle in my body ached. The next day, however, I woke up in a terrific mood and somehow managed to push the negativity and doubts out of my mind. Not even ten minutes after leaving the starting line, however, my CR250 began sliding around as if I'd just hit a patch of ice. I looked down to discover that my rear tire was completely flat! This was not good, and my verbalization of the fact certainly bore this out. I pulled over and proceeded to repair the flat tire on the side of the trail, knowing full well that any chance at a gold medal was now over. Reminiscent of Kamloops, I finished the day with an additional 600 points against my total score. There was some saving grace: I was still within a mere five minutes or 300 points of silver-medal pace. My goal now was to make up the time and finish with a silver medal. That meant, assuming I stayed on time between each checkpoint, that I needed to ride 300 seconds faster than silver-medal competitors in the next eight special tests. Unfortunately, by the end of day six, I was mere seconds short of a silver medal. Nevertheless, I counted the experience as a victory. I achieved my goal to finish the grueling event, never mind bagging a bronze medal. When I subtracted the time lost from getting the flat, I found solace in the fact that I would have been in contention for a gold medal, meaning my special test times were among the top ten percent of the world.

http://montejperepelkin.com/photos-14

Finishing the ISDE was another career highlight and a milestone in my life. After all, it was no small feat to accomplish this, especially for a first-time entry. When my racing experience at the six-day event in Tulsa was over, however, I learned something valuable about my ability, or lack thereof, when measured against the world's best. Although my cross-country special test times in Tulsa were often among the top ten percent, my motocross times were considerably less efficient. Therefore, before embarking on my rookie season in the Canadian Pro Cross-Country Championship series in 1995, I decided to take a year off from cross-country to race motocross instead. I knew I needed to improve my motocross skills and figured—with its multitude of obstacles and high-intensity racing on relatively short tracks—competing in motocross was the best way to achieve this. I also decided to enlist the services of Chris Bonneau, a local pro motocross racer who held riding clinics. Having a stellar reputation for teaching riders to improve their motocross skills, Chris had a long list of successful pros on his resume, including Dean Wilson, who went on to enjoy a successful career in the United States. Since I already had the speed and skills of how to ride a motorcycle, after a few one-on-one lessons with Chris, I noticed a dramatic improvement in my lap times. And because Chris went to nearly every motocross in Alberta, he would watch my races and give me riding tips afterward. Chris not only became my motocross mentor, but he would also become a very close friend—the same friend who would be such a huge support for me after my arenacross crash, which was at this time looming on the horizon, some four years away.

CHAPTER

29

Mixing Business with Racing

Being a married man and father, dirt bike racing wasn't the only thing taking up space in my life. Family and my real job still needed my undivided attention, regardless of my racing aspirations. It was a balancing act—to say the least. Early in 1995, my mom and dad had moved to Wetaskiwin, Alberta—roughly a two-hour drive from Calgary. After some years of physical distance between us, this would bring them back into my world on a more regular basis. Since turning over a new leaf in pursuing a more honest lifestyle, the relationship I had with my parents no longer suffered from the strains that my restless and delinquent youth had brought upon us. Dad acquired a sales position at Denham Ford in Wetaskiwin. His success selling Fords at Formo Motors in Preeceville, Saskatchewan, during the late 1970s and early eighties apparently superseded his reputation as a reflexologist; Denham hired Dad on the spot, over the phone, no less. After a ten-year career in the field of reflexology, it seemed Dad was ready for a change in scenery.

Meanwhile, I was finding my way quite successfully within the trade of finish carpentry, picking up regular contracts of my own with local home builders. Paul, my apprentice, moved on in early January, which meant I was on my own. That was until Burt Petersen, another fellow dirt bike enthusiast, enquired to see if I was interested in hiring a new apprentice. I'd known Peterson to be an easygoing, likeable guy through racing; therefore, the decision to hire him was easy. As it turned out, Burt would prove to be the best student of carpentry I ever had the pleasure of working with. He learned and caught on to things quickly while possessing a very necessary virtue that is required in becoming a skillful carpenter...patience. However, unfortunately for me, after just two years of working side by side with him, Peterson was educated enough and pretty much ready to work on his own. My young protégé gave me his notice, and I was flying solo again.

Throughout my years of working as a finishing carpenter, I had the privilege of teaching three full-time apprentices, all of whom went on to achieve successful careers within the industry. The one thing I noticed in all three of those instances was that the apprentices certainly took for granted the fact that they were learning a valuable trade while getting paid at the same time. In a sense, they were getting paid to go to school. When these guys first started out, they literally didn't even know how to properly hold or use a hammer, let alone how to case a window, use a miter saw, or work with air nailers. The first six months of working with any apprentice will almost always prove to be a financial loss—because of all the time spent teaching—but it's an investment that you hope will eventually pay off. What's even worse, hiring an apprentice comes with the clear understanding that the time will come when the student knows enough to go find his own work, eventually becoming your competition. Although somewhat different circumstances, I know the situation with Pete, hiring me to work for his dad, was similar. And if I'm honest with myself, I probably didn't show the gratitude I should have, considering the opportunity he'd afforded me as well. Sadly, especially in this day and age, gratitude seems to be a virtue that many of us neglect to display. Although I can't say that I ever enjoyed a measurable degree of financial advantage from working with apprentices, I did enjoy the teaching aspect. While finding reward in watching each individual learn and progress with the trade of carpentry, I also enjoyed the comradery and companionship of working with someone.

* * *

When an office renovation contract, which I'd picked up from a local business downtown, entailed a substantial amount of painting, I subcontracted a newly arrived Polish immigrant to do the work. His name was Eric. Eric was a well-known and very successful speed skater back in his homeland, with a legitimate dream of one day representing his country in the Olympics. That is, until he blew out his knee, ending that dream and altering his life path to make his way to Calgary. He was extremely driven in life and business, and that was what drew me to Eric. I saw something in him that persuaded me to want to help the guy out. I gradually taught Eric the ropes of contracting in the Great White North, and in return, I made money from the painting jobs I would subcontract to him. The situation was a win-win partnership for both of us. I even helped sponsor his parents when they migrated from Poland to Canada. The one thing about me that I believe irritated Eric at times was that I was extremely picky when it came to mistakes, especially with regards to painting. Never letting anything slide, I expected perfection. Eventually, my demand for perfectionism, from myself and others, rubbed off on him. Eric went on to become a very successful painting contractor in Calgary, joining an exclusive club of those with seven-figure incomes. All things being equal, he went on to be more successful than I. To this day, I consider Eric to be a lifelong friend, with whom I share a mutual respect.

* * *

In April of 1995, I made my motocross debut in the 125 Intermediate class. It would be the first season of racing in which I sustained an injury that actually kept me sidelined for a couple of weeks. Up until that time, the worst abuse my body ever received was a few minor bumps and bruises. This injury, however, was a cracked rib, and it hurt to breathe, never mind ride around on a motocross track. There's a saying in motocross that every racer knows all too well: When it comes to injuries, *it's not if…it's when*. The only question that remains is *how badly*? By the end of the season, I could definitely see an improvement in my motocross skills. My lap times were becoming consistent with the top five of those in the provincial pro class, and that would give me the confidence to feel as ready as ever to take a run at the Canadian National Pro Cross-Country series the following season.

The 1995 racing season saw Nicole and I loading up our RV nearly every weekend and heading to the races with Danielle and our rambunctious dog, Skye. During the week, I was putting in a lot of hours in my finish carpentry business while Nicole was being a stay-at-home mom. Traveling to different locations all over Alberta and parts of British Columbia became a family adventure. Alberta had a thriving motocross community during the 1990s, with events held in every quadrant of the province. And because I was racing motocross strictly to improve my riding skills for cross-country competition, acquiring championship points wasn't on my radar. I didn't have to worry about attending every race on the schedule. There were over thirty events to choose from all season, so we could pick those destinations that appealed to us most, skipping races here and there to take a well-earned weekend break. That's not to say I didn't race to win. As a very competitive person by nature, I always gave it one hundred percent when on a race track. I just had a different focus from the rest of the guys, who were out to make a name for themselves in motocross. I wanted to make a name for myself in cross-country; motocross was just a device for me towards that end.

Nicole would regularly race the women's class, and she progressed quite rapidly into becoming a consistent top-three provincial competitor herself. Often times, it seemed she took this racing stuff more seriously than even I did. I remember watching one of her motos, when she and another woman collided after the start, leaving them both on the ground. Inferring from their body language, as they were too far away for me to hear their discussion, I could tell they weren't happy with each other. The other girl must have said something somewhat unwise, thus motivating Nicole to up and wallop her in the head. Good thing they were both wearing helmets. I was holding Danielle in my arms—she was about two at the time—as I watched this scenario unfold, and I thought to myself, *That can't be good.* Apparently, the race adrenaline chemical that our body produces has the same effect on women as it does on men.

That particular season marked the first year I received notable sponsorship from Honda Canada and Calgary-based Blackfoot Motosports. The motorcycle dealership, which would evolve into one of the largest in Canada, sold me a bike for cost and even provided me with some free riding gear. Quite frankly, considering I was still in the motocross amateur ranks, it was more than I ever expected. In retrospect, it was an honor to have been associated with Blackfoot. Although the dealership was a minor player in the motocross scene at the time, Blackfoot would emerge as the winningest motocross team in Canadian pro motocross between 2000 and 2007, first as the operator of Honda Canada's official racing efforts and then as Yamaha Motor Canada's contract team.

My first race as a CMA 125 Intermediate was in Bruderheim, Alberta, where I finished fifth overall among a full gate of over thirty riders. In outdoor motocross, there are two separate races—known as motos—during the course of a day. The combined finishes of these motos count towards an overall position for the day. In a title hunt, regardless of the class or whether it's a provincial or national championship, points are awarded on the strength of each moto finish. The next race on my schedule was in Medicine Hat, Alberta, home of Canadian motocross/supercross legend Ross Pederson. I acquired my first overall win at this event, with two second-place finishes, no less. In motocross, it's not unusual to win the overall without scoring a moto win; it's the combined finishes of the two motos that determines your overall position.

I rode some hare-scramble off-road events as a pro in 1995 and had a blast. I even got my very first overall win at the last hare-scramble that fall. It's always different when you're not under the pressure of HAVING to perform in order to appease your sponsors…never mind your own ego. At the top level, when you're racing on a factory team or a top-notch, heavily sponsored private team, you're basically only as good as your last race. Sure, you can have a bad race here and there, but too many of those, and you'll be looking for new sponsors next year, unless you're fortunate enough to have a multi-year contract.

Towards the autumn of 1995, Nicole and I decided it was time to develop the basement in our Huntington Hills bungalow. After practicing for the past seven years on everyone else's homes doing renovations and finish carpentry, I had a fairly decent sense of what would look appealing from a design perspective. Sparing no expense, I went all out building and installing custom solid-wood cabinets, railings, and doors throughout. To complete the perfect man cave, I added a slate billiards table, big-screen TV, Luxman sound system with

Nuance towered speakers, and, of course, a workout center. It would be disingenuous of me if I didn't admit that it was certainly nice having money, especially having earned it honestly.

Throwing parties wasn't something Nicole and I were known for, but with our freshly renovated basement just finished, we decided to baptize our new pad with a New Year's bash that year. With Nicole's parents now living in Calgary, we knew who to call when we required babysitting service. New Year's Eve afternoon, Nicole and I dropped off Danielle at their place, with no intention of retrieving her until at least the following afternoon. We loved our daughter dearly, but sometimes it was nice to have a break and just let loose, something Nicole and I rarely did. Besides, my in-laws loved their granddaughter to the hilt and no doubt, when we weren't around, spoiled her rotten.

Just a few weeks before New Year's, Nicole and I drove down to Wetaskiwin to visit my parents. Since Dad was selling vehicles there and I needed a new truck, it seemed like a cool thing to do—go buy a truck from the man who raised me. I'll never forget the moment when he actually used a couple of his clever sales lines on me, the same ones I remembered him using on people when I was a kid and went to work with him on Saturdays. At one point, while negotiating the price, he said to me, "If I had your money, I'd burn mine." Then, a little while later, "You'd sure look good driving that F-150." I couldn't help but snicker...*Yeah, right Dad!* Surprisingly, even though I knew full well he was simply being a salesman, I'd be lying if I said his cliché lines didn't have an effect on me. It wasn't so much of what he was saying, but how he said it. No wonder Dad was successful at selling; he had the psychology of it figured out perfectly. Strange how easy it is to manipulate one's ego, even though we know it's a tawdry attempt at influential communication. Somehow—when delivered properly—it still works. Human psychology has always fascinated me.

During the course of my transaction of buying this truck from Dad, however, Nicole was chatting with my mom about the festivities we had planned for New Year's. Upon hearing this, they decided to crash our little party—I believe they were curious as to what a New Year's party hosted by their son consisted of. I'm not sure what their imagination was presupposing, but they were likely disappointed if they were expecting to find drunk people running around naked. Mom and Dad would have had to have crashed our 1999 party to have seen those kinds of shenanigans, but that's a story I'll save for later. Our '95 New Year's Eve celebration simply consisted of a few slightly intoxicated dirt bike racers sitting around watching Crusty Demons of Dirt videos while retelling exaggerated stories about racing. We were a fairly tame bunch of characters that evening.

* * *

Looking forward to campaigning the 1996 Canadian National Pro Cross-Country Championship, I began a new training schedule on January 1st. Every weekday morning, I'd get up earlier than usual, at 5:00 AM, in order to work out for an hour before heading out to do my real job. Getting up at that time of day was certainly difficult at first, but after noticing how amazing I felt afterward, I soon got used to the routine and even looked forward to the workout session. Then, in the evenings during the winter months, when riding wasn't an option, I'd run and climb stairs at a local park for cardio exercise. I took my training regimen quite seriously and devoted a lot of time, expense, and energy towards it. I believe that most people, without realizing how much effort it actually takes, look at successful athletes with envy and think that it's an easy life full of nothing but fun and excitement. My brush with athletic achievement was that of a meager off-road racer who enjoyed limited success. I can only imagine what

NHL players go through in a year, having to play eighty-two games a season plus practices.

While working out in my basement gym, I had a tendency of letting my mind wander, thinking about a varying degree of subjects. On one particular occasion, I remember the subject quite vividly: Is there really a God out there? After debating the subject back and forth in my mind while doing bench presses, suddenly the doorbell rang. The reason I remember this distinct memory so vividly is because of what happened next. I ran upstairs to answer the door...and there they were, two Jehovah's Witnesses. After a brief but courteous introduction, the gentleman ended with this question, "Do you believe there is a God?" Not wanting to get engaged in a lengthy conversation, however, I simply told them about how I'd been raised as a JW but wasn't interested. Before they left, I was handed a piece of literature that supposedly explained the existence of a Creator, which I crumpled up and tossed into the garbage basket as soon as they left. When I went back to my workout session, I felt a little freaked out by what had just happened and couldn't help but wonder, *Did God send them here to help me answer that question*? The skeptic in me concluded how kooky that actually sounded and chalked it up to another one of those strange coincidences in life. Besides, I was still more or less convinced that God was nothing more than a myth.

After racing the 1995 motocross season in the Intermediate division and winning several races, I officially turned pro for the 1996 season. I would now be riding with the top dogs of the sport, both in motocross as well as cross-country. Early in the new year, I secured my first ever factory-backed sponsorship deal with Yamaha Canada, through Pro-Am Motorsports. Factory rides in Canada are usually channeled through a motorcycle dealership. In this case, the dealership agreed to provide me with a brand-new YZ250 to contest the 1996 Canadian Pro Cross-Country Championship, along with a cash contingency package based on performance. Any modifications I made to the bike, however, was on my own dime. Although I raced to win, I had no aspirations to becoming rich from racing motorcycles. Winning races or finishing in the top ten meant you earned some prize money, and with the contingency bonus, it could add up to a pretty penny, but nothing life altering. For that simple reason, nobody I know of ever got into motocross or other off-road disciplines in Canada for monetary reasons. Besides, I considered finish carpentry my career, not racing dirt bikes. Being a pro rookie, however, I was doing all right with the bike sponsorship, which was topped off with a full riding gear and accessories package, not to mention a modest parts budget. I had received sponsorship deals in the past as an amateur, but no one had ever given me a free bike to ride. The Yamaha deal was sweet!

By early February of 1996, I wanted to get some saddle time in as part of my training for the cross-country series. Short of heading to California, which was not an option that year, and with the outdoor season not happening until springtime, arenacross was my only alternative. The problem was that I hadn't been able to set up my new YZ 250 or even had the chance to take it for a spin yet. So when Yamaha gave me permission to ride my Honda CR125 at the double-header 1996 Lethbridge Arenacross in mid-February, I was relieved. Technically, I was now under contract to Yamaha, and riding a competing brand was a no-no. But riding a brand-new bike out of the box at the pro level is just downright dangerous, especially indoors. It takes weeks of rigorous testing and tweaking to accomplish proper setup, and my CR125 was already dialed in perfectly. Hence, Yamaha approved this one 1996 season race on a bike that wasn't one of theirs.

Normally, I wasn't prone to being nervous about entering a race, but this was my first pro arenacross. I knew full well there was only room for ten guys in the main event, which meant I had to qualify. And because pro qualifying rounds are held in front of a crowd as part of the show, it creates an atmosphere that any first-timer would be somewhat apprehensive of. Sure enough, those pesky pre-race jitters got the best of me during Friday's qualifying rounds, and I found myself in the LCQ (Last Chance Qualifier). I managed to finish second, taking the last transfer spot to the final. Despite having last gate pick, I made it! Sitting on the starting line for the main event that evening had to be the most unnerving experience I can remember, and not because of the few thousand spectators in the stands. I was lined up on the far inside gate next to 1994 Canadian 125 and 250cc Motocross Champion Blair Morgan. The Prince Albert, Saskatchewan native was in the early stages of his meteoritic rise to stardom, which would see him claim six more national motocross titles as well as multiple World Snowcross Championships and five snowcross gold medals at the Winter X-Games. By the end of the fifteen-lap main event, I'd finished in eighth place and unfortunately gotten lapped on the last lap by none other than Mr. Motocross himself, Blair Morgan. The one thing I hated most about racing was getting lapped. There is just something about it that's demoralizing, even if it is at the hands of a national champion.

Saturday night's event had me qualify right out of the first-heat race. By lap five of the fifteen-lap main event—after just passing another rider—my pit-board girl for the evening, Nicole, held up the white board informing me I was in third place, with up-and-coming young motocross phenomenon Bart Stephenson just behind me. Underneath, in big black letters, she'd written "FOCUS!" Every lap that I passed by the pit area, Nicole would write something encouraging, like "Look ahead, not behind you" and "Ride smooth." On lap six, after passing him two laps earlier, Stephenson closed the gap and was showing me his front wheel in every tight corner. Because we were racing so closely to each other, I could often read Stephenson's board as well, which at one point read "Monte Who?" implying that I was a nobody. Of course, reading that on Stephenson's pit board just gave me extra incentive during our battle—not that it wasn't true, as I was a nobody in the sport of arenacross, but it definitely triggered my ego. Finally, after battling ferociously for the better part of ten laps with the Calgary native, he passed me on the next-to-last lap when I stalled my motorcycle in a corner...a rookie mistake! Then, while restarting my engine, another rider got by me as well, leaving me to coast across the finish line in fifth position. Truth is, by lap thirteen, I was exhausted, and my arms were aching to the point that I could barely hang on, never mind negotiate a clutch with my fingers. My legs felt as if they were made of jelly, and if I hadn't known better, I would have sworn someone had tied a grand piano to my butt for the last two laps. I don't even recall who won the race, but I was more than pleased with fifth for what was only my second pro arenacross race. There was no question about it, though: I needed to keep training and work on my endurance if I was going to have a say in the cross-country title chase.

* * *

When the 1996 Canadian National Cross-Country schedule was finally released early that spring, I was disappointed to see only four events making up the entire series. Four races at roughly three hours per race meant a national champion would be crowned after twelve hours of racing. In a sense, this would have been equivalent to a twelve-round motocross series. However, with only four separate races making up the national cross-country title hunt, it meant there was very little room for error.

My reputation as a cross-country racer was that of a solid rider who was consistent and didn't often crash. But I was never someone—I believe—who would be considered a threat to win EVERY race I entered. Because of my consistency, however, I could be considered a threat to win a championship as far as cross-country and hare scrambles were concerned. Arguably, out of the entire field of pros that year, there were probably five of us who had a legitimate shot at winning the title. From a competition standpoint, this was great. It more or less guaranteed that one guy wasn't going to run away with it and make for a boring season. Nevertheless, with only four races, consistency would be paramount. I concluded that finishing in the top three at each round should be my main focus. Multi-time AMA National Motocross and Supercross Champion Ricky Carmichael let it be known that "You win championships on your worst days." A statement that would prove to reflect my pursuit of the 1996 Canadian National Cross-Country crown.

After spending hours upon hours at the track, testing different settings on my Yamaha YZ250, my suspension sponsor Pro-Action and I finally had the bike dialed in perfectly. Being the type of racer who was meticulous about every little detail and could feel every nuance of his motorcycle, I left no stone unturned. My engine performance specialist, Dennis Kaltenbruner, beefed up my motor by installing a long rod kit to give it a few extra horsepower. When all was said and done, I was extremely pleased and convinced that I unquestionably had the best and fastest machine on the starting line of every race.

The first national was Porcupine Hills, where I started in third place right behind former Alberta Champion Julien Cerny; two-time National Champion Doug Beers trailed behind me. After a few minutes, I moved by Cerny into second place and focused my attention on catching the leader, who was none other than Paul "Spodey" Petrin, my former carpentry apprentice. The motorcycle felt and was handling phenomenally, the weather was perfect for racing, and I was feeling supraliminal in my element. Every once in a while, I would see dust lingering in the air, indicating that I was just seconds behind Petrin. I rode as hard and fast as I could in an effort to reel him in, yet I couldn't ever catch sight of him. By the two-hour mark, however, I was no longer seeing any sign of Paul and could feel my focus starting to dwindle. I often found it difficult to maintain a blistering pace when riding alone for an extended period of time. Even though the next few riders might only be thirty seconds behind me, because they were never visible, it felt as if I were all alone out there. I'm sure most racers share this sentiment. Then, not even two minutes from the finish line, I made a minuscule error and tipped over in a corner. Sure enough, Cerny, who'd been in third place, came up from behind and blasted right by me. Starting the bike, I quickly chased him down, but it was too late to even attempt a pass…the race was over!

Afterward, I found it quite fascinating how three racers, Petrin, Cerny, and I had been able to ride for nearly three hours, all the while just seconds apart, with Doug Beers a couple of minutes behind us. The on-track positioning contributes to the validity of how closely matched in terms of speed we were to each other. I walked away slightly frustrated because of the rookie mistake that had cost me second, yet I was content sitting third in the points after the first race.

The next national would be Moose Mountain, where I would take the lead early, with the wily veteran Doug Beers hot on my tail. For the entire contest, he and I raced up front, swapping positions every time one of us lost track of the racecourse flags. Each time I had the lead, a relentless Beers kept hounding me until I would lose the marked course or make a mistake. Then I would return the favor by ruthlessly shadowing his every move until he would mess up or lose track of the course. This went on for nearly the entirety of the race until roughly ten minutes from the finish, when the two of us mistakenly headed off course down a steep and narrow downhill. By the time we were back on the proper course—not knowing if anyone behind us had taken over the lead—I could see down a long narrow cutline that Beers had roughly a ten-second lead on me. Knowing we had to be near the finish line, I dug deep and rode my heart out in an effort to catch the former champ. With each passing minute, I could feel and see that I was just slightly gaining ground on him. As I proceeded down a long grassy hill into a meadow, there was Beers, not even five seconds ahead of me. But that didn't matter now. He had just crossed the finish line in first place, leaving me to claim a still respectable second place. But in racing, second place is the first loser. Still, the points I collected that day made up for not winning. With two rounds remaining, I was still on target and in the game to snatch the brass ring. It was all a matter of remaining consistent and not choking when the pressure was on.

After two races in the history books, I was sitting one point out of first place, with twenty-two points, while Beers and Petrin were tied for first with twenty-three points each. The next race, the notorious Green Meanie, was located roughly two hours southwest of Calgary. The Green Meanie had the reputation for being the most difficult race on the cross-country circuit. I could distinctly recall from previous races at this event riding down a rockslide over a field of boulders the size of large picnic coolers and microwave ovens and then along the side of a mountain on a trail a mountain goat would have had a hard time negotiating. If I was ever going to beat Beers and Petrin I knew it would likely be at this event. As technical races such as this were my specialty, it would HAVE to be at this event, not only to collect maximum points, but to score a moral victory over these two hotshots as well.

When the starting pistol went off, I quickly launched into the lead with a clean holeshot. Shane Cuthbertson—who hadn't been much of a threat thus far in the series—was trailing close behind me, and the two of us swiftly pulled away from the rest of the pack. Without ever challenging me for the lead, Cuthbertson hung back just far enough so he could capitalize on any mistake I made. At this point, not unlike me, the Airdrie, Alberta, native was still in the early stages of his pro-level career, but he would go on to win seven Alberta Regional Championships and become a national- and international-caliber contender. He ended up securing top titles such as the Canadian Hare Scrambles Championship and a gold and silver medal at the ISDE.

By the two-hour mark, I hadn't seen or heard hide nor hair of Doug Beers or Paul Petrin. And with Cuthbertson still in tow, from a championship perspective, this was shaping up to be the perfect scenario. Then, I made a slight bobble, and veered off course just enough for Cuthbertson to stick a pass on me. Fortunately for me, he made a slight oversight himself and became tangled up in some old fence wire, giving me the opportunity to repass him. Not realizing there wasn't enough room to get by him on the trail, though, I found myself toppling over on top of a hapless Cuthbertson and his motorcycle. Beers, meanwhile, appeared out of nowhere and came up from behind, passing Shane and me in one fell swoop. With Cuthbertson pinned under me and my bike, we couldn't help but start laughing. If there were a comedy of errors written into the Green Meanie scenario, this was definitely one of them. Knowing how close I was to Beers in the points chase, however, Cuthbertson said, "Get the hell off me and go catch him!"

After getting untangled from Cuthbertson, I went after Beers like a bat out of hell. But we were a lot closer to the end of the race than I had calculated. I never got the opportunity to make the pass and crossed the finish line, again in second place, just seconds behind Beers. As disappointed as I should have been with yet another error costing me a victory, surprisingly, I wasn't at all. I recalled how, just three years prior to this, I watched Doug Beers compete against the top Canadian cross-country riders at the nationals and how exceptionally fast they were. I remembered wondering if I would ever get to their level. Yet here I was, sitting solidly in second place for the championship after three rounds. I was pretty cool with that!

With one more round remaining, Beers sat atop the standings with thirty-eight points; I was trailing in second place, with thirty-four points. This meant that in order to win the championship, I needed to win the last round and have Beers finish third or worse. If I didn't win, he would have to finish three positions behind me, which was a highly unlikely scenario unless he experienced a mechanical breakdown. A DNF for Beers would be helpful, but I didn't want to win the championship that way. I wanted to beat him fair and square. Besides, you don't wish for your opponents to forfeit a race due to a bike problem. The hand of fate could see it happen to you instead. My old apprentice Spodey, meanwhile, was no longer a major concern in the title quest: He'd had bike issues at the Green Meanie and barely finished in the top ten. The final race was the Crowsnest National, staged in the Crowsnest Pass of the Alberta Rockies, in the southwest corner of the province. Although the odds were decidedly against me, I had won twice as an amateur at this visually stunning place. Therefore, given my track record at this event, I was liking my chances. I was keeping the faith, and I knew choking was not an option. It was time to shake a classic case of grace under pressure out of my sleeve.

Before the race started, Beers came up to me and shook my hand. He wished that we would both have good races. I was honored and somewhat impressed by his sportsmanship; I sort of wished that I had thought of making this overture. However, I did take note and learned from the experience: Winning isn't everything. Ready and focused on the task ahead, I lined up at the starting area. I have to admit I was a little nervous. There was, after all, a lot at stake with the entire season coming down to this one race. Everything I had worked toward rested on the outcome of the next three hours. Finally, the starting pistol sounded. Seconds later, I found myself in fourth place—my worst start all year—right behind Beers.

For what seemed like an eternity, I followed Beers closely, never losing sight of his rear wheel. We reached the first fuel stop together, and he pitted to gas up. Having a bigger tank, I didn't need to stop and conveniently took over third place at Beers's expense. Soon after, the course led us along a ridge that was muddled with loose rocks. I suddenly found it extremely difficult to keep my motorcycle on the trail, let alone maintain a good race speed. The front end of the bike was bouncing around, ricocheting off every rock. Several times, I looked down to see if maybe I had a flat tire, but that wasn't the case. I was unaware of this at the time, but one of my front fork tubes was bent. While dealing with my finicky suspension, Beers easily caught up to me and reclaimed third place. My determination to not let him pull away surpassed the capabilities of the damaged motorcycle I was piloting, and I soon found myself kissing the hard ground. With a vast majority of the Crowsnest National consisting of rocky trails, I soldiered on as briskly and safely as possible to the end, only to find out that I was just seconds behind the lead pack. But it was all for naught. I had been disqualified—unbeknownst to me until the end of the race. It turned out that the first gas stop, which I'd bypassed, was also a checkpoint. Be that as it may, I would have finished third, right behind Doug Beers. Shane Cuthbertson won the race, and Paul "Spodey" Petrin crashed out. In the end, I was left finishing the 1996 Canadian Cross-Country Nationals as runner up.

Considering the hard work and effort I put into that season, I was certainly disappointed with a disqualification at the last round. It didn't affect the final results, though…so all's well that ends well. Besides, in the spirit of truthfulness, excuses aside, I would have to concede that the championship was deservedly won by the best rider that year, Doug Beers. To sum up my entire 1996 season, consistently finishing top-three among the best off-road riders Canada had to offer was fine by me. Never in my wildest dreams could I have imagined ascending to such a level. It was my personal best, and I had nothing to be ashamed of or embarrassed about. As much as I wanted to win that championship, being a pro cross-country racer was not my career, it was my hobby. I took care of my family and myself as a finish carpenter…that was my career.

* * *

After the 1996 Cross-Country season wrapped up, a much-needed break from riding was on the agenda. This particular season, as exciting as it was, had worn me down mentally. First and foremost, I raced for fun, and for the first time in my brief racing career, I found myself not having any. When something like that stops being fun, it means it's time to move on. I wasn't bitter or feeling sorry for myself by any means. Fact is, I loved racing and have a multitude of awesome memories of riding in the mountains with some phenomenally talented riders, and not because I believed I was at the same level as my competitors. In my opinion, achieving the success I did was simply because of my ambition, which, by the way, far exceeded my talent. But I never thought of it like that at the time…being a top-three competitor, that is. Sure, I wanted to win every time I went to a race, but not to prove anything to anyone else. It was more about the personal challenge from within.

Looking back, I suppose finishing top-three in all of Canada is kind of a big deal, at least to those of us who pursue the sport of off-road motorcycle racing. In the grand scheme of things, dirt bike racing doesn't even register on the Canadian national sports radar, regardless of the discipline. Hockey, baseball, and football rule. That's no surprise, considering the number of people participating in those sports and the fan-bases they attract. Unless you live in a place that hosts a motocross national or arenacross event, you won't find anything about the sport in the print media or the sports news on television. In a medium where copy is at a premium, it just isn't newsworthy or financially feasible; hence, it doesn't get any attention. Today, however, there are a number of websites dedicated to Canadian motocross, including http://www.cmrcracing.com; http://www.mxpmag.com; http://www.mxnationals.ca; and http://www.directmotocross.com.

Accordingly, with the genuine sentiment of giving credit where it's due and to name a few notably gifted riders that I had the pleasure of competing against and learning from throughout my cross-country career, I'd like to give a "big shout out" and "thank you" to Doug Beers, Paul Petrin, Burt Peterson, Pete Issler, Pete DeGraaf, Julien Cerny, Guy Parrett, Adam Galbraith, Shane Cuthbertson, Wayne Vantighem, Dylan Cartwright, Carl Kuster, Craig Stappler, Ken Voutier, Dennis Bennett, and Brian Pierson. These remarkable men—some of them still active today—made cross-country racing a great sport in Canada at the time I was active in it. Even though to the majority of the population, dirt bike racing is something noisy, smelly, and dusty or muddy...and dangerous, I was thrilled to be a part of it.

CHAPTER

30

The Perfect Life

With the 1996 racing season over and done, Nicole and I started talking about the next move in life. The first thing we agreed was that it was time to have another child. Since our first was a girl, in my mind, as if I actually had a say in the matter, I determined this one was going to be a boy. Both of us having practiced extensively—throughout our marriage—at our baby making skills, it wasn't long before Nicole became pregnant. By late January, we already had a projected due date of mid-August 1997. That was easy!

The next prospect that Nicole and I were parallel in our thinking with was living on an acreage. My construction business kept gaining momentum as each year went by, and we were definitely in a financial position to finally make this dream a reality. Our arduous task of searching for the ideal location was set in motion. After viewing a number of properties around Calgary, we couldn't find anything that was even close to what we were looking for. Being a contractor/finish carpenter as well as a perfectionist made it difficult to find anything that lived up to or came close to our standards…well, at least my standards. We concluded that buying suitable land and building our own house was the only solution. In March of 1997, we purchased a quaint piece of land just ten minutes south of Calgary consisting of roughly seven acres, complete with a panoramic backdrop of the beautiful Rocky Mountains.

After viewing a number of show homes and sifting through a multitude of designs, I chose to create my own blueprints and custom build the house to incorporate our own conceptualization. In a joint effort with New Way Homes, one of the builders I did finish carpentry for, we broke ground and commenced construction later that spring. One of the most enjoyable components of building our dream house involved the process of choosing exactly where on the property our house would sit and what precise direction it faced. When all was said and done, we had a gorgeous 2,100-square-foot, three-bedroom, two-story home consisting of custom-built knotty pine kitchen cabinets, curved solid-wood staircase, large master bedroom with a walk-in closet, ensuite with Jacuzzi tub and separate shower stall, as well as his and her sinks, wraparound veranda, and, of course, a heated triple-car garage. To absorb the picturesque landscape just west of us, the architectural design within the great room/living room area incorporated fourteen-foot-high picture windows that captured the scenic backdrop of the striking Alberta Rockies.

http://montejperepelkin.com/photos-15

As for the remaining six or so acres towards the rear of our property, well, that would, of course, be used for the next phase of my riding career. After losing interest in racing off-road, my focus shifted to motocross. For that reason, with the skills acquired from running a Caterpillar while working for K-Line as a teenager, I rented the necessary equipment and built my own personal motocross track on those six acres of land. And as you may have already guessed, one third of our triple-car garage became my motocross fortress of solitude. A leftover from our family room in the previous house, a Martha Stewart-type floral design sofa—not exactly what I had envisioned—ended up as the seating area in my motocross lounge. While getting changed to go riding in the backyard, sometimes I would pinch myself to make sure I wasn't dreaming. Then, as I looked over at the latest copy of *Racer X Magazine* lying on that flower-embroidered sofa, I would realize that this was not a dream, but a dream come true!

On August 8, 1997, Nicole went into labor with our second child. When we had Danielle, we knew she was a girl, but for our second, Nicole and I decided to leave the sex of our child a mystery. While pregnant with Danielle, Nicole's belly hung low. But with this child, the baby rested much higher; they were two completely different pregnancies, convincing both of us it was a boy. And with Nicole having to endure just six hours of labor, this delivery was a breeze compared to Danielle's, which had lasted thirty-six hours. When the doctor finally delivered the baby, though, I looked down, and something wasn't right. *Wait a minute!* I thought to myself. *That's not a boy! That's a GIRL!* This is not to say that I was disappointed, of course; surprised would be more accurate. Being my second go-round with having children, this time, I rolled up my sleeves and got right in there to cut the cord as tears streamed down my face. No one would have ever guessed, but yeah, I'm a softy. We named our second daughter Haylee Macglory

Perepelkin. And those same cherished feelings of unconditional love I'd experienced when Danielle had been born came flooding over me once again. Becoming a parent is one of my most treasured passions in life and never seems to lose its luster.

Nicole and I seemed to have an uncanny habit of picking the most inopportune times in planning the birth of our children. Danielle was born two days before we moved into our Huntington Hills home; Haylee was born just two weeks before moving into our acreage home. With all that was going on in our lives, building a house and the birth of Haylee, racing took a backseat that year, but not completely. Yamaha— through Pro-Am Motorcycles—sponsored me for a second season. I finished consistently in the top ten, with a few top-five finishes for good measure, in regional Alberta pro motocross. In cross-country competition, the one thing I disliked was that often times, you were riding by yourself during the race. In motocross, however, whether riding with the frontrunners, in mid-pack, or at the back of the back, you were almost always battling for position in a field that usually had no less than twenty riders and up to a full gate of forty. This made it far more exciting—not to mention that having some spectators lined up around the track to watch added to the allure. Motocross has the longest history of all the off-road motorcycle racing disciplines, dating back to the mid-twenties in England. It was originally known as "scrambles" and drifted over to Europe by the early thirties, where it became known as motocross. Although in Canada it is a marginal sport, in many European countries—especially Belgium, the Netherlands, France, Germany, Italy, and, of course, the UK—it is a top spectator sport with a very deep talent pool to feed the various divisions and sanctioning bodies. Now that I had my own personal practice track in my backyard, it meant I was home more often as well. Life couldn't get any better!

Barely a couple of months after moving into our new acreage home, once again, those pesky JWs came knocking on my door. *These people are everywhere*, I thought to myself and wondered, *How on earth do they keep finding me?* Not a single year ever passed by, since moving to Calgary, that they hadn't knocked on my door. No matter where I lived, they always seemed to find me. I couldn't help but wonder if they had some kind of tracking device planted on me. Sometimes I would hide and not answer the door; other times, I'd simply say I wasn't interested.

Shortly after moving into our beautiful new acreage home, we discovered our family dog, Skye, had cancer. She was barely eight years old when I noticed a large bulge on her neck. Normally, when Nicole and I retired for the evening, Skye would sleep at the foot of our bed. Strangely, knowing she was sick, Skye would no longer come into the house at night. Instead, she would sleep in the grass behind our home. I could see her eyes glowing from a distance as she lay in the grass, watching the house. Finally, one evening when the cancer was worsening to the point that Skye could barely walk, I carried her into the house and placed her at the foot of our bed. Sadly, our beloved pet and family member chose to stumble towards our walk-in closet and sleep there instead. The poor dog was in so much pain it was becoming difficult, not to mention heartbreaking, to see her suffer.

The next day, I knew what we had to do. As long as I live, I'll never forget that afternoon when Nicole and I took her to the vet to have her put to sleep. I've endured some fairly heart-wrenching moments throughout my life—most of which were self-inflicted—but this one with Skye had to be one of the worst. The memory of holding her tightly in my arms as the vet injected the needle into her vein, left a deep and lasting imprint on me. Just as the needle entered, Skye let out a short yelp and looked at me with those big brown eyes of hers, as if to say, *What are you doing to me, Daddy?* After feeling the life leave her body, I ran out from the vet's office to my truck as tears uncontrollably bled from my eyes. Grasping for comfort, Nicole and I sat there for several minutes, holding each other.

It is strange how attached we can become to an animal. Often coming to work with me, Skye was like a best friend. Because the sound of my air nailers hurt her ears, she would hang out in the back of my cube van. I would leave the rear door open, and Skye would sleep in the back while I worked. With the door to the house also open, every once in a while, when she couldn't hear any disturbances coming from the house, she'd come to check and make sure I was still there. On one particular afternoon, however, Skye chose to go looking for mischief. Being a typical garbage dog, even though she knew darn well it was wrong, she just couldn't help herself—which reminded me of myself in some ways. I was working in a new home on the outskirts of Calgary. Meanwhile, in usual fashion, Skye hung out in the back of my cube van. Or so I thought. After running out of nails, I headed out to my truck to get a fresh box. And there was my naughty K-9 lying on the floor in the back of the truck, chewing on a huge hambone. Knowing she was in trouble, she stopped chewing, and without moving her head, she looked up at me from the corner of her eye with a look that said, *Uh Oh*! Wondering where on God's green earth she'd stolen this bone from, I hung my head around and out the back of my cube van. That was when my heart sank in disbelief. It turned out this was garbage day, and every house in the cul-de-sac had their trash bags sitting on the curb in front of each house. Only thing was, every bag was now ripped open, and trash was strewn all over the street. I spent the next hour picking up garbage and putting it into new bags.

http://montejperepelkin.com/photos-16

As frustrating as Skye was at times, I wept every day for more than a week, after her passing. The pain of losing her was something I never wanted to experience again. As a result, I never allowed myself to get attached to another pet. When living on an acreage, however, owning a dog is almost mandatory—if for nothing else, for protection and safety. Knowing them to be obedient, mild-tempered, and unlike Skye, less hyperactive, I was always fond of the German Shepard breed. As much as I loved Skye, her level of energy was a little more than I could handle. Nicole and I located a beautiful six-week-old German Shepard pup, and she was adorable. Nicole named her Neesoo, an aboriginal term meaning number two. Considering the circumstances, that was the perfect name.

During the time we were building our house, I sold our holiday trailer and purchased a brand-new thirty-one-foot class C motorhome complete with a separate ten-foot area in the back that even had a roll-up overhead door on the rear. With bikes loaded up in the back, this RV—state of the art at the time—was perfect for going to the races. At twenty-eight years of age, having two beautiful daughters, a gorgeous wife, and a luxurious house on an acreage, with my very own private motocross track in the backyard, I felt like I had it all. The perfect life! With my business consistently earning upwards of 250k each year, I was living the dream life. And after having children, it was evident that Nicole and I had become closer to each other and our relationship had improved significantly. I noticed her dedication to being the best mom she could be, and that impressed upon me a new respect for her. That she cared so much about our children really made me love my wife even more, with the added side-effect of influencing me to want to be a better husband and father. Being home every evening after work, I always made a point of spending daddy/ daughter time with them, whether it was horsing around on the living room floor, doing something outside with them, or telling one of my made-up, good-lesson, comical stories before they went to bed. Then, after the girls went to sleep, Nicole and I would spend quality time together before we went to bed. Of course, it wasn't like that every single evening, but more often than not, that was our routine.

As I sit at my desk writing this, their graduation pictures hang on the wall to the right of me, and I can't help but wonder where those years went. It seems just a short time ago I was coming home from work to find Haylee waiting by the front door for me to chase her into the living room, where I would gently tackle her to the floor and blow zerberts onto her little belly. Time certainly seems to have a way of getting away from us.

* * *

Early January of 1998, Bart Stephenson, JC Seitz, and I drove my motorhome down to California to do some riding and testing before the upcoming arenacross season. California, long considered center stage to the world's motocross scene, was a notorious hotspot for Canadian pros looking to get some practice time in during the winter months. There was a variety of challenging tracks scattered throughout southern California, and every weekend, there was a race somewhere. I wanted to make the two-week trip with my wife and daughters, but Nicole had no interest in such an adventure. With Haylee having been born barely five months prior, I couldn't exactly blame her. She wasn't exactly thrilled about my leaving for two weeks, but that never stopped me before and wasn't about to in this instance either. A man's gotta do what a man's gotta do. I worked hard for my family, and I didn't think it was selfish or unreasonable to once in a while just take care of my own needs or wants.

While in California, Bart and I were adamant in finding a riding area known as Cottonwood. Why? Because of an infamous, large step-up jump that had been highlighted in the recent Steel Roots Freestyle video featuring supercross legend Jeremy McGrath. The video grandstands various riders, including McGrath, jumping an astronomical step-up jump roughly thirty vertical feet from take-off to landing, the landing being at the top of a cliff. In order to accomplish this outrageous leap, we knew it was necessary to hit the jump at the bottom as fast as the bike would go. There was no way I was attempting it first. Stephenson, my arenacross nemesis from a few years earlier, volunteered to tackle this jump, which looked even scarier in real life. Bartman, as he was fondly known, cleared the monstrous jump perfectly. After witnessing firsthand someone else accomplish the feat, I felt confident enough to jump the obstacle. Besides, I wasn't going to chump out and be upstaged by Bart. Approaching the take-off as fast as my motorcycle would carry me, and then feeling the bike float to the top with a solid wall in front of me, sent a fear-inspiring rush through my body like I had never felt before. But I did it! It was by far the biggest jump I, and Bart, ever conquered on a motorcycle. JC was filming while adding his own commentary as we, for good measure, jumped this crazy step-up three or four more times each. JC admittedly conceded on video that he was too much of a chicken to attempt the jump.

Over the years, especially during my school days, I had heard a variety of colorful monikers as an attempt at making light of my lengthy, often difficult-to-pronounce last name. Some of these include what sounded like Pair of Pelicans, Purple licken, and Purple Pelican. Interestingly, while adding his own commentary in filming Stephenson and me that day, JC, in an attempt to inject his own sarcastic flavor to the occasion, began making light of my last name in a way I had never heard before. Strangely enough, throughout the forty-five-minute video of us jumping that afternoon, JC kept referring to me as Monte Paraplegic. Readily accustomed by now to the play on words people would often use in reference to my last name, I wasn't offended by any means, and I thought it was quite clever, actually. The irony in that little narration wouldn't hit home, of course, until some twelve months later.

http://montejperepelkin.com/videos/

Near the end of our trip to Southern California that year, the three of us went to a local riding hotspot located in the famous California hills. The area consisted of mostly dry brush, clay, and sand, with huge rain ruts carved into the landscape from notorious torrential rains during the winter months. Wanting to scope out the place, I unloaded my bike and put on a helmet, and before changing into riding gear, I decided to take a little cruise. Not two minutes later, while put-putting around in first gear, my front wheel fell into a rain rut, thus bringing the motorcycle to a dead stop and sending me to the ground. As my speed was no more than five miles per hour, you would assume a worst-case scenario might result in a minor scratch or two. After all, I had experienced get-offs at fifty mph that had resulted in less. When I hit the ground, however, a perfectly shaped boulder was there to break my fall and knock the wind out of me. After a few seconds of gasping for air, I was finally able to breathe, but the pain wasn't going away. Upon returning to the motorhome, I told the guys what had happened and went inside to lie down for a while—hoping the pain would eventually go away.

Fortunately, about twenty minutes later, JC and Bart came back from riding to check on me. By then, I was already sleeping. After they were finally able to wake me up, I remember not being able to see very well. My vision had gone all black from lack of blood pressure, and the pain was even worse. The boys quickly loaded up the bikes and drove me to the nearest hospital. After explaining what had happened to an emergency doctor, I was immediately scanned in the area the pain was emanating from and then rushed to surgery. Turned out my spleen was severly ruptured. While lying on the operating table, waiting for the doctor, I became extremely sleepy, but the nurse kept saying, "Don't go to sleep, Monte. You have to stay awake for us." It felt so good to close my eyes, though, so peaceful, like the best sleep of my life was waiting for me. The next thing I remember was waking up to a bright, piercing ray of sunshine pouring through my hospital room window, stinging my eyes. I lifted the blanket to find a row of stainless steel staples that began two inches below my navel and went straight up to my sternum.

A short time later, the doctor came into my room, and the first thing he said to me was: "You are one lucky guy." Not knowing what to say, I answered, "Yeah, why is that?" Apparently, my heart had stopped in surgery, and they'd been skeptical at best that I could be revived. The doctor went on to reiterate how it was a good thing my friends had brought me in when they did. If it had been even two minutes later, he assured me, I wouldn't have lived. Calling it no small miracle that I was alive, he patted me on the shoulder and told me to take it easy from now on. Not sure of how to take the doctor's words, I knew one thing for sure: There was no way I was telling anyone. If Nicole ever got wind of this, she'd never let me ride again. First question I asked the doctor was: "When can I go home?" He, of course, wanted to keep me for a couple of days.

Bart and JC came to see me shortly after the doctor left, wisely bringing me a change of clothes—they must have read my mind. Knowing full well that hospital stays in the U.S. cost an arm and a leg—I hadn't bought travel insurance—I was busting out of there. *If I can walk, then I can leave*, was my reasoning. Besides, except for feeling a little dizzy when I stood up, I was fine. I crawled out of bed, put my clothes on, and walked out of the hospital. It was the last scheduled day of our trip, so we climbed into the RV, and the boys drove straight through to Canada while I slept in the back. Arriving home sweet home late Sunday afternoon the next day, I was already feeling much better. Nicole, having talked to the doctor by phone, had some knowledge as to what had happened. But I downplayed the whole event as a simple splenectomy. "They removed my spleen. It was no big deal. Every doctor wants you to believe they saved your life," I explained in a tone that suggested that was the end of the conversation about my misadventure. Besides, other than the eight-inch row of staples holding me together and the fact that I was feeling a tad nauseous, I was fine. Ecstatic to see my daughters, I put on a pair of pajamas and cuddled with them on the couch. After nearly two long weeks, however, I especially missed Nicole. When we finally went to bed that evening, I desperately needed to make love to her, but after a valiant effort on my part, I just couldn't—it hurt too much.

In the morning, I woke up, showered, and got ready for work. The one downside to owning your own business—there's no one to fill in for you. Fortunately, it was a light day, and I got through it just fine. Within a few days, I was back to full capacity…more or less. However, because of the staples holding my stomach together, I had to miss competing at the '98 Lethbridge Arenacross, which was held a week later. Nicole and I still went, and she competed in the women's class. I was her mechanic and pit board guy for the weekend. Over the course of the racing weekend, I think she enjoyed all the attention on her for once. It was the perfect distraction from what had happened to me in California.

To this day, I don't know if the doctor was exaggerating about my close call. But it did kind of lead me to re-evaluate my life. I mean, twenty-eight-years old is not exactly an age at which a man who's got everything should be kicking the bucket. I was definitely glad to be alive. Not riding or racing dirt bikes anymore, however, didn't really enter my mind. Fatal crashes or life-altering injuries were the kind of stuff that happened to other people.

* * *

The 1998 season saw me dive head first into outdoor motocross. Needing a change in scenery—still with Yamaha—I switched to getting my bikes from Airdrie Motorsports, a bike shop that did suspension work, motor modification, and could supply all my riding gear from under one roof. With Canada finally enjoying the success of a nationally televised motocross series, I had a silent goal of sharpening up on my motocross abilities to contest the 1999 250 Nationals. After a long slide of the sport under CMA sanctioning during the 1980s, and a protracted sanctioning war with a new kid on the block during the early/mid 1990s, Continental Motosport Club (CMC), later to become Canadian Motosport Racing Corporation (CMRC), motocross in Canada was on the rise. Looking ahead, I planned to retire from professional racing at the end of the 1999 season, hoping to at least score a top-ten national ranking as the icing on the cake of what had been an exciting and fun pro hobby career. By the end of 1998, I was consistently finishing in the top five among Alberta's best riders and the top fifteen at the nationals I campaigned. Therefore, my top-ten national ranking objective for the following season seemed like an achievable goal.

During the winter of 1998 I decided to build an ice rink on our acreage. After constructing a wooden curb to hold in the water, I hired a local water truck to flood the rink. At roughly three-quarters the size of an NHL rink, it turned out quite well. I even built a homemade miniature Zamboni that I could pull behind our lawn tractor, put up lights for night skating, and bought a couple of hockey nets. To celebrate my somewhat successful attempt at building a rink, Nicole and I decided to throw a New Year's bash. Looking to keep the festivities tame, we only invited about ten people. Nevertheless, before the evening was over, a naked guy could be seen doing laps around the skating rink on my snowmobile…and it wasn't me.

January of 1999 rolled around, and this time of year being notoriously slow in the construction industry, I headed for sunny California again. This time, I went with Kevin, another friend of mine who was into dirt bike riding. My intention was to further sharpen my motocross skills. While there, we had the pleasure of staying with world-famous motocross legend, Gary Jones. Jones holds the distinction of winning the first three AMA 250cc Motocross National Championships back to back to back from 1972–1974. Each year, he pulled it off on a different brand of motorcycle, a feat that has never been repeated. Contributing to his legend, in 1972, Jones was a member of the first team to represent the United States at the prestigious Motocross des Nations. While staying with Gary at his home in California, he took me under his wing and gave me a few pointers on how to garner more speed on the racetrack. We covered everything from tricks on the starting line to motorcycle maintenance secrets. By the end of the week-long tutorial, I felt as if I had reached the next level in my riding ability. Now I was even more looking forward to the upcoming 250cc Canadian Motocross Nationals.

Returning to Canada, first up on the racing calendar in late January through early February were three arenacross races: Red Deer, Saskatoon, and then Lethbridge. Unfortunately, I blew a clutch in Red Deer, ending my weekend of racing there. My good friend Chris Bonneau agreed to come with me and be my mechanic for the following weekend in Saskatoon—Nicole stayed home with our daughters. During this trip, Chris and I opened up to one another about our personal lives for the first time in our friendship. He and I had hung out in the past and even gone to races together, but this was the first time we really talked about anything meaningful. He told me about his true feelings and plans to ask his girlfriend, Anne, to marry him. And I related some of my personal joys of having children. During our six-hour journey to and from Saskatoon, the subject of God even came up. I'm not sure what prompted us to engage in such a heart-to-heart exchange, but in light of upcoming events, I'm glad we did.

It was a double-header event, and something quite comical happened in Saskatoon during the second night of action. Wanting to try out a new trick I was practicing, and because it paid quite well, I entered the jump contest. Upon introducing me before my jump, I rode out, trying to be a showman, and proceeded to perform a little stunt known as a "stoppee." This is when a rider zips along on a flat surface, grabs the front brake, leans forward, and, before coming to a complete stop, balances the motorcycle on its front wheel—sort of like a reverse wheelie. However, due to a slight miscalculation, I ended up going over the bars and landing gracelessly in the dirt. Of course, with a stadium full of fans watching, everyone began applauding. Meanwhile, with my face red as a fire truck, I quickly remounted and carried on as if it was all part of the show. It was an embarrassing moment for sure. In the actual races, I turned in third and fifth place finishes respectively on the two nights.

The following weekend, I was headed to the Lethbridge Arenacross. As this race fell on Valentine's Day weekend, the plan was to have Nicole's mom stay at our house to babysit Haylee and Danielle. This would give us some well-deserved and needed alone time. With a somewhat slow week ahead of me work wise, I took advantage of the opportunity to spend a little extra time at home. Danielle and I went to our very first movie together at the cinema. We saw *Jack Frost*, and we both got teary during the climactic ending. Coincidently, the movie was about a father, played by Michael Keaton, who puts a music career ahead of his family. Then he gets killed in an automobile accident while returning home—where he should have been in the first place. The following winter, however, Jack returns in the form of a snowman to comfort his grieving son. Ironically, one of the lines from this movie had a profoundly accurate lesson attached to it: *Snow Dad is better than no Dad*. Even though he was a snowman and couldn't do what other dads could do, he could still be a great father to his son.

Later that evening, Danielle and I went skating on our ice rink. Putting her up on my shoulders, I skated around while she giggled at my mimicking funny voices. After that, we went back into the house, and I played with Danielle and Haylee for an hour before they went to bed. Upon tucking them in, I told the girls one of my homemade stories about a mischievous bunny rabbit who befriended a well-behaved porcupine. Adding my usual funny faces and comical voices to the narrative, they both listened attentively, hanging on my every word. The moral of my little bedtime stories usually revolved around how important it was that young ones listen to their parents and keep their room tidy.

The next day, being a Thursday, Nicole and I were planning to leave for Lethbridge later that afternoon for the 213-kilometer drive. All I had to do was finish a small job in the morning and then make a quick stop at the bank to make a deposit, which was the fee I was to collect after completing a three-month-long carpentry job. After that, I was free for the entire weekend, allowing me to focus on my racing at the Canada Games Sportsplex. As circumstance would have it, all of my current construction projects were completely wrapped up. Nothing was left unfinished—a first for me since becoming a contractor.

Upon driving home that afternoon on February 11, 1999, once again, I thought about the privilege I enjoyed of living such a perfect life. I really couldn't imagine it being any better than it was. I didn't take it for granted. I was thankful for being such a fortunate man. Then, as the western sky was illuminated by a blazingly colorful sunset, I loaded up the bikes and kissed my daughters goodbye. Nicole and I climbed into our vehicle and headed south to Lethbridge for a date with destiny, for a weekend of racing, eating out, and alone time. It was a weekend we were both looking forward to.

Cue music: "Lovers in a Dangerous Time" by Barenaked Ladies

https://www.youtube.com/watch?v=k_oOc3Zj0KU

CHAPTER

31

Inspiring Words

My goal upon moving to Calgary had been to make an honest and decent middle-class living, buy a house, and raise a family. Then, within a few years or so, depending on how things transpired, I hoped to build a nice home for Nicole and myself on an acreage near the outskirts of Calgary. The old adage, *You can take the boy out of the country, but you can't take the country out of the boy*, certainly applied to me. I didn't mind big-city life and understood that to get ahead sometimes, that was where you need to be. But I missed the rural life. So, when the opportunity presented itself to move far enough from the city, to some wide-open spaces, while remaining close enough to carry on my business without a long commute, I really couldn't have asked for anything more. I felt truly blessed. With Nicole and I being the proud parents of two beautiful daughters, our marriage problems rectified, and both of us equally enthusiastic about racing dirt bikes, we were about as happy as we could be. Then the bottom dropped out. Was I being punished for my youthful misdeeds? A victim of circumstance? Or simply a recipient of cause and effect, which, in this case, was the miscalculation of a tricky racing obstacle? After all, I wasn't the first to succumb to such a disaster and certainly not the last. Or was it the fulfilment of a prophecy I'd been told as a thirteen-year-old boy working away in his parents' backyard? Heady questions indeed. Questions that some days I feel I have the answers to, while other questions remain a mystery. If I hadn't raced dirt bikes, would I still be walking? Or would I have become paralyzed in some other fashion? I do believe that I was meant to become a quadriplegic. There were lessons to be learned, lessons I could only learn by being confined to a wheelchair. The how and whys are irrelevant. The only things that are relevant are the facts. Now that I was paralyzed, I wasn't sure about what goals to set for myself. Part of me wondered if I would ever have fun again. But then those old expectations would set in, expectations to be the best I can be and push the envelope to, if at all possible, surpass them. So, one of the things that kept me going and had me trying to remain as optimistic as possible was to be the best quadriplegic I could be. My stint writing for *MXP* had been a great help to bridge my past life to my future. Keeping busy at something that would challenge me mentally was the best therapy there was.

With a couple of weeks in the rear-view mirror since my bid to exit this world by downing a bottle of sleeping pills, my soon-to-be ex-wife reluctantly decided the right thing to do, for the sake of everyone's sanity, was to find a place for her and the girls to live and let me stay in the house. Considering the circumstances and pressure we were under, by this point, the worst in each of us was bubbling to the surface. To put it mildly, she and I were displaying our least-favorable behavior toward one another—just short of wanting to push each other in front of a bus. I was upset and angry at her for not wanting to try and make our marriage work in some shape or fashion. And she was upset and angry with me for getting injured and disrupting our lives in the first place—never mind for also trying to off myself. I couldn't really blame her. Adding more fuel to the sea of flames we had to navigate through every day, Nicole's family felt her decision to move out was outright ridiculous. They believed I should have done the honorable thing and moved out, paralyzed or not. As a result, Nicole's father looked me square in the eyes one day and fiercely called me Satan! For not moving out, of course. Truth is, not exactly thrilled with the situation myself, I felt like he might be right. After all, aren't we supposed to sacrifice ourselves for the betterment of our family?

Every time I did enquire about moving into a facility, however, I kept hearing the same response: There's a waiting list. And after explaining my situation, I was steadfastly advised not to move out of my home. Because I had care already in place, I should try to live on my own for as long as I could. Apparently, the self-managed government care program I was enrolled with was indefinitely put on hold around this time. Only existing clients such as myself were being maintained. In other words, once I dropped out of the program to live in a long-term care facility, there was little chance of ever getting back on home care. And I was certainly not in any position to cover costs on my own. The situation seemed hopeless. For all these reasons, and many more, is why I'd resorted to suicide in the first place. Confirming my assumption that Nicole was different from most of her family, however, and that the deep love we had shared had not totally eroded, the following spring, I received an unexpected visit from her. She confirmed as much when she thoughtfully explained, after considering the situation with a clear mind, how me staying in the renovated home was the right thing to do. Afterward, we discussed settling up financially in a manner that would allow her to buy a modest home for her and the girls to live in.

That afternoon, the two of us finally reached a mutual understanding of everything we had gone through. To love your spouse as much as we loved each other and then to have your world turned literally upside down is an experience that is difficult to articulate for the benefit of others. It is something only the actual experience itself can provide answers to what it's like. And it's something you don't wish upon others. The dynamics of love and the intricacies of human behavior make it impossible to satisfactorily examine the situation even for oneself without asking, *Why did this happen?* From an outsider's point of view, it can be easy to judge Nicole negatively and feel ill will toward her for wanting to dissolve our marriage. I would be lying if these thoughts didn't cross my own mind. Or to say the blame lies with me, because I chose to pursue a dangerous sport and paid the price. That was said and certainly thought. But to dwell on those things is pointless and counterproductive. Fortunately, this is something I grasped sooner rather than later, sparing myself and those around me a lot of grief. The fact that Nicole gave our marriage a second chance—risking everything she had financially and against fierce opposition from her family—is testament alone to her character as a person. The fact that she was honest with me and herself about not being able to continue with our relationship—early enough for both of us to move on—credits her with immense strength and courage.

The circumstances we were up against were simply more than our relationship could bear. And we weren't alone. The divorce rate after spinal cord injury is considerably higher than the national average. The dream I had while in prison about only being able to get the ring halfway on Nicole's finger at our wedding ceremony sometimes haunts me. If there is such a thing as a prophetic dream, this could be considered one. We had always planned on having four children—we ended up having two. We made it halfway. Nicole voiced her opinion that if I hadn't been injured, our marriage probably would have endured to the end. I believe that as well. A freak accident, one that was prophesied, no less, changed the course of our lives in a way that no one could ever understand. Whenever I think back on these things, it stirs my soul and leaves me feeling somewhat melancholy. But I'm a survivor, and I tuck away those thoughts almost as quickly as they arise. I'm too busy living my life, curiously looking forward to what awaits me next, to sit around playing the *what if* game. That gets a bit too tedious for me. What's important is that we endured through what could only be described as a marital nightmare and made it out the other side, meanwhile raising two beautiful daughters in the process. As I write this, Danielle and Haylee are in post-secondary education and doing quite well. I consider that a huge accomplishment, for which I am thankful to God, proud, and equally content with.

Before Nicole left that afternoon, she noticed my lawn needed cutting, so she mowed the grass and did a few chores for me. Then, while saying goodbye, with heartfelt sincerity, she stated, "You know, if you're ever stuck or in a bind with finding care, you can always count on me." Feeling both touched and thrilled by her gesture, in the end, I was content with the fact that we were able to part ways amicably, especially taking into account we still had two daughters to raise together. Later that summer, following a brief and cordial litigation process, we agreed on a cash settlement. . And I would pay her $300 per month for child support. It wasn't much, but it was all that I could afford. I remortgaged the house to pay her out, and sometime thereafter, she purchased a home about a ten-minute drive from me. Knowing what a struggle it was at first for my ex-wife to live life as a single mom raising two daughters, I have the deepest respect for her. Even against extraordinary odds, Nicole was always an exceptional mother. The decision to choose her to be my wife and mother of our children is one that I have no regrets over.

Not long after our divorce, Nicole remarried and had another child with a man who is, much to my relief and joy, a great stepdad to my daughters. With myself not being able to contribute as much financially as I would have liked, I'm eternally grateful to him for stepping up the way he did. These days, they live together on a small acreage in Saskatchewan with horses—a life Nicole always wanted. And I couldn't be happier for her.

* * *

Having a nice backyard to get around in with my wheelchair, warmer weather and the summer months quickly became my favorite time of year. Before my accident, I loved all four seasons, as each one offered something special. Like everyone else born in a temperate climate, seasonal changes were a way of life. Only during my brief time in Vancouver was I spared the full onslaught of cold, snowy winters. On the prairies and in Calgary, frigid winters and plenty of snow were something I looked forward to because it meant snowmobiling. Once I was wheelchair bound, snow no longer held the appeal for me it once did, for all the obvious reasons, nor did cold weather. What inclement weather meant was that I wasn't just confined to a wheelchair; I was confined mostly to my house. I wasn't immune to cabin fever just because my feet couldn't roam. After being stuck inside for any length of time, my spirit longed for the outdoors. And the option of spending the winter months in the Southern United States didn't really appeal that much to me either, even if I could afford it, which I couldn't. I just wanted to be near my children and the comfort zone of my handicap-friendly home.

While Nicole attended nursing school or worked a secular job, whenever possible, I would look after our daughters during the day. The best investment I ever made was buying a digital camera in the spring of 2002. This was before every smart phone came equipped with one. With a little ingenuity and some Velcro, I took a ton of video and pictures of my daughters that summer. Pretending I was interviewing them for a magazine article, with the camera rolling, I would ask each of them a series of questions about their lives. What's your favorite movie? Who's your best friend? What do you want to do when you grow up? They loved it! Over the years, I have collected a compilation of digital paraphernalia of them as they've grown up. Now that they are both adults, every now and then, when they come for a visit, we'll watch the videos together and have a good laugh or shed a nostalgic tear or two.

Having a reliable vehicle to get around in, the girls and I would constantly be venturing out to the zoo, various waterparks, fairgrounds, and several kids' movies. One of the benefits of being in a wheelchair is "rock star parking" everywhere I go. It's a seemingly small consolation for being paralyzed…but it's a perk nonetheless. Spending all that one-on-one time with my daughters was definitely the most advantageous element of this new life. If I had lived my entire adult life like most able-bodied mortals, I would have been busy working, racing, and just being busy *being* busy in this hectic world we live in. And like so many parents, I wouldn't have really had the time to spend enough of the quality time that is so important to a growing child. As a result, I've been able to maintain a close relationship with both my girls, an aspect of my life for which I am eternally grateful.

After successfully renovating my own house from the confines of a wheelchair, I decided to use this unique frame of reference and help other wheelchair users make their homes optimally accessible. With my experience as a contractor, combined with firsthand knowledge of using a wheelchair, accessibility renovations were my focus. Eventually, I started a non-profit business I called Barrier Free Solutions and constructed a website to advertise my services. The first job I did was for a fellow quadriplegic who shared the same caregiver with me. The project went well and was finished on schedule. But not being able to lift a finger—physically speaking—left me feeling somewhat frustrated. Over the years, I transitioned to more of a consulting role, where I would meet with clients and give them cost-efficient ideas on how to proceed.

One afternoon during summer holidays, my youngest daughter, Haylee, would teach me a much-needed valuable lesson when dealing with frustration. Being home alone with me while Danielle was over at a friend's house, Haylee was hungry and requested Kraft Dinner for a snack. Considering what an easy chore it is to whip up, I suggested giving her verbal instructions while she substituted as my hands. Haylee agreed, and we headed into the kitchen. After gathering a few necessities and boiling a pot of water, the next step was to open the cardboard box and pour the noodles into the boiling water. Being just six years old, however, she was struggling to get the box open. After several failed attempts at getting her to try different strategies, I unknowingly began to grow impatient, and my poor daughter, trying earnestly to open this box with her little hands, was sensing the frustration in my voice. At this point, I happened to catch a glimpse of the steady flow of tears streaming from her eyes as she endeavored to conceal her face from me, at which point my heart instantly sank about six inches lower in my chest. To see my innocent little girl trying so hard to hide her emotions—for fear of letting me down—damn near broke my heart in two.

In the aftermath of that heavy-hearted afternoon with my youngest daughter, I came to the sobering conclusion that patience was an aspect of my personality that definitely needed some improvement, if I was going to successfully navigate through this new journey in a wheelchair. As a result, whenever that vein in the middle of my forehead begins to pulsate, I think back to my little girl in tears, trying so hard to please her daddy. That usually adjusts my perspective posthaste. Eventually, I learned a verifiable truth: Time moves at the speed of time, not at the speed of my expectations. It was a difficult but necessary lesson that has served me well—when I remember to follow it, that is.

* * *

Newly divorced and living on my own, admittedly I was feeling somewhat isolated from the world. After having had a companion for more than a third of my life, being by myself definitely felt unfamiliar. When Nicole left, I pretty much resolved in my heart that I was destined to be single for the rest of my life. After all, if my own wife—who already loved me—couldn't handle me being a quadriplegic, how on earth could anyone else? Besides, how is any prospective date supposed to get to know the real me when all they see is a wheelchair? My relationship status appeared to be permanently etched in stone. But just when I think something is impossible, it seems life has a way of teaching me otherwise. This time, the impossible was reversed by none other than Nikkita, the attractive nanny whose services were greatly reduced after my family was no longer living in the house and my three other caregivers were taking care of all my personal needs. Given the situation, Nikkita moved out a few months later, though not before expressing romantic interest in me. Thinking she was simply being sympathetic to the guy in the wheelchair whenever she flirted with me, I'd been oblivious to her advances for the longest time. That was how hopelessly convinced I was of the hopelessness of my situation. In the end, our relationship never amounted to more than a brief fling, but Nikkita was the very first able-bodied woman to show an interest in me, which certainly ignited the spark of hope inside me.

The next indicator signaling that I still had a chance in the dating world showed up a few months after Nikkita moved out. When I say, "showed up," I mean that literally, as in "on my front doorstep." Having to replace one of my personal caregivers, who was moving on to a full-time career in nursing, I placed an ad in the newspaper to fill the position. The next day, I received a call from a woman named Shelley. We scheduled an interview later that afternoon. From the moment I opened the door to let her in, there was no question I was in big trouble. There she stood, five foot six, 120 pounds, green eyes, with long, curly blond hair draping over her pretty face. And she was quite well proportioned. Like magnets to steel, we were instantly attracted to each other. Surprisingly, because she was there for a caregiver job, any inhibitions I might have had about being in a wheelchair were completely gone. I was just me! So much so that what was supposed to be a job interview, I believe, ended up being our first date—I decided to date Shelley and hire someone else. Two years younger than me, easy on the eyes, liking the same music, and being an awesome cook to boot, Shelley seemed straight out of a romance novel. I remember her baking me the best apple pie. It was like heaven in my mouth. Unfortunately, she and I only dated for about a month before the idiosyncrasies of life got in the way. She was a smoker, and of course, I was not. No matter how hard I tried—as beautiful and vivacious as she was—there was no getting past that, which, considering I was the one in a wheelchair and Shelley was willing to look past that monster-truck-sized obstacle, made me feel incredibly guilty.

One of my favorite memories with Shelley took place at a local amusement park. We had taken my kids along, and it felt like a regular family-type outing for me. While waiting for Danielle and Haylee to finish one of their rides, Shelley and I were sharing an ice cream cone. Then, when I went to take a bite, she willfully pushed the ice cream right into my nose. On purpose! My first reaction was that of frustration, but after swallowing my pride enough to see the humor, I soon realized that was exactly what I would have done if the situation were reversed. In the end, we shared a good laugh. That was when I realized how painfully on guard I constantly was about appearing "normal" in public, so much so that I never let down my defenses to have any fun. Although a work in progress, being around Shelley thankfully introduced me to that necessary adjustment.

Just in case I wasn't quite convinced that life in a wheelchair wasn't a roadblock to having a real relationship with a woman—desperate and psychologically disturbed excluded—my next liaison would definitely be the clincher. Not long after the breakup with Shelley, I found myself in slightly uncomfortable territory... Her name was Ingrid. She was strikingly gorgeous. But she was twelve years younger than I. Uncomfortable territory. Although it was true that Priscilla, my first venture with a new woman, had also been twelve years younger, somehow her being in a wheelchair had put us on a level playing field. Perhaps because we'd had that one thing in common, Priscilla's age had seemed less important. This, in itself proves, that even people in wheelchairs aren't immune to stereotyping people in wheelchairs. Introduced to me by a friend, Ingrid took over a once-per-week dinnertime shift on Saturdays to earn a few extra bucks during the summer downtime from her university studies. That was when I suddenly began looking forward to Saturdays more and more. Over the course of the next two months, our times together slowly evolved into feeling more like dates than employer/employee scenarios. Not long after, the two of us entered a relationship together.

Given our age difference and the fact that she was returning to university in the fall, we knew there wasn't a real future for us. Nevertheless, Ingrid, with all that young, vibrant energy flowing inside her, was a great motivator in getting me out and doing things I probably never would have considered. In doing so, she introduced me to a multitude of activities I never would have embarked on. At the same time, she enlightened me as to how truly beautiful Alberta was and there to enjoy, regardless of my mobility status. Obviously, I already knew Alberta was a beautiful province, but seeing it through Ingrid's eyes made it more special. As a result, I no longer took the scenic wonder of my adoptive province, whose sobriquet is Wild Rose Country, for granted, as I had done in the past. Constantly going on day trips, visiting numerous lakes, rivers, mountain trails, and waterfalls, all within a few short hours of Calgary, made the summer of 2003 certainly memorable. The inevitable, of course, put an end to this fairy-tale-like time for me. Once university began that fall, it was back to the books for Ingrid and back to the status of single for me. But I certainly owe this wonderful woman a debt of gratitude for rejuvenating me, and she will always remain a cherished memory.

* * *

Dating from a wheelchair probably isn't on anyone's bucket list, but without even trying, I was off to a fairly decent start. This in itself provided me with just enough confidence to put myself out there and embark on my next adventure: meeting someone online. Online dating, with the instant-rejection component built right in to the dynamics of meeting someone in cyberspace, can be unnerving for anyone. Entering that same arena as a quadriplegic, well, that's another story altogether. Be that as it may, no one wants to be alone either, unless they're confirmed loners, which I'm not. With that sentiment, I scripted a poetic yet honest representation of who I was and what I was looking for, posted a picture, and held my breath. Admittedly, receiving my first message darn near gave me a full-on anxiety attack before opening it. Being that I enjoy talking about the deeper things in life and wasn't simply looking to get laid, it took a few weeks before finally meeting someone who piqued my interest. Her name was Caroline.

Caroline was a grade six French emersion school teacher. As she was an intellectual person, we hit it off right away. For our second date, we went to a Nickelback concert. The band, which hails from Hanna, Alberta, was still gaining a lot of momentum to eventually becoming one of Canada's most commercially successful recording and touring acts. Going to the concert was my idea, and I still enjoy some of their music to this day, particularly "When We Stand Together," off their 2011 album *Here and Now*.

Meeting Caroline in person for the first time, from the vantage point of being paralyzed from the neck down, was by far the most apprehensive aspect of the entire process. On top of that was the question: Where and how do we meet? Normally, in a first-time meet-and-greet scenario, a neutral location with people around would be chosen. That way, in case your date ended up being a psycho, you could run for the hills. Here, though, the option to simply hop in my vehicle and drive anywhere I wanted, whenever I wanted, wasn't exactly available. And being an extremely discreet person when it came to my personal life, asking one of my caregivers or friends was out of the question. Besides, having to explain how someone had to drive me to our date—in my opinion—projected an image of helplessness. Surprisingly, after getting to know each other briefly online and considering my circumstances, Caroline, and each prospective date thereafter, was willing to rendezvous at my crib. Although convenient for me, it was rather trusting of them and probably a bit discomforting.

Getting ready for a date was an ordeal all in itself, and not because it needed to be either. Regularly wearing designer jeans and stylish brand-name collared shirts—with a couple of squirts of cologne—I probably cared a little too much about my appearance. As a result, I nearly drove my poor caregivers to madness making sure every little detail was just right, as if a tiny wrinkle that looked out of place might stand out above and beyond the fact that I was a quadriplegic. But hey, I wanted to look good. Besides, doesn't every girl love a sharply dressed man?

The one undesirable element of my physical condition that was most bothersome—when meeting anyone new—was the muscle spasms. The definition of a muscle spasm is this: energy that builds within muscle tissue from lack of movement that needs to release, causing one's arm or leg to shake involuntarily. And being an anti-drug advocate, I refused to take medication to eliminate the spasms. Besides, spasms worked great for maintaining muscle tone. However, while sitting and conversing with a date, my worst nightmare was that one of my arms or legs would suddenly begin doing the funky chicken right in front of them. Unfortunately, it has happened more times than I care to remember. Once I became more comfortable with my situation, I learned to utilize the awkward moment as an opportunity to deliver a flirtatious comment: "My arm only does that when I'm anxious about a beautiful woman sitting in front of me."

There's an old saying: *Something good always comes from the bad.* Well, as I'm sure anyone else in my situation can attest to, one of the unique characteristics of being paralyzed to this degree is that our perceptibility becomes progressively fine-tuned. By taking away something as profound as physical movement, it's as if other sensory inputs try to compensate by becoming increasingly more sensitive. In turn, the mental connection I was able to establish with a girlfriend was quite unique. Just as the adage purports: *Stimulate a woman's body, and she will love you for five minutes; stimulate her mind, and she will love you forever.* Through the process of intellectually revealing conversation, a prospective girlfriend was able to experience firsthand that I consisted of much more than what my physical body couldn't do. After all, our physical bodies are of small consequence as to who we are and how we love. This is not to say that I believe I'm an extraordinary person by any means; it is simply a fortunate byproduct of my disability. Neither am I implying there wasn't plenty of rejection. There was…for sure, and if the situation were reversed, I might have done the same. But I have no negative feelings toward anyone. Personally, I'd sooner be rejected for being paralyzed than anything else. Given that we all have different expectations in regard to what we want or need from a mate, it's completely understandable that some people would never choose to be with someone who was paralyzed from the neck down.

Not surprisingly, the number one question every girl was dying to ask but afraid to was: "Can you still have sex?" followed by, "How does that work?" That was when the jokester in me would reply, "Well, men have what's called a penis, and women have a vagina. Now, when a man and woman decide to have sex, the man puts his…" Upon hearing this, laughter would usually ensue. I know that most people wonder the same thing: *How does that actually work?* Having sex with a quadriplegic, that is. Well, your imagination will have to suffice, because I'm not about to reveal the finer details of how I make love to a woman. Fair enough? To broach this subject with a prospective mate, however, when the time was right, I'd write her a romantically inclined, detailed story of what our first time together might be like. Given the power of the written word, that particular method seemed quite effective.

As for Caroline and I, we dated for roughly three months. Sadly, my feelings weren't progressing, and for that reason, I had to end our relationship. Unbeknownst to me at the time, something inside me was broken—psychologically speaking. Not recognizing that fact, I kept repeating the same pattern over and over. Time after time, my first priority was to get the girl to fall in love with me, meanwhile failing to evaluate my own feelings until it was too late, which resulted in a revolving door of failed relationships and a lineup of broken hearts in my wake. Truth be told, each and every time I had the very best of intentions. But good intentions don't solve real-life psychological issues.

* * *

Four years after Caroline ceased to be part of my life, and following a string of two- to three-month romances that ended in tears and me feeling like a predator, the ambition I once felt in finding a romantic partner was seriously beginning to diminish. Wondering if true love might be nothing more than a fantasy, I found myself straying in and out of the jaded corridor of cynicism. Then, like a hurricane that dissipates over landfall, SHE blew in to my life. Her name was Laurie. With a cast on one arm and a barrelful of heartbreaking stories in the other, Laurie was my perfect damsel in distress. And being a cross between Heather Locklear and Meg Ryan, she was a beautiful damsel indeed, precisely what my confused heart was yearning for: to be needed! Finally, I'd met someone who actually needed ME! Less than five months later, on May 7, 2006, Laurie and I were married. We had a small ceremony in front of a few friends and family at the Banff Springs Hotel. Our wedding song was "Nothing Else Matters" by Metallica. It was a happy day.

Unfortunately, neither of us realized the serious psychological baggage we both carried, issues that clashed like nitroglycerine and fire. This led to several rifts in our marriage, with seemingly no solution—at least, no solution either of us were capable of figuring out. After two virtuous attempts to reconcile, we divorced four years later. Be that as it may, my relationship with Laurie was definitely the most fun I've ever had with a woman, and not surprisingly, evoked the deepest love I may have ever felt for a mate. Extremely self-sacrificing and always willing to go that extra mile, in many ways, she was the perfect wife. If asked for ten minutes, she wouldn't hesitate in giving me an hour-long neck massage every time. Quite honestly, Laurie was the type of woman who made it impossible for me not to love her. She definitely gave me more than I was able to give her—physically speaking. Sure, I'd write endearing emails and love letters to her, but that paled in comparison. Wanting to do so much more, in my mind, I was rubbing her feet, throwing her playfully into a snowbank, or picking her up and carrying her to the bedroom. As a consequence, often times, I'd end up in that secret little room inside my head, feeling inadequate— an undesirable state of mind that often dominated my mood around her. Without question, for me personally, the hardest part of being paralyzed from the neck down is being someone I'm not. I was never the type of person who could sit around all day, and having to watch my spouse do everything was extremely frustrating. To this day, I've yet to conquer that psychological reflex of being a quadriplegic.

One of the favorite side effects I retained from my life with Laurie involves her love and natural ability to photograph the beauty within the world we live. She has a way of capturing the artistic element of just about anything she points her camera at. Laurie definitely has a gift. As a consequence, she introduced me to a new and fascinating perspective in viewing the magnificent reality we are so very fortunate to experience, a reality I never recognized with the naked eye before I met her. Being a quadriplegic, this was a gift that I have cherished ever since and am thankful for. In the aftermath of everything she and I went through together, I have to say that it was both a dishonor and disservice to each of us that we couldn't get past our weaknesses and enjoy how nearly perfect we were for each other. The day our relationship ended was a sad moment for anyone who believes in true love, as I do.

* * *

Not more than a couple of weeks after my brush with suicide, I took the advice of my Indian doctor about seeing a therapist to make sure there weren't any loose screws rattling around inside my noggin. Unexpectedly, the counselor to which I was assigned had a somewhat brilliant evaluation of my circumstances. During one of our sessions, she said, "Sometimes it's not about what you ARE doing, but rather what you're NOT doing." For me, that meant, *These are the cards I've been dealt. Now, what do I want to do with this life?* My first and obvious response was to find a spouse, and considering my physical limitations, preferably an able-bodied one. During my final session with this therapist, she gave me a lengthy poem to read. In it, I found some much-needed inspiration.

The Invitation (By Oriah)

It doesn't interest me what you do for a living. I want to know what you ache for and if you dare to dream of meeting your heart's longing.

It doesn't interest me how old you are. I want to know if you will risk looking like a fool for love, for your dream, for the adventure of being alive.

It doesn't interest me what planets are squaring your moon... I want to know if you have touched the center of your own sorrow, if you have been opened by life's betrayals or have become shriveled and closed from fear of further pain. I want to know if you can sit with pain, mine or your own, without moving to hide it or fade it or fix it.

I want to know if you can be with joy, mine or your own, if you can dance with wildness and let the ecstasy fill you to the tips of your fingers and toes without cautioning us to be careful, to be realistic, to remember the limitations of being human.

It doesn't interest me if the story you are telling me is true. I want to know if you can disappoint another to be true to yourself. If you can bear the accusation of betrayal and not betray your own soul. If you can be faithless and therefore trustworthy.

I want to know if you can see Beauty, even when it is not pretty every day. And if you can source your own life from its presence.

I want to know if you can live with failure, yours and mine, and still stand at the edge of the lake and shout to the silver of the full moon, "Yes."

It doesn't interest me to know where you live or how much money you have. I want to know if you can get up after the night of grief and despair, weary and bruised to the bone, and do what needs to be done to feed the children.

It doesn't interest me who you know or how you came to be here. I want to know if you will stand in the center of the fire with me and not shrink back.

It doesn't interest me where or what or with whom you have studied. I want to know what sustains you from the inside when all else falls away.

I want to know if you can be alone with yourself and if you truly like the company you keep in the empty moments.

Cue music: "Let Her Go" by Passenger

https://www.youtube.com/watch?v=RBumgq5yVrA

CHAPTER

32

The Road's Still Long

Ever since my second departure from married life, I have been extremely reluctant to pull the trigger on a committed relationship. Though engaged once after divorce number two, I saw it necessary to back out and have since chosen to remain single. In terms of relationships, I've learned that life as a quadriplegic comes with an array of psychological effects that I'm still figuring out to this day. As a result, my willingness to commit to a third marriage or partnership is somewhat unenthusiastic. Someday perhaps, but for now, I'm content with being single.

During the course of this eventful life and until my fortieth year on this planet, I had never lost anyone close to me in death, except when my dog, Skye, passed away in 1997. But losing a pet, as hard as it is, can hardly be compared to a human being. Before my forty-fifth birthday, however, three people who were extremely important to me would die. First, my stepdad, Bill, passed away from a heart attack in 2009. Never having had to process the psychological effects of losing someone close to me through death, his abrupt departure from my life left me in a state of confusion for the longest time. Then my longtime friend Chris Bonneau died from a brain tumor in 2011.

In 2013, Ada, my grandmother on Mom's side of the family, fell asleep and never woke up again. Although Bill and Grandma died in quick, merciful ways, Chris, unfortunately, suffered before being set free from the pain his illness inflicted on him. He fought the cancer that would fell him heroically and courageously. He wasn't the type to just throw in the towel. It was a heart-wrenching time for his family, friends, and motocross industry colleagues. When the moment of his passing came, it was almost a relief. He was finally at peace. Chris left behind his beautiful wife, Anne, and two young children, Christopher and Brooklyn. He also left a gap in the Canadian motocross scene to which he'd devoted a good deal of his forty-five years. It hit me particularly hard because Chris was the friend who'd stepped up to the plate for me after my accident. He'd shown his true character as a human being, becoming the brother I never had, while I was first dealing with the aftermath of my injury.

When Chris died, I couldn't help but wonder why a man of such noble character had ended up with the short stick in life. As a result, his passing bothered me to the point where I felt anger. I'm not even sure exactly where my frustration was focused; I just felt his death was incredibly unfair. Having to hear how death was simply a part of life everyone must accept didn't provide me with any comfort at all. Besides, are life and death not the opposite of each other? Then, how can they be a part of each other? Bill and Grandma went out like the proverbial light. Here one moment...gone the next! That provided some consolation in dealing with the loss. Besides, Grandma had lived a long, full life. Her death still stung, but it was easier to rationalize. Although not really that old, Bill wasn't exactly a spring chicken either, and he had lived a relatively full life as well—compared to the average person.

Shortly before Ada passed away, something peculiar happened that I'm quite certain many can relate to. Not more than a month before she died, I hadn't spoken to her in twelve years. This was not for any particular reason; time just flew by, and I wasn't counting the years. Being busy with life and the geographical distance between us—she lived in Saskatchewan—simply got in the way and took precedence. Same goes for the relationship between my sister, Nikki, and me—a sad state of affairs, really. There is no excuse for not picking up the phone and making a quick call to say, "Hello, how's things?" One day, out of the blue, however, I did just that. I felt the strong inclination to give my dear old grandma a phone call. She was ninety-six years old, virtually blind, and living in a care facility, yet she was still sharp as a whip. Upon answering my call, she said, "Hello," in a strong voice that belied her age. I replied, "Hello, Grandma." From those two words, she somehow immediately recognized my voice and responded, "Hi, Monte! I wondered when you were going to call me." Needless to say, we enjoyed a lengthy and beautiful conversation together. Then, four weeks later, she passed away.

A great memory I have of my grandma is when cousin Duane, Aunt Beverly, and I were playing Old Maid—the card game—with her. I would have been roughly eighteen years old at the time. While the four of us were sitting around the table playing cards one evening, I orchestrated my play so that Grandma ended up with the Queen of Spades, the one and only card you really don't want when playing this particular game. Well, Grandma got so mad at me for giving her the queen that she jumped up from her seat and started chasing me around with a broom, trying to clobber me over the head. Everyone laughed, but Grandma wasn't very happy. We had some fun card games together, creating many cherished memories.

Interestingly, not unlike the experience with my grandmother, a similar situation unfolded with my dad three weeks before he died. After returning to our old home in Tadmore to enjoy retirement, Mom, for some strange reason encouraged Dad to drive out to British Columbia and visit his Mom—a widow by this time. In doing so, Bill made the effort to also visit with each one of his siblings. Then, on his journey back to Saskatchewan, he stopped for a visit with me in Calgary. Though he and I talked regularly by telephone, we hadn't seen each other in roughly two years before this particular visit. Roughly three weeks later, the phone rang. It was my sister, Nikki, calling to inform me that Dad had just passed away from a heart attack. Needless to say, the phone call caught me completely off guard. I was devastated beyond belief. For the longest time, all I could think about was the conversation he and I had had about him wanting to get me into a boat and go fishing that summer. To have those plans fade to black in my memory left me staring at the ceiling in my bedroom with tears in my eyes more times than I care to remember. Unable to arrange the necessary means to attend Bill's funeral, I wrote this eulogy for his memorial service, which was read by Gary Rudabaugh—a friend of Dad's.

July 17th, 2009

I want to thank everyone here today who came to celebrate the memory of my dad. Bill was an amazing father who always did his best to raise my sister and me with kindness, fairness and integrity. I credit many things to my dad: he taught me how to catch a baseball, how to shoot and stick handle a puck, how to golf, and how to fish. Throughout my childhood, we went on several holidays and fishing trips together all over western Canada. In the process, we caught hundreds of fish together, thus creating a multitude of memories that I'll forever cherish.

But most of all, Bill never gave up in trying to teach me what it meant to be a man in pretty much every aspect of life, most of which he did through example. For instance, the manner in which Dad treated my mother taught me how to treat women. And through his trustworthiness, he taught me about honesty. As many of you know, however, I didn't always utilize these lessons and pushed every boundary there was during my teenage years. As a result, I found myself in more than a fair share of trouble. Yet deep inside my core, his teachings were there. It just took me a while to recognize them. Thanks to him for never giving up on me. Everything I am today is a result of his efforts. For that, I am eternally grateful.

There is one secret he never did teach me, though. Therefore, I have a little story I want to share with everyone. As anyone here might remember, I was a fairly cocky teenager. Well, one summer after the last day of school, I came home with a conglomeration of ribbons pinned to my chest—it was track and field day. I was probably twelve or thirteen at the time. Dad, while working on a few things to get ready for a fishing trip, noticed me feeling somewhat proud of all the track and field ribbons pinned to my chest and said, "I see you have a first-place ribbon. What's it for?" In a prideful tone, I answered that it was for winning the fifty-meter race. Then, with a smile on his face, he asked, "So, you think you're pretty fast?" To which I replied, "Well, the first-place ribbon says I'm the fastest."

A few moments later, Dad summoned me to the back lane behind our house, where he pointed and explained, "From here to the end of the lane is about fifty meters, wouldn't you say?"

I laughed and retorted, "You want to race ME?" Meanwhile, I'm thinking, He's old! I don't want to embarrass the poor guy. Except, then he started egging me on and teasing about how badly I was about to lose, even going one step further to say that if I won, I didn't have to cut the lawn all summer. Well, that did it. I was no longer feeling sorry for him. "Okay, lets race!" I said. "Whenever you're ready, just say GO," he told me. Suddenly, Dad said to me, "Wait a minute, what do I get if I win?"

Believing he didn't have a snowflake's chance in hell of actually winning, I told him to name anything. After suggesting that I wax his car and clean out the garage, I agreed. The only thing on my mind was the sweet pleasure of watching him cut the lawn all summer long and rubbing this victory in his nose every chance I could. At that, we got ready, and I said, "GO!"

To this day, I've never been able to figure out how those short, stubby legs of his were able to move so fast. Not only did he win the race, he kicked my butt! It wasn't even close. Consequently, for a taste of my own medicine, Dad never let me forget the outcome of that race.

The most important information that Bill ever taught me, however, was in regard to God. First and foremost, my stepdad strived to put God first in his life. And with a willingness to help just about anyone, he educated me about what it truly means to love your neighbor. If you needed a hand, Dad was the first to drop everything and help out. In terms of generosity, if all he had was $20 to his name and you were hungry, Bill would buy you a meal. That's the sort of man he was. As a result, I will forever miss and remember my stepdad as the kindest man I ever knew.

Cue music; "Torn to Pieces" by Pop Evil

https://www.youtube.com/watch?v=e8A9J94UWI8

* * *

Over the years, I have often been asked to visit newly injured people at the hospital and speak with them about life after injury: how to live on your own and how to avoid some of the pitfalls. In September of 2015, I was invited by Spinal Cord Injury Alberta to speak at their 2015 Peer Conference. I considered it an honor to join them at their conference and speak to those in attendance about how I coped with life after my spinal cord injury and how I managed to live successfully on my own for so many years. Spinal Cord Injury Association Alberta, which has its office in Edmonton, has been helping Albertans with spinal cord injuries and other physical disabilities for more than fifty-five years. The association is a leader in offering support, direct service, information, and advocacy to people who have been impacted by SCI, so I was more than happy to contribute to their ongoing cause.

The people who had gathered at Calgary's Carriage House Inn for the Peer Conference consisted of both able-bodied and paralyzed people. In addition to my talk, I showed a brief video of me at home, demonstrating how I use my ability to move and utilize my head to the max, something able-bodied people never really give much thought to as they go about their daily lives. I was rather nervous, because I had never spoken in front of a large group, but once I got rolling, I enjoyed the rapport I had with the audience. Rather than delve right into the serious stuff, I decided to start off my talk with a joke, to loosen up not just myself, but the audience as well.

A middle-aged woman, roughly forty years of age, travels into the city with her five-year-old daughter and husband for the first time. This woman has never been to the city in her entire life. The reason for her trip to the city is because a relative recently passed away and left her a sizable inheritance. Therefore, to receive the inheritance, she has to travel to the city and sign some documents at the lawyer's office. When they drive up to the office building where the lawyer's office is located, the woman and her daughter head in to the building together—the husband sits in the truck and waits in the parking lot. Upon walking in the main lobby of the building, the mom and daughter spot the elevator, but having lived on a farm her entire life, mom has never seen an elevator before—neither has her five-year-old daughter. While standing in front of the elevator—at a distance—a rough-looking man in a wheelchair rolls by just as the metallic elevator doors part in the middle and open. The man rolls into the elevator, and the doors close behind him. Meanwhile, mom and daughter stand there holding hands in bewilderment. Above the elevator door, a number slowly counts from one to ten, then back down to one, and the metallic doors once again part in the middle and open. Then a young, attractive, and very fit man wearing a suit steps out of the elevator. Mom and daughter look on in absolute amazement. They cannot believe their eyes! To them, a rough-looking older fellow in a wheelchair went in to a little room that counted to ten and transformed him into a young, healthy man. The daughter looks up to her mom and says, "Too bad daddy isn't in a wheelchair." Her mom replies, "That's okay. Let's go get him and put him in there anyway!"

This bit of humor, perhaps perceived as politically incorrect in some quarters, worked well for everyone concerned, including myself, and set the stage for me to get in to the serious stuff. My talk summarized quite accurately what I have come to learn while living the past seventeen years as a quadriplegic.

We all want that perfect life, don't we? Everyone wants to be happy. Most often, however, our pursuit for that happiness leads us to wanting more than what we need or something different than what we already have. For some, that means having more money. Others want a different or better body, and some people just want an attractive spouse. People in wheelchairs want nothing more than to be cured of their impairment. When I was in the hospital, I started out on a ventilator and prayed every day for that one level of recovery so that I could breathe on my own. Well, I got that one level and recovered the ability to breathe on my own, but it wasn't enough. Then I wanted one more level so that I could use my arms, which I knew would improve my life immensely. I would finally be able to feed myself. And I spent the next three months feeling sorry for myself waiting for that recovery. As humans, it seems we never stop wanting more. Quite simply, we all lack contentment.

Understandably, many people just want a life free of pain or disease. And sometimes the biggest obstacles people face are invisible to everyone else. A very close friend of mine, who is a good, honest-hearted, and humble man, is the perfect example of this. He has a beautiful family and gorgeous wife, is in relatively perfect physical health, and he's a carpenter just like I was. A lot of people would look at my friend and say to themselves, "I would trade places with that guy in a heartbeat." What people do not know, however, is that sometimes my friend cannot even get out of bed in the morning because he suffers from depression. Not every day, of course, but some days, his depression incapacitates him completely. He once told me that it paralyzes his mind to the point that he can no longer function.

Addictions and psychological challenges, because we cannot physically see them, are viewed differently by members of society than they do someone who is physically paralyzed and confined to a wheelchair. Because the people who suffer from such things are up walking around and appear completely healthy on the outside, we cannot help ask, "What is wrong with him? What is his excuse? Just stop being sad and get on with life!" But that is not how life works. My point is that we all face obstacles. Just because an obstacle is not visible does not mean it doesn't exist. Everyone has limitations. The best athletes in the world have limitations and face obstacles in life. People look at my life, see my wheelchair, and think that because I am severely disabled, I am at a disadvantage compared to most people. But I do not believe that. Anyone, regardless of their situation, who believes they are disadvantaged is sentencing themselves to continually living a disadvantaged life.

Getting into an elevator and figuring out how I am going to push that stupid button, sometimes that's my biggest obstacle of the day. Having a caregiver help me do things from day to day can be viewed as an obstacle. Or maybe it's just an inconvenience. After all, what I need to get done is still getting done. I get out of bed every morning, wash my face, brush my teeth, and eat breakfast just like everyone else. I just need help doing it. To me, that is a minor inconvenience. What most people who live life from a wheelchair or any other debilitating encumbrance do not realize is that they possess above average mental strength. The fact that you got out of bed this morning proves that you have the drive and determination that my able-bodied friend who suffers from depression wishes he had. For people with disabilities, that mental strength comes natural to us. It's that survival instinct that most of us are born with. The will to survive.

When my youngest daughter told me how she was glad I was in a wheelchair because she could spend more time with me, let me tell you, that changed my perspective. How could it not? Only your child could be that brutally honest with you. First thing a life like this will teach anyone is patience. Otherwise, that vein in the middle of your forehead is sure to explode one day. The next thing this life will teach anyone is humility. When I look in the mirror and see myself sitting in this chair, it takes humility to go out in public and risk being accepted for the way I am—either that or live like a hermit and never leave the house.

Society would have us believe that fame, money, and power are the ingredients to happiness. Many people believe that to be true. See yourself as successful, and you will be successful! Everyone has heard that philosophy. But anyone who has experienced an extreme personal loss knows that success is not the main ingredient to happiness. If given a second chance, how much differently would you live your life? I know that I sure would. What seemed important to me before my injury is not as important to me anymore. That new understanding is a gift that many people go through their entire lives without ever learning. Unfortunately, this type of knowledge cannot be taught in textbooks. It can only be gained by life experience. If you possess this knowledge, then live in appreciation of that knowledge. That awesome cup of coffee in the morning. The perfect song at just the right moment. Watching a beautiful sunset. Those are the little things that most of us take for granted every day. Find that little piece of contentment in your life, and I guarantee you will live your life wider and deeper than ninety-nine percent of the people around you. Stop focusing on what you can't do. Everyone has limitations as to what they can and cannot do. Focus on what you can do and what you can control.

One of my favorite movies is The Shawshank Redemption. *In the movie, Tim Robins says, "Get busy living or get busy dying." Does that mean you either live a happy life or take a bottle of pills and check out? Not at all. It means getting out of bed in the morning and looking forward to the day, as opposed to getting out of bed and dreading the day. Get busy living or get busy dying! My paralysis is an inconvenience that I cannot do anything about. Therefore, I focus on what I can do. And I choose to live my life with the advantage of what it has taught me: to be content and thankful for what I do have. Remember this: If you live your life believing you are disadvantaged, then you will live a disadvantaged life.*

* * *

Throughout my life, I've struggled to answer the question…*Is there a Creator?* I even presumed to plead with God for proof of His existence at the age of thirteen, when, for a brief moment, I wondered if what I'd experienced was actually real and if the revelation of becoming paralyzed would prove to manifest itself at some point in the future. In the end, those events, the image my cousins and I saw on our garage door and the strange sounds I heard with my mother, never convinced me either way. I simply labeled it as a cool story to tell while sitting around a campfire. And the revelation of living life from a wheelchair was forgotten before I woke the next morning.

Looking back at my life—which may at times resemble what some would choose to describe as a nightmare—I have come to realize that this long journey I took to get where I am today was actually a gift. I'm eternally grateful to have had the opportunity to experience the many roads I ventured down, especially the one that led me to walk into the Canada Games Sportsplex on February 12, 1999, and leave on a stretcher with a broken neck, simply because, without it, I never would have come to learn what I have since that fateful night: knowledge that is exceedingly more valuable than any prosperous material life I may have lived as an able-bodied man.

As a result of having long intervals of free time with nothing more than my thoughts to occupy my mind, I would definitely concede that being paralyzed at thirty years of age has taught me the most about life. Although originally beginning in late 2005, it wasn't until my stepdad's passing that the unstoppable thirst for real answers to life's true purpose and that of a Creator became ignited inside me. Further fueling that desire was the death of my close friend Chris Bonneau and dear grandmother Ada. I admit that in this autobiography, I've often contradicted myself when it comes to believing in God or a Creator. In one paragraph, I affirm that there is no God, and then in the next paragraph, I say a prayer. Truth is, since that first visit to Sunday school at six years old, there has always been a burning desire inside me to probe for an answer to that question. Then, in late 2005, I was paid a visit by a man about ten years my senior dressed in everyday street clothes who introduced himself as Wayne. He was a Jehovah's Witnesses, but there was something different about this guy; I got the impression that he wasn't canvassing the neighborhood. Instead of blowing him off as I would normally have done, I invited him in. I soon learned that Wayne was an elder from the local congregation my dad attended when visiting me in Calgary and had been asked by Dad to stop by and see me. Dad, who over the years had returned to the JW faith, had tried on a few occasions to rekindle a Bible study with me, which I'd told him I had no interest in doing. By sending a local congregation elder to speak with me, he was no doubt hoping someone else might succeed. Even though I was hard-nosed in my conviction against the Jehovah's Witness way of life, I liked Wayne right away—probably because he never once brought up the Bible or God during that first visit. We got together a few more times after that and just talked like a couple of new friends about our lives. Religion didn't enter the picture. Wayne proved to be an interesting man, without any pretenses or character traits that came across as self-important.

Finally, during one of our get-togethers, Wayne asked if I believed in God. Because I considered us friends, I wasn't put off by his question and explained that I had struggled my entire life for a satisfactory answer without ever arriving at one. The clever elder then challenged me to a Bible study, where he would attempt to prove to me there is a Creator. He assured me I could end the session at any time and there would be no hard feelings. Believing this could be the perfect opportunity for me to quench my thirst for an answer to that question once and for all, I accepted his challenge. Admittedly, the Bible does provide a solid debate in concluding that there is a Creator. Being open minded and a searcher, however, I needed reality-based, factual answers that didn't entirely rely on one book—a book that seemingly has religion tied to it, no less. For the next ten years, I became a voracious reader of scientific research. Meanwhile, I delved into a number of Bible-based topics with three experienced elders who, one by one, took on the challenge of studying with me. First, Wayne, then a fellow named Albert, and, finally, Stanton.

Scientific research is certainly interesting, and the theories and counter-theories to explain our planet and the life it harbors—never mind the universe—keep changing at a rapid pace. Even the theories of the venerable Albert Einstein, who was not an atheist, have not escaped scrutiny. And just like Plato's view of the universe, they are not infallible and subject to endless debate. The more the scientific community purports to know about the origins and fate of the universe, the less they seem to know. Simple words such as "maybe," "possibly," and "perhaps" often accompany their statements. Theories, after all, are just that…theories. One question answered creates two or more questions in its place.

Although I'm sure most scientists, astronomers, theoretical physicists, etc. are not out to prove the existence of God, there is plenty of physical evidence out there that indicates a Creator is responsible for the universe we inhabit and this thing called life. Evidence uncovered by geneticists, physicists, and mathematicians dramatically proves that we are the result of intelligent design. The code found in DNA, for example, is a case in point. It didn't just evolve; it was purposely put there. Microsoft's Bill Gates told us that "DNA is like a computer program but far, far more advanced than any software ever created." For me, the wonders of the DNA code, much more complex than the ones and zeros of our human-developed computer codes, is just one aspect of what led me, in addition to the Bible, to accept that there is indeed a Creator. My journey to that conclusion, however, given my propensity for learning everything the hard way, took me a long time, only finally coming together during the remnants of the past decade or so.

As a culmination to my search, on March 7, 2015, I dedicated my life to our Creator by getting baptized as a Jehovah's Witness. The truth within the Bible has since been scored more deeply upon my heart than I could have ever imagined. Shortly after my decision to get baptized is when the memories of everything that transpired when I was thirteen years old and why I felt the eerie sensation of déjà vu the evening of my injury finally became crystal clear. At forty-six years of age, as if a switch was suddenly flipped on inside my head, I suddenly remembered the revelation made to me that fateful afternoon in 1982. That was also when I realized that I had an agreement to fulfill.

The Perfect Life, however, was not written for that purpose. I wrote my autobiography with the purpose of sharing the story of my life before and after becoming a quadriplegic. I wanted to illustrate that there is indeed life after losing the ability to perform the everyday actions that we humans assume to be our birthright and take for granted. Upon completion of my autobiography, I was inspired to document what convinced me about the reality of a Creator in a book entitled *Truth and Reality*—without the influence of religious beliefs and doctrines. It was a book that at age thirteen, I promised to write. If you find yourself faced with a dilemma similar to the one that perplexed me for the majority of my life, I invite you to read the follow-up to *The Perfect Life.* For more information, please visit my website:

https://www.truthandreality.org

* * *

Tom Cochrane, who, like me, is a son of the Canadian prairies, released the song, "Life is a Highway." It was the lead single on Cochrane's album, Mad Mad World, released in 1991. "Life is a Highway" was a number one hit in Canada and his biggest ever hit. Admittedly, it is a cleverly written piece of lyrical poetry, but I would have to disagree with Tom. As I'm sure everyone can attest, life is anything but a highway. We identify "highway" with smooth traveling on an obstacle-free road from one place to the next—at least when there are no traffic jams. But our journey through life is anything but obstacle free and smooth; it's more like traveling on a winding road through the jungle, with plenty of potholes to bump us around and even stop us dead in our tracks if we're not careful. I know, because I've found myself stuck in a few of those potholes. Therefore, I will end this book with some inspiring words that I believe the world could seriously use right now: Never give up! The true value of life is a gift worth learning about and experiencing.

I'm not sure what inspired the artist to pen the lyrics for this final song—perhaps a reflection of his own life—but in consideration of where I came from, where I've been, and where I'm going, this final piece of music sums up the perfect ending to my autobiography…

Cue music: "The Road's Still Long" by Cinderella

https://www.youtube.com/watch?v=EIJ7zKkiaSs